Hope Against History

The Ulster Conflict

Jack Holland

CORONET BOOKS
LIR
Hodder & Stoughton

Copyright © 1999 by Jack Holland

The right of Jack Holland to be identified as the
Author of the Work has been asserted by him in accordance
with the Copyright, Designs and Patents Act 1988.

First published in Great Britain in 1999
by Hodder and Stoughton
First published in paperback in 2000
by Hodder and Stoughton
A division of Hodder Headline

A Coronet Lir Paperback

10 9 8 7 6 5 4 3 2 1

A CIP catalogue record for this title
is available from the British Library

ISBN 0 340 73910 X

Typeset by Hewer Text Ltd, Edinburgh
Printed and bound in Great Britain by
Clays Ltd, St Ives plc

Hodder and Stoughton
A division of Hodder Headline
338 Euston Road
London NW1 3BH

In memory of Martha Holland (1910–1998)
and Margaret McNicholl (1947–1998)

'Too late for tears: thinking'

John Berryman, *Dream Songs*

Contents

List of Illustrations

Dominic McGlinchey
The New Ireland Forum, 1984
Loyalists protest at the Anglo-Irish Agreement, 1985
PLO villa in the Middle East
Paddy Hill
A prison 'comm'
Peter Brooke
Martin McGuinness
Mitchel McLaughlin
Martin Mansergh
Bill Clinton, Albert Reynolds and Jean Kennedy Smith
Sean O hUiginn
Bill Clinton
Gusty Spence
David Ervine
George Mitchell
Mo Mowlam
Gerry Adams, 1998
David Trimble, 1998
Seamus Mallon
All-party talks at Stormont
Billy Wright
A member of the Orange Order

Acknowledgments

Much of the material that went to the making of this book was gathered over the course of many years of reporting on and writing about Northern Ireland. To all those who spoke to me, gave of their time, and shared their information, I record my gratitude, though most cannot be named.

I would like to thank David McKittrick for permission to use our unpublished history of the UDA, *The Assassins*. My thanks are due to "Joseph" who has proven to be an invaluable guide to the paramilitary underworld. My thanks, too, to Dr. Susan Phoenix for her generous assistance. And once again I, like so many others who have written about Northern Ireland, must say thank you to Yvonne Murphy at the Linen Hall Library, Belfast, for her unstinting efforts to uncover needed matter.

On a more personal note, I would like to thank Marcia Rock for her helpful criticism of the manuscript. To my wife, Dr. Mary Hudson, I can only repeat what I have said before in so many acknowledgements, that without her it would not have been possible.

Preface

The Northern Ireland conflict has produced a whole library of books. Yet there was lacking a concise, readable account that told the story of the last thirty years, with enough detail to give it depth and authority but without overburdening the narrative. And the essence of history, after all, is narrative.

Hope Against History is an attempt to meet that need. It is, as far as I have been able to make it, a non-partisan account. Its perspective is derived from the experience of some twenty-five years writing about the Troubles, during which I have met and in some cases come to know many of the participants – republicans, loyalist paramilitaries, civil rights activists, politicians, undercover police officers and soldiers. I have endeavoured to weave something of their experience into the narrative, hoping it will illuminate a situation where though the chief protaganists are so remarkably similar, there is strikingly little curiosity about the views and experience of the 'other'. They run along parallel tracks and never meet. The peace process has not made much difference to this aspect of the situation. In fact, if anything it has made it more obvious.

Also, the fact that I grew up in Belfast has deeply influenced my perspective for the simple reason that I have (to some extent) lived the Troubles as well as written about them. And to quote Aristotle: 'Experience is the knowledge of detail.' My hope is that the following pages will reflect that axiom.

New York,
January 1999.

PROLOGUE

An Irish Rip van Winkle
Goes to Washington

I f an Irish Rip van Winkle had been roused from his slumbers after twenty years and transported to Washington, DC, on the evening of St Patrick's Day, 1995, he would have scarcely believed what he saw.

Unusually warm weather had brought the daffodils out in bloom, and the capital was bathed in the russet colours of sunset. Spring had come early, and the clement weather had already encouraged a few people to cast off their jackets as they strolled along the city's wide boulevards. But it would not have been the weather which would have arrested the attention of the visitor transported from Ireland's recent, troubled past.

President Bill Clinton, in his third year in office, was holding an Irish party to celebrate the feast day of Ireland's patron saint and its national holiday. In the small theatre in the East Wing of the White House, under three ornate chandeliers, the Irish tenor Frank Patterson sang the sentimental Irish parlour song 'The Rose of Tralee'. The party had become a tradition since the days of Ronald Reagan. Clinton, however, had taken the occasion beyond the level of a

1

sentimental get-together and celebration of shamrockery, though it retained something of those elements.

Even before he became President, the former Governor of Arkansas had committed himself to putting the Ulster question on his administration's agenda. Most other Presidents before him had preferred to avoid the issue. It was seen as a political quagmire in which the United States should not become stuck. As one US Senator said in 1978: 'It's too hard to tell the good guys from the bad guys.' Even Presidents Jimmy Carter and Ronald Reagan, who had addressed the problem, had done so intermittently, and certainly did not allow it to assume anything like the importance that it was to acquire during Clinton's first term in office. Certainly, for Clinton, there was a political calculation involved. He was anxious to solidify support among the so-called 'Reagan Democrats' – conservative, mostly Catholic, Irish American Democrats who had been appalled at what they viewed as the ultra-liberal agenda of their party in the 1980s. Ireland was an issue that would strike a chord with them. But the President's Irish agenda was driven primarily by his own interest in the situation – he had been in England almost thirty years earlier when the first Northern Ireland civil rights demonstrators were marching in Belfast and Derry to protest against discrimination towards Catholics in housing and jobs.

Beneath the low stage on which Patterson sang, a hushed crowd listened intently. But they were not the usual gathering of prominent Irish and Irish American politicians, businessmen and entertainers invited for the St Patrick's Day shenanigans in Washington – far from it. This was an historical occasion – one that would make our Rip van Winkle from across the ocean rub his eyes in disbelief, perhaps thinking that he had been placed under a charm.

Directly behind the table where the President and Mrs Clinton sat next to Paul Newman and his wife Joanne Woodward sat a tall, lean, bearded man with his hands

2

folded in front of him. The Irish Rip van Winkle would have recognized him as Gerry Adams, President of Sinn Fein, the political arm of the outlawed Provisional Irish Republican Army. Twenty years before, when Rip van Winkle went to sleep, Mr Adams was locked up in Long Kesh prison camp near Belfast, jailed as a leading member of the Belfast Provisionals. Since the early 1970s Adams had been a key figure in the campaign of the Belfast PIRA, an organization dedicated to driving the British government out of Northern Ireland and uniting the country as one socialist republic. Now the picture of the bearded, beady-eyed intellectual, he had risen through the IRA ranks to a national leadership position and had taken command of its political structure, Sinn Fein, as well.

In those guerrilla days, Adams looked for support to the Sandinistas, the PLO and the ANC, and was more accustomed to ballads of revolution and rebellion than parlour songs served up at St Patrick's Day galas in America, a country from which he had been barred for decades on the grounds that he was associated with terrorism. But thanks to Bill Clinton, in January 1994 Adams had been granted the first of several visas to visit New York City, which he did for three days. Throughout that brief period, he had received an enthusiastic welcome from the Irish American honchos of the corporate world, among others, who made it clear that they were ready to support a genuine peace move; it depended on a vital decision from the Provisional IRA to end its twenty-five-year campaign of violence.

Adams's reception in the US helped convince him that the time had come to press for a more peaceful approach to resolving the Ulster crisis than the one with which he and his organization had been traditionally associated. What Adams did not tell his Irish American backers was that the Provisionals were in desperate straits, their campaign increasingly frustrated by the success of the undercover counter-terror strategy of the security forces. They were looking for a way

3

out, one that would allow them a graceful exit without being forced to admit defeat. This could not be achieved without compromise, of course, and if it meant joining in a sing along to Frank Patterson's rendition of 'God Bless America', so be it – the former guerrilla chief could get dewy-eyed about it with the most patriotic American.

The day before St Patrick's Day, Adams had shaken the hand of President Clinton at a lunch with Newt Gingrich, the Speaker of the House. He was to do so again that evening. On neither occasion were photographers present to record the historic conjunction of violent Irish republicanism and the political establishment of the most powerful nation on earth.

Adams's visit of March 1995 was his fourth to the United States. Not only had the visa ban been lifted, but the authorities now allowed him and his colleagues in Sinn Fein to fund-raise in America – a change that would have been unimaginable twenty years earlier when the energy of Federal government agencies was devoted to blocking money and arms being sent from PIRA's US support network to the gunmen and bombers ambushing troops and police in the lanes and back streets of Ulster.

Not far from where Mr Adams stood listening to Patterson sing the praises of Mary, the Rose of Tralee, our freshly awakened visitor from the past might have picked out a pallid, round-faced young man staring straight in front of him. Gary McMichael was the head of the Ulster Democratic Party, the political wing of the Ulster Defence Association, at one time the largest paramilitary group in Ulster, dedicated to keeping it British. He did not look at Adams nor did Adams look at him. Indeed, they studiously avoided eye contact. Twenty years ago, the UDP did not yet exist, but the UDA did and was engaged in a vicious sectarian war directed mainly at Northern Ireland's Catholic population, which left hundreds of them dead. The UDA killed in the belief that such terror would frighten Catholics into abandoning their support for

4

the Provisional IRA and its goals. If Rip van Winkle did not recognize Gary McMichael at first glance he would, if he was an astute observer, have noted a certain familiarity about the young man's appearance. Gerry Adams certainly would have. Mr Adams's colleagues in the Provisional IRA murdered Gary's father John, a leading member of the UDA, in December 1987.

At a table not far from McMichael sat Joe English, a short bull-terrier of a man with clipped spiky hair. When Rip van Winkle had fallen asleep, English was no more than a local activist in the UDA's ruthless North Belfast death squads, which helped make that part of the capital city of Northern Ireland perhaps the most dangerous place in the country. By the early 1990s, he had become the chairman of the organization. Under his leadership there was an upsurge in UDA violence against Catholics which had prompted one leading Belfast IRA man to lament, 'We were being slaughtered.' Roughly speaking, for every British soldier the IRA killed between 1992 and 1994, the UDA killed eight Catholics. But violence seemed far from English's mind that evening as he sipped his Irish whiskey, seemingly enraptured by the sickly-sweet Victorian melody that held the guests in the East Wing in its thrall.

Our Irish Rip van Winkle would have begun scratching his head at this point, looking around for explanations as to how such dedicated enemies in an ancient war found themselves in Washington, as guests of an American President, at that most green of occasions. Searching for answers he might have approached the squat, bespectacled, middle-aged man who sat not far from the Clintons. John Hume, the leader of Ulster's largest nationalist party, the Social Democratic and Labour Party, had the agitated look of a man in a hurry, a slightly dishevelled, untidy appearance which reminds one of the schoolteacher he was before becoming involved in the Northern Ireland civil rights movement thirty years earlier.

5

Since those days of street protests and riots, which first drew the world's attention to the Ulster situation, the former teacher of French had earned a reputation as a fearless defender of basic democratic rights for Northern Ireland's Catholic minority, and as an opponent of the paramilitary organizations like the UDA and the Provisional IRA. Once upon a time, McMichael's colleagues in the UDA had slashed to death Senator Paddy Wilson, one of Hume's fellow SDLP members, leaving his body and that of Irene Andrews, a woman friend, mutilated with knife wounds. One of the killers involved had described to a reporter how thrusting a knife into her breasts was like stabbing a pillow.

The Provisional IRA had also targeted SDLP party members, whom it regarded as collaborators, ready to compromise with the British government in its attempts to stabilize Ulster. Hume's home in Derry had been attacked more than once. In 1976, an enraged mob of Provisional IRA supporters had driven Gerry Fitt, Hume's predecessor as the leader of the SDLP, from his house in North Belfast. As of 1995, things had changed, 'changed utterly'. Hume had formed a close liaison with Adams. Later, in Washington, he would be seen sharing a drink with John White, one of the UDA men who was convicted of the murder of Wilson and Andrews.

In certain periods during the decades of violence, Hume had been more welcome in Washington than in parts of Northern Ireland. He had built up a solid following on the Hill, with contacts among all the leading politicians, including the President himself. Thanks to this, he was able to construct a powerful and influential Irish American lobby to bring pressure to bear on the British government to throw its support behind a daring new peace strategy which he had helped initiate three years before when he opened secret talks with the Provisional IRA. Without him, that St Patrick's Day evening in Washington in 1995 would never have taken place.

Giving vital support to Hume's efforts was another important guest – John Bruton, the Irish Prime Minister. For years, one Irish government after another had condemned and imprisoned IRA members, and campaigned in the United States to try to persuade Irish Americans to stop sending money and arms to republican organizations in Ireland. But Hume had persuaded Bruton's predecessor, Albert Reynolds, that the Provisionals were changing, and that their leaders were genuinely seeking a way out of the bloody morass they called the armed struggle, where they had been stuck for decades, slugging it out with the forces of law and order in a dirty little war of attrition. The Irish government was convinced. Reynolds swung his support behind Hume's efforts. For the first time in over seventy years, all strands of Irish nationalism – the militant republicans, the moderates in Ulster, the government in Dublin, and the powerful Irish American lobby in the US – were united. The fruit of this unity was christened the Pan-Nationalist Front – a front that for years had been Adams's goal. But it was not viewed with sympathy by everyone in Ireland.

If the Irish Rip van Winkle looked around him carefully he would have noticed several absences. There was no representative of the Ulster Unionists in attendance. The largest party in Northern Ireland, representing the aspirations of the Protestant majority, had stayed away, using the excuse that invitations to the affair had been sent out too late for it to respond. Most knew, in fact, that the Unionists were deeply unhappy at the spectacle of the apotheosis of Gerry Adams, whom they regarded as a cunning terrorist who had simply changed tactics temporarily. Though they welcomed the cessation of violence, they remained convinced that the Provisionals and their allies were as dangerous as ever – if not more so, now that they had the approval and support of the Irish and US political establishments.

Nor was there anyone present from Her Majesty's Government. The Conservative Party under Prime Minister

John Major had fought bitterly to keep Adams out of the US in the first place, and had suffered a resounding diplomatic defeat. Clinton had telephoned Major after taking his decision to grant the first Adams visa waiver in 1994 to explain why he had broken with precedent. Major did not return the call for three days. It took a while to get used to the fact that in the post-Cold War world, Britain's influence in Washington was on the wane. For decades its massive diplomatic establishment in Washington had been a formative influence on US policy towards Ireland and the crisis in Ulster. Their line had been consistent and simple: Ulster was Britain's business and the United States should concentrate on what the British government saw as the Federal government's only role – blocking illegal arms shipments to the Provisionals and curtailing Irish American fund-raising efforts on their behalf. But by St Patrick's Day 1995, all the roles had changed.

Six months before, on 31 August 1994, the Provisional IRA had declared a 'cessation of military operations' – its first long-term halt in twenty years to its campaign of political violence and terror. Six weeks later, on 13 October, the loyalist paramilitary groups, the UDA and the smaller Ulster Volunteer Force and Red Hand Commandos, followed suit. For the first time in the history of the Ulster crisis all its chief paramilitary antagonists had stopped the killing.

The Irish government had moved fast, inviting Adams to Dublin, where the then Prime Minister, Albert Reynolds, met with Hume and the Sinn Fein leader on the steps of Leinster House – the seat of the Irish parliament, the Dail – in an historic handshake that many hoped presaged a future of peace and political progress. Before long, Adams and other party members had travelled to New York to meet with American supporters. They were followed that October by loyalist paramilitary representatives, speaking for the first time in New York to Irish Americans, whom they had traditionally viewed as the hopelessly naive backers of their hated enemy, the Provisional IRA.

Even a year or two earlier, such developments would have been unthinkable. In 1992 a leading historian of the Troubles had deemed the Ulster crisis 'intractable' – a problem without a solution. A feeling of inertia had set in long ago. A former British cabinet minister had characterized Britain's policy as reducing the Ulster troubles to an 'acceptable level of violence'. But as the loyalists' ceasefire followed that of the republicans, euphoria had replaced resignation and despair, the characteristic emotions generated by the Ulster crisis.

The euphoria was evident that night in the East Wing as the sunset turned vermilion and Frank Patterson burst into 'The Town I Love So Well', a song about Derry city, Northern Ireland's second largest, which Protestants refer to as Londonderry. For hundreds of years, the seventeenth-century walled city has been a symbol of Protestant colonial might and determination in Ireland, since it withstood the long siege of the Catholic King James in his struggle to defeat the Protestant William of Orange for the English throne in 1689. 'The Town I Love So Well', written by Derry songwriter and entertainer Phil Coulter, has become almost as well known as that other song that Derry inspired, 'Danny Boy', known formally as 'The Londonderry Air'.

Coulter's song describes the destruction of Derry during the years of political violence, years of 'armoured cars and bombed out bars', of shootings, car bombings, ambush and assassination, riots, raids and arrests – years symbolized by barbed wire and the crumpled bodies of the thirteen unarmed demonstrators British troops gunned down on 30 January 1972 in a massacre known for ever as Bloody Sunday.

Derry is John Hume's city, where thirty years earlier he had been a leader of the civil rights movement that first sparked world media interest in the Ulster crisis. The black-and-white images of Hume, drenched by a police water cannon or battered by their batons, or thrown against a wall by British troops, still occasionally flash across the screen as film-makers retell the story of those early civil rights struggles. But just as importantly for Hume, Derry is also the first city where the Catholic majority, so long excluded from municipal power, finally assumed the reins of government. In doing so, they gave him a model of how the Ulster crisis might eventually be resolved, with Catholics and Protestants rotating the position of mayor. By 1995, Derry was the model of civic responsibility and power-sharing. Hume wanted to apply its lessons to the whole of Northern Ireland.

As the evening wore on, as happens in any Irish occasion, the guests took over the entertainment. Hume and Adams got up on the stage and formed a duet. Not surprisingly, the audience wanted to hear another rendition of 'The Town I Loved So Well'. Clutching microphones, the representatives of the two strands of Irish nationalism, the constitutional and the violent, for seventy years in bitter confrontation with each other, joined together in song. The other guests linked arms. Some were moved to tears at the sight. As the duet wound up, one veteran observer of the Ulster situation remarked with characteristic Ulster sarcasm: 'Adams should've been singing "The Town We Bombed So Well".' After all, he said, it was the Provisional IRA's bombing campaign in the early 1970s which reduced much of the city centre to a wasteland of bombed buildings and boarded-up shops. Sarcasm and irony long ago became part of the mental armoury of the Ulster temperament; they serve to ward off any temptation to become too optimistic and enthusiastic about the future.

By the time the two wings of Ulster nationalism had united in song, President Clinton and his wife had retired. So had the Irish Prime Minister. So also had the representatives of Ulster loyalism, John McMichael and Joe English, along with their companion Billy Blair. They had stolen out just before the Adam–Hume duet got started. In spite of the evening's claim to be a celebration of the new consensus that was said to be emerging in Ireland, no one had thought to include in the scheduled entertainment a song from the loyalist, Protestant tradition. There had been no rendition of 'The Sash' – the Protestants' most stirring song.

It had been, in the end, in spite of all the euphoria about a new era dawning, a very nationalist occasion, with the Protestants there almost as an afterthought.

In a minor way, this was an indication of underlying problems that as yet had not surfaced, though they lurked not far beneath the bubble of euphoria and would soon test its thin skin. From 1993 onwards, the entire peace process had been very much a nationalist-generated affair. Britain stood suspiciously to one side, waiting, watching, mistrustful of the Provisional IRA, which it had grown grudgingly to respect as a wily if vicious opponent, adept at changing tactics to ensure its survival. Meanwhile, though the Ulster Protestants were prepared to make their case in the US and elsewhere, given the opportunity, they were not entirely happy with what they saw going on around them – years of violence had deepened the sense of paranoia in a community that believed it was under constant threat from Irish republicans bent on breaking its links to Britain and absorbing it into a new, Irish state. That paranoia, centuries old, which various campaigns of IRA violence had reinforced, was not going to be overcome by a few visits to the White House and a St Patrick's Day party.

Nor was there much euphoria outside the White House at the spot where two solitary protesters from Northern Ireland, Thomas Clark and Lisa O'Hagan, maintained a picket. They were drawing attention to the fact that in spite of the Provisional IRA's 'cessation of military operations', it continued to attack alleged criminals. Customarily, the Provisionals carry off the suspects, beat them with cudgels and baseball bats,

11

and/or shoot off their knee-caps. (On occasion they 'execute' them by blowing their brains out.) Thomas Clark explained that this son Malachy was one such victim. After the Provisionals beat him, he had killed himself in despair and fear.

'We're not here to harass Clinton,' said Clark, 'but just to give Gerry a spin.' When asked why Malachy had been singled out, his father replied: 'He was found with a bag of glue in his pocket.'

Glue-sniffing is a favourite escape for many youths in the poor neighbourhoods of Belfast where unemployment is endemic and welfare a way of life as a second generation of the unemployed come of age. The Provisionals act as a kind of surrogate police force, trying to control drug-dealing, petty crime and what they deem 'antisocial' behaviour, which can include allegations about anything from glue-sniffing to child-molesting. They have fulfilled this role since the early 1970s, when it became impossible for the Royal Ulster Constabulary – the Protestant-dominated police force – to operate in a normal fashion in the Catholic ghettos.

Thomas Clark's son Malachy is not listed as a victim of the Ulster crisis. Yet in some ways he was as much a victim as any of those deliberately gunned down or blown up. Twenty-five years and more of relentless violence, concentrated mostly in working-class areas, had taken its toll, morally and psychologically, as well as economically and socially.

There were the obvious signs that accompany social and economic disintegration. There was a marked rise in crime, for instance, in once closely knit neighbourhoods where a few years before it would have been possible to go away from home for the weekend with the front door left unlocked without fear of a robbery. In circumstances where it was a common occurrence to see people gunned down for their political or religious affiliations, petty thievery or drug-taking must have seemed a small enough offence to unemployed youths with no hope of a future.

Behaviour had changed in other, quite radical ways. Profound sexual repression and conservatism had given way to a confused hedonism. There was a rapid rise in out-of-wedlock births, with schoolgirls having babies at ages as young as fourteen and fifteen. As one sixteen year-old pupil at a Belfast Catholic girls' school remarked to a film-maker: 'Our school is going to need a maternity ward next to it.'

People were left to lament the loss of the old decencies and customs that had once characterized life in the poor quarters of Belfast, both Catholic and Protestant, while still being uncertain and fearful of what if anything had replaced them. The Victorian world of hard work and worship that produced those decencies seemed as far away and out of date as the grainy black-and-white photographs of the *Titanic* sitting in its dock in Harland and Wolff, the Belfast shipyard that built it.

The guests that attended the White House St Patrick's Day party that evening paid little attention to the protests of Thomas Clark and his companion Lisa O'Hagan. Nor could they address the underlying social and economic ills that they represented. It was not the time to stop and take heed of such details. Their minds were focused on the bigger picture – what they saw as the first real chance of peace since the Troubles began all those long, blood-bespattered decades ago. They were convinced that an historic breakthrough in Anglo-Irish relations was in the making such as had not been seen since Ireland was partitioned more than seventy years earlier.

There was surely cause to be optimistic. By March 1995, the Provisional IRA's ceasefire had endured for more than six months; the loyalist groups too had succeeded in keeping their men under control, creating the longest cessation of paramilitary violence that Ulster had experienced. But those who looked closely at the Ulster situation noticed several disturbing signs – not only did the Provisional IRA continue its 'policing' role, as it inflicted vicious violence on those such as Malachy Clark who displeased it. Even as celebrations were

13

being held in the White House, plans were being hatched in Belfast to launch a campaign against alleged drug dealers that would soon lead to a wave of murders which the IRA carried out under the pseudonym 'Direct Action Against Drugs', known by the acronym DAAD, with all its connotations of sinister patriarchal violence.

Meanwhile, in the poor working-class Protestant neighbourhoods, the old sectarian hatreds had not gone away. Late in December 1994, a Catholic student called Noel Lyness had drifted into a loyalist area of Belfast, drunk. Next morning, his battered body was found dumped in an alleyway. The underlying tensions and fears that had characterized Ulster for generations remained.

As the guests headed back to Ireland, plans were being drafted for a Northern Ireland Investment Conference to be sponsored by Clinton in Washington the following May. There was talk of the first ever US presidential visit to Belfast before the year was out. Hopes were high. But in Ulster, history is a stubborn ghost that is not easily laid to rest. It would haunt the hopes of the peacemakers.

The violence had ended, more or less. But the conflict remained. The politicians and paramilitary chiefs left the East Wing of the White House to go home to the difficult task of dealing with the roots of that conflict. The conflicting claims and aspirations of Catholic and Protestant, nationalist and unionist, republican and loyalist, had somehow to be resolved before the fault lines that lie deep within Ulster society began to grind against each other again, bringing the potential for renewed death and destruction. Hope was not enough to deal with history. It rarely is. In Ulster, history has vanquished hope so often that it seems an act of folly to expect it to be otherwise.

Why this should be, and how it came about, is the aim of the following pages to elucidate. They will do so based on the premise that the Troubles, usually described in accounts as

14

one seamless period, which some begin in 1969, others in 1968 and still others in 1966, in fact breaks down into three fairly distinct phases – 1966–77, 1977–94, and 1994 to the present.

A few of those who were at the Washington party in March 1995 had been formative influences in the first two, 1966–77 and 1977–94, and were there to shape the third, perhaps final phase. In each of these phases the nature of the Troubles changed in noticeable ways, though the underlying conflict remained the same.

PART ONE

The Troubles

1966–77

CHAPTER ONE

Return of the Gunman: 1966–69

1

The conflict known as the Troubles began ingloriously in a Belfast side street with the murder of an old woman. Two drunk men emerged from an alleyway, their raincoats pulled up around their faces. One of them hurled a Molotov cocktail across the street at a Catholic-owned off-licence. He missed and hit the house next door, the home of Matilda Gould, a seventy-seven-year-old Protestant widow who lived there with her son. Unable to climb the stairs, she slept in the front room on the ground floor where the bomb landed.

The first sounds of a conflict that would endure for more than thirty years were the crash of glass from a breaking window, the whoosh of flame as a petrol bomb burst, and the screech of pain as the burning liquid splashed over Mrs Gould. Rescuers found her crumpled behind the door, burning.

It was 10.40 p.m. on 7 May 1966. And Northern Ireland was, technically speaking, at peace.

Within weeks of the fire-bombing, there were two more fatal attacks. This time, both victims were Catholics, more or

19

less picked at random. The first was a drunk man called John Scullion, shot on his way home singing an Irish republican ballad. The second was Peter Ward, an eighteen-year-old bartender, ambushed as he left an after-hours drinking den in the Protestant Shankill area of Belfast in the early morning of 26 June.

The Troubles, most assumed, were a thing of the past, a name given to the turmoil of the early 1920s, when the Irish Republican Army fought to drive the British out of Ireland. The IRA succeeded in securing twenty-six of the thirty-two counties. Unionists wanted no part of an independent Ireland. They formed their own six-county state, Northern Ireland, carved out of the nine historic counties of the northern province of Ulster, where loyal Protestants possessed an overall majority, imposing their will through violence and intimidation on a recalcitrant Catholic minority. Belfast became its capital, an industrial boom town, a jewel in the crown of the British Empire, and a bulwark against the nationalism that was threatening to engulf the whole of Ireland.

Between 1922 and 1966 Northern Ireland settled into two more or less homogenous blocks, nationalist and Unionist, Catholic and Protestant. In many ways, they were mirror images of each other. The nationalists were exiles from the Irish nation; in their exclusion they clung to their religion as a mark of cultural identity; politically, they dealt with the Northern Ireland state by ignoring it. The Unionists were also a community under threat – a minority within the island of Ireland. In 1920, Lord Edward Carson, the founding father of Northern Ireland, did his sums and calculated that three of the nine Ulster counties with a Catholic majority, Monaghan, Donegal and Cavan, would have to be ditched. But Counties Derry, Antrim, Tyrone, Armagh, Fermanagh and Down would give Ulster Protestants the homeland they sought. Unfortunately for Ulster Unionists, the prospect of a uniformly 'loyal' Northern Ireland proved illusory. There were loyal parts, a majority of them, but in other places in Northern Ireland Catholics formed a local majority. Northern Ireland was a state based on numbers, and numbers by their very nature have a habit of changing. With this in-built insecurity, separated from their parent nation, Britain, Protestants clung to the symbols of their Britishness – the union jack flag, the Royal Family, and their own particular rituals which celebrated their triumph over Popery and nationalism. The most famous of these were the parades organized by the Orange Order – a 'brotherhood' of Protestants which had been created in the eighteenth century to fight Irish republicanism – culminating on 12 July. That is, Northern Ireland was comprised of two communities who shared the same area but owed their allegiances to different nations. This difference was the fault line on which the state rested.

By 1966, the IRA numbered its adherents in Belfast on the fingers of two hands. Northern Ireland's Catholic population had failed to respond to its last summons to arms when in 1956 it launched a border campaign to 'free' the remaining British-controlled corner of Ireland. The IRA's sporadic attacks against police stations, cross-border bridges and bus stations sputtered out, barely noticed, in 1962. A liberal Unionist Prime Minister, Captain Terence O'Neill, was now leading Northern Ireland's parliament at Stormont, promising reform and the integration of the minority Catholic population into the economic and political life of a province that Protestant Unionists had completely dominated since its foundation in 1921. It was the 1960s, after all, the age of the Beatles, Muhammad Ali, John F. Kennedy, manned space flight, free love, and civil rights. Never in human history had change occurred at such a rapid pace. But for some in the back streets of working-class Protestant areas of Belfast, that was precisely the problem.

Matilda Gould, John Scullion and Peter Ward were the

21

victims of a small group of working-class Protestant loyalists who called themselves the Ulster Volunteer Force and whose professed aim was to defend Northern Ireland against Catholic subversion.[1] The fiftieth anniversary of the 1916 rebellion stirred their fears; their Prime Minister's overtures to Catholics and appeals that they should be treated with 'due consideration and kindness' were seen as evidence of weakness and betrayal. Their idea of 'defence' was to vandalize Catholic-owned premises in Protestant areas, scribble anti-Catholic graffiti on Catholic property – just prior to the fire-bombing, *Popehead* had appeared on the Catholic premises next door to Mrs Gould's home – and kill 'IRA' men.

A statement issued in the name of the UVF in May declared: 'Known IRA men will be executed mercilessly and without hesitation.' However, in 1966 IRA men were rare in Belfast, and when the UVF's half-hearted attempts to find them failed, it did what loyalist extremists have always done – killed the most vulnerable Catholic. Anyway, to loyalists, such as Andrew Augustus Spence, known as Gusty, the founder of the UVF, a Catholic was by definition an IRA man.

Spence was a lantern-jawed former British soldier who had served as a military policeman in Cyprus. He worked as a steel-fitter in Harland and Wolff shipyards, whose workforce was almost entirely Protestant and the biggest employer in Belfast.

When Spence and his gang were arrested in connection with the killing of Ward, of which they were later convicted, one of them, Hugh McClean, blurted out: 'I am terribly sorry I ever heard tell of that man Paisley or decided to follow him. I am definitely ashamed of myself to be in such a position.'

The Rev. Ian Kyle Paisley was a big, braying anti-Catholic fundamentalist preacher, who told men like Spence what they wanted to hear – that the Catholic threat to Ulster was real, part of a vast conspiracy organized from Rome. Its agents were the IRA, liberal Unionists such as Terence O'Neill, the ecumenical movement as represented by the World Council of Churches, communists and socialists, its conspirator-in-chief the Pope. 'Go into any Roman church in this city,' begins a typical specimen of Paisley's preaching, *circa* 1964, 'and what do you see? It's like Madame Tussaud's in London. Legions of graven images! Gaudy and vulgar, and an abomination in the sight of God. Equally rank in the nostrils and nauseating are the sanctuary lamps and candelabras placed before the sickly prints of the Virgin and other saints. These are the trappings of the great whore of Babylon and the Scarlet Woman . . . Are you prepared to be party to this base surrender, to be Lundies and Papists?' (Lundy was a seventeenth-century traitor to the Protestant cause.) Paisley's favourite trick was to wheel on an ex-nun to regale his outraged congregation with pornographic tales of convent life, a mixture of sexual fantasy and dubious theology that exercised an irresistible charm over a handful of mostly repressed social misfits.

Paisley drew most of his support from the fringe of the Protestant community, a murky world of crackpot religious extremists, bigots and gunmen, who set up paramilitary organizations that were usually unknown to anyone other than the handful of men that formed them. This was part of a hallowed Ulster Protestant tradition where the need for unofficial militias went back to the eighteenth century. There were at least three different groups using the name UVF. Paisley formed the Ulster Protestant Volunteers in the spring of 1966, the same year in which Spence set up his version of the UVF.

Though many of Paisley's associates ended up behind bars for violent crimes, Paisley himself spoke out against acts of violence and avoided arrest on anything more serious than an offence for disorderly behaviour. But his followers clearly regarded his public condemnations of violence as a mere fiction and acted accordingly. They used the UPV headquarters in Belfast to hide their arms. When Paisley discovered weapons there, he ordered the UPV member who had hidden them to remove them at once. The preacher possessed the presence of mind to make sure his follower carried them out the back door, not the front, which he believed was under police surveillance. 'If you let those fellows get away with the likes of that, they'd finish us all,' he is reported to have remarked, somewhat disingenuously.[2]

A visitor to Belfast at any time since about the mid-1880s would have found gangs of men like those around Spence and Bible-thumping bigots of Paisley's type. It was a hive of fundamentalist faiths and apocalyptic visionaries whose doomsday rhetoric stirred up poor Protestants against the increasing number of Catholics flooding into the city after the Famine of 1847. Catholics were also hungry for jobs and houses. Their large families swarmed in the narrow streets of the Falls Road, just a few hundred yards away from their Protestant neighbours on the Shankill. Moreover, the new-comers traditionally aligned themselves with Irish national-ism. Tension led to clashes and widespread rioting, which in 1886 became so bad as to 'assume the character of a civil war'.[3] With the rise of the shipbuilding, ropeworks and linen industries, Ulster became more closely bound economically to Britain and the Empire. The severing of those bonds, Protes-tants feared, would mean the destruction of Ulster's prosper-ity and status as the only industrially developed part of Ireland.

It remained in 1966 a Victorian city, conservative, pious, and industrious, with work and worship dominating the lives of its citizens, both Catholic and Protestant. The working classes lived in the narrow streets which clustered around the mills and factories in little two-up, two-down redbrick row houses with black slate roofs. It was a city that even then still smelt of coal smoke and candle wax, tobacco and hemp. They were a God-fearing people, reared on religious as well as political dogmas, to whom sin and damnation were as real as the shriek of the factory horn that called them to work in the morning. On Sunday, Belfast shut down. Pubs, restaurants and cinemas were closed. The children's parks were locked, the swings chained. Like the God of the Old Testament, Ulster had a low opinion of pleasure.

Political change or perceived change made the fault line between the Protestant and Catholic communities shift a little, and the tension released itself in outbursts of rioting and sectarian murder, as much a feature of Belfast life as the gaunt industrial chimney stacks and the church spires that dominated its skyline.

Beyond the low hills that surrounded the city was a world of small, mostly ugly nineteenth-century towns. As in the city, the two communities rubbed against each other, close together yet segregated. The pattern of land distribution dated back to the seventeenth century, when James I began the Plantation. English and Scottish settlers supplanted the local, rebellious Celtic warlords. Though the cultural and linguistic links between Scotland and Ulster were far older, the Plantation was a traumatic change, representing the overthrow of the old order of Celtic aristocracy. Protestants farmed the valleys, and Catholics for the most part were left with the smaller, poorer farms among the hills, wresting a meagre living from a few stony fields. 'Every bullet and every bomb exploded in Northern Ireland,' wrote a local historian, 'is laid to the blame of a monarch dead these three centuries.'[4]

In 1966, the Northern Ireland Unionist Party was celebrating almost fifty years in government. Northern Ireland was, in effect, a one-party state, unique in western Europe. Voting patterns were as fixed as the Plantation. Of the state's 1.5 million population, around 65 per cent were Protestants, the rest Catholic, which kept the Unionists in power, year after year, decade after decade. Though a substantial and growing minority, Catholics were politically passive. Nationalist politics was embodied in the Nationalist Party – though embodied, suggesting life of some sort, is perhaps the wrong word. By the mid-1960s the party was effectively a corpse, killed off by its own verities, one of which was its steadfast refusal to recognize the reality of the Northern Ireland state. Its politicians, when elected to the parliament at Stormont, refused to deal with their Unionist counterparts or act as an opposition in any way. Its goal of achieving a united Ireland through ignoring partition was as far away as ever. And during the entire period from 1921 until the 1960s, the Nationalist Party failed to get any reform passed that would benefit the Catholic population or address their grievances.

Catholics were still barred from certain jobs, such as in the Harland and Wolff shipyards; few found their way into the civil service and those that did remained on the lower scales. By 1966, only 4 per cent of those earning £2,000 were Catholics. In Derry, Northern Ireland's second city, with a large Catholic majority, only 32 of the city's 177 municipal employees were Catholics. Northern Ireland's housing standards were among the worst in the United Kingdom. With outdoor toilets and no bathrooms, some houses dated back to the 1840s. For working-class Catholics the situation was made worse because some local housing authorities, dominated by Unionists, favoured their fellow Protestants when it came to the allocation of new homes. This was especially noticeable in the west of Northern Ireland, where there was an overall Catholic majority. In Co. Fermanagh, for example, of 1,589 postwar houses built, 1,021 went to Protestants, 568 to Catholics.[5] The distribution of houses had profound political implications in areas where Catholics were in the majority but Unionists still managed to hold on to the running of local authorities, which allocated jobs and houses. It enabled the Unionists to gerrymander the ward system to ensure that more Unionists were elected than nationalists. Thus in Derry, Unionists, though in the minority, were able to hold twelve of the twenty council seats. However, discrimination was an accepted part of Ulster society, and practised on both sides. In some areas where nationalists held power, such as Newry in South Down, that they should hire 'their own' was taken for granted.[6]

Catholics lacked political leadership. A twenty-seven-year-old teacher of French, John Hume wrote in *The Irish Times*. 'Weak opposition leads to corrupt government. Nationalists in opposition have in no way been constructive . . . leadership has been the comfortable leadership of flags and slogans . . . There has been no attempt to be positive, to encourage the Catholic community to develop the resources they have in plenty to make a positive contribution in terms of community service.' Hume founded the Derry Credit Union to help working-class Catholics save money in order to buy their own homes. He was a new type of nationalist that was emerging in the mid-1960s. His mother worked in a shirt factory, and his father was unemployed. Discrimination barred young working-class Catholics like him from skilled manufacturing jobs. A growing number took the route of higher education, effectively moving into the middle class, to become lawyers, teachers, journalists and academics. They wanted wider horizons than the narrow, sectarian politics of Northern Ireland seemed to offer. And thanks to British education reforms enacted in 1944 and later extended to Northern Ireland, Hume was able to go to university, where he studied French. One of the first times Hume spoke in public was in a college debate in 1959, when he argued in favour of Ireland joining the Common Market (later the European Community). One of the benefits, he said, was that it would gradually make the border irrelevant. Traditional nationalist politicans regarded such arguments as heretical. How could partition not be relevant? It was like telling a Catholic that there was no such thing as original sin. But Hume's contemporaries were as impatient with nationalist verities as they were with the status quo and the unaddressed grievances on which it rested. They wanted change. The problem was, there existed no vehicle to effect that change. But in August 1966, just as Spence and his gang were going to trial for the murder of Peter Ward, a small group of republicans and political activists quietly met to create one.

An urge to make an old vehicle of change, the IRA, relevant to modern Ireland inspired the meeting. Since the débâcle of the 1956–62 border campaign a powerful group had arisen within the IRA who saw the trench-coated gunman – the symbol of the IRA's ethos – as a prop that must be carried off the stage of Irish history and dumped. The romantic nationalism that came out of the barrel of his gun would have to be replaced with something else, something more relevant to a country whose most popular television show was *Top of the Pops*, on which swarms of miniskirted young women and long-haired young men gyrated once a week to the music of the Beatles and the Rolling Stones. At the August meeting, a handful of disgruntled IRA men, left-wing intellectuals, Communist Party members and a few trade union activists talked of infiltrating the trade unions to make contact with sympathetic Protestant workers. Like Hume, they were convinced that the old sectarian barriers that divided Catholic from Protestant would crumble. All that was needed was a programme around which both Catholics and Protestants could unite. It was an optimistic, progressive vision, based on the left-wing assumption that given the opportunity Catholic and Protestant workers would realize that they shared common economic interests that outweighed the old nationalist ideologies and sectarian beliefs still dividing them.

The unity of Catholic and Protestant workers was the holy grail of Irish socialism and, to a lesser extent republicanism. Progressive left-wing republicans had pursued it since the beginning of the twentieth century. And each time, they failed to find it. But in 1966, it seemed right to try again. There were hopeful signs. A Labour government was in power in Britain under the leadership of Harold Wilson. Several Labour Party MPs were known to be keen to reform Northern Ireland and expose its abuses. In February, the Catholics of West Belfast had elected Gerry Fitt to Westminster. Fitt was a member of the small Republican Labour Party. He was a bluff and jovial former dock worker, a life-long trade unionist, the sort of Belfast man that looks as if he was born wearing a cloth cap, with a pint in one hand and a betting slip in the other. In Westminster, Fitt formed alliances with interested Labour MPs to press for the British government to take a more active role in Northern Ireland affairs. For left-wing republicans this seemed to be part of the general movement towards change that was in the very air in the 1960s.

On 29 January 1967 a second meeting was held, this time in Belfast. The original group had expanded considerably to include members of the tiny Ulster Liberal Party and the Northern Ireland Labour Party. A liberal Unionist was co-opted on to a steering committee. Out of this, the Northern Ireland Civil Rights Association (NICRA) was born.

Its constitution proclaimed its goals:

1 To defend the basic freedoms of all citizens
2 To protect the rights of the individuals
3 To highlight all possible abuses of power
4 To demand guarantees of freedom of speech, assembly and association
5 To inform the public of their lawful rights.

The group also demanded the abolition of the Special Powers Act, draconian security legislation enacted in the early years of Northern Ireland when the IRA was still a menace. This allowed the Northern Ireland police, the Royal Ulster Constabulary, wide powers of arrest, including detention without trial. There were also calls for the abolition of the B-Specials, a part-time constabulary set up during the Troubles of the 1920s, whom Catholics regarded as sectarian.

NICRA's tactics of marches and sit-downs would be based on the campaign for black civil rights which at the time was reaching its climax in the US.[7] In 1968 it took to the streets as a result of a housing protest. Austin Currie, a nationalist MP for East Tyrone, wanted to draw attention to the case of a nineteen-year-old Protestant woman, a secretary for a local Unionist, who had been allocated a house over the heads of 269 people on the waiting list, many of them Catholics with large families. Attempts to raise the matter in Stormont proved fruitless. Currie recalled the advice of Labour MP Paul Rose, who was active on the Northern Ireland issue. 'No British government, including this one, will intervene to remedy injustice in Northern Ireland unless you people there force it to,' he told Currie. On 20 June 1968, Currie, his wife and a local farmer broke into the disputed house and squatted.

'The media arrived within the hour . . . after three and a half hours the bailiffs arrived with a sledge hammer. The door was smashed down and we were ejected none too gently into the lenses of the waiting media. That night the BBC news from London for the first time carried a report of injustice in Northern Ireland. Paul Rose rang to congratulate me. The process of forcing the British government to intervene to remedy injustice in the North had begun.'[8]

Two months later, in support of Currie, NICRA organized its first protest march, from Coalisland to Market Square in Dungannon, Co. Tyrone. A minister in the Unionist government, John Taylor, declared that Dungannon town centre was 'Unionist territory'. The Rev. Ian Paisley and his supporters immediately organized a counter-demonstration, which occupied Market Square to prevent the civil rights protesters from entering. This was a clash of 1960s culture with fundamentalist, conservative Ulster. But it was occurring on traditional ground. That is, it was the form of the protest as much as its content which spurred Protestant reaction. The issue, as the Protestants saw it, was territorial. To march in Ulster is to stake a claim on a territory. It is to say: 'I have a right to march here because this is mine.' For this reason traditional parades such as those taking place around 12 July each year are basic expressions of the underlying conflict and over the years have provoked much violence. Now the civil rights movement was marching to draw attention not to territorial claims but to fundamental issues concerning injustice and the nature of the state. Their struggle was aimed at a public, legal sphere, where they hoped a consensus could be created on the need for change. But to Paisley and his followers, and to other less militant Protestants also, it was an expansion by the enemy into territory that was not theirs. And they responded as Ulster Protestants always have to perceived threats – with blockades, counter-marches and, ultimately, extreme violence.

NICRA's next march was an attempt to show that its campaign was not about territory but about bridge-building. It was planned for 5 October in Derry city. It would proceed from the Protestant Waterside district, and cross a bridge into the west side of the city, which was predominantly Catholic, for a rally in Guildhall Square. However, a few within NICRA and on its fringes had different intentions and effectively took over the organization of the event. A small group of Derry socialists hoped 'to provoke the police into over reaction and thus spark off mass reaction against the authorities'.[9] The IRA, which had been taking a back seat in these events, also got involved. Their volunteers were ordered to act as 'stewards' of the march. When it was announced that a few prominent Labour politicians from Britain would be taking part, the IRA instructed its men to ensure that 'if the police lashed out they would connect with newsworthy skulls'.[10] When the authorities banned the march, the organizers

31

declared their intention to go ahead, and the scene was set for a nasty confrontation.

Four hundred marchers, far fewer than expected, gathered on a grey Saturday afternoon, near the Derry railway station. But British and Irish television cameras were there as the Royal Ulster Constabulary blocked the route. Several protesters approached the police cordon to remonstrate with the officers. A baton was thrust into the stomach of one and he collapsed, writhing in pain. The RUC waded into the marchers' ranks, clubbing them to the ground. Westminster MP Gerry Fitt's head was split in front of the television cameras. Meanwhile, a second line of RUC men took the marchers in the rear. A water cannon drenched respectable MPs and militants alike. The demonstrators fled in confused panic into the Catholic west side of the city, the RUC in pursuit. The police were met with stones and petrol bombs in sporadic attacks that lasted into the early hours of Sunday morning.

For many television viewers in Britain, their first sight of Northern Ireland was that of a policeman batoning a peaceful protester. Their ignorance of the Ulster situation was profound, most assuming that the Irish problem had been settled decades ago. They were shocked not only by the pictures of the violence but by the fact that, unlike the English 'bobby', the RUC were armed, more like a paramilitary unit than a civilian police force. NICRA effectively exploited the coverage with such slogans as 'British Rights for British Citizens'. As a result, Northern Ireland was suddenly thrust on to the Wilson government's agenda. For the British, after almost fifty years of keeping the Irish problem at arm's length, it was an unwelcome intrusion.

Wilson ordered the Northern Ireland Prime Minister, Terence O'Neill, along with two of his more prominent ministers, William Craig and Brian Faulkner, to London, where he impressed upon the Unionists the need for reforms. O'Neill announced on his return that the Special Powers Acts would be abolished as soon as it was safe to do so, housing allocation would in future be based on a points system, the company vote, allowing businessmen more than one vote, was to be abolished, and there would be reforms in local government, including the abolition of the Unionist-controlled Derry city council. An ombudsman was to be appointed to handle complaints. Craig, a hardliner who resented British interference, was furious, and once back in Belfast stirred up Unionist resistance to the changes with increasingly violent speeches. He depicted the whole civil rights movement as a stalking-horse for the IRA. Faulkner, more wily and driven mainly by ambition, bided his time with his eye on replacing O'Neill as Prime Minister.

After five years as head of government, O'Neill was in an invidious position. His problems stemmed partly from the fact that he was not a typical Unionist. Educated at Eton, he looked and sounded more like an upper-class Englishman than an Ulsterman. For all the ferocity of their claims to be British, Ulster Unionists deeply suspected Britain, with its changing, multicultural society, its more easy-going morals and liberal opinions. O'Neill, by accent, education and class, was tainted and distrusted. His political gestures deepened that distrust among the more hardline elements in Unionism. In 1965, he had invited Sean Lemass, the Irish Taoiseach (Prime Minister), to Stormont, a harmless gesture in any but the Ulster political context, with watchtowers and gates as its symbols and betrayal as its rallying cry. He visited a Catholic school and was photographed speaking with nuns. But in fact, for most of his time as leader, O'Neill had made no serious attempts at addressing Catholic grievances. Instead, he concentrated on economic changes, based on attracting outside investors into Northern Ireland to replace its flagging industries. He hoped that a new prosperity would result which would dissolve traditional sectarian differences, and Catholics would live like Protestants as contented Ulstermen and women. By 1968, however, it was too late for such long-term solutions. O'Neill was trapped between his enemies within Unionism and the growing anger and impatience of Catholics.

'Patiently endured so long as it seemed beyond redress, a grievance comes to appear intolerable once the possibility of removing it crosses men's minds,' observed Alexis de Tocqueville of the days leading up to the French Revolution and the end of the *ancien régime*. 'For the mere fact that certain abuses have been remedied draws attention to others and they appear more galling.'[11] O'Neill's promise of change unleashed forces that the *ancien régime* of Unionism could not contain.

NICRA branches mushroomed all over Northern Ireland. Other groups sprang up. More militant left-wing students, among them a young woman called Bernadette Devlin, created People's Democracy. John Hume, worried that left-wing republican influence was too strong in NICRA, established the Derry Citizen's Action Committee. More demonstrations followed and O'Neill appealed for calm. 'Ulster stands at the cross-roads,' he said on a television broadcast as 1968 came to a close, 'our conduct over the coming days will decide our future. For more than five years now I have tried to heal some of the deep divisions in our community. I did so because I could not see how an Ulster divided against itself could hope to stand . . . What kind of Ulster do you want? A happy and respected province in good standing with the rest of the United Kingdom? Or a place continually torn apart by riots and demonstrations and regarded by the rest of Britain as a political outcast?'

NICRA responded favourably to O'Neill's speech and said it was temporarily halting its demonstrations. But People's Democracy declared it was to hold a long march from Belfast to Derry, beginning on 1 January 1969. One of its leaders said that it would be modelled on Martin Luther King's march in 1966 from Selma to Mongomery, Alabama, which 'exposed

34

the racist thuggery of America's deep south and forced the US government into major reforms'.[12]

The PD's was a self-fulfilling prophesy. On the fourth day of the hundred-mile trek, with an RUC escort, the marchers reached Burntollet Bridge, outside Derry. A mob of loyalists, several hundred strong, lay in wait. According to Bernadette Devlin: 'a curtain of bricks and boulders brought the march to a halt. From the lanes burst hordes of screaming people wielding planks of wood, bottles, laths, iron bars, crowbars, cudgels studded with nails, and they waded into the march beating the hell out of everybody.'[13]

The police did little to protect the marchers. As they staggered into Derry, bloodied and battered, riots erupted in the Catholic Bogside district where vicious clashes occurred with the RUC. Three hundred people were injured, and Catholics accused the police of running amok.[14]

O'Neill succumbed to British government pressure to set up an inquiry into the disturbances. His enemies within his own party saw their opportunity. Brian Faulkner resigned from the Cabinet, accusing O'Neill of abdicating the powers of the Stormont government. Craig attacked him for not standing up to the British and being unable to lead the Unionist Party. Almost fifty years of single-party rule at Stormont, during which Unionists were left to their own devices, made some forget that sovereignty lay not in the Belfast parliament but in Westminster. In a desperate bid to bolster his position, O'Neill called a general election for 24 February.

For the first time since 1920 and the divisive debate over whether or not Northern Ireland should comprise six or nine counties, the Ulster Unionist Party began to fragment. Pro-O'Neill Unionists stood against anti-O'Neill Unionists and former colleagues bitterly denounced each other. Paisley stood under the label of Protestant Unionist, and challenged O'Neill in his own constituency. A similar fragmentation occurred on the nationalist side. Civil rights campaigners

35

such as John Hume and Austin Currie ran in constituencies formerly the domain of the old Nationalist Party. In Belfast, Gerry Fitt's Republican Labour sought to broaden its base among nationalists and trade union activists.

The election result was a failure for O'Neill and the moderate Unionists. Though his majority – twenty-seven pro-O'Neill Unionists as against twelve anti-O'Neill MPs or undecideds – seemed solid, it was not the overwhelming endorsement of his policy he felt he needed. Most embarrassingly of all, Paisley, his nemesis, came within 1,500 votes of taking his seat. Catholics also failed to support pro-O'Neill Unionists. His attempt to build a bridge between moderate Unionists and moderate nationalists collapsed under Paisley's jeers that 'bridges like traitors go over to the other side'. The election dubbed the 'cross-roads' election (after O'Neill's speech of the previous December) showed that a significant block of Ulster's Protestants were taking the road of extremism. It also showed that nationalists were following a different road from that of the old Nationalist Party. Its vote dropped catastrophically to 6 per cent. Civil rights activists, including Hume, took three seats from Nationalist Party MPs. In Belfast, where the party had never been strong, it ceased to exist. Republican Labour with two seats was now the voice of Belfast nationalists.

The realignment that took place in February 1969 would set Northern Ireland's political mould for the coming decades. Two months later, it saw the election to Westminster of Bernadette Devlin, the youngest MP for fifty years. The left-wing IRA leadership supported her campaign as a way of bringing civil rights issues right into the heart of the British political establishment. Her maiden speech was a fiery attack on British government policy; she warned that if British troops were sent to Ulster 'I should not like to be either the mother or sister of any unfortunate soldier stationed there'.

Wilson, perhaps misreading the February election result as a clear-cut victory for moderate Unionists, continued to press O'Neill to make reforms, especially to introduce one-man-one-vote for local elections. O'Neill moved to introduce the reform. Militant loyalists were more frustrated than ever. O'Neill was still in power, bending to British pressure, as ready as ever, as they saw it, to sell out. On the gable walls in Protestant areas of Belfast was scrawled: 'Gusty Spence Was Right'.

After Spence was imprisoned for life, his organization, the UVF, merged with two smaller groups on the Shankill Road using the same name. One of these was no more than a gang of street thugs who liked to beat up any Catholics that wandered into their area. Among its members, however, were Davy Payne and Jim Craig, men who would later rise to prominence in loyalism's violent underworld. In the spring of 1969, UVF elements linked up with members of Paisley's Ulster Protestant Volunteers. On 21 March, they bombed a Catholic church in Co. Antrim. On 30 March, an electricity substation in Protestant East Belfast was struck. Three weeks later, a few days before O'Neill was to announce the abolition of the property vote in local elections, a wave of explosions rocked Ulster. The targets as before were water and electricity utilities, including Belfast's reservoir.

Paisley alleged it was the work of the IRA. But RUC intelligence pointed in a different direction, and O'Neill was told that the attacks were the responsibility of Protestant extremists linked to the UVF. O'Neill had banned the UVF in 1966 after the first wave of murders. It now exacted its revenge. On 28 April, demoralized and disheartened, his hope of a moderate centre embracing Catholic and Protestant broken, O'Neill resigned.

At the trial in April 1970 of one of those accused of taking part in the bombing campaign it was revealed that the bombing conspiracy also involved members of Paisley's

UPV. It was stated that the defendant, Sam Stevenson, a UPV man and a member of Paisley's Free Presbyterian church, 'was not the man who conceived the idea, nor had he a mind subtle enough to consider the long-term implications of his conduct'.[15] It was suggested that the mysterious mastermind behind the plot to remove O'Neill was Paisley himself. Over the years, though he has been associated with violent organizations, there has never been hard evidence to connect Paisley to violent acts. He himself condemns violence. But there is evidence (see above) that he knew that members of his UPV were acting illegally at times. The organization's constitution, which forbade Catholics to join, advocated using whatever 'legal' means necessary to uphold the constitution. However, it contained a clause that stated 'when the authorities act contrary to the Constitution the body will take whatever steps it thinks fit to expose such unconstitutional acts'.[16] This was easily interpreted by extreme loyalists as meaning that through violence they could rid themselves of someone like O'Neill, whom they considered a 'traitor'.

Faulkner lost the Unionist leadership contest to James Chichester-Clark. Right-wing Unionists who hoped for stronger leadership were soon disappointed. Chichester-Clark would face the same dilemma as his predecessor, caught between insecure and angry loyalists, British government pressure for reform, and increasingly belligerent nationalists, some of whom began thinking that if Protestants could use violence to achieve their aims then perhaps the age of the trench-coated gunman was not yet past.

2

For most Catholics, the IRA was a derisory organization, real only to a handful of old men, superannuated republicans and a few paranoid loyalists. By the 1960s it was being kept alive in Belfast thanks to a handful of republican families such as that of Gerry Adams, whose father was an IRA veteran imprisoned in the 1940s. But it was politics as well as family tradition which pushed Adams to join while still a lanky teenager. The attempt to make the IRA relevant again attracted Adams and a few other working-class Belfast Catholics. The new left-wing politics the IRA leadership in Dublin espoused made sense, as did the republican movement's involvement with the burgeoning civil rights campaign, as a way of broadening the IRA's appeal beyond the romantic images of gun battles on picturesque hillsides and stoical martyrs facing firing squads for 'the cause'. 'The civil rights movement had done more in a few weeks to damage Unionist structure than decades of IRA activity,' observed one republican activist.[17]

However, for many older veterans the new course was a dangerous diversion away from the main aim of the IRA, which was to fight for the thirty-two-county republic they believe was betrayed in 1921 with the partition of the country. Belfast IRA men like Billy McKee and Joe Cahill, whose republican creed was forged in the 1940s and 1950s, believed the politicization process would mean the end of the IRA. According to McKee: 'The IRA would've been phased out but for the Troubles. By 1969, it was bankrupt.'[18] Money was being used not to buy weapons but to keep the movement's newspaper, the *United Irishman*, from closing. The veterans' discontent intensified as the civil rights movement came under attack from extreme loyalists. They had some support among the leaders in the South. Sean MacStiofain, who was head of the IRA's intelligence-gathering department, sympathized with their predicament. He complained bitterly that 'the Irish Republican Army had been bogged down in politics to the point where young girl students from Northern universities had left it far behind in revolutionary initiative'.[19] MacStiofain, an Englishman by birth and a former corporal in the RAF, was a fanatical republican and Irish language devotee who had served a prison term in England in the 1950s for stealing arms. He demanded that the IRA take retaliatory action against police officers who had been seen hitting demonstrators during riots. He said they should be shot. Fortunately, cooler heads within the IRA's ruling body, the Army Council, quickly squashed that proposal, realizing it would play right into the hands of right-wing Unionists. But in April 1969, under growing pressure from their more militant members, the Army Council placed all volunteers on full alert and sent a number of fully-equipped units north to take up 'defensive' positions. This sounded more impressive than it actually was – the number of men involved was no more than a few dozen at the most. However, in Belfast the IRA ignored the leadership's caution and early on moved from 'defensive' into 'offensive' mode. Between 20 and 21 April their younger activists carried out a series of fire-bomb attacks on post offices.

The Unionist response to the civil rights movement had moved the situation beyond NICRA's demands for reform and brought 'the existence of the six-county state into question'.[20] MacStiofain agreed; without informing other members of the Army Council, he collected ammunition from arms dumps in the South, as well as a few hand grenades and guns, and quietly transported them to Belfast, where they were handed over to the IRA's intelligence officer in the city.[21] The authority of the Dublin leadership was being further undermined as individual republicans, convinced that a major confrontation was looming, set up secret training camps.

Summer is always the most dangerous time in Ulster, when thousands of Orange parades take place. As the evenings lengthened, riots erupted and spread beyond Belfast and Derry to rural towns such as Armagh, Lurgan and Dungannon. Those parades that passed Catholic areas came under attack from bottle- and stone-throwing youths. Orange halls were torched. Not since the 1880s had rioting occurred on such a scale. Northern Irish Catholics, aroused from their stupor, sensing change was in the air, were no longer content to sit back, spectators forced to put up with a display of Protestant hegemony designed to humiliate them. In Belfast fierce sectarian street battles broke out along the fault line where the two communities met – Unity Flats, a Catholic apartment project at the foot of the loyalist Shankill, Ardoyne, one of an archipelago of Catholic ghettos in loyalist North Belfast, and near the streets which joined the Protestant Shankill to the Catholic Falls. Adams spent his lunch hours touring the threatened areas, helping locals, he says, prepare for their defence. He did so without the support of the IRA Army Council, which 'in no way was prepared for any sort of military defence, never mind an offensive. It was, instead, engaged in political semantics.'[22] MacStiofain implored Cathal Goulding, the IRA Chief of Staff and one of the architects of the new republican strategy, to 'take heed of the warnings we were relaying from our threatened comrades in the North. On the very brink, the "politicals" still refused to do anything.'[23]

Goulding, a left-wing Dubliner, deeply distrusted the militant Belfast republicans. It was a feeling shared by many southern radicals that went back to the 1920s, when the IRA in the northern capital emerged as 'defenders' of Catholics first and republicans second, retaliating against Protestants for attacks on Catholic streets. In the 1930s, Peadar O'Donnell, like Goulding a socialist republican who wanted to turn the IRA into a radical left-wing movement, commented: 'We haven't a battalion of IRA men in Belfast, we just have a battalion of armed Catholics.'[24] He might have been expressing Goulding's fears that an injection of arms into the city would be like throwing petrol on a fire. The IRA leadership wanted to avoid a sectarian conflict, not provoke one – especially as they knew they could not protect isolated Catholic areas should they come under sustained attack.

Belfast republicans, however, saw armed action as a

deterrent against attack – a way of letting their enemies know they were able to defend themselves. In July, in the maze of narrow streets near the Falls Road, RUC patrols were attacked with handguns and hand grenades. Though there were no serious injuries, it made the police nervous and convinced angry loyalists that the old enemy was back, getting ready to strike at them. In mid-July, at the height of the Orange marching season, a Catholic mob tried to burn down an Orange hall in Dungiven, south Co. Derry. The police intervened and killed Francis McCloskey, a sixty-seven-year-old Catholic, during the riot. On 17 July, another Catholic, Samuel Devenney, whom the RUC had injured in a confrontation in Derry three months earlier, died. Their deaths provoked further demands within the IRA for stronger action as the police was increasingly viewed as anti-Catholic and not to be trusted with the protection of nationalist areas.

Young IRA activists in Belfast, including Adams, led Catholic mobs in attacks upon RUC stations on the Falls Road in early August, in one case battering down the station door with a telegraph pole. Loyalists revenged themselves on vulnerable Catholics. Unity Flats became a favourite target. In rioting around the flats on 2 August, involving loyalists, Catholics and the RUC, the police fatally injured a sixty-one-year-old Catholic, Patrick Corry.

The resources of the three-thousand-strong police were being stretched. Paisley and other Protestant extremists demanded that the part-time constabulary, the B-Specials, be deployed to aid the RUC. However, Chichester-Clark hesitated, knowing that this could produce a backlash from enraged Catholics, who hated the Specials as a thoroughly sectarian unit.

The Apprentice Boys was a Protestant group, a 'Loyal Order', rather like the Orange Order, but older. It was formed to commemorate events dating back to the seventeenth-century war of succession between the Protestant King William of

Orange and the Catholic King James II, during which Catholic forces besieged Williamite Derry and legend has it were kept successfully at bay thanks to the action of thirteen loyalist apprentice boys. The Apprentice Boys held its main march on 12 August. Traditionally, the marchers' route took them along the city's seventeenth-century battlements, which looked out over the impoverished Catholic neighbourhood of the Bogside. Some marchers contemptuously hurled pennies at the Catholics in the streets below. As the march came to an end it was met with a torrent of stones, bottles and nails. The RUC moved against the Catholic rioters, who had erected barricades around their district. The Bogsiders were prepared, with thousands of petrol bombs ready. The worst riot so far of the Troubles resulted, lasting two days. For the first time, the RUC, exhausted and stretched to near breaking point, lobbed tear gas canisters into the rebellious streets. But the rioters quickly found an antidote in water and vinegar. The Northern Ireland Prime Minister, facing the worst crisis in the state's history, sent units of the B-Specials to Derry to relieve the weary and demoralized police force. This led only to a further deterioration of the situation. On 14 August, the Northern Ireland authorities requested the intervention of British troops.

In the Northern Ireland capital, meanwhile, an even more disastrous breakdown occurred. As news spread about the riots in Derry, NICRA called for demonstrations throughout the province. Local IRA men helped organize mob attacks on police stations along the Falls Road. Rioters set fire to a few vulnerable Protestant businesses, including a car salesroom and a flour mill. Their aim was to take the pressure off the besieged and barricaded Catholics in the Bogside, which was now being proclaimed Free Derry. But sectarian animosity in Belfast was always more deadly.

Mobs of loyalists from the Shankill descended on the Falls, torching Catholic homes along the streets linking the two thoroughfares, only a few hundred yards apart. Gunshots reverberated along the narrow streets. A few armed IRA men were spotted flitting from alleyway to alleyway. Billy McKee began evacuating Catholic families along Divis Street, at the foot of the Falls. Along with three other IRA veterans, Seamus Twomey, Liam Burke and Liam Price, he took up position in a primary school which commanded a view of the streets leading into their area from the loyalist district. They were joined by seven or eight local teenagers. Between them, they possessed six handguns and an old submachine-gun. As the loyalist mob approached, the IRA men opened fire, wounding eight Protestants.[25]

The RUC, jittery, expecting an IRA ambush, riddled the Divis Flats, a Catholic apartment block, with a general-purpose machinegun mounted on an armoured car, blowing the head off a nine-year-old boy, Patrick Rooney. As the boy was whisked away in an ambulance, his father was left to scrape his son's brains off the bedroom wall with a spoon.[26] Rooney was one of eight killed in Belfast during the night of 14 August and the early hours of the following day. They included a Protestant, Herbert Roy, shot dead not far from the school where McKee and his men were stationed, and an off-duty British soldier, Hugh McCabe, who like Rooney died in the Divis Flats complex as a result of police gunfire.[27] A fifteen-year-old republican, Gerard McAuley, was among the dead, killed by a loyalist sniper during an attack on Bombay Street, which was Catholic and close to the border with the Shankill area. Thirty-eight houses of the sixty-three in the street were destroyed. As the day dawned over the smouldering ruins in street after street, the scene resembled the aftermath of the Blitz.[28]

When British troops took up positions in Derry on 14 August, then in Belfast on the next day, things calmed down. Catholics welcomed them with open arms and cups of tea. A few people returned cautiously to the streets to go back to the homes from which they had fled the night before. Nineteen-year-old Geraldine O'Regan, a Catholic, was due to be married in two weeks. She found her home a burnt-out ruin. 'I walked down this street, and I seen all the destruction around me and . . . you couldn't really understand it, you couldn't take it in . . . our house was burnt to the ground and all the houses around it were burnt. And the Protestants . . . were shouting down at us and laughing at us . . . My whole political thinking changed at that point.'[29]

The politics of hope hatched in the early 1960s, which envisioned a different world where Catholic and Protestant would live side by side, were reduced to ashes. It was the figures rooted in the violent past, once derided as historical anomalies, who now shaped events.

CHAPTER TWO

Out of the Ashes: 1969–72

1

The charred shells of homes and factories smouldered between the Falls and Shankill roads, the smell of smoke and burning petrol everywhere. Gaunt streets of gutted houses stood abandoned.

Troops patrolled the uneasy city, uncoiling rolls of barbed wire to separate the Protestant and Catholic working-class communities, where the mood of uncertainty was mixed with anger. Where was the legendary IRA and the UVF when they were needed most? As usual, Catholics and Protestants looked at the same events and came to opposite conclusions. The burnings proved to Catholics that the IRA was woefully inadequate as a defence force. The killings of two Protestants meanwhile convinced loyalists that they had been right all along: the IRA was back on the offensive.

Resentment was turned on their leaders.

Paisley blotted his copybook in August 1969. I remember when it was still pretty hairy, when there was still fighting going on in Percy Street [between the Shankill and the Falls] and he was saying, 'Let me down there to my people, I'm going down to my people'. Women were holding on to his arm and saying, 'No, you can't go down there.' He wasn't making much attempt to get away from them. Men were just standing there with their arms folded looking at him and saying, 'Look at that eejit.' After that, people said: 'Where were you when we wanted you? You started this thing, and then where were you when we needed you?'[1]

Around the Catholic streets the slogan 'IRA=I Ran Away' appeared on gable walls. The Dublin leadership was blamed and accused of being out of touch with the realities of Ulster. The IRA Chief of Staff, Cathal Goulding, committed to transforming the IRA from a cabal of militarists into a left-wing organization relevant to modern Ireland, came under attack from two different generations. IRA veterans such as Billy McKee regarded as folly the efforts of the reformers to 'phase out' the IRA when it was most needed. 'Money was being used to keep the *United Irishman* [newspaper] going instead of buying arms. The first rule of the IRA was defence of the people.'[2] McKee's reputation, gained from the twelve years or so he had spent in jail for IRA activities, was enhanced as one of the 'defenders of the Falls' in St Comgall's school. Younger republican activists like Gerry Adams, less than half McKee's age, were at one with him in feeling that the Army Council in the South could no longer be trusted to take the necessary steps to protect Northern Catholics.

According to Adams, 'The republican movement of the 1960s had proved incapable of responding adequately to events as they evolved in the Six Counties.'[3] They believed that the movement would have to reverse its course if it was to survive. A consensus developed between the young street fighters of Belfast and the ageing traditionalists, who after years of isolation and derision suddenly saw the prospect of an IRA reborn. But in the meantime, it was galling for them to look on powerlessly as Catholics welcomed British troops with cups of tea as their saviours from loyalist mob rule.

The British government too saw its approach to 'the Irish question' go up in smoke in the fires of August 1969. Since the 1920s, Britain's aim had been to insulate itself from the Irish question, which from the 1880s on had proved so disruptive to British political life. Partition was a means of keeping the problem at a safe distance. The Unionist parliament in Belfast was left to run things much as it liked, while the Irish Free State suppressed the remnants of militant Irish republicanism south of the border. Over the decades, Ulster was kept firmly on the margins of British political life. In 1923, the Westminster parliament ruled that 'matters of administration for a minister in Northern Ireland could not be discussed' in the British parliament.[4] Even among educated English people, not much was known about Northern Ireland, not even if it was still a part of the United Kingdom.[5] The main link between the two parliaments was financial, with Britain shoring up a failing Ulster economy through yearly disbursements from the British Treasury. But even that relationship was left mostly undiscussed. According to Richard Crossman, who was a minister in the Wilson government: 'Neither Jack Diamond [Chief Secretary to the Treasury 1964–70] nor the Chancellor knew the formula by which Northern Ireland gets its money. In all these years it has never been revealed to the politicians and I am longing to see whether now we shall get to the bottom of this very large and expensive secret . . .'[6]

With Harold Wilson in power from 1964, Labour Party activists among others felt that the party should press for a united Ireland. The Prime Minister was known to be in favour of a united Ireland, at least in principle. His government was, after all, one of reform, which some in the party thought should encompass changes in Northern Ireland. But Wilson was effectively overruled. Any kind of intervention – other than nudging Terence O'Neill to do the right thing – was regarded as too risky. As the crisis deepened, Unionists were warned that if they requested troops, Stormont would have to be suspended and direct rule imposed. However, this was a threat meant only to discourage Stormont from seeking such aid. Direct rule would have breached the British principle of minimal intervention. When the crisis broke in August 1969, and intervention became inevitable, it was delayed, and when it came it was minimal. Committing the Prince of Wales' Own Regiment to the Bogside in Derry on 14 August, and the Second Battalion of the Queen's Regiment to the streets of Belfast the following day, was viewed as a holding operation, no more. The troops were there to give the Unionist government time to push through the necessary reforms. Once confidence in the police was restored, they would leave. If Britain could be said to have had a strategy, that was it. When the troops did go in, they were under the control of the Unionist government, though their legal status was somewhat confused.

On 19 August, Wilson's government tried to reassure jittery Unionists that the status of Northern Ireland within the UK was not threatened and that 'the border is not an issue'.[7] This, the first Downing Street Declaration, at the same time welcomed reforms in local government elections, public housing allocation, and other steps to ensure that equality of treatment for all the people of Northern Ireland would be guaranteed. It was a reminder to the Unionists that while Northern Ireland was still part of the UK it would have to change.

The Northern Ireland Prime Minister, Chichester-Clark, undertook a sweeping security review. Lord Hunt (the conqueror of Mount Everest) chaired a commission on the police. It recommended that the RUC be disarmed and civilianized, and the B-Specials abolished, replaced by a reserve force. A locally recruited military unit, the Ulster Defence Regiment, would be raised under the control of the British Army.[8]

Loyalists were already in a state of agitated insecurity, convinced that the IRA was active again. At the beginning of September, Jackie Todd, a Protestant vigilante, was shot dead near a barricade in North Belfast – the third Protestant to be murdered within as many weeks. Soon arms, including .45 Smith and Wesson long-barrelled revolvers, .32 and .38 pistols, were being sold on the Shankill. During the riot on 9 October with which loyalists greeted the Hunt Commission's recommendations, the British Army fired on the crowd, killing two Protestants. Loyalists replied using the recently acquired weapons and shot and killed Constable Victor Arbuckle. Thanks to the Hunt reforms, Constable Arbuckle was unarmed at the time.

Arbuckle's death was a reminder of the crucial role loyalists have played in creating the Ulster crisis, a role that tends to be forgotten. Between 1966 and 1969, they launched a murder campaign, bombed a Prime Minister out of office, burnt down hundreds of homes, and killed a policeman.

The only organization on the Shankill that contributed to the violence was the Shankill Road Defence Association, a gang of vigilantes under John McKeague, a blond-haired Paisleyite with a taste for teenage boys.[9] Other Shankill Road Protestants, vigilantes also, but less prominent and certainly less flamboyant, began quietly to meet in local clubs to plot a course of action.

The meetings were divided into two parts, the first devoted to recruiting those who were prepared merely to man the barricades, and the second to identifying those prepared to take the war into the Catholic areas, who believed that attack was the best form of defence. Charles Harding-Smith, a lorry driver and hod carrier, dominated these gatherings, which were attended by a handful of local toughs and street fighters. While not a hard man himself, he knew how to attract them.

Throughout 1970, the Protestant vigilantes remained a ramshackle amalgam of different defence groups. There was no centralized command, and not even an agreed name. Harding-Smith wanted the loose alliance to be called the Ulster Volunteer Force, but since there were already organizations using that hallowed name. This would have caused confusion. Eventually McKeague's idea of calling the collection of vigilantes the Ulster Defence Association was accepted. The loyalist vigilantes established a training camp in the little fishing port of Kilkeel in South Down in June 1970. The training mainly consisted of arms drill under the guidance of Jim Finlay, a former British soldier. It was not much use for men who were about to become assassins, but it built up a camaraderie among them. As Harding-Smith's power grew, he clashed with the volatile McKeague, accusing him of stealing funds. McKeague was expelled but still continued to cause trouble. He set up his own group with a comic-book name, the Red Hand Commandos. As a warning, Harding-Smith's men fire-bombed the shop above which McKeague lived with his ageing mother. Mrs McKeague was burned to death and the UDA claimed its first victim – a Protestant old-age pensioner.

The violence of August 1969 also provoked a crisis within the IRA and Sinn Fein, which brought to the surface the underlying tensions and distrust between the Dublin leadership and the majority of republican activists in Belfast. The uncertainty and distrust the Dublin IRA felt went back to the 1920s. Even when the IRA was at the height of its power under Michael Collins, it balked at the prospect of a full-scale assault in Ulster. IRA men from the North advised Collins against it, pointing out that the kind of guerrilla war the IRA fought successfully in parts of southern Ireland – especially in West Cork and Kerry – could not be sustained in Ulster, where most of the population was hostile to republicanism. The ever-present prospect of loyalist counter-terror directed against innocent Catholics (particularly in Belfast) was also an important factor in restraining the IRA's activities in the North. During the civil disturbances following the formation of the Northern Ireland state, the IRA's actions in Belfast provoked a ferocious Protestant backlash. Republicans retaliated with attacks on Protestants. Left-wing activists such as Peadar O'Donnell had long regarded the IRA in the North as a Catholic defence force with reactionary potential.[10] He fiercely criticized the Belfast IRA for its failure to build relations with the Protestant working class and accused it of possessing 'a bigotry that is dangerous to the cause they have at heart'.[11] O'Donnell's expectations were absurdly high – like all left-wing republicans, he completely misunderstood the nature of the Ulster Protestants' connection to Britain, seeing it as an 'artificial' link that could be broken if the right socialist policies were presented to them. In the 1960s, the IRA leadership again took up this line, arguing that militant loyalism would die out because British imperialism no longer had any use for it. It was only a matter of time before the Protestant working class would be won over to revolutionary socialism – provided the republican movement could make them see its relevance. In the intervening thirty years, the IRA in Belfast went into a disastrous decline, partly precipitated by the defeats of the 1920s. It played no part in the 1956 border campaign. And it was peripheral to the republican analysis that followed the collapse of that campaign in 1962.

For Goulding, faced with a new crisis and many republicans clamouring for a Northern campaign, the lessons of the 1920s still applied. He and his supporters on the Army Council pressed ahead with their politicization programme, demanding that the movement change its constitution to allow elected Sinn Fein members to take their seats in the parliaments in Belfast, Dublin and London.

Infuriated, in Belfast the anti-Goulding faction of the IRA staged a coup against his supporters and replaced Liam McMillen, the Officer Commanding the IRA in the city, with Billy McKee. The Belfast IRA then announced that it was breaking off relations with the Army Council in Dublin.

An extraordinary convention of IRA delegates was held in mid-December 1969 to debate the leadership's proposals to recognize the three parliaments – in effect, to accept the reality of the 1921 settlement. The traditionalists asked that a two-thirds majority should be required if such drastic changes were to be enacted, but were overruled. The IRA's Intelligence Chief, Sean MacStiofain, warned that if the change came about 'those who accepted it would forfeit the right to describe themselves as the Irish Republican Army'.[12] But the main proposals were passed with a simple majority.

Opposition to Goulding crystalized around MacStiofain, the forty-one-year-old Londoner. Hurried meetings followed with opponents of the new course, including McKee and Seamus Twomey, who had taken part in the St Comgall's school action in August, and two prominent veterans of the 1956–62 campaign, Daithi O Conaill and Ruairi O Bradaigh. A new IRA emerged from these gatherings, intent on remaining faithful to traditional republican goals and methods. O Conaill was elected its first Chief of Staff but he declined the post. MacStiofain was then chosen – the first time in the history of the republican movement that an Englishman had filled that role.[13] Because a full-scale army convention had yet to formalize the new structures and personnel, the organization called itself the Provisional IRA.

Murals soon appeared in working-class Catholic areas of Belfast showing a crudely drawn phoenix rising from the flames. Under it was written, 'From the ashes of '69 arose the Provisionals'. The name stuck.

The Provisional IRA was a dangerous mix of dogma and determination. Purist republicans from the South such as O Bradaigh and O Conaill joined forces with embittered and angry Belfast men like McKee. They shared a contempt for conventional, parliamentary politics. The holy grail of a united Ireland would never be obtained through surrendering to the temptations of compromise, however alluring. To their zeal was added the impatience of the young left-wing activists of Adams's generation, who wanted action. As did the third element in the mixture – the recruits from the local Catholic defence groups that manned the barricades in embattled areas such as Ardoyne in North Belfast and were ready to retaliate against Protestants. The ethos of the early Provisionals was decidedly Catholic – McKee, the first commanding officer of the Belfast organization, was a daily communicant. The dogmatism of the pulpit and the narrowness of the Belfast ghetto made for a ruthless combination.

However, for Belfast activists like Adams the most important thing was that there was now a leadership in Dublin in sympathy with their need for guns. Shortly before the split, he and a few like-minded republicans took measures into their own hands and attended an unauthorized arms training camp across the border in Co. Leitrim. On the way back to Belfast, their car crashed and one of his companions, IRA man Liam McParland, was killed. Adams was suspended from the IRA. But by then the Goulding faction in Belfast was already under siege and his suspension was soon lifted. Though Adams joined the Provisional faction, he maintained friendly contacts with many who stayed with Goulding and was suspected of leaning in that direction by McKee, who said that Adams once told him that 'the split was right but for the wrong reason'.[14]

In January, at the Sinn Fein *ard fheis*, the two sides fought it out again at a political level. Once again, the majority voted in favour of the Goulding proposals. Sinn Fein split, and O Bradaigh led 257 delegates out of the convention to form Provisional Sinn Fein, of which he became President.

The Goulding IRA became known as the Officials, and then the Stickies, thanks to the adhesive Easter Lily emblem that its members wore and distributed during the commemoration of the 1916 Easter Rising.[15]

Among the first tasks the Provisionals set themselves was the acquisition of an arsenal. Like earlier generations of Irish republicans, they turned to the United States. In New York, George Harrison, a fifty-four-year-old Brinks security guard who traced his roots back to Co. Mayo in the west of Ireland, was watching the developments in Ulster with interest and concern. An uncompromising republican, Harrison became involved in supplying weapons to the IRA in the 1950s. His main link was through another American-based republican activist, Eoin McNamee, from County Tyrone. In August 1969, McNamee wrote to Harrison from the Bogside, at the height of the riots, with the smell of burning petrol in his nose, asking for assistance. Harrison raised and dispatched several thousand dollars – perhaps the first money from the US to reach nationalists in this phase of the conflict. Later, McNamee, who supported the Provisional faction, arrived in New York, and Harrison handed over what few weapons were left from the early 1960s. McNamee shipped them back on a regular Aer Lingus flight from Kennedy Airport. 'The inspection at the airport was easy at the time,' said Harrison.[16] McNamee helped set up a meeting between Harrison and Daithi O Conaill, who came to New York in January 1970. Harrison and Liam Cotter, another exiled republican who was part of the 1950s arms smuggling network, met with O Conaill in a restaurant near Central Park. O Conaill asked if they would be prepared to help with the 'armed struggle'. 'There's no problem with that,' they told him.[17] O Conaill met with other Irish Americans like IRA veteran Michael Flannery, who agreed to start a fund-raising organization, Irish Northern Aid. Harrison and Cotter kept their activities far apart from those of the fund-raisers and succeeded in establishing a regular supply of guns and ammunition that gave the Provisionals the fire-power to take on the British Army.[18]

2

The cosy relationship between Catholics and the British Army deteriorated rapidly during the early months of 1970. Restless and aggressive youths challenged the army, which, having replaced the RUC, was forced into a policing role it was not equipped to handle. The first serious confrontation took place in Derry in March, when a crowd attacked an RUC station and injured twelve soldiers. But it was the windswept and desolate housing developments on the outskirts of Belfast, places like Ballymurphy, where Adams lived, which saw the worst violence. These sprawling estates, erected in the early 1950s, were areas of high unemployment where the Provisionals quickly gained a hold over their large populations of bored and listless young men.

In Ballymurphy, relations between the people and the troops became strained after Adams and other local Provisionals organized a picket of the nearby army base to protest against soldiers inviting local girls to their weekly disco.[19] Pent-up frustration and daily friction between youths and troops boiled over at the beginning of April. Mobs of Catholics and Protestants who lived near by confronted each other, with the army in between. Local residents armed with hurley sticks, clubs and rocks fought hand to hand with the soldiers. Other army units lobbed CS gas canisters into the streets. Army snatch squads would suddenly dash from the ranks to seize an identified mob leader and drag him back. Youths turned this tactic against the army. They deliberately lured snatch squads into cul-de-sacs, which they sealed with barbed wire, trapping the troops and pelting them with stones and bricks. Many Protestants who lived in or near Ballymurphy were driven from their homes.

In June 1970, to the dismay of nationalists, the authorities failed to ban an Orange parade that skirted Catholic streets in North Belfast. Serious riots flared up on 27 June. Provisional IRA snipers opened fire on the Protestant rioters and killed three. The same night, in the east of the city, loyalists attacked the isolated Catholic Short Strand area. Billy McKee arrived on the scene to support the local IRA and a gun battle broke out around St Matthew's Catholic church. Another two

Protestants were shot dead, along with one Provisional IRA man. McKee was wounded and smuggled across the border to hospital. The next day, loyalists ejected five hundred Catholic workers from their workplace at the Harland and Wolff shipyards.

The intervention of the Provisionals confirmed their primary role as a Catholic defence force, strongest in areas like the Short Strand and North Belfast, were Catholics felt most vulnerable.

The situation continued to deteriorate throughout the spring and summer of 1970. In April, the General Officer Commanding in Ulster, General Freeland, warned petrol bombers that they would be shot. In June he warned that anyone seen carrying a weapon would be shot on sight.

Increasingly, Catholics saw the British Army as just another instrument of Unionist rule, no better or even worse than the RUC.

On 2 July, the army made an arms find in the lower Falls district, an area loyal to the Official IRA. A mob trapped the search team, and snipers fired on troops surrounding the neighbourhood. General Freeland decided that a show of force was needed and launched a rescue mission. Troops went in firing CS gas, sending residents choking through the narrow streets. Soldiers smashed their way from house to house, kicking down doors and tearing up floorboards. They hauled off a small horde of weapons, 281 pounds of gelignite, over 20,000 rounds of ammunition, and made 337 arrests.[20] The Official IRA 'took on' the army to show they could defend their area as well as PIRA, wounding eighteen soldiers. The army killed four civilians during the operation, including a visiting photographer from England.[21]

Freeland imposed a curfew which was not lifted (except for two hours to allow women to shop) until 9 a.m. on 5 July. He later justified the Falls raid as a major success, because of the arms found. However, in Northern Ireland it is the political consequences of every military or violent act, not its tactical efficacy, which determines whether it is judged a 'success' or otherwise. By this measure, the Falls Road Curfew, as it came to be known, was a political disaster for British policy in Ulster:

'It can be argued that the failure to ban the 1970 Orange parades, and the massive arms searches and curfew in the Lower Falls area which followed, was the last chance to avoid the catastrophe that has since engulfed Ulster . . . Until the spring of 1970, most Catholics regarded the troops as their protectors. The Lower Falls operation changed everything, though the Army was merely doing its job and reacting to events . . . Following the events of early July, PIRA grew from fewer than 100 activists in May–June to roughly 800 in December 1970.'[22]

Embarrassingly for the government, it was discovered that the curfew had been illegally imposed.

The momentum was now behind the Provisional IRA. Though the Provisionals concentrated on 'defensive' operations, they had occasionally carried out more aggressive actions, in January 1970 bombing an RUC station on the fringes of West Belfast. Two weeks after the Falls Road raids, a no-warning bomb exploded at a bank in the heart of the city, injuring thirty people, two of them seriously. A UDR vehicle was blown up near Derry and two soldiers were injured. When the British GOC warned rioters that they would be shot, the Provisionals countered that they would retaliate. At the end of July, troops shot dead nineteen-year-old Daniel O'Hagan during a riot in North Belfast. On 11 August a booby-trapped car left near Crossmaglen in South Armagh exploded and killed two RUC men, Constables Samuel Donaldson and Robert Millar.[23] They were the first members of the security forces to die at the hands of the IRA in the current Troubles. They were the exception. Of the nine victims of the Provisional IRA in 1970, seven were civilians, five of them Protestants. The disproportionately high number of civilian deaths would remain a characteristic of the ensuing conflict.

A second Provisional army convention was held in September 1970, ratifying the decisions taken the previous December and re-electing MacStiofain as Chief of Staff. In the meantime, in Belfast the Provisionals prepared to go on the offensive. Many of those joining the organization were former British soldiers, who brought with them valued experience in weapons training.

The Provisionals began to enforce their own version of law and order in Catholic areas of Belfast. Ordinary crime was comparatively rare in the city, but where it appeared the Provisionals knew that there was a likelihood also of felons informing, offering information in return for leniency. Arthur McKenna and Alexander McVicar, two petty criminals operating in Adams's area, were shot to death on 16 November. The killings served as a warning that there was a new arm of law enforcement in the district and that it would deal brutally with transgressors. The following year, 1971, began with the murder of the first alleged informer, John Kavanagh, a neighbourhood drunk who was accused of speaking to the police. The Provisionals dragged Kavanagh to the banks of a polluted river in West Belfast, shoved a gun into his mouth and 'executed' him.

3

Throughout 1970, violence pushed civil rights issues into the background. Northern Ireland was seen more and more as a security problem, a trend that gained strength when the British general election of 18 June brought the Conservative Party to power, with Edward Heath as the new Prime Minister. Unionists and Conservatives were traditional political allies. Unionists could expect a more sympathetic hearing from London to their argument that the fuss over civil rights was merely a front for the IRA. But the Conservative government shared with its Labour predecessor the same aversion to becoming more involved in Ulster than was absolutely unavoidable. The new Home Secretary, Reginald Maudling, arrived in Northern Ireland on 1 July to be greeted by a swarm of conflicting views and opinions. He left a few hours later, exasperated and confused. Insofar as he was able to formulate a consistent policy it was one of letting the Unionists get on with whatever it was they were doing. On the return flight to London he exploded: 'For God's sake, bring me a large scotch. What a bloody awful country!'[24]

'With the advent of a new British government,' wrote one of the founders of the civil rights movement, 'there appeared to be changed attitudes. The Unionists' "harder line" directives went into the Catholic areas to re-establish "law and order". Force was met by force . . . The army was now according to them, and with appropriate support from Westminster, acting in a proper way and doing what every loyalist and Unionist required . . . beating the minority back into submission.'[25]

Against the background of militarization, within the nationalist community a major political realignment took place. Civil rights leader John Hume had long called for 'a new political movement based on social-democratic principles . . . that must provide what has been severely lacking at Stormont – a strong energetic opposition to conservatism – proposing radical social and economic policies'.[26] Hume made the constitutional status of Northern Ireland central to the new political movement he envisioned. But any change in that status would only come about with the consent of the majority. This was heresy to traditional nationalism, which saw partition as Britain's way of retaining control over part of Ireland. Hume's view implied that partition was a product of the Protestants' wish to stay out of a united Ireland, not of a British desire to dominate.

Gerry Fitt, the Republican Labour MP, shared Hume's view, as did Paddy Devlin, a former IRA man and member of the Northern Ireland Labour Party. In August 1970, they got together with a few members of the old Nationalist Party (by then almost defunct) and civil rights activists to form the Social Democratic and Labour Party.

The SDLP was woven from three different political strands within nationalism represented by left-wing trade unionists, the civil rights activists and the former members of the Nationalist Party. Unlike the Nationalist Party, the SDLP would actively engage with Unionists and, if elected, its members would take their seats in both the Belfast and London parliaments.

Among the party's aims as embodied in its constitution were 'to organize and maintain in Northern Ireland a socialist party . . . to promote the cause of Irish unity based on the consent of a majority of the people of Northern Ireland'. It aligned itself with other social democratic parties 'at an international level' and would 'co-operate with the Irish Congress of Trades Unions'.[27]

Fitt and Devlin gave the new party a base among the Catholic working class in Belfast. Both were blunt-speaking, working-class politicians, with strong links to the unions. Austin Currie, whose house squat had helped start the civil rights movement in 1968, brought into the party some of the rural bastions of the Nationalist Party for which he was an MP. Hume's popularity in Derry gave the SDLP an almost impregnable base in that city among Catholics of all classes. Other prominent members of the new alignment were Paddy Wilson of Republican Labour, and Ivan Cooper, a Protestant and a leading civil rights activist. But the SDLP never succeeded in attracting more than the occasional Protestant. The Alliance Party, founded in the same year, siphoned off many politically moderate Protestants, some of them former supporters of Terence O'Neill.

Because of his position as a Westminster MP Fitt was appointed SDLP leader, with Hume as his deputy.

In 1971 Hume wrote: 'To create a truly united country we need a truly united people, not a united piece of earth. In that task we need not to overcome the Northern Protestant but to seek his co-operation, help and assistance.'[28] The creation of the SDLP was an attempt to translate that vision into practical politics. It was a struggle to introduce rational politics into what was fundamentally an irrational situation where the clash of conflicting absolutes drowned out reasoned argument. It was not that the Provisionals did not have politics as such – they did, and a political programme for a new Ireland, *Eire Nua*; it was that their aim had become secondary to the methods they were using to achieve it.

The Provisional IRA despised SDLP pragmatism as weakness and cowardice. The moral basis for its vision was a semi-mystical incantation of sacrifice and martyrdom where absolutes reigned: the absolute right of a vague entity, the 'Irish people', to an independent united Ireland, and the IRA's absolute right to use violence to achieve it. Provisional leaders scorned the SDLP as the 'Stoop Down Low Party'.

4

In the eighteen months between August 1969 and January 1971, the IRA was brought back from the verge of extinction. The Provisionals alone could now muster about 1,000 activists, mainly concentrated in Belfast, the Officials somewhat fewer. Opposed to them were 7,000 regular British troops, 4,000 Ulster Defence Regiment members and just over 3,000 RUC officers, aided by about 600 reserve constables. The struggle over civil rights was transformed into an incipient guerrilla war, with Belfast as its cockpit. The city's three

battalions were the first to organize and the first to demonstrate a willingness to 'defend' their areas with violence. They
were also the first to go on an all-out offensive. The strategy
was two-pronged, consisting of attacks against soldiers and
policemen, in tandem with a bombing campaign aimed at
'economic' targets. The aim was to make Britain's link to
Northern Ireland so expensive that it would be forced to
withdraw.

MacStiofain believed that if the British Army lost forty
men, the government would come under irresistible pressure
to pull out. This assumption was naïve, but typical of the
failure of the Provisionals' mainly Dublin-based leadership to
realize the crucial role that Protestants played in the equation.
The strength of their resistance to British withdrawal was not
taken into account. Instead, the Provisional leaders believed
that once soldiers started coming home in boxes, the clamour
would be so great in Britain that the link would be cut. But
even those republicans with a more sceptical view of this
programme were swept along by the desire for sheer revenge
that gripped the nationalist ghettoes in the wake of army
raids, searches and general harassment.

However, the most important factor which would deter-
mine the course of the Provisionals' campaign was one that
had little to do with strategies worked out in Dublin or the
political analysis of ideologues. The Provisionals were a
ghetto force first and foremost and responded to events in
their neighbourhood, often taking actions that disregarded
the leadership's instructions. After all, it was far away in
Dublin. According to McKee, MacStiofain, though Chief of
Staff, 'knew nothing about what was going on in the
North'.[29]

Though MacStiofain liked to give the impression that the
decision to kill British soldiers was not taken until February
1971, in fact the Provisionals had been targeting them since at
least the summer before.[30] That they did not succeed in killing

any was as much a matter of luck as policy. That changed on 6 February. After a series of vicious riots, a patrol of the Royal Artillery came under Sterling submachine-gun fire on the New Lodge Road in North Belfast. The hail of bullets killed twenty-year-old Gunner Robert Curtis, the first British soldier to die in Ireland in over fifty years.

'At long last the step had been taken.'[31]

His killer, Billy Reid, had never used a Sterling before.[32] He was a member of the Provisionals' 3rd Battalion in North Belfast, the most active of the three that made up the Belfast Brigade and the most dangerous IRA unit in the whole of Northern Ireland. Of the fifty-nine security forces fatalities that year, twenty-one died at the hands of the 3rd Battalion, including seven RUC officers. Snipers killed most, using the back alleyways to escape. But the 3rd Battalion showed it was flexible when it came to tactics.

A Scottish regiment stationed in North Belfast soon gained a reputation for harassing the locals, and even provoked complaints from some Protestants. On the night of 10 March, three members of the regiment, two of them brothers, were drinking in a city-centre pub, where they met three IRA men from the tough Ardoyne neighbourhood in North Belfast. They were lured to an isolated roadway with the promise of women. The three soldiers were urinating at the side of the road when their drinking companions shot them dead.

The IRA issued a statement denying responsibility. Mac-Stiofain claimed that his men only targeted on-duty military personnel. As usual, however, the Dublin leadership was being left to try to explain events over which it exercised little control. It was later admitted that the Belfast Provisionals had lied in the hope that the killings would be blamed on Protestant extremists to cause friction between them and the British.[33] The incident led to a widespread investigation during which Billy McKee was arrested. He was charged and convicted of possession of explosives.

The killings provoked a crisis for the Unionist government. Four thousand workmen downed tools at the Belfast shipyards and marched on the city centre to demand the introduction of internment without trial for the IRA. Many Unionists agreed with them. The British resisted, partly because the army advised against it, and partly owing to a fear of being sucked more deeply into the Ulster morass. Unionist Prime Minister Chichester-Clark then asked London for 3,000 more troops. When the Heath government sent him 1,300, he resigned.

Frustrated and still determined to get internment, the Unionist Party turned to Brian Faulkner. A dapper little businessman and a cunning politician, Faulkner had made his name in two areas – commerce and security. During the IRA's border offensive, Faulkner had used internment without trial to break the back of the campaign. In the 1960s, as O'Neill's Commerce Minister, he helped bring new industry to Northern Ireland. But it was his reputation as a 'law and order' man which won him Unionist support in 1971.

The Provisionals' other tactic, the bombing campaign, was also bringing the Northern Ireland government under pressure from those who wanted a quick solution to the worsening security situation. There were 16 bombings in January, 38 in February, 31 in March, and 38 in April. May saw 43, and June 44. In July the number of bombing attacks jumped to 94.[34] The attacks were often reckless. On 25 May, a Provisional bomber threw a suitcase packed with explosives into the hallway of the Springfield Road RUC station, in the Falls area. A group of women and children standing near by were ushered to safety just before it exploded, killing Sergeant Michael Willets, of 3 Para, who was between them and the blast. A baby on the opposite side of the street was flung from its pram and buried under the rubble. Miraculously, it survived with a fractured skull. When the fatally wounded soldier was being carried out of the station on a door, used as makeshift stretcher, a crowd of youths began to jeer and scream obscenities. 'My reaction was one of total disbelief that anyone could be so inhumane,' commented Lieutenant-Colonel Peter Chiswell, who was in command of the unit at the time.[35]

The rapid growth of the Provisional IRA caught the RUC unawares. It was overwhelmed; its Special Branch had dwindled to a 'crimes special' unit, lacking informers. A new generation of gunmen and activists was emerging, about which the police possessed only a few clues. This lack of reliable information made the British hesitate to use internment.

However, Faulkner was besieged. The IRA menace was growing, and without some drastic action how could the government prevent the prospect of a militant Unionist backlash? Secretary of State for Defence, Lord Carrington, thought there might be a way of actually utilizing internment to gain the much-needed information. He reached an arrangement with Faulkner and the police. Army intelligence officers would instruct the RUC in secret methods for extracting information from a group of prisoners who would be specially selected from the internees.[36] They were sensory deprivation techniques, used in every colonial war that Britain had fought since the late 1940s, although this fact was not widely known.[37]

The Provisionals were expecting internment. From the beginning of the summer members were ordered to take the necessary precautions, the most obvious being not to stay at home. IRA operatives watched the airport and seaports, noting the steady influx of troops. However, the British still hesitated. It was only after an army swoop on 28 July failed to disrupt IRA operations that the final decision to go ahead was taken. The operation was code-named Demetrius.

At around 4 a.m. on 9 August people in the Catholic areas of Belfast and Derry awoke to a deafening noise. Women were banging dust bin lids on pavements, the traditional signal that the security forces were approaching. Thousands of troops stormed into the ghettoes, with a list of 452 suspects; 342 people were lifted, including a few members of NICRA and the student group People's Democracy. According to Mac-Stiofain, only 56 Provisionals were caught in the net.[38] Gerry Adams was one of those most sought. But he watched quietly from a distance as soldiers wrecked his home, dragging off his father and a younger brother.[39] The Catholic districts were raked with gunfire as battles broke out between loyalists, the IRA and the army. Within a few hours, fifteen people lay dead, all but one of them civilians. They included a Catholic priest, Father Hugh Mullan, and a fourteen-year-old boy, Desmond Healey. Two thousand five hundred Catholics were driven from their homes near Protestant areas, and in North Belfast Catholics drove out Protestant neighbours. Whole streets were ablaze. In the Ardoyne, Protestants burned down two hundred houses as they evacuated them rather than hand them over to Catholics.

'By now the entire area was in a state of insurrection,' wrote Adams of Ballymurphy.[40]

One third of those arrested were released within two days. Twelve of the remaining 237 were hooded, and flown by helicopter to an old Royal Air Force base in Ballykelly, Co. Derry. For six days they were subjected to the nightmare of sensory deprivation. Spread-eagled against a wall for up to sixteen hours at a stretch, always hooded, denied sleep, while a noise like the roar of a jet engine drowned out the sound of everything else, they were beaten if they fell, then dragged before Special Branch officers for questioning, before being sent back to the wall again. During the six days they were kept on a diet of bread and water. The effect was to induce a kind of psychosis. 'I thought I was going mad,' said one victim, nineteen-year-old Joe Clark from West Belfast.[41]

When details about the treatment began to emerge, there

were demands for an inquiry, which led to the setting up of a committee under Lord Parker. A member of this committee, Lord Gardiner, declared that the techniques were illegal. For this reason, he argued, the army could not have used them in any authorized fashion. 'If any document or Minister had purported to authorize them, it would have been invalid because the procedures were and are illegal by domestic law and may also have been illegal by international law.'[42]

Yet no charges were ever brought against those involved in what was one of the most egregious acts of illegality in the Troubles. It was part of a pattern that would lead to further, bloodier violations of human rights.[43]

The political cost of internment far outweighed whatever intelligence-gathering benefits may have been gained. It was aimed solely at the Catholic community – not one loyalist was interned.[44] The authorities defended themselves by arguing that loyalists did not pose a significant threat at the time. Catholics, at the receiving end of UVF sniping attacks, were not convinced. Internment succeeded in alienating the entire nationalist community from the state and its security forces. From August 1971, the IRA's grip on the working-class nationalist neighbourhoods tightened, turning them into no-go areas for the army and police.

The SDLP had walked out of Stormont on 8 July in protest against a British Army shooting in Derry. Though it was uncomfortable with the abstentionist tactic, internment made it impossible for the party to re-enter Parliament without losing all credibility with nationalists. It organized a rent-and-rates strike in protest at internment, but the initiative still lay with the Provisionals.

Internment was a political disaster for Faulkner, partly because it was so obviously a military failure also. Within days of its introduction, practically the entire Provisional Army Council held a press conference in a school in Bally-murphy to flaunt their freedom. And British Army casualties were rising drastically. Between 6 February and 9 August, eleven soldiers were killed; in the weeks following internment, thirty-two died. The IRA was emerging in other areas where it had lain dormant for years, such as South Armagh. On 29 August the Provisional IRA shot dead a British soldier, Ian Armstrong, in Crossmaglen. Other units became active in Tyrone, Fermanagh and Down. The number of explosions soared; 179 took place in September, the highest till then. Among the targets attacked was a Protestant pub on the Shankill Road which was bombed on the 29th of that month, killing two customers and injuring thirty.[45] The Provisional IRA leadership again denied responsibility, but it was suspected that the North Belfast units were involved. The sectarian element that was present in the Provisionals from the start now asserted itself. Another Protestant pub was bombed a few days later, but fortunately with no fatalities.

Because internment was so obviously a failure, it did nothing to placate Unionist and loyalist militants. If anything, it convinced loyalists that they would have to take the 'offensive' themselves to thwart the IRA menace. The pub bombings, in the heartlands of loyalist Belfast, were added provocations.

The loyalists who gathered around Charles Harding-Smith were getting ready to strike back. 'We were trying to sort out the wheat from the chaff – establishing who had what weapons, who was prepared to do what. It was a weeding-out process,' said one of the UDA men who attended the meetings that were taking place in loyalist areas.[46] The organization was building crude bombs. A premature explosion in September killed two of its men, John Thompson and Jim Finlay, the ex-soldier who had been a UDA training officer. Immediately after their funeral, a UDA meeting was held in a school hall to discuss the organization's future. Harding-Smith and a gang of his backers walked up the hall and unbuttoned their jackets, revealing an array of pistols. It was the first time that the UDA militants had publicly displayed their weapons. The two hundred people in the hall began to applaud. The time for action had come. Harding-Smith was elected chairman and began amalgamating the loosely co-ordinated defence groups into a sectarian murder machine.[47]

Loyalists revenged themselves for the pub attacks. At the beginning of October 1971, UDA men threw a bomb into a pub known for traditional Irish music, but the only fatality was Winifred Maxwell, a forty-five-year-old Protestant. On 4 December, after an IRA sniper shot dead a Protestant teenage girl, loyalists targeted a pub known as an IRA haunt. *En route*, they panicked and left the bomb at McGurk's Bar, the nearest Catholic pub. At 8.45 p.m. one of the thirty customers in the bar shouted: 'Somebody has put a stink bomb in here.' Seconds later an explosion brought the building down. An underground gaspipe erupted, asphyxiating and burning those trapped in the rubble, from which fifteen corpses were eventually dug, including that of the owner's wife Philomena and fourteen-year-old daughter Marie.

A week later, the Provisionals bombed a furniture store on the Shankill, killing four people. As rescuers dug out the dead, they found the remains of one-year-old Colin Nicholl and two-year-old Tracey Munn, along with that of an old-age pensioner, Hugh Bruce, and twenty-nine-year-old Harold King.

The dark winter months closed in rapidly as 1971 drew to a close, with no sign that the security forces were making any progress against the republican uprising. The city centre emptied before evening fell, and people fled home along roads rendered pitch black because the streetlamps were out, often forced to make the journey on foot as public transport collapsed because of hijackings, burnings and riots. A make-shift service of taxis was struggling to replace the buses. Among Catholics, thousands of families disrupted by internment and evictions faced Christmas without a father or a home. By the beginning of 1972, over nine hundred Catholic men were being held without trial, leaving women to struggle as best they could.

And worst of all, the killings continued relentlessly. Catholic children, Protestant children, old-age pensioners, teenage girls – their broken bodies littered Ulster's landscape as the New Year dawned.

CHAPTER THREE

The Blood-Dimmed Tide: 1972–77

1

In Derry, Northern Ireland's second city and the scene of the first civil rights clashes, the IRA took longer to organize. With a solid nationalist majority, the city did not have the sectarian problems that haunted Belfast, and therefore the Provisionals were not called upon as a 'defence' force to guard against loyalist attacks. Their rivals in the Official IRA thrived in the city's lively left-wing political environment, where Trotskyists, communists and Marxist militants of various varieties debated against traditional republicans. It was not until 10 August 1971 that the Derry IRA managed to kill a soldier.

The authorities were notified that on 30 January a NICRA march against internment would be held in the city's Catholic Bogside, followed by speeches from Bernadette Devlin and other MPs and civil rights activists. The government had banned all marches in Northern Ireland from 9 August 1971. But Chief Superintendent Frank Lagan, the head of the Derry RUC, advised Major-General Robert Ford, the new GOC British forces, that the march should be allowed to proceed and the organizers prosecuted later. In his estimation the police would be able to control the situation and the army would not be needed, as intelligence suggested that the IRA would not be involved in the demonstration. Technically speaking, the British Army was in Ulster as an aid to the civil power, which gave Chief Superintendent Lagan as head of the police the authority to order the army's intervention or not. However, Lagan was informed that the military had orders to 'contain' the march within the Bogside. On 24 January, Ford told Lt-Col. Derek Wilford, the commander of the 1st Battalion of the Parachute Regiment, to prepare to conduct an 'arrest operation' for 30 January which would mean going after the 'hooligan element' if it should attempt to penetrate the streets on the fringes of the Bogside that led to Derry city centre. But 1st Parachute Battalion was given a standing order not to engage in running battles down the streets that led into the Bogside itself, for fear of falling victim to IRA snipers. Lagan had been superseded, his advice ignored. Major-General Ford would be in Derry himself to observe.

The decision to overrule Lagan was taken at a high political level, though the actual responsibility for this has never been determined. Nobody would ever be held accountable for the disastrous events that followed.

Frank Lagan's prediction of a relatively uneventful demonstration seemed to be proving accurate. By about 4 p.m. on that Sunday afternoon the several hundred youths who had earlier indulged in the ritual stone-throwing at the security forces on the border of the Bogside began to disperse as the main crowd gathered to listen to the speakers at 'Free Derry Corner' in the heart of the nationalist area. Then the first army units arrived.

Since internment, barricades had effectively sealed off the Bogside. The first of these lay a few hundred yards away from where the crowds were milling around, moving towards Free

Derry Corner. As the troops crossed the first barricade they opened fire, wounding two civilians, one of whom, John Johnson, a passer-by, died months later of his wounds. The troops continued towards the Bogside, with others arriving in a convoy of ten vehicles. Debouching from their armoured carriers, the paratroopers fanned out in a rapid and disciplined deployment, some towards nearby blocks of flats. It was 4.10 p.m., and already the wintry twilight was setting in. It was then that the 'arrest operation' began in earnest. According to Agnes Hume, the sister of the SDLP leader: 'One Saracen knocked a man on the ground and a soldier jumped out. He kept the man on the ground by battering him with the butt of his rifle and another soldier shot at this man from very close range. Then the soldiers seemed to go berserk and were shooting everywhere. Women and children were running for cover, screaming.'[1]

At the same time, unknown to the crowd below, members of the Royal Anglian Regiment were in position on the walls overlooking the Bogside. At least two of them were equipped with snipers' rifles.

Seventeen-year-old Jackie Duddy was the first to be shot dead that afternoon, hit in the back as he ran up the street towards Free Derry Corner. Within minutes, and in the same area, others would follow. Patrick Joseph Doherty, aged thirty-one, was crawling along to avoid the paratroopers' guns when he was shot in the buttock and died. Hugh Gilmore, a teenager, died next, after being shot possibly by two different soldiers. Forty-one-year-old Bernard McGuigan had taken cover not far from where Gilmore was hit. An eye-witness, Geraldine Richmond, said that she heard a wounded man cry out 'I don't want to die [by] myself, I don't want to die [by] myself'. McGuigan responded, 'I can't stand this any longer. If I take a white handkerchief out they will not shoot me.' He did so. But as he crossed to aid the wounded man he was shot in the head.

The force of the bullet that killed him was such that it blew off the back of his skull.[2]

John Young, William Nash and Michael McDaid were killed immediately after McGuigan as they stood at a barricade near Free Derry Corner, picked off from the walls overlooking the Bogside, where the Royal Anglians were stationed.[3]

As the paratroopers moved swiftly towards Free Derry Corner they killed Michael Kelly and Kevin McElhinney, and cornered James Wray, Gerald Donaghy, Gerald McKinney and William McKinney (no relation) with a group of terrified demonstrators in a courtyard. Eye-witnesses saw William McKinney being shot while (like Bernard McGuigan a few minutes earlier) he was going to the aid of a wounded man, and claim that Donaghy and Gerard McKinney were gunned down from point-blank range even though they had their hands on their heads in a gesture of surrender. Gerard McKinney's last words were 'Don't shoot, don't shoot'.[4]

The shooting finally stopped at about 4.30 p.m. But the lying about what happened had just begun. It was to last some twenty-five years.

At first the British Army claimed that eight of the thirteen dead were wanted, known terrorists and found with weapons. Within hours, this claim was modified to four wanted IRA men; one of the dead, Gerard Donaghy, who was in fact a member of the IRA's youth wing, they said had been found with four nail bombs in his pocket. Within two days, even these claims were almost totally abandoned as it was admitted that none of the dead were on any wanted list nor had any been found with weapons; the claim against Donaghy was repeated at a subsequent inquiry but later retracted. However, this did not discourage the British from asserting that the troops had been fired on first, if not by those shot dead, then by IRA snipers operating either from behind the barricades or from the surrounding buildings. GOC Major-General Ford was categorical: 'There is absolutely no doubt that the Parachute Battalion opened up only after they were fired on.'[5]

There is evidence that republican gunmen were present that afternoon. A man firing a pistol was seen by some civilian witnesses. In December 1991, Channel Four claimed that the Official IRA had fired at soldiers. A week after Bloody Sunday, as nationalists were calling it, the author spoke with a wounded man who said he was in the Official IRA. He asserted that soldiers had shot him in the buttock after he had opened fire on them. But he claimed that he only fired after the British troops had begun shooting. There is no way of determining the accuracy of this last claim. But the fact that not one soldier was injured during the course of the operation suggests strongly that there was no concerted IRA effort (either Provisional or Official) either to lure the troops into a gun battle or engage with them in response to their raid into the Bogside.

Civilian eye-witnesses rejected allegations of an IRA presence or any attempt to use the demonstration for cover in order to launch an attack on the army. Their version was simple: soldiers murdered people without provocation, in cold blood. The clash between these two versions of the events of 30 January would last for decades. A British government inquiry into the shootings headed by the Lord Chief Justice of England, Lord Widgery, did not resolve it. In a report published in April 1972, his sharpest criticism of the behaviour of British troops was in his conclusion. He wrote:

Each soldier was his own judge of whether he had identified a gunman. Their training made them aggressive and quick in decision and some showed more restraint in opening fire than others. At one end of the scale some soldiers showed a high degree of responsibility; at the other, notably in Glenfada Park [where James Wray, Gerard Donaghy, William McKinney and Gerald McKinney were shot] firing bordered on the reckless. These distinctions reflect differences in the character of the soldiers concerned . . . None of the deceased or wounded is proved to have been shot whilst handling a firearm or bomb. Some are wholly acquitted of complicity in such action; but there is a strong suspicion that some others had been firing weapons or handling bombs in the course of the afternoon and that yet others had been closely supporting them.[6]

Widgery arrived at his conclusions through studiously ignoring the statements NICRA collected from some five hundred civilian eye-witnesses, choosing instead to rely on the testimonies of the soldiers and their officers. Most importantly, he avoided the question of who held the overall responsibility for ordering the troops into action. The testimony of Chief Superintendent Lagan, who had said that the use of the army would not be required on 30 January, was kept until the very last days of the inquiry. Though Lord Widgery acknowledged that the decision to override the civil authority had been taken at a level higher than that of the Chief Constable and the GOC, he did not pursue the question of who it was who had defined the task of the paratroop battalion. Widgery offered no explanation as to how it was that the troops exceeded their orders not to penetrate the Bogside. As with the question of the authorization of the illegal five techniques of sensory deprivation, the question of who bears the ultimate responsibility for the massacre that afternoon in Derry has never been fully answered.

However, in a statement in the House of Commons two days after the event, Prime Minister Edward Heath admitted that the plan to 'contain' the 30 January demonstration had been drawn up in consultation with the Joint Security Council chaired by Northern Ireland Prime Minister Brian Faulkner, and was known to ministers in the British government. Of these, Reginald Maudling, the Home Secretary, and Lord Carrington, Defence Secretary, would have been the most crucial in formulating Ulster security policy. Carrington had already given the go-ahead to one illegal procedure, the use of the five techniques, nine months earlier. It was he who would have had to have sanctioned the use of 1st Para in Derry on 30 January for the aggressive 'arrest operation'.

For nationalists, the most damning aspect of the Widgery inquiry and report was the failure of the Lord Chief Justice to decide on whether the soldiers had acted illegally. When it came to the Ulster question, Britain's pre-eminent legal authorities seemed to have dozed off between 1970 and 1972, substituting disingenuous and tautological arguments for objective evaluations of what happened.

It took over twenty years for evidence to emerge that would wake them up. In *Eyewitness Bloody Sunday*, journalist Don Mullan compiled a series of eye-witness statements collected in 1972 but never admitted as evidence before the Widgery tribunal. New evidence also emerged. At the beginning of 1997 a paratrooper later known as Para AA, who had served with 1st Para, approached an Irish journalist claiming that he had been on duty on 30 January in Derry and had witnessed several of the killings. He said that the previous day an officer had told them to get some 'kills'. His statement, which was passed on to the Irish government, confirmed civilian eye-witnesses' accounts of unarmed demonstrators being shot while wounded or trying to surrender. He also stated that Widgery tribunal members doctored soldiers' original statements to make them conform to an acceptable version of what happened. Para AA continued:

I was then interviewed in an office by two Crown lawyers on Lord Widgery's team. I rattled off everything I had seen and had done. The only thing I omitted were the names and the manner in which people had been shot, apart from that I told the truth which I wanted to convey. Then to my utter surprise one of these doddering gentlemen said 'dear me Private 027, you make it sound as though shots were being fired at the crowd, and we can't have that can we?' And then proceeded to tear up my statement. He returned ten minutes later with another statement which bore no relation to fact . . .

Para AA was informed that this would be the statement he would use when going before the inquiry.[7]

Channel Four News compiled an investigative report that was broadcast on 17 January 1997, including tapes made of army and police radio messages in Derry on 30 January 1972 and a medical expert's analysis of some of the forensic evidence relating to the killings of Young, Nash and McDaid. The radio intercepts gave no indication whatsoever of any nail bombs being thrown, nor of shots fired at 1st Para. Instead they indicated that soldiers were firing from Derry's walls. The medical examination supported the allegations that the shots that killed Young, Nash and McDaid were fired from a position or positions on the walls overlooking the Bogside.

Twelve days later, on 29 January 1997, Channel Four News reported that a member of the Royal Anglican Regiment had confirmed that at least one army sniper was operating on the walls. Like Para AA he has not been named. But their versions of events of Bloody Sunday were supported not only by other eye-witness accounts but also by independent forensic and ballistic evidence and constituted an overwhelming case for reopening the Bloody Sunday inquiry. At the beginning of 1998, the new Labour Prime Minister, Tony Blair, announced that the case would be re-examined. By the summer of that year, preliminary hearings had begun.

The impact of Bloody Sunday reverberated throughout Ireland. On 2 February 1972, a mob attacked the British embassy in Dublin and burned it to the ground. Thousands of workers went on strike in protest. In Australia, dockers refused to unload British cargo ships. In the US, Irish Northern Aid's money-raising efforts met with increasing success. Figures filed with the Justice Department show that between

January and July 1972, NORAID collected $313,000 compared to $128,000 for the previous six months. (This figure is but an indication of how much was actually raised, since considerable sums were brought into Ireland by hand and never declared.) Meanwhile, the Harrison arms network in New York was getting into its stride, and by the end of 1972 was sending between two and three hundred rifles and several hundred thousand rounds of ammunition a year to the Provisionals.

Bloody Sunday's most important impact was at home. On 22 March 1972 the British government informed Brian Faulkner that it was taking over full security powers for the province. When Faulkner responded that Unionists could never accept this watering down of the Stormont regime's authority – already his own right wing was coalescing around a new militant movement called Vanguard – the British Prime Minister announced on 24 March the imposition of direct rule from London and the suspension of the Northern Ireland parliament. Six days later, the 1920 experiment came to an end and Britain took full responsibility for the bloody mess it had helped create. Internment marked the failure of the ordinary system of law and order to cope with the security crisis. The end of Stormont meant the collapse of the political structure that had sustained that system.

Over the next quarter of a century Britain would try other versions of devolved government for Ulster but the old majority-rule regime that had been in place for over fifty years was gone for ever.

2

Before the suspension of Stormont, murder had already become part of Ulster's daily routine. Between August 1971 and 30 March, 1972 there were over 1,130 bomb explosions, and over 2,000 shootings. These claimed the lives of 158 civilians, 58 soldiers and 17 RUC men, while 2,505 civilians, 306 soldiers and 107 policemen were injured. However, in the six months following the suspension of Stormont, violence increased drastically. There were 9,536 shooting incidents, 264 civilians died, as well as 108 soldiers and nine RUC members, with 2,634 civilians, 535 soldiers and 195 policemen injured. Only the number of explosions showed a slight decline.[8]

There were two main reasons why violence rose sharply. Both were linked to Stormont's suspension. The first was that the Provisional IRA took credit for bringing down the Unionist government and assumed that suspending Stormont was a sign that Britain was weakening in its commitment to Northern Ireland. As a result, the Provisionals' leaders were encouraged to launch an all-out offensive while at the same time opening up contacts with the government in the hope of negotiating a British withdrawal. Meanwhile, loyalist paramilitaries viewed the end of Stormont as an appalling betrayal, the inevitable consequence of the perfidious policies of successive British governments which had abolished the B-Specials, disarmed the RUC, cosseted the civil rights movement, and failed to deal successfully with the IRA menace. They were confronting the end of Ulster as they knew it. Loyalists would respond to the crisis with the most vicious sectarian campaign that Northern Ireland had yet experienced. It would last for almost twenty-five years.

From a small band of neglected old men, the IRA in Belfast had become, by early 1972, stronger than at any time in its entire history, with hundreds of recruits and many thousands of supporters. Most of these new republicans came from non-republican backgrounds, and almost all were working-class. Middle-class Belfast remained largely unaffected by the trauma that was going on around it. The quiet, prosperous avenues in the south of the city and along its eastern fringes by the Co. Down coast rarely had their tranquility disturbed.

One of those most eagerly overseeing the republican movement's rapid growth was Gerry Adams, who throughout 1971 and early 1972 was commanding officer of the Provisionals' Second Battalion, based in the mid-Falls area. He established his republican credentials during a feud with the local Official IRA in which one of their Ballymurphy members was shot and seriously wounded. The man remained paralysed for the rest of his life. In mid-1971, on the run from the security forces, who had already snatched his father, and at various times would put his brother, two of his cousins and his uncle Liam Hannaway behind bars, Adams took time off from guerrilla warfare to get married to Colette McArdle in a church in West Belfast. Outside troops scoured the streets, with Adams near the head of their wanted list, as the ceremony proceeded.

What few rules the Provisional IRA established to give its war a moral context began to dissolve, and with increasing rapidity, following internment and Bloody Sunday. At the beginning of the campaign there was a rule about only attacking members of the security forces while they were on duty. Any pretence about obeying it was abandoned after internment was introduced. The Provisionals targeted the local militia, the UDR, whose members were easy to locate. One of the first to be murdered at home was Sean Russell, who lived in the Ballymurphy area, Adams's stronghold. Gunmen from the Second Battalion shot him dead on 8 December 1971. In the very first week of 1972, gunmen from the Second Battalion struck again. Raymond Denham, an off-duty RUC reservist, was shot while at the factory where he worked near the Falls Road. Over the following days, the Provisionals in North Belfast killed another off-duty UDR man and an off-duty policeman.

Seventeen days after Bloody Sunday, Provisional gunmen in Derry kidnapped a Catholic bus driver, Thomas Callaghan, who was also a part-time member of the UDR, and 'executed' him. At first, there were cries of horror that men should be gunned down out of uniform, often in front of their families. But within months each had become just another routine Ulster killing.

A novel contrivance – so simple it now seems incredible that anyone had actually to invent it – helped propel the Provisional IRA to new heights of violence – the car bomb. It would change terrorist tactics throughout the world. It first devastated Derry city centre in March 1972. The same month, a hundred-pound car bomb killed seven people – two of them old-age pensioners – and wounded a hundred in Donegall Street in the centre of Belfast. For the first time, television viewers came home to scenes of policemen scooping burnt and unrecognizable bits of human beings into plastic bags. The Provisional leadership justified the tactic, saying that it tied down hundreds of troops and policemen, drained the British coffers of money in compensation payments, and that, anyway, they always gave warnings. But the telephoned warnings were frequently inaccurate or confusing. In the Donegall Street bombing, the warnings actually led the police to shepherd people into the street where the car bomb was waiting to explode. The storm of condemnation that followed the blast contributed to the leadership's decision to call a temporary truce, lasting seventy-two hours. It was also a signal to the British, now directly embroiled in the Ulster crisis, that they were dealing with a disciplined movement that could, under the right conditions, bring about a permanent halt to the violence. The Provisionals, having got rid of Stormont, now wanted face-to-face negotiations with the 'real' enemy.

The violence resumed with even greater fury in April 1972. On the 14th, there were twenty-three explosions across Northern Ireland. Provisional IRA snipers in the narrow streets of West and North Belfast continued to pick off troops on foot patrol on almost a daily basis. In rural areas, especially Armagh, the Provisionals favoured land-mines, which soon made the roads around the south of the county unusable for the security forces.

While the Provisionals were going for a final push, their former comrades in the Official IRA stumbled from one disastrous mistake to another. After Bloody Sunday, their Operations officer, Seamus Costello, dispatched a bombing team to Britain to wreak revenge on the Parachute Regiment. A former British paratrooper drove a van bomb to the gates of the regiment's headquarters in Aldershot. When it went off, it killed six cleaning ladies and a Catholic chaplain. Shortly afterwards, Joe McCann, an Official IRA leader from Belfast, along with two other gunmen, attempted to assassinate the Stormont Minister for Home Affairs, John Taylor. Though hit over twenty times, Taylor survived, thanks to the inaccuracy and low velocity of the antiquated Thompson submachine-guns the gunmen used.

McCann was as militant as any Provisional but had stuck with the leadership of Cathal Goulding for political reasons. However, he remained close to Adams – the two had joined the junior wing of the IRA at around the same time. In May 1971, McCann ambushed an army patrol in Belfast, killing Corporal Robert Bankier, the first fatality the Official IRA claimed. During internment, McCann made a name for himself as one of the most dangerous operators in Belfast in a series of gun battles with British troops. By 1972 he was on the army's most-wanted list. Under the circumstances, his decision to return to his native Markets area near Belfast city centre seemed foolhardy, especially since he refused to disguise himself. On 15 April, police spotted McCann as he got off a bus. A patrol of paratroopers gave chase. McCann, unarmed, dashed down a side street, desperately trying to push through one front door after the next. On that day all the doors happened to be locked. He died in a hail of bullets.

When news of McCann's death spread, working-class areas of Catholic Belfast and Derry erupted in a series of gun battles. Within twenty-four hours, the Officials killed three soldiers. It would be their last show of strength against British forces. The Official IRA Army Council had made up its mind that political violence in Northern Ireland was counterproductive. Already, there were worrying signs of growing loyalist militancy, with a series of 'unexplained' murders of innocent Catholics in Belfast. Goulding and his supporters on the Army Council feared the violence would provoke a Protestant backlash.

The Official IRA in Derry gave Goulding the excuse he needed. William Best, a young Derry Catholic who was in the British Army, came home on leave to the Bogside where a group of Official IRA men kidnapped him. Pleas for his release were ignored. His body was found dumped on waste ground. The killing outraged local Catholics, who marched to the Official IRA's Derry headquarters to demand that they get out of the area. Eight days later, on 29 May, the Official IRA announced an open-ended ceasefire. It said it was doing so in compliance with the wishes of the people it represented in Northern Ireland, but warned that it reserved the right to retaliate against the British troops or 'sectarian' forces. The decision left many members of the Officials unhappy, and suspicious of Goulding's long-term intentions. This was especially so in Belfast, where the leadership's overtures to loyalists in its attempts to link up with the Protestant working class were regarded as naïve.

Two weeks after the Official IRA ceasefire, the Provisionals met with John Hume and Paddy Devlin in Derry. For Hume, and for the SDLP, the period since internment had been one of continuing frustration, as ordinary politics became impossible. But there had been feelers put out between the recently appointed Secretary of State for Northern Ireland, William Whitelaw, who effectively ruled the province, replacing the Stormont government, and the Provisional Army Council. Hume acted as a go-between, and passed on to the British the

Provisionals' terms for talks. The most important was that IRA prisoners should not be treated as common criminals but granted 'political status'. Billy McKee was leading a group of republicans on a prison hunger strike to win special privileges, such as the right to wear their own clothes and to refuse to do prison work. Political status, a traditional IRA demand, was an acknowledgment that its acts were politically motivated. In the eyes of republicans, it was recognition that they were prisoners of war. The Provisionals also wanted an independent observer at the meeting, and demanded that it not take place at Stormont. The Heath government conceded all their demands. The Provisionals responded with a declaration that they would call a ceasefire on 26 June. Ulster held its breath.

Earlier, on 14 March, just ten days before Stormont's suspension, Adams's life on the run had come to an end when troops raided the house in which he was hiding. He was taken to Springfield Road RUC station where a Special Branch officer eventually identified him. For thirty-six hours he was punched, slapped and kicked around; a Special Branch officer threw a fit, went for his gun and, overcoming his colleagues' efforts to restrain him, attempted to shoot the prisoner. The gun was unloaded, which suggests that the police were indulging in histrionics. Adams was interned but the Provisional IRA ceasefire entailed a happy consequence for him. In June he was whisked from prison to freedom as one of the delegates the Provisionals named to meet with the British government.[9] The others were Army Council members MacStiofain, O Conaill and Seamus Twomey (a veteran from the 15 August shoot-out in Divis Street), Belfast IRA leader Ivor Bell, Adams's Derry contemporary Martin McGuinness, who had graduated from the Officials to command the city's Provisionals, and a Sinn Fein representative, Myles Shevlin.

On 7 July, *en route* to Belfast airport where an RAF helicopter awaited the delegation, one of the two cars carrying them broke down.[10] It was an omen. The delegates were flown to Oxfordshire and then taken to Chelsea, where at the gracious home of a junior minister in the Northern Ireland Office they came face to face with the British government's supremo in Northern Ireland, William Whitelaw, who listened with some bemusement to MacStiofain's main demand for a British declaration of intent to withdraw by 1975. His other demands, such as the reduction of the military presence in Catholic areas and the ending of internment, were possible under the right circumstances – in fact, the British had already begun to release those held without charge. But Whitelaw put it to MacStiofain that the Protestants might react violently if Britain were to announce an intention to pull out. MacStiofain dismissed this fear. The Provisionals' fundamentalist republicanism had no place in it for Protestants, other than that of dupes of British imperialism who would come to their senses when the British told them to. They saw the threat of a Protestant backlash as a bluff Britain used for its own insidious purposes. The gulf between these two positions was unbridgeable. The Provisionals would maintain this view of Ulster's Protestants, refusing to acknowledge that there is legitimate, indigenous opposition to republicanism within Ulster – opposition that exists independent of Britain's interests. It is of course a self-serving incomprehension, allowing republicans to prolong the fiction that they are fighting on behalf of the whole Irish nation.

After the meeting Whitelaw commented with undisguised disdain: 'The meeting was a non-event. The IRA leaders simply made impossible demands which I told them the British government would never concede. They were in fact still in a mood of defiance and determination to carry on until their absurd ultimatums were met.'[11]

Adams kept his counsel at the talks, saying nothing. He had not wanted the meeting in the first place, and cautioned the Southern IRA men that the British were more interested in gathering information about them than in seriously negotiating. Both he and Ivor Bell, who was a close friend and a committed socialist, dressed down for the occasion to show their scorn for it. In contrast, MacStiofain and O Conaill saw themselves as being in a similar position to that of Michael Collins, when he went to meet the British in December 1921 to negotiate the Treaty, except, of course, they were now going to end the partition that came about as a result of those talks.

The reality was that, unlike Collins, the Provisionals had no political machine to translate whatever military strengths they possessed into an expression of popular support – Provisional Sinn Fein hardly existed as a political organization. The Provisionals had sprung from a 'purist' republican tradition that regarded politics and the fighting of elections rather as Paisley regarded the Catholic Church – as a source of tempta-tion and vice. The blandishments of constitutional politics had to be spurned at all costs as they would lead to compro-mise. The Belfast Provisional leader Billy McKee expressed it best when he called Sinn Fein 'a bloody anchor around our neck'.[12] Nor, in the end, did MacStiofain and O Conaill have a military machine anything like that which stood behind Collins. Events would soon expose their crippling military and political weaknesses.

The British were supposed to report back with their re-sponse to MacStiofain's demands inside a week. But within two days of the London meeting the ceasefire collapsed. Given the Provisionals' dismissal of Protestant opposition as irrele-vant, it was ironic that what ended the slim hope of peace was the UDA. It blocked a Catholic family from occupying a house a Protestant family had vacated. The British Army refused to intervene to break up the UDA blockade of the street. On 13 July, the Provisionals fully resumed their cam-paign, killing three soldiers in West and North Belfast. Loy-alists were threatening to impose their own 'no-go' areas unless the British dismantled the IRA's strongholds. The

British did not sit back for long. Four thousand extra troops were sent to Ulster to take part in a huge invasion of the Catholic working-class no-go areas. Militant Protestant action had forced the British to act yet again.[13] The republican barricades were dismantled on 31 July without the IRA firing a shot. Its forces melted away to resume their campaign of hit-and-run.

By July 1972, the feared Protestant backlash had begun, though many, including the British, the RUC and the IRA, each for their own reasons, refused to recognize it. For the next two years it would dominate the future of Ulster, acting as a check on nationalists' ambitions and frustrating Britain's most ambitious attempt to reach a settlement and extricate itself from the Irish quagmire.

3

John White was nineteen years old when rioting and burning consumed West Belfast in 1969. One day, shortly after the August upheavals, White was stopped at a Catholic barricade near the Falls Road and given a bad beating. He became a Protestant vigilante. In 1971, White was still a vigilante, manning barricades in the Shankill area, attending meetings of the various defence groups that were coming together slowly to form the UDA. Then two events hardened him. The first was the bombing of the Four Step Inn on the Shankill Road in September 1971 (see Chapter 2), which killed a friend, Ernie Bates. White had lived next door to Bates's family. 'The Four Step Inn was a paramilitary hang out,' White admits, 'but Ernie was just an Orangeman.' No one claimed responsibility for the attack, but it was almost certainly the North Belfast Provisionals' work. Then, the following December, White encountered the funeral of one of the two 'Balmoral babies' killed in the Provisional IRA bombing of the Balmoral furniture store. 'I saw the father carrying the little coffin,' White remembers. He joined the UDA shortly afterwards. 'I wanted revenge, I wanted to protect my community and I wanted to stop the IRA,' he said.[14]

Within a month he was involved with UDA strongman Charles Harding-Smith in a gunrunning effort. A local gun dealer had put the UDA in touch with an English dealer, who told the loyalists that he had access to a large haul of AK-47s, the powerful Russian-made automatic rifle that would later become the Provisionals' trademark. With the guns going at £250 each, the UDA raised half a million pounds for the deal, mostly, says White, from members' subscriptions. After a few meetings in London, everything seemed ready to go. The UDA made the arrangements to have the arms shipped to Belfast.

In January 1972, White, Harding-Smith and the English gun dealer met at the Hilton Hotel in London to clinch the deal, along with another man, who turned out to be a member of the RUC Special Branch. Harding-Smith and White were arrested. White is convinced that the English contact was in fact a member of MI5.

He and Harding-Smith spent eleven months on remand in Brixton Prison, only to be acquitted in court on the grounds that they had been 'entrapped'. When they got back to Belfast in December 1972, White was amazed at the change in the ramshackle league of vigilantes that he and Harding-Smith had left behind.

Throughout 1972, the Protestant backlash was manifesting itself in two ways. In public, disaffected Unionist Party politicians such as William Craig set up rival political organizations. Paisley had established his own party, the Democratic Unionist Party, in September of the previous year. Craig, who since 1968 had been the chief voice of right-wing obstructionism within the UUP, launched the Vanguard Movement on 9 February 1972, threatening 'if and when the politicians fail us, it will be our duty to liquidate the enemy'.[15] On 18 March he held a mass rally in Belfast with leather-jacketed men in serried ranks, with motorcycle out-riders escorting his car, as if in an ominous revival of 1930s fascism. But in spite of the impressive numbers – sixty thousand showed at the first rally – and violent talk, Protes-tant resistance did not coalesce around Vanguard, which tried to bridge the gap between paramilitary menace and political respectability, ground the Rev. Ian Paisley already occupied.

The real backlash began in a much more low-key but far more deadly manner on the day before the founding of Vanguard. On 8 February a forty-nine-year-old Catholic called Bernard Rice was walking along the Crumlin Road, North Belfast's main thoroughfare, when gunmen shot him dead from a passing car. There was no claim of responsibility. The RUC issued a statement calling it a 'motiveless murder'. Mrs Rice thought differently. Two days after her husband's death she said that he had been killed 'because he was a Catholic'.[16] Mrs Rice was right. The killers were members of the Red Hand Commandos, John McKeague's virulently sectarian organization. For a time, they operated out of the UDA's office on the Shankill Road. The bigger organization occasionally lent them guns.

By then the UDA itself was ready to go into action. Behind the vigilantes lurked four killer squads, comprising thirty-eight men. The biggest team was in White's area of the Shankill Road, with twenty members; its leader was an ex-British soldier and former UDR man. His second-in-com-mand was Davey Payne, on whom his colleagues would soon jokingly confer the nickname 'Psychopath'. The North Belfast UDA had a smaller team of six gunmen. A third group was based in the oldest loyalist area of Belfast, Sandy Row, near the city centre. It also had six members, as had the fourth hit team. It operated across the Lagan in East Belfast, where Tommy Herron, the former hotel doorman who had become UDA vice-chairman, held sway.

These men would kill approximately 80 of the 121 victims

of sectarian assassination (the vast majority of them in Belfast) that helped make 1972 the worst year of the conflict. The Provisionals murdered most of the rest.

The aim of the UDA's death squads, according to White, was 'to terrorize the terrorist. It was one community attacking another'.[17] At first, victims were gunned down on the street or at home. But in May, when the UDA set up a series of no-go areas in response to those in the Catholic districts, the nature of the killings changed. A more frightening pattern emerged with the discovery of the body of Gerard McCusker, a twenty-four-year-old Catholic, on a vacant lot in the Shankill area. His hair had been pulled out, his face was badly bruised and his wrists were broken. According to the UDA, McCusker's killers believed that he knew the names of IRA men, and he was brutalized in order to force him to talk. As the summer weeks passed, this kind of brutalization grew even more ferocious. Herron's UDA squad in East Belfast kidnapped twenty-three-year-old Henry Russell, one of the few Catholics to have joined the UDR. On 13 July, his badly beaten and almost naked body was found with burn marks and with a cross branded on his back. Terror began to take hold of the Catholic community, who feared that a loyalist Jack the Ripper was prowling the streets. The torture and beatings were a feature of all four death squads. Nine days after Russell was murdered, the rumours had more sensational material on which to feed. In the early hours of 22 July, the UDA stopped local Irish folk singer Rose McCartney and her boyfriend Patrick O'Neill at a roadblock on the Crumlin Road. Both were taken to the UDA's Shankill Road headquarters, above a pub called the Bricklayer's Arms, where their heads were covered while 'the Psychopath' set about interrogating them, badly injuring O'Neill's hand in the process. Present in the room was East Belfast supremo Tommy Herron. Unfortunately, the cover slipped from one of the victims, who caught a glimpse of Herron. This sealed their fate. After making McCartney sing a song, their killers bundled the two into the back of a car, drove to a patch of waste ground and machinegunned them to death.[18]

Rose McCartney was the first Catholic woman to fall victim to the Shankill Road UDA, and rumours spread throughout West Belfast that the 'Ripper' had struck again, inflicting terrible mutilations on her.[19] White's theory about 'terrorizing the terrorist' at least worked in so far as it terrified the population that supported the Provisional IRA. But since working-class Catholics did not trust the security forces to protect them – between 31 July and 31 December only three Protestants were charged with murder – sectarian killings may have enhanced the position of the IRA. Nor did the UDA's killings do anything to curb the Provisionals' campaign, which kept going throughout 1972 with increasing recklessness. Nine people were killed in a series of twenty-two bomb explosions in Belfast on 21 July on a day of panic and death known as Bloody Friday. Ten days later, another nine died when three car bombs exploded in the peaceful village of Claudy, in Co. Derry. Included among the dead were two children. A sectarian element was noticeable in this atrocity, as all three bombs were left near Protestant-run businesses.[20]

In the closing months of 1972, the Provisionals' armed campaign showed the first signs that it was running out of steam. In each month for the first eight months of the year, the Provisionals detonated well over a hundred bombs, reaching a peak of 196 during the bloody days of July. But in the last three months, the average fell to under a hundred. In December there were only sixty-four IRA bombings.[21] The army's saturation of Catholic areas made it increasingly difficult for the IRA to mount bombing runs. Perhaps more importantly, they were losing the moral ground they had held since internment. The slaughter of civilians in Provisional bombing attacks, whether 'accidental' or not, undermined whatever claim they might have had to being the 'defenders' of Catholics. It allowed the Dublin government which, thanks to internment and Bloody Sunday, was reluctant to clamp down on the movement to adopt a more stringent approach.

On 19 November they arrested Sean MacStiofain, the Provisionals' Chief of Staff, and sentenced him to six months in jail for IRA membership. He went on a hunger-and-thirst strike, which he abandoned after a week. Though he refused food until January, it was a futile exercise, invoking less and less sympathy even among Provisionals. Meanwhile, the introduction into the Provisionals' arsenal of a new weapon, the RPG-7 rocket-launcher, while potentially deadly, did not halt the group's military decline. But it did signal the beginning of a relationship that in the coming years would prove very fruitful for the IRA. A consignment of these Russian-made weapons was flown from Libya to a small airstrip in Kerry, where they were unloaded and sent north. Army Council member Joe Cahill had made the contact with Colonel Gaddafi. A Canadian had piloted the consignment. He and his plane were later lost over the Atlantic when, it is believed, he ran out of fuel. The rocket was first used on 28 November in an attack on an RUC base in Fermanagh, which killed a police officer. Fortunately for the security forces, in the Provisionals' hands the device proved erratic and unreliable.

As a sign of the Irish government's increasing confidence, it introduced the Offences against the State Act, a draconian new bill which allowed the authorities to jail anyone as a member of an illegal organization simply on the word of a policeman. The debate on the measure went on against the background of the UDA's campaign, which spread beyond Belfast to Derry – where UDA gunmen murdered five people in a machinegun attack on a pub – and into the Irish republic. After bombing a pub and a soft drinks factory in Donegal, the UDA issued a rare statement in which it claimed responsibility for the incidents. It concluded: 'We warn the Eire Government to clamp down on the IRA. Every time the IRA strike in the North we will strike twice as hard in the south.'[22] During the debate on the new antiterrorism bill in the Dail (the Irish parliament) on 1 December, two car bombs exploded in Dublin, killing two men and injuring eighty. The Belfast UVF was responsible, though it never publicly acknowledged the attacks.

In the panic following the bombings, parliamentary opposition to the Offences against the State Act collapsed, and it was made law.

When White returned to Belfast from London shortly after this, he shared the satisfaction of the UDA leaders, who looked upon the last twelve months as a period of great advancement for the organization. It had been instrumental in forcing the British to dismantle the nationalist no-go areas, blocking the government from making concessions to the IRA, and frightening the Irish political establishment into taking a harder line with militant republicans under its jurisdiction. The Protestant backlash was achieving results – the problem was that few seemed to recognize it, at least publicly. The RUC persisted in describing the sectarian killings as 'motiveless murders', and the IRA insisted that they were the work of undercover British agents. Neither the British nor Irish governments rushed to proclaim Protestant involvement in widespread terrorism.

Each had their own reason for ignoring the facts – the security forces because they did not want to be distracted from their war against the IRA, the British because they did not want to be forced to start introducing internment against Protestants for fear of provoking a bigger backlash – and anyway, in late 1972 they were phasing out internment. The Irish government was afraid to recognize Protestant violence in case it should legitimize the Provisionals' claims to be the Catholics' defenders.

As for the Provisionals and the Officials, they both refused to accept the extent and depth of Protestant opposition to their goal of 'uniting' all Irishmen; they preferred to ascribe the sectarian killings to the sinister machinations of their 'real' enemy, the British. So it was that in early 1973 Johnny White began thinking of ways of making the point that loyalists were behind the murder campaign, and were prepared to continue until the IRA stopped.

White had rejoined the Shankill Road section of the UDA, which was now organized, like the Provisionals, into a pseudo-military structure consisting of 'companies'. The Shankill Road unit became 'C' company. By early 1973, White was third in command, and soon afterwards became 'C' company's representative on the Inner Council, the UDA's ruling body. According to White, 'C' company was responsible for 'ninety percent' of all the sectarian killings in the West Belfast area from 1972 until about 1976.[23]

The UDA campaign escalated in February 1973, with a hand-grenade attack on a bus carrying workers to an East Belfast factory. By then, the UDA had murdered almost a hundred people. It had also engaged in several gun battles with the British Army, after riots in Protestant areas that left two civilians dead, provoking Tommy Herron, the UDA's vice-chairman, to declare: 'The British army and government are now our enemies.'

Yet of the 364 people who were being held without trial as of 3 February 1973, not one was a loyalist. The police argued that this was because loyalist violence was neither sufficiently 'organized' nor systematic enough to warrant such a response. The authorities maintained that 'maverick' gangs were carrying out the killings. Herron, fearing internment, did his best to reinforce this notion. As a ruse, he issued a statement 'warning' the killers that unless they stopped, the UDA would act against them. In fact Herron had been one of the murder campaign's main organizers. As White's testimony reveals, this was a politically convenient fiction, which the police chose to accept. After the hand-grenade attack, however, the outcry from nationalists forced the authorities to act for political reasons, regardless of whether or not their security arguments about the nature of the sectarian campaign were legitimate. On 5 February, the first two loyalists were interned. Within a few days, five more were lifted. Among them was John McKeague, the erratic leader of the Red Hand Commandos, and several UVF members, though their contribution to the sectarian violence was slight. There was a burst of protests from the Protestant community, with marches, demonstrations and a series of strikes, which quickly degenerated into widespread rioting, looting and general disorder, antagonizing ordinary, respectable Protestants who anyway regarded their own paramilitaries with suspicion if not outright hostility. There was no foundation of sympathy on which the UDA could build a coherent protest movement against internment.

The introduction of internment against loyalists highlighted the UDA's dilemma about acknowledging its responsibility for the sectarian murder campaign. If it claimed the killings, then the authorities would have no other option than to crack down harder on the organization, interning its leadership and declaring it illegal, as they had done the UVF and IRA. But by not claiming responsibility, the political point of the murders was lost. In May 1973, the UDA held a conference in an East Belfast hotel, attended by some fifty leading members. There was a battle for the chairmanship between East and West Belfast, with Herron and Harding-Smith being the respective contenders. It was resolved with the election of a 'compromise' candidate, Andy Tyrie, a founding member of the organization in West Belfast. Tyrie, portly and bespectacled, moustached like a Mexican bandit, was a quiet background figure. To Herron and Harding-Smith he seemed malleable enough to serve as a puppet. It was after his election that the contentious issue of claiming responsibility came up again.

Johnny White and another UDA man suggested a simple solution. Invent a different name for the UDA's hit squads. The name they came up with was the Ulster Freedom Fighters.

Tyrie agreed. In fact, this fitted in with his own plans. He appointed an overall 'military' commander to take charge of the 'UFF'. He would choose those men from the four murder gangs regarded as the most reliable and ruthless to head UFF cells in each area. Things would be systematized. Members of the West Belfast unit were given instructions on, among other things, the use of the knife. One of their commanders, who favoured this method of killing, demonstrated how the victim was gripped from behind and the jugular cut across from left to right. 'The assassin must always make sure to stand behind the victim to avoid being drenched in blood,' he said.[24] He acknowledged that only a few men were capable of killing with the knife.

A death list of SDLP politicians was drawn up, with Gerry Fitt at its head. A UFF cell from 'C' company, with White in charge, waited to abduct Fitt from a bar in central Belfast. When he didn't show up, they grabbed his election agent and SDLP city councillor, Paddy Wilson, along with his companion, a Protestant woman, Irene Andrews, with whom Wilson was having an affair. They were taken to a remote quarry outside Belfast and stabbed and shot to death. Andrews was stabbed over twenty times in her head and body; Wilson had over thirty stab wounds and his throat had been cut from ear to ear. One of the killers remarked that stabbing a woman to death was like 'sticking a knife in a pillow case'.

At 1.30 a.m. on 26 June a call to a Belfast newspaper in the name of 'Captain Black, Ulster Freedom Fighters' gave the location of the bodies. They were found three hours later. According to White, this was the first time that the name 'UFF' was used to claim responsibility for a murder. 'There will be more deaths in reprisal,' said the caller.[25]

Shortly after the double murders, White was arrested and

detained without trial. One of the UDA's most prolific killers would remain behind bars for two years. From August, the sectarian murder rate began to drop drastically as more of the UDA's hit-men were deposited in Long Kesh, reaching a peak of around thirty. This put considerable strains on the UDA's economic resources, since the organization was expected to contribute money to the families of its interned and imprisoned members. It was shortly after a fund-raising drive for prisoners' families that Herron disappeared, only to be found murdered in a ditch along a country road south-east of Belfast on 16 September. The murder fuelled conspiracy theories for decades, and to date remains unsolved.[26]

By the end of the year there were around seventy-five loyalists interned, as well as over five hundred republicans. In December 1973 there was only one sectarian murder in Northern Ireland. Internment was hurting both the UDA and the Provisionals. The decline of the paramilitaries allowed the British government to launch a daring political initiative to solve the Ulster crisis, one that would give Catholics governmental power and an institutional link to the Irish Republic.

4

It was always the intention of the British government to keep Northern Ireland on the margins of British politics. Its first instinct, having removed Stormont, was to put something in its place that would have the support of the nationalist population. Following the announcement of Stormont's suspension, Prime Minister Heath appealed to Northern Ireland's Catholics: 'Now is your chance,' he said in a television broadcast. 'A chance for fairness, a chance for peace, a chance at last to bring the bombings and killings to an end.'[27] Britain could only reinstate a devolved government that would keep Ulster at arm's length with the help of the moderate nationalists, whom the SDLP represented. But the party ignored a British appeal to all the parties to meet to discuss political options in Darlington, England, in September 1972. Only the UUP, the Northern Ireland Labour Party and the Alliance Party showed up. As long as internment existed, the SDLP's room for political manoeuvre was limited: it could not ignore the alienation of the Catholic population. However, Britain's professed intention of ending internment as soon as it was feasible, and its publication of a plan that advocated an assembly with a power-sharing executive and an Irish dimension for a future Northern Ireland government, allowed Fitt and Hume to lead their party in June 1973 into elections for the proposed new assembly. The Provisionals opposed the plans, calling on nationalists to boycott the elections. They accused the SDLP of a sell-out – after all, the party had pledged itself not to take part in any Ulster political institution until internment ended. But Hume and Fitt had calculated wisely. Sinn Fein had not one single elected official in Northern Ireland. Southern traditionalists like O Conaill and O Bradaigh dominated the Provisionals' thinking at this time, and a moribund Sinn Fein reflected their scorn for the ordinary political process. Their boycott proved ineffective, and the SDLP won nineteen of the seventy-eight proposed seats, which represented 22.1 per cent of the vote. As Michael Farrell has pointed out, this made the SDLP 'the biggest anti-Unionist parliamentary party in the history of the state'.[28] The SDLP could claim four positions on the power-sharing executive.

Things were more confused, and more difficult, on the Unionist side. Faulkner, the UUP leader and Northern Ireland's last Prime Minister, was ambivalent about the British proposals; eventually he committed himself to supporting them but with the intention of changing them so that they would be more palatable to Protestants. Ex-Unionist Party member William Craig and the Rev. Ian Paisley opposed the plans vociferously. A poll in March, which the British included as part of the overall plan and which showed an overwhelming majority in support of partition, did not appease loyalist fears about long-term British intentions. And loyalists were especially incensed at the idea of a Council of Ireland, linking Northern Ireland to the Republic. Craig and Paisley ran against the plan, as did a group of Unionists led by John Taylor, who had survived the Official IRA's assassination attempt the year before. The Unionist result boded ill for the future of the proposed executive. The anti-power-sharing Unionists won twenty-seven seats, while Faulkner's supporters took twenty-two. As Britain would find time and time again, the struggle to create a moderate consensus among Unionists would prove much more difficult than it would among nationalists, who were more willing to compromise. Still, Heath pushed ahead, trying to make Faulkner into a Terence O'Neill for the 1970s.

A four-day conference was held at Sunningdale beginning on 6 December 1973. In attendance was the SDLP, the Faulkner Unionists, the Alliance Party, British government ministers and ministers from the Irish government, led by William Cosgrave, whose Fine Gael-Labour Party coalition had just ousted Jack Lynch. An agreement was hammered out making the Council of Ireland a fourteen-member body responsible mainly for economic and social matters. In return, the Irish government agreed to recognize the right of the majority in Northern Ireland to remain part of the UK for as long as they wished. Britain undertook to review internment and release more prisoners by Christmas, and to make the RUC more acceptable to Catholics. The Irish agreed to intensify the offensive against the Provisionals – an undertaking very congenial to Cosgrave, whose Fine Gael party was traditionally anti-republican. Its partner, the Irish Labour Party, was hardly less enthusiastic.

In the words of Farrell: 'Sunningdale was the high point of British strategy in Ireland. It was a masterpiece of balance and ambiguity.'[29] But for over twenty years the Sunningdale Agreement would stand more as a gloomy reminder of the dangers of ambitious reform than as a beacon showing the way forward.

Unionist opposition quickly hardened around the United Ulster Unionist Council. Its members disrupted the assembly with noisy protests, which intensified when the executive took power in January 1974. Brian Faulkner was appointed Chief Executive and Gerry Fitt was his deputy. John Hume held the post of Minister for Commerce, with his colleagues Paddy Devlin and Austin Currie holding the ministries of Health and Social Services and Housing, respectively. It was poetic justice that Currie, who started the civil rights protests in 1968 by squatting in a house, should have ended up in charge of all housing allocation in Northern Ireland. Unfortunately, no one had the time or the inclination to savour it. Faulkner resigned as Unionist Party leader in January 1974 after a vote of the party's leadership body rejected the power-sharing settlement. The SDLP did not help matters by trumpeting the new arrangements as a triumph for nationalism. In a speech in Trinity College, Dublin, on 17 January, SDLP assembly member Hugh Logue proclaimed the Council of Ireland as 'the vehicle that would trundle the Unionists into a United Ireland', to the discomfiture of Faulkner who was desperately trying to convince his demoralized supporters that it was a defence against a united Ireland.

A British general election the following month gave the anti-Faulkner Unionists a chance to show their strength. They did so, triumphantly. United Ulster Unionist Council alliance candidates dominated by Paisley and Craig took eleven of the twelve Westminster seats, leaving Faulkner's supporters without any; Gerry Fitt was returned as the sole pro-power-sharing representative. The SDLP split the nationalist vote in two marginal constituencies, Fermanagh-South Tyrone and Mid-Ulster, with the result that anti-power-sharing Unionists took the seats from independent nationalists Frank Maguire and Bernadette McAliskey (née Devlin). McAliskey's defeat marked the end of the era of the 'new' nationalist politics based on civil rights demands.

The election also returned a Labour government, under Harold Wilson, who had been out of office since 1970. He appointed Merlyn Rees as the Northern Ireland Secretary of State. This was not the confident Labour Party that had tackled the Ulster crisis in 1969, pushing reforms through in spite of loyalist ire, but one that seemed mainly peeved that the situation had not yet gone away – in fact had become much, much worse. Tension in loyalist parts of Belfast spilled over into riots and gun battles with the British Army. The Ulster Volunteer Force, dormant for two years, resumed its campaign of sectarian violence, murdering sixteen people in the first months of 1974, mainly in Belfast, and threatening further havoc if the British tried to enforce the power-sharing agreement. But Wilson, on a visit to Northern Ireland in mid-April, responded to Unionist threats with a flat statement saying there was no alternative to the Sunningdale Agreement.

On 23 March 1974 a hitherto unheard-of loyalist group, the Ulster Workers Council, issued a statement demanding fresh assembly elections and warning that there would be widespread disruption if its demands were not met. The UWC was in fact a small group of loyalist workers, which had recruited trade union shop stewards from the power stations. It had the support of the UDA, as well as several smaller loyalist paramilitary groups. At first, it was ignored. Unionist politicians like Craig were wary of being linked to loyalist working-class militants; their last attempt to organize work stoppages in February 1973 in protest against the internment of Protestants had collapsed in disorder. When the UWC announced the beginning of a 'constitutional stoppage' or general strike on 14 May, to oppose the power-sharing executive, it was greeted with a certain amount of scepticism. However, what was happening became startlingly clear soon thereafter, when hooded UDA men appeared on the streets of the Protestant port of Larne and forced shops to close in 'support' of the UWC's call. UDA roadblocks soon appeared all over Protestant areas of Belfast, forcing workers to return home. Factories and shops began to shut down. Meanwhile, UWC supporters in the main power plant near Larne began running down the province's electricity supply. On 16 May, Craig declared that Sunningdale must be scrapped and that its supporters had to realize that if it was not 'there will be further actions taken against the Irish republic and those who attempt to implement the agreement'.[30]

The following morning, 17 May 1974, the UVF in Belfast hijacked two cars on the Shankill Road and stole a third from the city's dockside. They drove the vehicles to South Armagh, where mid-Ulster UVF men loaded them with bombs. The cars continued south towards Dublin. That afternoon, a fourth car was stolen from a carpark in Portadown. It too was taken to South Armagh and loaded with explosives.

In a carpark just outside Dublin, at around 5 p.m., the bombs in the three cars from Belfast were armed and, with their timers ticking away, driven into the city. Two were left on the north side, in Parnell Street and Talbot Street. The driver of the third car bomb seems to have been trying to get close to the Irish parliament in Kildare Street on the city's south side. A bus strike may have complicated matters for the UVF team, and the car was parked instead on nearby South Leinster Street by the side wall of Trinity College, on the other side of which was the university's playing fields.

People were leaving work for home, getting ready to face the tribulations and confusion of the bus strike, when at 5.27 p.m. the two bombs in Parnell Street and Talbot Street exploded almost simultaneously and without warning. Six minutes later, the South Leinster Street bomb went off.

The explosions were heard all over Dublin, as black clouds of dust and debris spiralled into the sky. The blasts shredded passers-by with tangled metal and slivers of glass as shop windows were shattered. Their force was such that the bodies of two victims, a man and a woman, hurled through a shop window in Talbot Street, were found fused together.[31] A young family, the O'Briens, was wiped out – the husband John, aged twenty-three, his wife Anne, aged twenty-two, and their two children Jacqueline, aged seventeen months, and five-month-old Anne Maire. Among the dead was a thirty-year-old Frenchwoman, Simone Chetrit, who was working as an au pair in Dublin and was planning to return to Paris on 19 May.[32] In South Leinster Street twenty-one-year-old Anne Massey was hurrying to meet her husband-to-be, who was to give her a lift home. She passed the car bomb just as it exploded.[33] Her body lay covered with a policeman's coat, only her platform boots protruding. Not far from her lay the body of a man, reduced to smouldering cinders. An old man lay near by, screaming, one foot missing and his legs smashed, as the ambulances raced through the traffic-jammed streets to the disaster zones, which reeked of sulphur, burning petrol and cordite.

At 6.42 p.m., as the stunned Irish capital was coming to terms with the horror, the fourth car bomb exploded in Monaghan town, outside a pub. It killed seven people, including two old-age pensioners. The death toll from the four explosions climbed as the hours ticked by and the corpses were identified. The final victim did not die until 24 June, bringing the toll to thirty-three dead, making 17 May 1974 the bloodiest day in the story of the Ulster conflict. The bombings remain the greatest crime in the history of the Irish Republic, a crime for which no one has been convicted.[34]

Meanwhile, the UWC, aided by the UDA, tightened its grip on the province's lifeline, choking off fuel, food and electricity supplies. People had to cook out in their gardens, making the best of the unusually sunny May weather. Rumours that the next stage of the loyalist plan to overthrow the government was to launch all-out attacks on vulnerable nationalist areas swept the Catholic districts of Belfast. Two Catholic brothers were shot dead in their bar near Balleymena on 24 May for refusing to close it. Faulkner, Fitt and two other executive ministers flew to London to plead with Wilson to send the troops in to dismantle the UDA barricades and take over the fuel depots and power plants. Wilson hesitated to use the army against the massed ranks of the UDA and UWC, especially since their support seemed to be growing. Instead, he launched a vituperative attack on the loyalists – on behalf of British taxpayers, who he said

> have seen the taxes they have poured out without regard to cost – over 300 million pounds a year with the cost of the army on top of that – going into Northern Ireland. They see property destroyed by evil violence and are asked to pick up the bill for rebuilding it. Yet people who benefit from this now viciously defy Westminster, purporting to act as though they were an elected government, spending their lives sponging on Westminster and British democracy and then systematically assaulting democratic methods. Who do these people think they are?[35]

Wilson's response to the UWC–UDA challenge was typical of his government – petulant and weak. Two days after his speech, the army took over twenty-one petrol stations, provoking the UWC, who warned that they would completely close down the power stations, water and sewage works. Ulster was on the verge of collapse when Faulkner begged Rees to open talks with the strike leaders. Rees refused, and on 28 May Faulkner resigned as the head of government – for the second time in just over two years. 'It is . . . apparent to us', he said, 'from the extent of support for the present stoppage that the degree of consent needed to sustain the executive does not at present exist. Nor, as Ulstermen, are we prepared to see our country undergo, for any political reason, the catastrophe which now confronts it.'[36]

When the news of the executive's collapse reached loyalist ears, bonfires were lit across the province, and Protestants took to the streets to celebrate. Faulkner, like O'Neill before him, was dispatched into the political wilderness for daring to compromise. He would not return.

Ironically, in Faulkner's footsteps went the UDA. Its role in the events of May 1974, though pivotal, brought it no political rewards; instead, Unionist politicians took credit for having 'saved' Ulster and made sure that the paramilitaries were kept out of mainstream Unionist politics. Andy Tyrie's successful management of the UDA during the strike made him the most powerful figure within the organization. Tyrie, embittered at the Unionists' treatment, launched his organization on a quixotic political quest, which would bring it to Libya and New York, and meetings with the SDLP and the Provisionals.

As for the SDLP, the fate of the power-sharing experiment was an especially bitter blow. Hume concluded that it was no use searching for a political solution within the confines of Northern Ireland. He began a long pilgrimage which would take him beyond London and Dublin to Brussels, Boston and Washington, looking for a way out of the bloody deadlock. His quest would last for twenty years.

Britain's most ambitious attempt to restructure the 1921 settlement had failed disastrously. Immediately after the collapse of the executive, the British announced a 'constitutional convention' in which all the political parties could take part, but it would be no more than a talking shop. In future, successive British governments would adopt a more cautious approach to searching for solutions to the Ulster problem. Indeed, there would be no more ambitious political schemes for the province for over a decade. Britain would concentrate on finding ways to contain the violence. For the British, Ulster had become primarily a security problem.

5

In the aftermath of the power-sharing executive's fall, the Provisional IRA was left to contemplate the new political landscape and completely misread it. Its leading ideologues, Daithi O Conaill and Ruairi O Bradaigh, came to the conclusion that Britain's failure to take on the UWC meant it was making ready to withdraw from Northern Ireland. They declared 1974 'The Year of Victory'.

It was a startlingly inappropriate declaration, given the state of the Provisionals' military machine in Ulster. Internment had cut a wide swath through its ranks, and most of the younger, Northern-based activists who had come to the fore in 1971 were behind bars. Adams, the O/C of Belfast, was grabbed (for a second time) in July 1973, along with Brendan 'The Dark' Hughes, the man who had taken over the Second Battalion, and Tom Cahill, Joe Cahill's brother and a prominent member of the Belfast brigade. After a heavy beating, Adams was sent to Long Kesh. Shortly afterwards, his successor as Belfast O/C, his close friend Ivor Bell, was arrested and joined Adams in the internment camp. By then, there were 578 prisoners held in Long Kesh without trial, all but 29 of them republicans.[37] The Belfast units were especially badly hit. As a result, by 1974 IRA activity in the city had dropped drastically. During the first six months of the year, only three British soldiers were killed in Belfast compared to sixteen in the same period the year before. In September, Billy McKee, who had been O/C of Belfast until his arrest in March 1971, was released. He says he was shocked at what he found. 'There was no IRA [in Belfast] when I got out, thanks to internment.'[38] For a period in the autumn, there was no one to take over as O/C. So how then was the Army Council in

Dublin going to deliver its 'Year of Victory'? The Provisionals were active, it is true, in rural areas such as Tyrone and South Armagh, where land-mine attacks were proving effective against British forces. Soon the South Armagh IRA acquired the kind of reputation that the North Belfast IRA had enjoyed in 1971 and 1972. But the Provisionals knew that however successful, the rural battalions were too easily isolated. The war would not be won unless they could strike at commercial and military targets in urban areas. With the Belfast brigade temporarily crippled, they looked towards England.

When MacStiofain was Chief of Staff, there had been no attacks in England. Under the brief reign of Joe Cahill, his successor, the Belfast Provisionals carried out a quick bombing raid in London to coincide with the border plebiscite in March 1973.[39] But it was under Seamus Twomey, who took over as Chief of Staff from Cahill, that England was first subjected to a concerted bombing campaign. An army bus was bombed in February 1974 as it drove along the M62 motorway, killing twelve people, nine of them soldiers. Among the dead were two children, aged five and two. In July, a bomb exploded at the Tower of London, killing a woman tourist. In October, the Provisionals bombed a pub frequented by British troops in Guildford, Surrey, and five people died, four of them off-duty members of the British Army, two of them teenage girls.[40] More attacks followed. Most occurred without warning. The worst incident took place in Birmingham towards the end of November.

Birmingham, with its large Irish population, was central to the IRA's 1970s English campaign. Explosives carried in cars from Belfast would arrive there on a regular basis. The Birmingham IRA had been responsible for thirty-eight attacks in 1973, causing only one fatality, an army bomb disposal officer. An effort had been made to concentrate on damaging property, avoiding civilian deaths. With the proclamation of 1974 as the 'Year of Victory', that changed. On the evening of

21 November, the Provisional IRA targeted two popular downtown Birmingham pubs, the Mulberry Bush in the landmark Rotunda building and the Talk of the Town, located underneath the tax office in nearby New Street. The bombing team of two men planted the first bomb in a duffel bag in the Mulberry Bush and, a few minutes later, left the other in a small brown suitcase in the Talk of the Town, three hundred yards away. Both pubs were packed that evening. At 8.11 p.m. a telephonist at the *Birmingham Post and Mail* received a warning: 'There is a bomb planted in the Rotunda and a bomb in New Street . . . at the tax office.' It came six minutes before the first blast at the Mulberry Bush. That blast killed ten people. It was heard at the Talk of the Town, just minutes before the bomb exploded there, killing eleven.[41]

Shortly afterwards, in a wave of anti-Irish sentiment, six Irish immigrants, Hugh Callaghan, Patrick Hill, Gerry Hunter, Richard McIllkenny, Billy Power and Johnny Walker, all long-time residents of Birmingham, were arrested. Five of them were picked up on the night of the pub blasts as they were on their way back to Belfast for the funeral of an IRA man who had earlier killed himself in a bungled bombing in nearby Coventry. They suffered severe beatings before being charged and later convicted of the worst mass murder in British history. Their convictions were overturned sixteen years later, following a long campaign to prove their innocence.[42]

The Provisionals denied responsibility for the bombings, though shortly before they occurred Daithi O Conaill had given an interview warning that the English campaign would be stepped up. Along with Twomey, he was convinced that this would finally persuade Britain to leave Ireland. The Provisional IRA commander in Birmingham, who ordered the bombings, was said to have remarked: 'Three or more of those and the Brits will pull out.'[43]

Britain's first response was to introduce the Prevention of Terrorism Act, which allowed police to hold suspects for up to seven days without charging them, and to expel people from Great Britain. In announcing the new bill, the Home Secretary, Roy Jenkins, said: 'These powers . . . are Draconian. In combination they are unprecedented in peace time. I believe they are fully justified to meet the clear and present danger.'[44] There was considerable irony in the fact that the Northern Ireland problem, which had developed as a protest against the lack of certain civil rights in one part of the UK, was now forcing the government to suspend many of the same basic rights throughout the whole of Great Britain.

Though the no-warning bombing campaign in England did not in the end force Britain from Northern Ireland, it undoubtedly had something to do with the reopening of contacts between the government and the Provisional leadership, if only with the aim of getting the IRA to stop. With Protestant clergymen acting as go-betweens, contact was renewed. The Provisional Army Council called a ceasefire on 20 December, 1974, its first since 26 June 1972. After a false start, followed by more bombings in London, the ceasefire was renewed indefinitely on 10 February, 1975. In return for a cessation of IRA attacks in Britain and on military targets in Ulster, the British agreed to release a hundred prisoners within two weeks with the aim of ending internment completely, withdraw between three and four thousand troops, de-escalate the British presence in Catholic areas, permit wanted IRA men to carry weapons and return to Northern Ireland without fear of arrest, and allow Sinn Fein to open seven 'Truce Monitoring Centres' throughout the province. The government also said it would hold further talks with the IRA and draw up a formal truce agreement. A further condition for the ceasefire, which was not made public, was the transfer of Gerry Kelly, convicted of the London bombings of March 1973, from an

English jail to Long Kesh – an indication of Kelly's status within the movement even at this early stage.

The British government's public acknowledgment of its arrangement with the Provisional Army Council alarmed the Irish government and the SDLP. Both were disturbed that the Wilson government had done a secret deal behind their backs, one that could provoke a vicious Protestant backlash and reprisals in the Republic by fuelling rumours of a British withdrawal plan. This is exactly the interpretation that Provisional leaders O Bradaigh and O Conaill were advocating, as they sought to deliver on their '1974 – Year of Victory' slogan.

For six months, a high-ranking British civil servant, James Allen, liaised with the Belfast O/C Billy McKee as Long Kesh was emptied of its inmates. Whatever the aim of the meetings, one thing was plain: they did not end the violence. On the contrary, it grew worse. Loyalists, anxious about the government–IRA contacts, launched another round of sectarian killings and the Provisionals responded in kind. Both the UDA and the UVF were now active, the UDA using its *nom de guerre* UFF, which the government had banned in November 1973. (This had prompted one UDA man to ask 'How can you be convicted of belonging to an organization which doesn't exist?')[45]

From late 1974, the Provisionals' campaign in Belfast ceased to be aimed at the security forces (between September and December 1974 not one police officer or soldier was killed); its guns instead were turned on Protestants. Nine were murdered in November, compared to eight Catholics.

The sectarian killings would get worse throughout 1975 and 1976, long after the ceasefire, such as it was, had collapsed. Of the 247 people murdered in 1975, only 30 were members of the security forces. The following year, there were 297 murders – making it the second-worst year in the history of the Troubles; of those, only 52 were police officers or soldiers.

This disproportion between the numbers of civilian and military victims would remain a constant feature of the Ulster conflict. In the single worst incident on 5 January 1976, the Provisional IRA in South Armagh stopped a bus-load of Protestant workers, lined them up and shot ten of them to death. The killings were in revenge for a UVF attack in Whitecross, South Armagh, during which three Catholic brothers were murdered.

The various paramilitary groups also fought among themselves. By late 1974, a faction within the Official IRA had formed around Seamus Costello. He feared that the organization's leadership was intent on completely abandoning the armed struggle and endeavoured to prevent it. His efforts failed, and he was court-martialled. On 8 December, 1974, the split became formal with the birth of a new republican organization. In its political, public guise it was called the Irish Republican Socialist Party. Behind the scenes, it was secretly organized as the Irish National Liberation Army. Costello's new alignment attracted much of the Official IRA's support in Belfast and Derry. When the Belfast Officials attempted to stamp out the new group, a feud erupted. On 28 April 1975 a sixteen-year-old gunman called Gerard Steenson shot dead the Official IRA's Belfast leader, Billy McMillen, a veteran republican. In the years to come, Steenson would earn a reputation as one of the most feared gunmen in Northern Ireland. Five republicans were killed in the feud.

Six months later, another feud broke out, this time between the remains of the Official IRA in Belfast and the Provisionals. It claimed eleven lives, including that of seven-year-old Eileen Kelly, whom Provisional IRA gunmen murdered while trying to shoot her father. It was hardly surprising that in August 1976 the war-weary population of Belfast, disgusted by what was seen as increasingly aimless violence, should marshal themselves behind two local Catholic women, Mairead Corrigan and Betty Williams, in a short-lived peace movement. It sprang up spontaneously, when soldiers shot dead a friend of Adams – IRA gunman Danny Lennon. His car crashed into Corrigan's sister Annie Maguire and her family as they walked along the street, killing three of her children, aged from six weeks to nine years. The women organized a march to demand an end to the killings. The marches, involving both Catholics and Protestants, grew in size throughout the late summer and early autumn, helped by intense media interest.

Some thought that the movement had the power to isolate the Provisionals, against whom its campaign was chiefly directed. It was wishful thinking. Many in the Catholic ghettoes felt the government was manipulating what was a genuine yearning for peace but had become a well-managed media event fronted by naïve women. Though the peace movement remained a news story for some months longer, by early 1977 it had actually spent itself. It brought Corrigan and Williams the Nobel Peace Prize, but it did not bring peace to Ireland.

From inside Long Kesh, Adams watched these developments with growing anxiety. At the core of his unease was his attitude towards the 1975 ceasefire. Adams suspected that the 1972 ceasefire had been a British ploy to lure the IRA away from the armed campaign with false hopes. He saw the 1975 ceasefire in the same light, except this time it was succeeding.[46] Adams would later claim that at this point the IRA was near defeat. Its drift into sectarian killing and internecine violence was playing right into the hands of British government policy. Though the peace movement was not a threat to hard-core republican support, Adams and others, like Ivor Bell, saw it as a worrying symptom. That hard core would always be enough to keep a campaign of some sort going, but it was not wide enough to provide a basis for the Provisionals to expand, leaving them in danger of isolation from the broader Catholic community.

Adams and his associates also came to another conclusion

which would drastically affect the future of the Provisional IRA: they concluded that contrary to what O Conaill and O Bradaigh believed, the British, far from preparing to leave, had merely changed their tactics and were ready to embark on a new offensive combining both legal and military means to isolate and finally defeat the republican movement. The changes were encapsulated in the terms 'normalization', 'Ulsterization' and 'criminalization'. A new legal system was being introduced, supported by a restructuring of the RUC to enable it to take the leading role in tackling the paramilitaries. The Provisionals would have to adjust their strategy accordingly.

The year 1977 was the turning point in the history of the conflict, as much for loyalists as for the IRA. Proof of this came in May, when the UDA attempted to duplicate its success against the power-sharing executive. This time, with the support of Paisley, the militants took aim at Britain's failure to return a majority-ruled government to Northern Ireland and its failure to defeat the IRA. Police and the army moved resolutely against the barricades, arresting obstructers, including Paisley himself. Protestant shipyard workers voted to stay at work. More importantly, so did the workers in the main power station. After ten days, on 13 May, the 'strike' collapsed ignominiously.

Ulster was entering a new phase. The most important sign was the drastic reduction in the yearly death rate – after 1977 it would rarely rise above one hundred.[47] Internment had ended, with the last detainee being released on 5 December 1975. The security forces' tactics were changing equally drastically. One indication was the number of houses searched annually, which fell from a high of 74,914 in 1974 to 20,724 in 1977. It would continue to fall. Widespread street disturbances and open confrontations between the Provisionals and the army became rarer. The no-go areas (with the possible exception of South Armagh) were no more, and civil rights protests had become a historical memory. The 'Troubles' in one sense were over. But in another sense they were just about to begin. Ulster was soon to be engulfed in a twilight war of covert action from which it would not emerge for almost twenty years.

PART TWO

The Twilight War

1977–94

CHAPTER FOUR

The Politics of Despair: 1977–81

1

By 1977, a pall of despair had settled on Ulster. The optimism of the civil rights days was spent; the destructive energy of the paramilitaries, which seemed for a time as if it might settle the question one way or another, was exhausted; a peace movement had come and gone without changing anything; as for the politicians, the faces of the new men who sprang up in the late 1960s promising change had become as dullingly familiar as the phrases they used to condemn the murders. The centres of the two main cities, Belfast and Derry, were dead after dark as those fortunate enough not to be touched by growing unemployment hurried home from their jobs to the safety of their ghetto – Catholic or Protestant, working-class or middle-class.[1] The Peace Line had become a wall fifteen feet high, dissecting West Belfast, a crude expression of the segregation that sectarian violence had imposed upon the city. The days of city-centre dance halls, cinemas and restaurants were a memory around which those born in the 1930s and 1940s could weave nostalgic stories about the time when Belfast was a 'real' city. Many of the Victorian working-class neighbourhoods that had sustained city life were being levelled as planners gouged out tracts of land for link roads to the motorways. Most of the lower Falls was gone, passing into history along with the linen mills where its people had worked for generations. Even the city-centre pubs fell silent in the evening, their doors barred. In the working-class districts along the main roads out of town, or in the surrounding housing estates, there were pubs, but they looked like miniature prisons. Metal cages protected the entrance. From inside, guards scrutinized monitors linked to security cameras trained on the street. Boulders or barrels filled with concrete and connected by iron rods ringed the pavement to prevent car bombers from parking too close to the premises. Drinking in a 'legitimate target' was not a very relaxing experience.

Shopping was hardly any better. Long lines formed in downtown city stores as security guards searched shoppers on their way in. They went through bags, pocket-books, parcels, and passed detectors up and around customers, monitoring them from head to foot. Belfast and Derry were probably the only cities in the world where customers were scrutinized more as they went into the shop than when they were leaving it. Because of car bombs, parking had long ago been banned from the city centre. As a result, commerce drained away to the suburbs. People followed, and the cities' population fell throughout the 1970s. Soon, Belfast began to resemble a Midwestern town in the United States, a place from which life fled after business hours. The ghostly atmosphere was augmented by the boarded-up buildings and half-demolished streets, the houses sliced in half with the tattered wallpaper exposed to the sky. Only the Europa, opened in 1969, and Belfast's last remaining downtown hotel, stood as a reminder of what other cities took for granted – that some of the minor pleasures of life were still possible, like dining out in the evening after a few cocktails in a cheery, anonymous environment. But dining in the Europa was not without its tribulations: by 1977, it had been bombed twenty-eight times.

By 1977 a feature of the cityscape of Belfast and Derry that startled visitors was the heavily armed foot patrols of British soldiers, edging their way slowly around the streets of the working-class housing estates, the constant whir of helicopters circling above them. At night the choppers would swoop low, searchlights blazing, wakening every baby for miles around. What could almost have been a normal vision of urban desolation was thereby transformed into something else – a scene from a war movie perhaps, though what kind of war it was hard to gauge.

For Gerry Adams, released from prison in March 1977, that was a question of supreme importance. He had had four years to think about it. The situation he confronted as he enjoyed his first days of freedom was very different from the one that had existed in 1973. The British government had put in place a whole new battery of legislation, following the recommendations in a report by Lord Gardiner, the man who in 1972 advised the government that the use of in-depth interrogation – the 'five techniques' – was illegal. His report came to several important conclusions. One was that the use of detention without trial 'cannot remain as a long term policy . . . the prolonged effects of the use of detention are ultimately inimical to community life'.[2] Another was that Special Category Status, conferred on paramilitary prisoners in July 1972, 'was a serious mistake . . . we recommend that the earliest practicable opportunity should be taken to end the special category'.[3]

A new court system had already replaced internment. A single judge, sitting without a jury, decided on the guilt or innocence of the accused. This followed on the recommendations of Lord Diplock, and the courts became known as the Diplock courts. The Emergency Provisionals Act (1973, 1978) replaced the old Special Powers Act, and allowed a more flexible interpretation of when confessions might be used in court as sole evidence to convict a suspect. Meanwhile, as Lord Gardiner had recommended, the old prison system of Nissen huts arranged in compounds, which had housed the sudden huge influx of prisoners since August 1971, was replaced by a new cellular prison near Long Kesh, renamed The Maze. The individual blocks were shaped like the letter 'H' and soon became known as 'H-Blocks'. It was said to be one of the most secure prisons in the world. As of 1 March 1976, no one convicted of a terrorist offence would be granted Special Status but would be incarcerated like any other 'ordinary' criminal in an H-Block cell.

The aim of these reforms was to 'normalize' the situation in Ulster by processing suspects through the courts. Putting prisoners in ordinary prison cells and depriving them of the privileges that came with Special Status 'criminalized' the paramilitaries, denying them the opportunity to present themselves to the world as 'freedom fighters' whose crimes were 'political'. The third leg of this plan, 'Ulsterization', meant withdrawing the British Army into the background and placing the chief responsibility for fighting the paramilitary organizations back in the hands of the RUC. In the long run, this would be the only part of the initiative that would succeed.

The new Northern Ireland Secretary of State, Roy Mason, who had replaced Rees in September 1976, was also a source of much concern to republicans. Mason was the opposite of Rees. If Rees looked somewhat like an indecisive, bumbling Labour Party intellectual, Mason had the appearance of a stocky, bluff coalminer. In fact he went down the mines at the age of fourteen, and liked nothing better than an opportunity to talk about it. Right from the start he wanted to 'take on the terrorists'. Even before he was appointed to the Northern Ireland post, as Secretary of Defence in the Wilson government in early 1976 he had ordered the army's élite undercover unit, the Special Air Services (known in security circles as the

Troop), into South Armagh after a series of bloody sectarian murders. Rees had been a student of Irish history. Mason was mainly concerned with winning the present war and not cogitating too much over the outcome of 'battles long ago'. Indeed, the battle had hardly begun when he declared that it was won, that the IRA was 'reeling', or was being 'squeezed like toothpaste from a tube'.

Neither did he endear himself to loyalists – in fact, he had a more pronounced success against them than against republicans. He sent the RUC in to smash their 'strike' in May 1977, dismantling barricades and arresting the ringleaders (see Chapter 3). Several of the most vicious UVF gangs were arrested and jailed, including the Shankill Road Butchers, who terrorized Catholics between November 1975 and March 1977. The gang's violence was so indiscriminate that of their nineteen victims, nine were Protestant.[4]

If certain kinds of murder can be said to be as revealing as poetry about the nature of the society in which they occur, then loyalism's deep-seated bigotry had found its most brutally eloquent exponent in gang leader Lenny Murphy. Murphy was a Shankill Road Protestant whose Catholic surname would have been enough to doom him at the hands of the kind of thugs he recruited. His reputation as Belfast's 'Jack the Ripper' rests on the series of frenzied cut-throat killings for which he and his gang became notorious.

In November 1975, Murphy and two others dragged Francis Crossan, a thirty-four-year-old Catholic, into a black taxi driven by Billy Moore, where he was beaten with a wheel brace, kicked, and had a broken beer glass shoved into his face. The gang drove him to an alleyway off the Shankill Road, where his semi-conscious body was laid out. Murphy then set about hacking his way through Crossan's throat with a butcher's knife until the spine was reached.

A detective who was among the first on the murder scene recalled it years later: 'It was a horrific sight and especially when the body was lifted off the ground because the victim's head was held to the trunk by tissue. I knew I was witnessing something different . . . a more personal type of killing.'[5] Thomas Quinn and Francis Rice were beaten and hacked to death in February 1976. Murphy was taken off the streets in March that year, charged and convicted of possession of a gun, which kept him locked up until 1982. But on his instructions his gang continued killing, hatcheting Cornelius Neeson to death in August 1976 and cutting the throats of another three victims – Stephen McCann the following October, Daniel Morrisey in February 1977 and Francis Cassidy in March the same year. After one of their intended victims escaped, the gang was finally identified and arrested. Following a sensational trial, in January 1979 eleven of them were convicted and given forty-two life sentences. Murphy, nicknamed the Master Butcher, emerged from prison three years later as eager as ever to resume his reign of terror. (See Chapter 5.)

After the collapse of the UDA strike in May 1977, and the break-up of the UVF gangs, sectarian killings came to a halt and did not resume until February 1978. Along with the Butcher's gang, among those removed from the loyalist paramilitary scene was John White, founder of the UFF. After his release from internment in 1975, he had rejoined the UDA, only to be lifted in July 1977. Detectives questioned him about the murders of SDLP man Paddy Wilson and Irene Andrews. White believes that one of the Shankill Butchers gang, who had been arrested at the same time, gave the police information. The interrogation lasted morning, afternoon and evening for three days, at the end of which White confessed. He was convicted and received a life sentence.[6]

When sectarian killings did resume, they were on a much smaller scale and would remain so for a decade. Like the Provisionals, the loyalist groups had been forced to retrench and consider their future.

The main target of the security forces remained the Provisional IRA. While Mason's declaration of victory was to prove premature, there was no doubt that he was having unprecedented successes against them. A new Chief Constable, Kenneth Newman, had helped restructure the RUC, setting up four Regional Crime Squads 'to target the most active members of terrorist organizations'.[7] The squads combined the resources of the Criminal Investigation Division with those of the Special Branch. They were also responsible for interrogating suspects at Castlereagh holding centre in East Belfast. In this they were helped in obtaining confessions by the court's interpretation of Section 6 of the Emergency Provisions Act, which stipulated that unless it could be proved that such confessions were obtained by torture or inhuman or degrading treatment, they were to be regarded as admissible in a court of law. It afforded the police interrogators room to apply a considerable amount of 'rough' treatment that did not fit the definition of torture or degrading treatment, though for those on the receiving end the distinction was academic. Confessions began to flow and the conviction rate soared. During 1976, out of 1,200 people charged with terrorist offences 900 were convicted, 80 per cent of them on the strength of confessions. In August, the government felt secure enough in Northern Ireland that Her Majesty the Queen made her first visit to the province in eleven years, defying Provisional IRA threats.

Certainly, a government that was taking such pains to reform its legal and prison system was hardly planning to pull out of Northern Ireland any time soon, regardless of what the Provisional IRA leadership might think. By the spring of 1977, that much was obvious to Adams, and to the younger Belfast and Derry activists who like him had been drawn into the movement in the 1960s. They realized from the evidence that was all around them that what they were now involved in was a long war of attrition, with little prospect of an immediate British withdrawal. As Adams saw it, while the Provisionals had been sitting around in their Truce Monitoring Centres waiting for a British withdrawal to begin, the British had pushed ahead with their efforts to normalize, criminalize and Ulsterize the conflict, bringing the IRA to the verge of defeat.

On his release Adams had taken up a leadership position on the GHQ staff, and was summoned South to work with Seamus Twomey, who had been Chief of Staff since 1973. Moves were begun to restructure the Provisional IRA and Sinn Fein. The public face of this initiative was revealed on 12 June at the Wolfe Tone Memorial in Co. Kildare. This is one of the two most sacred occasions on the Irish republican calendar (the other being Easter), when devotees look to Tone, the leader of the 1798 rebellion and the man they regard as republicanism's founder. The event has been frequently used as an opportunity for the leadership to announce fresh policies or a new departure. Goulding did so in 1967, proclaiming the republican movement's rededication to left-wing political action. Ten years on, the message was not much different. In a way, it harked back to Adams's days as a political activist in Belfast, prior to the 1969 upheaval, when he and his colleagues were involved in housing action and other forms of social protest. In order to avoid accusations (which came anyway) that this was a return to the Official IRA 'Marxist' line, the man chosen to deliver the speech was Jimmy Drumm, a contemporary of Cahill and McKee, a founding member of the Belfast Provisionals and a veteran of the 1950s campaign.[8]

Drumm cautioned that the war could not be won if it was fought solely on the issue of the withdrawal of the British Army. It had to be broadened into a political struggle, with links forged throughout Ireland to other revolutionary and socialist groups. Clearly, this meant that Sinn Fein would play an important role. But there would be no cessation of the armed campaign, which was to remain the 'cutting edge' of the struggle.

Meanwhile, behind the scenes, the secret reorganization of the Provisional IRA had begun. It was not without its casualties. McKee, who had been Officer Commanding the Belfast Provisionals since June 1975, was brought to Dublin and placed in charge of sorting out 'internal problems'.[9] Others were given a rather more violent send-off. Jack 'Fingers' McCartan, who for years ran a social club in West Belfast – a republican front operation – and was involved in corrupt housing schemes, was shot dead one night as he left his club. The killing was blamed on the British Army, but it was the Belfast IRA who removed him as part of their 'clean-up' campaign.

Just how thoroughgoing the reforms were was revealed in December that year, thanks to the arrest of Seamus Twomey. After four years as Chief of Staff and one spectacular escape, when he and two other IRA leaders were lifted by helicopter from Mountjoy Prison yard in Dublin, Twomey's run came to an end on the southern outskirts of the Irish capital, when Irish police stopped his car and arrested him. In a follow-up search of his apartment, they discovered the plans for the restructuring of the republican movement under the title 'Staff report'.

It began by sounding an alarm: 'The three-day and seven-day detention orders are breaking volunteers, and it is the Irish Republican Army's own fault for not indoctrinating volunteers with the psychological strength to resist interrogation. Coupled with this factor, *which is contributing to our defeat* [author's emphasis], we are burdened with an inefficient infrastructure of commands, brigades, battalions and companies. The old system, with which the Brits and Branch are familiar, has to be changed. We recommend reorganization and remotivation, the building of a new Irish Republican Army.'[10] After advocating the creation of the post of

Education Officer as part of the GHQ Staff for training recruits in how to resist interrogation techniques, the report continued: 'We must gear ourselves towards long-term armed struggle based on putting unknown men and new recruits into a new structure. The new structure shall be a cell system.' It would consist 'ideally of four people. Rural areas we decided should be treated as separate cases to that of city and town areas where the majority of our operations are carried out and where the biggest proportion of our support lies anyway.' The cell system was then described. Each cell was to be under the control of

> the brigade's/command's intelligence officer . . . Cells must be specialized into IC cells, sniping cells, execution, bombing, robberies, etc. The cell will have no control of weapons or explosives, but should be capable of dumping weapons overnight (in the case of a postponed operation). The weapons and explosives should be under the complete control of the brigade's/command's Q[uarter]M[aster] and E[xplosives] O[ffi-cer] respectively. Cells should operate as often as possible outside of their own areas; both to confuse Brit intelligence (which would thus increase our security) and to expand our operational areas.

The report went on to deal with Sinn Fein, the almost non-existent political wing of the movement that Provisional activists held in contempt. That would have to change. According to the staff report:

> Sinn Fein should come under army organizers at all levels. Sinn Fein should employ full-time organizers in big republican areas. Sinn Fein should be radicalized (under army direction) and should agitate about social and economic issues which attack the welfare of the people. Sinn Fein should be directed to infiltrate other organizations to win support for, and sympathy to, the movement. Sinn Fein should be reeducated

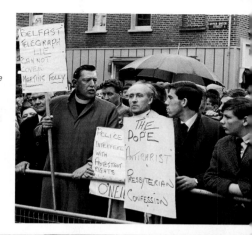

The Rev. Ian Paisley at an early demonstration in 1966 against a meeting of the Presbyterian General Assembly in Belfast city centre. Paisley had set up the Ulster Protestant Volunteers that year, and established his paper, *The Protestant Telegraph*. He was a fierce opponent of liberal Unionist Prime Minister Terence O'Neill and would soon turn his fundamentalist rhetoric against the civil rights movement, leading counter demonstrations to block civil rights marches. *(Victor Patterson Archive/Linen Hall Library)*

An early civil rights demonstration in Derry. On the left is John Hume, and on the right, wearing dark glasses Ivan Cooper. Hume and Cooper become founding members of the SDLP in August 1970. Cooper, a Protestant, had originally been a member of the Young Unionists. *(Barry Doherty)*

Bernadette McAliskey (née Devlin) was an icon of the 1960s student protest movement in Northern Ireland and in 1969 became the youngest MP in over a century to be elected to Westminster. Her campaign was supported by the new-look left-wing IRA led by Cathal Goulding. Here she is seen at a meeting in 1997 to protest the arrest of her daughter Roisin who was wanted in Germany in connection with an IRA mortar attack on a British army base there. Extradition proceedings were later stopped. *(Ronnie Close/Photocall Ireland)*

Cathal Goulding, the last Chief of Staff of the IRA, before it split in late 1969 into Official and Provisional wings. Goulding became Chief of Staff of the Official IRA and helped steer it away from armed struggle. He died in 1998. *(Courtesy of the Irish News)*

Opposite above left Seamus Twomey, founding member of the Provisional IRA who was its Chief of Staff from 1973 to 1977. He was described as one of the most 'aggressive' leaders of the Provisionals, under whom no-warning bomb attacks were carried out in England. Twomey died in 1989. *(Victor Patterson Archive/Linen Hall Library)*

Above Joe Cahill and Daithi O Conaill, founding members of the Provisional IRA. Cahill was briefly Chief of Staff and remained on the organization's leadership body, the Army Council, for almost thirty years. O Conaill was originally chosen as the Provisionals' first Chief of Staff but declined and became Adjutant General. He was also instrumental in setting up the US arms network for the IRA. He split with the Provisionals in 1986 and set up the Continuity IRA. O Conaill died in 1991. Cahill became a supporter of the peace process. *(Eamonn Farrell/Photocall Ireland)*

Right Gerry Adams, at the funeral of Provisional IRA man Francis Liggett, shot dead during an attempted robbery on 18 January 1973. Adams at the time was a high-ranking member of the Provisionals' Belfast brigade. He was arrested in July that year and reemerged in early 1977 determined to restructure the whole Provisional movement. *(Kelvin Boyes)*

Below Davey Payne, who was involved with various loyalist fringe groups in the late 1960s and became a founding member of the UDA. Nicknamed the Psychopath by his colleagues, he was one of the most active members of the UDA's 'C' company, based in the Shankill Road. He was responsible for most of the sectarian assassinations in North and West Belfast between 1972 and 1976. Payne fell out with his colleagues in the late 1970s, but then rejoined the UDA. In 1988 the RUC arrested him with a large arms haul destined for the UDA. (Victor Patterson Archive/Linen Hall Library)

Below right Johnny White and Gary McMichael. White became head of the UDA's 'C' company, and was one of those who thought up the Ulster Freedom Fighters, using the name 'Captain Black' to claim responsibility for murders. One of the most feared paramilitary activists, he was convicted of the double murder of SDLP man Paddy Wilson and his female companion Irene Andrews. White later became strongly identified with the peace process and an active member of the UDA-linked Ulster Democratic Party. McMichael, whose father John was murdered by the IRA in 1987, is the UDP leader. Both men are seen shortly after the UDP was suspended from the all-party talks in January 1998 because of a renewal of UDA violence. Both stood for the assembly elections later that year but failed to win any seats. (AP Photo Ben Curtis)

John McKeague, a founding member of the Shankill Road Defence Association which later helped form the basis of the Ulster Defence Association. McKeague, a former Paisley-ite, later set up his own terrorist group, the Red Hand Commandos, and was among the first Protestants to be interned in February 1973. He was a notorious paedophile. He turned informer, working for British army intelligence until he was murdered by the INLA in January 1982. (Victor Petterson/Linen Hall LIbrary)

The first Provisional IRA car bomb to cause multiple deaths. It exploded in Donegal Street near Belfast city centre on 20 March 1972, killing seven people. The IRA's warning misidentified the location of the device, and civilians were directed towards the car containing the bomb. It was the first of numerous fatal bombings which the Provisionals referred to as 'mistakes'. *(Victor Patterson Archive/Linen Hall Library)*

Below left After internment in August 1971, working-class Catholic areas of Belfast became 'no-go' areas for the security forces. Here, Official IRA men are seen on 'patrol' in Turf Lodge, one of their strongholds in West Belfast. The photograph was taken just after the shooting of OIRA leader Joe McCann on 15 April 1972. A month later, the OIRA called a permanent ceasefire. *(Victor Patterson Archive/Linen Hall Library)*

Below right In the spring and summer of 1972, angered by the suspension of Stormont and the Provisional IRA's campaign, the UDA set up its own 'no-go' areas in Belfast. Checkpoints like this were often used to snatch victims who were taken for 'interrogation' and then murdered. Among those who suffered this fate were folk singer Rosemary McCartney and Patrick O'Neill who, the day after Bloody Friday, were taken to the UDA headquarters on the Shankill Road where they were beaten before being killed. 1972 was one of the worst years in the history of the Troubles for sectarian killings, with 121 such murders, the majority of which were carried out by the Belfast UDA. *(Victor Patterson Archive/Linen Hall Library)*

Pictures of the Bloody Sunday victims, overlooking Derry City and the Foyle River, being carried into the city. The murder of the 14 demonstrators traumatised Ireland and led to a sharp growth in support for the IRA. A 1972 official enquiry into the massacre failed to satisfy nationalists and a fresh enquiry was launched by Labour Prime Minister Tony Blair in 1998. *(Ronnie Close/Photocall Ireland)*

Right above Paddy Wilson, a founding member of the SDLP, who was the first victim claimed by the UFF on June 1973. His female companion, Irene Andrews, was murdered with him. His throat was cut from ear to ear and he had over 30 stab wounds. Andrews was stabbed more than twenty times. According to Johnny White, who headed the UDA gang involved, the couple were repeatedly stabbed because the knife used had a short blade. *(Victor Patterson Archive/Linen Hall Library)*

Right middle George Harrison, the veteran republican and leading member of the New York-based arms smuggling network in the US which supplied the Provisional IRA with most of its weaponry until the late 1970s. *(Photo courtesy of Irish Echo)*

Right Liam Cotter, who along with Harrison was a key figure in the Provisional IRA arms network. He was shot and killed in New York in 1976. *(Private collection)*

Far right Owen McNamee, a former high-ranking IRA member, otherwise known as the Emissary. For many years he acted as the go-between for Harrison's arms network and the Provisional IRA's GHQ in Dublin. He eluded capture and died in 1986.

UDA chairman Andy Tyrie (on left) with former unionist government minister William Craig (centre) and UDA spokesman Glenn Barr (right), in June 1974 shortly after the fall of the power-sharing executive. Paisley is in the background. He and other unionist leaders were reluctant to support the move against the government until they saw that it was going to succeed. Tyrie had been chairman of the UDA for just over a year when he became central to the efforts to bring down the new government, headed by Brian Faulkner and Gerry Fitt. Barr and Craig received much of the media's attention, whilst Tyrie was ignored. Tyrie was partly responsible for setting up the UFF. He remained chairman of the UDA for 15 years. From 1977 onwards he oversaw a de-escalation of the organization's sectarian campaign. He was removed from office in 1988 after threats to his life from restive, younger UDA members. *(Victor Patterson Archive/Linen Hall Library)*

Above right Gerry Kelly, Belfast Provisional IRA, who was convicted of bombing London in March 1973. His transfer to a prison in Northern Ireland was one of the conditions of the Provisional leadership's declaration of a ceasefire in late 1974. He escaped from the Maze in September 1983. Later, he became a member of the Provisional's Army Council and second-in-command to the Chief of Staff. His support of the Gerry Adams-Martin McGuinness peace moves in the early 1990s was crucial to their success. He is seen here at the all-party talks in February 1998. He was elected to the new Northern Ireland assembly in June 1998. *(Leon Farrell/Photocall Ireland)*

Below The Maze Prison. Built near the site of the old Long Kesh internment camp, the Maze was declared the most secure prison in Europe. Paramilitary prisoners were treated like ordinary criminals there from 1976 onwards and in protest republicans refused to wear prison uniforms. The protest escalated into a "dirty" protest and then to a hunger strike in which ten prisoners died in 1981. The Long Kesh/Maze Prison suffered

two major breakouts. In 1976, nine INLA me escaped, and in 1983, 38 IRA members broke out. By 1991, it held around 400 prisoners and cost £42,000,000 a year to run. By late 1998, about half of its inmates had been released thanks to the Good Friday Agreement. *(Kelvin Boyes) bove* IRA pallbearers at the funeral of Bobby Sands who died after 66 days on hunger :rike on 5 May 1981, following his election to Westminster. Another nine hunger :rikers died between then and 20 August. The hunger strikes galvanized working-class ationalists and created a base of support for Sinn Fein. *(Photocall Ireland)*

elow Disturbances inspired by the hunger strikes spread from Northern Ireland in the ummer of 1981. On 18 July a serious riot occurred in Dublin, outside the British mbassy, which had been burned down in early protests after the Bloody Sunday 1ootings in 1972. One hundred-and-twenty Irish police were injured and 80 protesters. *Eamonn Farrell/Photocall Ireland)*

Dominic McGlinchey, Chief of Staff of the INLA 1982-1984, during which period it carried out some of its bloodiest attacks. He was nicknamed 'Mad Dog' by the press after claiming he had been involved in some 30 murders. He was shot dead in February 1994 by South Armagh republicans in revenge for an earlier murder. *(Courtesy of The Irish Times)*

Sinn Fein's press officers Rita O'Hare and Danny Morrison. In the hunger strikes' aftermath, Morrison proclaimed that the IRA would take power in Ireland with a ballot paper in one hand and an armalite in the other. For a time, Morrison was head of CAT, the IRA's informer hunting squad. He went to jail in 1990. O'Hare was wanted for a shooting attack on an army patrol in 1971. She became head of Sinn Fein's Washington office in 1999. *(Eamonn Farrell/Photocall Ireland)*

Gerard Steenson, one of the most feared gunmen in Northern Ireland. He claimed his first victim aged 16 and went on to become a leading member of the INLA in Belfast. The press nicknamed him 'Dr. Death'. He was involved in about 12 murders. This was taken a few days before he himself was shot dead in a feud on 15 March 1987.

and have a big role to play in publicity and propaganda depts, complaints and problems (making no room for RUC opportunism). It gains the respect of the people which in turn leads to increased support for the cell.[11]

When these ambitious plans for Provisional Sinn Fein's role were drafted, there seemed little or no chance of their being realized. Sinn Fein as a unified organization had not fought an election in Ulster since the mid-1950s. After the republican movement split, Official Sinn Fein, whose own strategy was similar to that outlined in the Staff report, had entered elections for the first time in 1973. The result was not auspicious. The Officials won only ten seats in the local elections of May and a derisory 1.8 per cent of the vote in the June assembly elections, winning no seats.

As well, there remained within the Provisionals a powerful current running against involvement in politics, particularly electoral politics. After all, one of the reasons for the 1969 split was disagreement with the Goulding leadership's ambitions for Sinn Fein to become a 'real' political party that would take its place in the Dail in Dublin, if elected. Men such as O Conaill and O Bradaigh who had fought this ideological battle in the 1960s were still powerful figures within the Provisional movement. In 1977, however, it is unlikely that anyone in the Provisionals thought that these issues would ever have to be faced up to again. Sinn Fein's prospects of fighting elections, never mind winning them, seemed remote, to say the least. But more importantly for the movement's immediate prospects, its ability to continue its armed campaign was being seriously challenged. It was a challenge that had to be met by a new Chief of Staff.

Twomey's successor as Chief of Staff was Adams's Derry contemporary Martin McGuinness. McGuinness was the first of the 1960s generation of Northern activists to head the Provisional IRA. Under him, the Derry active service units had devastated the city, reducing its downtown area to streets of bombed and boarded-up buildings. They had also been among the first to carry out a ruthless murder campaign against off-duty UDR men. McGuinness was a devout Catholic, who guarded the Provisionals' Derry domain jealously. As a result, the Derry IRA did not tolerate rivals easily. When the IRSP/INLA started to organize there, the Provisionals tied one of its leaders to a lamppost and covered him with tar.

McGuinness faced severe problems, thanks to the new security initiatives. In the first eight months of 1977, compared with the previous year, bombings were down 52 per cent, shootings 33 per cent and the death toll had fallen by 62 per cent. The statistics show that September 1977 was the first month since October 1970 in which no civilians were killed in Northern Ireland as the result of political violence. Attacks on the British Army and the RUC declined drastically. The Provisionals' campaign became restricted to attacking off-duty UDR men at home or at work. Between September and December only one member of the security forces was killed while on duty – Paul Harman, an undercover soldier shot dead in Andersonstown, West Belfast, on 14 December. The IRA's plans to regroup suffered a serious setback when a large arms shipment acquired from PLO sources and destined for the Provisionals was tracked from Cyprus and intercepted in Antwerp, Belgium, at the end of November. As the year ended, *The Irish Times* quoted Mason as declaring that 'the tide has turned against the terrorists and the message for 1978 is one of real hope'.

The pattern of striking at soft targets persisted into 1978. It was a particularly prominent feature of the Provisionals' violence in rural areas such as Fermanagh, Tyrone, Armagh and Derry, where off-duty UDR and RUC men were more vulnerable, often living on isolated farms. On 8 February, part-time UDR officer William Gordon got into his car, with his ten-year-old daughter Lesley sitting next to him. When he started the engine, it detonated an undercar booby-trap bomb (UCBT) which killed them both. Such killings especially angered local Protestants, who viewed them as part of a deliberate IRA campaign to drive Protestant farmers off their land in areas where Catholics were in the ascendant.[12]

Car bombs for the time being became a thing of the past. Instead, the Provisionals used incendiary devices to burn down cinemas, hotels, offices, shops and department stores. Women were the key to this tactic. The cigarette-sized bombs were often smuggled into stores inside the soles of the platform boots so fashionable at the time. Throughout the first months of 1978, the Provisionals mounted a concentrated campaign of fire-bombings, determined to prove that Mason was over-optimistic. By February there had been more than a hundred explosions. On the evening of 17 February 1978, the Northern Ireland Collie Club and the Junior Motor Cycle Club were holding their annual prize-giving functions in the La Mon House hotel in the Castlereagh Hills, a low range of drumlins patchworked with fields overlooking East Belfast. Just before 9 p.m. a warning came that a bomb had been planted. As the staff rushed to clear the dining room, two bombs attached to cans of gasoline and hooked on to security grilles outside the main function room exploded. A huge fireball engulfed everything in front of it as dozens of guests were sprayed with burning fuel which stuck to their clothes and flesh. Twelve people were burned to death. Pictures of their blackened, charred remains – hardly recognizable as human beings – were distributed around the country in an effort to make those who still supported the Provisionals realize the cost of their campaign and to remind those who opposed them of the need to continue doing so.

When reporters asked the Chief Constable if he still thought that the Provisionals were beaten he replied tersely: 'I never made that claim.'[13] The message was clear to Mason: neither should he have made it. Declaring victory was a dangerous business in an unconventional war in which winning or losing was more a matter of perception than established fact.

Something significant emerged in the days following the La Mon House atrocity. In spite of the horror of the bombing and the fact that all of the twelve dead were Protestants, there was no loyalist retaliation. This was the first time since 1971 that the UDA and the UVF refrained from answering a republican outrage with one of their own. The UDA's Supreme Chairman, Andy Tyrie, maintained that this was because the organization no longer targeted ordinary Catholics but was more selective.[14] The La Mon bombing did lead to a crackdown, however. Among twenty-one republicans arrested in the aftermath was Gerry Adams. He was charged with belonging to an illegal organization. After eight months on remand, the court accepted his lawyer's argument that there was insufficient evidence to convict him of the charge and he was released. (The evidence consisted of speeches Adams made and pictures of him taking part in an IRA parade in prison.) Sinn Fein turned the situation to their advantage and for the first time went on the propaganda offensive, claiming that the British government was using the La Mon House bombing as an excuse to impede their legitimate political activity through harassing and arresting Sinn Fein members and workers. The party's new feistiness was a sign of things to come.

Another offensive against the Provisionals was under way, and in the end it would prove to be much the most effective one. RUC recruitment had increased. Between 1975 and 1979 around eighty-five recruits entered the force each month, compared with a dozen or so per month in the years before. The Special Branch, or 'E' Department, was restructured in line with the government's 'Ulsterization' plans, the key to which was re-establishing the primacy of the police in security matters. Traditionally, E Department's function had been more or less restricted to gathering information from informers. In the 1970s, the department was subdivided into different sections, each with its own specialization. The handling of the human sources of intelligence became the responsibility of E3. Later, a surveillance unit, E4, was developed, specializing in technical sources of intelligence. It oversaw the use of various types of bugging devices and wiretaps to monitor arms dumps and premises used by suspects.[15] These operations were carried out in collaboration with MI5, Britain's internal security service. MI5 agents were tasked to plant listening devices in targeted buildings under RUC supervision.

In 1976, a subdivision, E4A, was set up, modelled on the British Army's surveillance unit known as 'Det'. RUC officers were trained in Close Target Recognizance (CTR) – surveillance techniques such as the use of disguises, selecting and establishing suitable observation posts (OPs), and the following of suspects. Police operators were sent into nationalist areas to maintain surveillance of IRA suspects often for weeks at a time. It was relatively easy to carry out these operations in rural areas, but in urban centres it was difficult and dangerous. Fortunately for the RUC, in the late 1970s the redevelopment of Belfast provided plenty of abandoned buildings in which E4A could set up OPs. The Special Branch also began working in close collaboration with the army's SAS, which had been in Ulster as a unit since 1976 (see above), though before that individual members of the Troop stationed there had been attached to other regiments.[16]

The Tasking Co-ordination Group (TCG) was created in the late 1970s to pool intelligence from police, army and MI5 sources and to co-ordinate a response to planned terrorist operations, 'locking together intelligence from informers with surveillance and ambushing activities of undercover units'.[17] The first TCG was established in Belfast. Later TCG South, headquartered in Gough Barracks, Armagh, and TCG North, based in Derry city, were created.

The RUC began making dramatic progress in the twilight war during this period, recruiting among others two key figures from the Belfast brigade who became informers. One, whose police nickname was 'DJ', was from West Belfast and was recruited after being arrested for a driving offence. DJ's information would frustrate many IRA bombing operations and lead to the apprehension of some of their top activists. The other 'tout' was Maurice Gilvary, the Operations Officer of the Third Battalion in North Belfast, who according to republican sources provided the information that allowed the SAS to ambush a bombing team as it was about to blow up a post office depot on 20 June 1978. Denis Brown, Jackie Mealy and James Mulvenna were shot dead in the single biggest strike the Troop had so far delivered against the Provisionals, who admitted that the men were on 'active service' but alleged that they were shot without warning and were unarmed. A fourth man, Billy Hanna, a Protestant, who happened to be passing at the time, was also killed. His death was an indication of the risks the authorities took in deploying the fire-power and aggression of the Troop in built-up areas. In the end, the SAS would be used mainly in the countryside. This operation and others like them highlighted the growing reliance of the security forces on accurate intelligence, which allowed them to anticipate paramilitary operations with deadly effect.[18] It also allowed the RUC Special Branch to build up a picture of the Provisional IRA command structure in Ulster from the late 1970s onwards.

At this point, the Provisional Army Council, under the growing influence of the Northern activists, had established two separate commands – Northern and Southern. The main responsibility of the Southern Command was acquiring and storing weapons, raising finance (at first through robberies, later through running front operations such as pubs and clubs), organizing the training of volunteers and transporting weapons to the 'war zone', where Northern Command ran the actual day-to-day operations. Gerry Adams's name was at the top of a list of twenty-seven the Special Branch made of

Belfast PIRA activists. He was listed as being on 'Northern Command'. Along with the names, the police had details of the licence numbers of the suspects' cars, their hair and eye colour, addresses, height, etc. (For instance, Adams is noted as being six foot one inch tall, and brown-haired.) The compilation was made for use by TCG Belfast.

The Provisionals were at a distinct disadvantage in the twilight war, a disadvantage from which they would never recover. In the 1980s it would cost them heavily – indeed, to a certain extent it lost them the war. It stemmed from the fact that they never penetrated the security forces and intelligence-gathering agencies. They had no one on the inside to give them the kind of information that would allow them to identify undercover agents operating against them. The disadvantage is all the more apparent when the Provisionals' campaign is compared to that the IRA conducted in 1919–21 under the command of Michael Collins. Collins's penetration of security force intelligence allowed him to mount a devastating counter-strike in Dublin on the morning of 21 November 1920. Fourteen undercover agents were killed and the heart ripped out of a major British intelligence-gathering operation.

There were a number of reasons for the Provisionals' weakness in this area. Partly it was due to their failure, early on, to grasp the nature of Britain's commitment to Northern Ireland. Their mistaken notion from 1970 to 1975 that one big push would force the British to leave meant they made no long-term plans to plant agents in the security forces, especially the RUC, who could later be activated as they rose in rank. Indeed, a sort of militaristic stupidity led them to do the opposite and to single out for assassination any Catholic who dared to join the RUC or UDR. They were also limited by the inherent sectarianism of Ulster society which discouraged the vast majority of Catholics from joining the police or UDR and prevented them from rising to high-level positions within the civil service. Finally, because the Provisionals' support base was almost entirely working-class if not lumpen-proletariat, they found it hard to recruit the kind of educated, middle-class activist who might have been able to provide a way into the relevant social strata.

However, briefly, in the late 1970s, the Provisionals in Belfast overcame this handicap. They recruited an English-born RUC detective whose code-name was 'Fox'. The RUC discovered his relationship with the enemy in the course of a surveillance operation in August 1979, which targeted the head of the IRA's internal security unit, known innocuously as the Civil Administration Team. Regardless of its name, there was nothing very 'civil' about CAT. It was responsible for uncovering and interrogating suspected touts, usually by brutal means. Suspects had their heads submerged in baths full of water, or were burned with cigarette ends. In 1979, the Special Branch recruited CAT member Peter Valente as an informer. He revealed that the head of CAT was in contact with a renegade policeman, who had a list of ten informers working within the Provisionals which he was prepared to sell for two hundred pounds sterling – that is, ten pounds a head.[19] 'Fox' was apprehended in October 1979 and dismissed from the force, but at the insistence of MI5 and some senior police officers, who feared a scandal, charges against him were never pressed. Several informers did not get off so easily. Included among them was Peter Valente, shot in November 1980. Valente may have lost his life as a result of the operation against Fox. It seems that before he died he was tortured into giving up the names of other touts. In January 1981, Maurice Gilvary's body was found near Jonesborough in South Armagh, an area where suspected informers were frequently held for long periods of interrogation. The purge of informers left a few still operating, including 'DJ', who would later play a crucial role in the undercover war (see Chapter 5).

2

While the twilight war was getting into its stride, constitutional politics was in abeyance in Ulster, where power-sharing had become a dead issue. But John Hume was intent on keeping it alive elsewhere. There was no better place than the world's most powerful nation, where something of a revolution was occurring in relation to the Ulster problem, mainly thanks to the SDLP leader and the efforts of the Irish government. Hume went to Boston in 1976, where he struck up a friendship with Thomas 'Tip' O'Neill and Senator Edward Kennedy. Hume convinced O'Neill and Kennedy of the need for a political solution based on power-sharing and opposition to the Provisional IRA.

The lure of Irish America had always been strong for all shades of Irish nationalism, who saw it as a potential ally. But for constitutional nationalists, the dangers were also evident. The IRA exercised a powerful, if mostly sentimental, appeal among some Irish Americans, who saw the conflict in Ulster as merely a continuation of the 1919–21 War of Independence. The Protestant dimension was usually ignored.[20] Senator Kennedy's earliest proclamations on Ulster in 1971, calling for a British withdrawal, had smacked of Provisional IRA sentiments, to the horror of the Irish government. The year that Hume was in Boston, the Irish government became alarmed again when the Democratic presidential candidate, Jimmy Carter, was approached by the Rev. Sean McManus of the Irish National Caucus, which Dublin believed to be a lobbying group for the Provisional IRA. Rev. Sean McManus was Ulster-born, and had attended Sean MacStiofain, the IRA Chief of Staff, during his hunger-and-thirst strike in late 1972. Carter had agreed to make human rights in Ulster an issue if elected. The human rights issue had always been a delicate one for Dublin to handle in the Irish American context, where it was easily transformed into support for the Provisionals.

Tutored by Hume, and Irish government diplomats, Washington's heavyweight politicians, O'Neill, Kennedy and Senator Patrick Moynihan of New York, immediately began a rescue mission to make sure that when Carter, the newly elected President, spoke on Ulster he was using the right script, not one crafted by a troublesome priest with unsettling connections to the Provisionals.[21]

Along with Senator Moynihan and New York State Governor Hugh Carey, O'Neill, now House Speaker, and Kennedy formed the Friends of Ireland. They began issuing St Patrick's Day statements that coupled demands for an agreed settlement with denunciations of those who supported the IRA's violent campaign. They also applied pressure on Carter to make a public statement on Ulster, but one more in keeping with the ideas of Hume and the Irish government.

For most of the twentieth century, successive US governments had accepted the British position that Northern Ireland was an internal British problem and the only contribution that the Federal government could make was stopping weapons and money going to the IRA from its American backers. In spite of pressure from Irish America, over the years successive US administrations practised a studied non-interventionist policy on Ireland – the 'Special Relationship' between the UK and the US, cemented by the Second World War and the Cold War, seemed unassailable. When British diplomats learned of moves to change this, they fought hard to prevent the President from saying anything about Ulster, other than making the ritual condemnations of violence. But British diplomacy failed, suffering a major defeat when on 30 August 1977, for the first time in US history, a serving President, Jimmy Carter, broke one of the golden rules of Anglo-American diplomacy and made a public statement on Northern Ireland. It represented the first real triumph of Irish government diplomacy in the US over the two forces that were aligned against it: the British embassy in Washington and the

Provisional IRA's sympathizers, backers and funders in organizations such as Irish Northern Aid.

President Carter began by recalling the contributions that Irish men and women had made to the United States. 'It is natural', said the President,

> that Americans are deeply concerned about the continuing conflict and violence in Northern Ireland. We know the overwhelming majority of the people there reject the bomb and the bullet. The United States wholeheartedly supports peaceful means for finding a just solution that involves both parts of the community of Northern Ireland, protects human rights and guarantees freedom from discrimination – a solution that the people of Northern Ireland as well as the Governments of Great Britain and Ireland can support. Violence cannot resolve Northern Ireland's problems; it only increases them and solves nothing.[22]

President Carter said that the US, while not wanting to impose a solution, would support a 'form of government in Northern Ireland which will command widespread support throughout both parts of the community'. In closing, he promised that 'In the event of such a settlement, the United States Government would be prepared to join with others to see how additional job-creating investment could be encouraged, to the benefit of all the people of Northern Ireland.'[23]

To most, it seemed like an unremarkable and uncontroversial statement, but a chip was knocked off the 'special relationship' that gave Britain global significance in the chilly postwar imperial twilight. The veiled references to power-sharing were unwelcome at a time when the Labour government, now under the leadership of James Callaghan (Harold Wilson having resigned), increasingly relied on the Unionist vote in Parliament to keep it in power. Callaghan had agreed to increase the number of seats Northern Ireland MPs held in Westminster from twelve to seventeen, knowing that most of them would go to Unionists. He did not need the ghost of power-sharing to haunt this particular banquet. Carter's speech was in fact a landmark on the long road to putting the Ulster crisis solidly on the US presidential agenda and taking the initiative away from maverick groups such as NORAID.

Irish Northern Aid had, since its foundation in 1970, striven to stir up anti-British sentiment in the US and involve sympathetic Congressmen in various gestures of 'solidarity' with the Catholics of Northern Ireland. They were joined by other groups, such as the Washington-based Irish National Caucus, and the more traditional Ancient Order of Hibernians, the organizers of the St Patrick's Day parade.

Some Irish American activists, whose Irish nationalism found a Bronx bar more congenial than the marbled corridors on The Hill, found other ways to tweak the lion's tail and irritate the Irish government at the same time. They approached Mario Biaggi, the Congressman for East Queens and the Bronx, who, when he was a New York policeman, chalked up more fatal shootings than anyone in the force's history. Biaggi's chief connection to Ireland had been an Irish American cop he once worked with who he said 'told me all about it' in 1942 or 1943.[24] The aim was for the Congressman to set up an *ad hoc* committee on Ireland. Biaggi agreed at once, and recruited seventy-nine members within weeks.

Specifically, the Ad Hoc Committee on Ireland was to press for congressional hearings on human rights violations in Northern Ireland and to look into such issues as the visa ban on Irish republicans, which prevented men like Ruairi O Bradaigh and later Gerry Adams from coming into the US legally. Dublin regarded the committee with a jaundiced eye as another way of spreading IRA propaganda, and detailed Tip O'Neill to police it. Biaggi's hearings never took place.[25]

Congressional manoeuvres were in fact a sideshow. In an unlikely concordance with the British, the Provisionals (while appreciative of any sympathetic propaganda) still saw the US primarily in terms of an arms source. George Harrison remained in place to make sure they were not disappointed. For him too the real business was making sure the weapons were acquired and reached the right hands. Harrison had survived federal detection by staying away from NORAID. His only contact with the Provisional Army Council for most of the time was Eoin McNamee, who would arrive in New York regularly with a 'shopping list' from GHQ. From the mid-1970s, Harrison's network was dispatching between two and three hundred weapons a year, mainly Armalites purloined from US military bases. One of his most successful acquisitions came in the spring of 1977, when an Irish American gangster, Eddy Connors from Philadelphia, approached him with an offer of six M-60 machineguns. Connors was linked to the Mafia which, in a joint raid with Irish American gangsters, stole the weapons from an armoury in Danvers, Massachusetts, in 1976. Connors got them for Harrison at a bargain price.[26] They left New York in July 1977 and arrived in Ireland in September, not long after President Carter had made his historic Northern Ireland speech.[27] GHQ was always on the lookout for a weapon that would escalate the struggle and give them even a temporary advantage over the increasingly well-protected forces of the Crown.

The M-60, the general-purpose machinegun of the US Army, was just that. Capable of firing six hundred rounds per minute and taking down a helicopter, it was even more deadly when trained on a foot patrol. It made its first appearance in January 1978, during a Bloody Sunday commemoration, when the Provisional IRA unveiled it. The M-60 claimed its first victims in Ulster four days before Christmas 1978 in Crossmaglen. As an army foot patrol was passing a parked van, its back door flew open and the Provisionals inside raked the soldiers with machinegun fire, killing three, before speeding away. The following year, on 28 October, an Active Service Unit (ASU) equipped with an M-60 ambushed a mobile patrol as it left Springfield Road RUC station in West Belfast, claiming the lives of a policeman and a soldier. It was used in several attacks on helicopters and on 24 May 1985 forced one to land after smashing its windscreen.[28]

The Harrison network was running smoothly enough, its chief figures, after Harrison himself, being McNamee, 'the Emissary' for the GHQ, Tom Falvey, who helped Harrison clean and store the weapons, and George De Meo, who acquired them. Harrison made a point of not going to NORAID sources for money. His network had its own resources, and occasionally McNamee brought money with him from the Provisionals in Ireland. (Harrison reckons that in his years as an IRA arms supplier he raised and spent about $1,000,000.) Things began to change, however, in the spring of 1978, with the arrival of Martin McGuinness and Ruairi O Bradaigh in New York, the two men having slipped into the country illegally. They stayed at Harrison's apartment in Brooklyn, in spite of the fact that on the premises a large arms haul was being prepared for shipment to Ireland. It might seem remarkable that the Provisionals' Chief of Staff should be prepared to take such a risk, but it is an indication of how confident the IRA was in the security of the Harrison network. Among the weapons were Armalites, some of the features of which Harrison demonstrated to his guests.

The McGuinness–O Bradaigh visit was to further the Provisionals' restructuring plans (see above). The organization was increasingly dominated by Ulstermen. Adams, Bell and McGuinness were gradually taking over its military and political structures and putting in place their own people – usually Northerners. McGuinness was also concerned that Harrison was not actually a member of the IRA – he had had a dispute with the leadership linked to the death in 1964 of a former Sinn Fein President, Paddy McLogan, who had been a close friend.[29] The Chief of Staff suggested to Harrison that he officially become a member. Harrison refused, citing the McLogan affair. There the matter was left – or so it seemed. But in the year following the visit, the Provisional leadership moved others into place in America, including a former IRA member from North Belfast who had been in the US since 1975 and who soon began making it generally known that he was the IRA 'representative' in New York. According to Harrison, things began to go wrong. Weapons were not moved on schedule. 'There were too many unnecessary telephone calls,' he said. 'The new people didn't have a grasp of the job.'[30] Though he said he felt 'something ominous in the air', he went ahead with another large haul, which was handled by the new IRA 'representative' and shipped to Dublin in the autumn of 1979. That was the beginning of the end. One of those involved made a telephone call to Dublin along a line that was tapped to notify GHQ that 'the Frigidaire was on its way'. The haul, consisting of 150 weapons – two of them M-60s – and 60,000 rounds of ammunition, was seized on Dublin's dockside. Eighty per cent of it came from Harrison. But worse was to follow.

'Markings weren't removed as they should have been,' according to Harrison, which allowed the police to trace part of the shipment to George De Meo. De Meo was arrested, charged and convicted of arms smuggling. However, he soon came to an arrangement with the federal authorities. In return for only having to serve half his ten-year term, and in a minimum security prison, De Meo would give up the IRA's main arms supplier in the US.

'I knew by 1979 that the old operation was gone,' recalled Harrison. 'It would have to be reorganized on a larger scale than before.' Though he had misgivings, they were not about his old friend De Meo, but about the mistakes that had been made in the last shipment. Harrison was considering getting out. 'I had always thought of leaving them plentifully supplied before I left the scene,' he said.[31] De Meo contacted him, saying that he would like to do something for him before he went to jail. Harrison agreed to meet to discuss it. They did. De Meo was wired. He told Harrison that he would introduce him to someone who had access to 350 MAC-10 machine-pistols and a quantity of AK-47s. That someone was 'John White', otherwise known as John Winslow, an undercover FBI operator. Instead of clinching an arms deal that would leave the Provisionals 'plentifully supplied', Harrison walked into a major FBI sting operation which netted Tom Falvey and three others, Danny Gormley, Paddy Mullins and Michael Flannery, one of the founding fathers of Irish Northern Aid. (Because of the unexpectedness of the deal with White, Harrison was in need of cash fast, and broke one of his cardinal rules about not approaching NORAID.) Harrison and Falvey were arrested on 19 June 1981, the others later. Harrison's arrest effectively meant the end of the IRA's most successful arms-smuggling network.[32] Its demise had come about at a disastrous time for the Provisionals, who were trying to intensify their campaign. The struggle over Special Category status, abolished in March 1976, had escalated into a major hunger strike which would change the face of Northern Ireland politics.

3

The story of the Ulster conflict is one that is riddled with ironies. But perhaps the supreme irony lies in the fact that the process that set out in March 1976 to criminalize the Provisionals within five years transformed them into a legitimate political force – and would eventually propel them to the threshold of the government of Northern Ireland itself.

No one, including the leadership of the republican movement, foresaw this when in September 1976 Ciaran Nugent, the first IRA man convicted under the new dispensation, refused to put on a prison uniform or otherwise be treated like an 'ordinary criminal' (see above). If they wanted him to wear one, 'they'd have to nail the clothes on my back,' he declared. He wore a blanket instead. The authorities responded by punishing him with loss of remission and the removal of furniture from his cell, so that he was forced to sleep on the floor. In spite of these hardships, the number of protesters steadily increased as more and more convicted Provisionals, along with members of the smaller INLA, draped themselves in blankets in rejection of the government's insistence that they, being ordinary criminals, should wear a prisoner's uniform. They became known as the Blanket Men. The protest escalated in 1978, when prisoners refused to leave their cells to empty their chamber pots, alleging excessive supervision and harassment from prison staff. They stuffed their excrement through the cell windows. The wardens hurled it back in. The protesters then began smearing the cell walls with it. An Irish journalist visiting the Maze was taken to a cell where he witnessed a well-known North Belfast IRA man, Martin Meehan, decorating the walls of his cell by painting palm trees with bits of rubber foam dipped in shit.[33] By 1978, over three hundred prisoners were involved in what was now called the Dirty Protest. At the beginning of August 1978, the protesters received an extraordinary publicity boost when Ireland's Cardinal Tomas O Fiaich (a native of the strongly republican South Armagh) visited the Maze. What he saw horrified him. 'One would hardly allow an animal to remain in such conditions, let alone a human being,' he said a few days later. 'The nearest approach to it that I have ever seen was the spectacle of hundreds of homeless people living in the sewer pipes of Calcutta. The stench and the filth in some of the cells with the remains of rotten food and human excreta scattered around the walls was almost unbearable.' In the women's prison in Armagh, republican inmates became involved in a similar protest, and soon their cell walls were covered with shit and menstrual blood.

Coincidentally, August 1978 saw the tenth anniversary of the first civil rights march. It would have been unthinkable, in 1968, that a struggle that had begun on the issue of housing and equal voting rights for Catholics should lead to a situation where people lived surrounded by their own excrement. But it was one sign that the problem had long ago left the sphere of the rational, where compromise is possible, to reside on the plane of conflicting absolutes.

In spite of the rising tide of concern and the increased publicity, the British government refused to budge: Special Category Status would not be reinstated. Indeed, the one quarter from which they were not coming under much pressure to do so was the republican movement itself. Sinn Fein had been slow to mobilize support for the protest, even though Adams claims he had conveyed its importance to the party president, Ruairi O Bradaigh.[34] Relatives Action Committees had been formed as early as 1976 to draw attention to the deteriorating situation in the prison, but the republican movement did not throw its weight behind them. In contrast, the INLA's political wing, the Irish Republican Socialist Party, had become active on the issue even before Special Category Status was abolished. 'Political prisoners status must stay,' its newspaper, the *Starry Plough*, had declared as early as December 1975. 'The attempt to do away with their special category status is intended to portray all political prisoners as common criminals, psychopaths, intimidators for personal gain, devoid of any politics.'

However, the Provisional leadership regarded the protest as a distraction from its main business – conducting the war. In an interview with a leading Dublin magazine published in August 1978, a spokesman for the Army Council did not mention the H-Block issue once – one indication of its low priority. The Provisionals had launched a murder campaign against prison officers, beginning on 8 April 1976, when they

148

gunned down a thirty-six-year-old warden, Pacelli Dillon, outside his home in Carrickmore, Co. Tyrone. But the idea of taking political action on the streets in conjunction with the RACs was resisted. Throughout their history, the Provisionals have shown a marked reluctance to get involved with any movement unless they can completely control it. In spring 1979 Bernadette McAliskey entered the elections to the European Parliament, making the prisoners' plight the single issue of her campaign. But even at this late date, not only did the Provisionals refuse to support her, they actively campaigned against her, advocating a boycott. In spite of this opposition, McAliskey won over thirty thousand first-preference votes. The proof that the issue could attract substantial support strengthened the hand of those who, like Adams, wanted some means of broadening the republican struggle.

In late 1979, a Smash H-Block Committee was set up with the Provisionals' backing, but first attempts to broaden its appeal foundered on their demand that all those involved must also support the IRA's armed struggle. This was later dropped, and the committee soon enlisted support from left-wing groups and some trade unionists, even attracting some attention from the Peace People organization, now much declined in strength from its peak in late 1976. The campaign was based on the prisoners' five demands – the right to wear their own clothes, to refuse to do prison work, to receive extra visits and food parcels, to freely associate with members of their own organization within the jail, and the restoration of remission lost because of their protest. By then, however, a formidable obstacle had risen up in the prisoners' path in the shape of the new British Prime Minister, Margaret Thatcher, who had earlier ousted the debilitated Labour government.

Even before Thatcher entered office, the Ulster conflict had bloodied her. On the afternoon of 30 March, just after Parliament was dissolved to prepare for the elections, Airey Neave, her close friend and adviser, who had helped engineer her takeover of the Conservative Party, got into his car, which had been parked in the underground carpark of the House of Commons. Neave, a fierce advocate of stern law-and-order policies, including greater use of the SAS, was designated to be her Secretary of State for Northern Ireland. As he drove up the ramp towards the street, a bomb attached to the floor panel under the driver's seat exploded, severing both his legs. It took thirty minutes to cut him free from the mangled wreckage. He died eight minutes after reaching hospital. The INLA claimed responsibility for what was one of the most daring assassinations in the history of the Troubles. The operation was the fruit of a true international terrorist conspiracy. The pink-coloured explosives that killed Neave were made in the Soviet Union, part of a shipment that came from the PLO, which also regularly supplied the INLA with mostly Soviet-made weapons, via East Germany. The information that helped the two-man team penetrate the House of Commons disguised as workmen came from leftist Labour Party activists who believed that Neave and Thatcher were about to lead a right-wing backlash. They told the INLA that security was slack as regards legitimate workmen engaged in renovations, and that security cameras were not monitored carefully. The sixteen-ounce chunk of explosive used in the bomb was carried in a lunch box and cost about five pounds.[35]

Thatcher, nicknamed the Iron Lady because of her reputation for refusing to compromise, was in no mood to listen to IRA and INLA prisoners' claims to be deserving of special treatment. She responded to arguments that the IRA and INLA were political offenders by stating 'A crime is a crime is a crime'; if the Blanket Men lived in their own filth, it was self-inflicted and obedience to the law would easily remedy it. Unionists were delighted that at last they had found someone as intransigent as themselves. The fact that most Catholics viewed the prisoners as having a legitimate grievance went unheeded. Neither Thatcher nor the Unionists could grasp the simple truth that while Catholics might not approve of the Provisional IRA or INLA actions, yet at the same time they saw them as the result of a historical struggle that conferred on them a certain legitimacy.

The conflict over the prisoners' status starkly revealed the depth of the dichotomy between nationalist and Unionist, as it did the extent of the incomprehension the British government showed about the nature of the republican movement and the kind of support it could invoke at certain times among ordinary Catholics. It also highlighted the capacity of the Provisionals for behind-the-scenes manoeuvring. At the height of the Smash H-Block campaign, when the IRSP, the Relatives Action Committees and various other organizations were galvanizing support, the Provisionals opened up secret talks with the British government, using a channel that had existed since the 1974/74 ceasefire. Some feared that the Provisionals were quite prepared to abandon the protest if they could get a separate deal for their own prisoners.

The secret talks came to nothing, and the protests dragged on inside the jails, counterpointed by the violence outside. In the most serious incident, on 27 August 1979, two Provisional IRA bombs killed eighteen soldiers, mostly members of 2 Para, near Warrenpoint, a beautiful seaside town in South Down – the highest number of fatalities that the British Army experienced in any single incident in the long conflict. The first bomb, estimated at five hundred pounds, exploded in a hay wagon at 4.30 p.m. as a convoy of paras drove past. The second, one thousand-pound device went off near by twenty-nine minutes later as more troops arrived to investigate the first. Both were detonated by remote control from a few hundred yards away across a narrow stretch of Carlingford Lough, which at that point separates Northern Ireland from the Irish Republic. So intense was the second blast that the remains of one officer, Lieutenant-Colonel David Blair, who was standing near it, were never recovered.[36]

That same day, a few hours earlier, another remote-controlled bomb claimed the life of Earl Louis Mountbatten, the seventy-nine-year-old uncle of the Queen, as his thirty-foot boat left the harbour of Mullaghmore near Sligo in the west of Ireland. With him died his fourteen-year-old grandson Nicholas, and Paul Maxwell, another teenager who worked on the boat. Dowager Lady Brabourne, aged eighty-two, who had also been on board, died later of her wounds.

The massacre of the soldiers provoked demands from the army that overall responsibility for fighting the Provisionals be returned to it, effectively ending the three-year-old policies of Ulsterization and criminalization. An appeal was made directly to Thatcher when she arrived in the province shortly after the bombings. To make his point, a senior army officer threw down in front of the Prime Minister the metal epaulettes worn by Lt.-Col. Blair, killed at Warrenpoint, announcing melodramatically: 'This is all that's left of one of my bravest officers.'[37] Given the Prime Minister's reputation, it might be thought that she would be sympathetic to the army's demand. But instead she listened to the Chief Constable, Sir Kenneth Newman, who was adamant that the policies that gave the RUC the primary security role represented the best hope of defeating the Provisionals and allowing the army to eventually withdraw. He demanded a thousand extra policemen and a strengthening of the RUC's role. Thatcher agreed. If ever there was any doubt that Britain was conducting anything other than a holding operation in Ulster, then this decision should have dispelled it.[38]

Meanwhile, Thatcher continued to meet the prisoners' challenge to 'criminalization' with undiminished intransigence. If the British Army could not budge her, then a collection of dirt-covered convicts draped in blankets certainly would not succeed. The H-Block protests depended mainly on one tactic – marches – and they were beginning to lose support, breeding a sense of apathy and increasing futility. As the protest went into its fourth year, the prisoners began to talk about taking the ultimate step – the hunger strike. This, the traditional weapon of last resort in the armoury of Irish republican prisoners, had been discussed as an option as early as 1978. The Army Council was reluctant to sanction it – Michael Gaughan had died in 1974 on a futile hunger strike in England trying to get the authorities to accord him Special Category Status, as had Frank Stagg two years later. Before that, MacStiofain's hunger-and-thirst strike had ended ignominiously. The only propitious precedent was that of Billy McKee, whose hunger strike in June 1972 had won the prisoners the concessions they were now fighting to restore. His example persuaded many of them that the tactic would work again.

Both Sinn Fein and the Provisional IRA leadership were afraid that a hunger strike would further divert resources away from the war effort, and that in the end the prisoners would be defeated, thus discrediting the whole movement. But in spite of their opposition, the prisoners' leader, Brendan 'The Dark' Hughes – who before his arrest had succeeded Ivor Bell as O/C of the Belfast IRA in 1974 – announced that he and six other prisoners (including one member of the INLA) would begin to refuse food on 27 October 1980. The strike lasted less than two months before coming to a confused end, with the prisoners believing that the British were prepared to make concessions, especially on the issue of clothes, and the British denying it. According to Adams, 'there was a feeling of despondency in the air' following the ending of the strike.[39] The prisoners had been outmanoeuvered and the issues remained unresolved as Ulster entered its fifth year of an increasingly bitter prison protest.

A series of loyalist assassinations and attempted assassinations of leading republicans associated with the H-Block protest deepened the gloom. The first to die was John Turnley, a member of the Irish Independence Party, shot dead as he was going to attend a political meeting on 4 June 1980. Three weeks later, the killer squads targeted Miriam Daly, a lecturer in economics at Queen's University, Belfast, and a former chairperson of the IRSP. For several years she had been a prominent speaker on H-Block platforms, along with her husband Jim, who was also an academic and prominent republican activist. Her ten-year-old adopted daughter came home from school on the afternoon of 26 June to find her bound hand and foot, a fatal bullet wound in her head, a bloodstained cushion that was used to muffle the sound lying near by. In the early hours of 15 October, gunmen sledge hammered their way into the home of Ronnie Bunting Jr, the Protestant republican and a founding member of the INLA who was the son of Paisley's former sidekick. They raced up the stairs and reached the door of his bedroom where he was sleeping with his wife Suzanne. The couple struggled to prevent them from getting into the room but the gunmen fired through a gap in the door. She fell back on the bed, shot in the hand. According to Mrs Bunting: 'The next moment two men were in the room and started shooting Ronnie . . . They wore those green, ribbed pullovers with suede patches on the shoulders and ski-type masks which covered their whole faces with only holes for eyes . . . They were cool and calm – like animals – without fear – they had no smell of fear about them.'[40] Before leaving, the gunmen shot dead Noel Lyttle, a guest in the Bunting home, as he slept in the next room. At the time of his death, Bunting was the O/C of the INLA in Belfast – the highest-ranking member of the republican movement to fall victim to loyalist assassins. His removal would have profound consequences for the organization.

Barely two weeks of 1981 had elapsed when three masked gunmen shot and seriously wounded veteran civil rights activist Bernadette McAliskey and her husband in their home in Co. Tyrone as they dressed their children for school. This time, however, the attackers were arrested as they left the scene of the crime by a squad of British soldiers who had been on patrol near by. The assailants turned out to be UDA men.[41] The Provisional IRA responded to these attacks with a murderous assault on the stately home of a prominent Unionist family in Armagh, the Stronges. Eighty-six-year-old Norman Stronge had been Speaker in the Stormont parliament. He died along with his forty-eight-year-old son James in a hail of IRA bullets.

Inside the shit-besmeared walls of H-Blocks minds were focusing on a different kind of struggle. A twenty-seven-year-old activist called Bobby Sands was now the commander of the IRA prisoners in the Maze. Forced out of his home in a loyalist area of North Belfast in 1972, Sands joined the Provisionals. He was not a very successful or lucky IRA member, his two brief bursts of activity leading to arrests. During his first period of imprisonment, from 1973 to 1976, he became friends with Gerry Adams when they shared the same hut. Just six months after his release, he was caught after a bombing attack on a furniture store and sentenced to fourteen years for possession of a handgun. This time, he was subjected to the new 'ordinary criminal' regime, and fought it, going on the blanket, then joining in the excremental war with the prison authorities. In spite of the hardships and horrors, he found time to write – poetry, ballads and accounts of his prison life, mainly in the form of 'comms.' – messages, stories and poems inscribed on tiny scraps of toilet or cigarette paper with a care and deliberation that would do credit to a medieval monk. They were smuggled out of the prison, often secreted in the visitor's anus and sometimes in a female visitor's vagina. In contrast to the unconventional means by which they were conveyed to the world, Sands's writings, especially the verse, are full of conventional sentimentality, but his prose description of prison life, *One Day in My Life*, is graphic and disturbing.[42] The writings are testimony to the romantic power the Irish republican tradition exercised on young men like Sands, with its mystification of sacrifice and ideal of martyrdom. It enabled them to endure the most obscene squalor and humiliating violations of their persons and, finally, to undergo an agonizing death. Perhaps, had Margaret Thatcher or some of her advisers read them, the confrontation that followed would never have occurred.

Sands notified the Provisional leadership that he was going to begin another hunger strike on 1 March 1981, the fifth anniversary of the abolition of Special Category Status. In contrast to the last effort, prisoners would begin it in stages. The next hunger striker, Francis Hughes, would join Sands on 15 March, and he would be followed a week later by Ray McCreesh and Patsy O'Hara, with others joining after shorter intervals until the British conceded their demands.

Adams made the Provisionals' position clear. 'Bobby, we are tactically, strategically, physically and morally opposed to a hunger strike,' he wrote to Sands.[43] A march took place on the Falls Road to support Sands, but the outside world paid little heed other than to condemn the action. The Catholic Bishop of Derry, Cathal Daly, stated that a hunger strike was not morally justified. *The New York Times* reported the event in one paragraph.

Four days after Sands began his fast, Frank Maguire, the Independent Nationalist MP for Formanagh-South Tyrone, died suddenly of a heart attack. The constituency had a Catholic majority and an agreed nationalist candidate had a very strong chance of winning it. Bernadette McAliskey announced that she would run as an independent on the H-Block issue, but would step aside in favour of an H-Block candidate. The idea was seized upon by Daithi O Conaill, who at a special republican convention held in Monaghan in April suggested that Sands should stand. What better way of refuting the government's propaganda that the prisoners were common criminals without support other than from a minority of republican fanatics? Of course, defeat could knock the heart out of the whole H-Block campaign, and discredit the prisoners' demands. The local Sinn Fein activists opposed the idea, but O Conaill prevailed. Sands was nominated. The Provisionals finally persuaded the two other nationalist candidates to step aside – though one was still threatening to put his name forward just minutes away from the close of nominations.

Sinn Fein's electoral limbs were pretty stiff from not having run in an election for years, but the party learned on the job, and quickly. The hope that a Sands victory would not only score an important propaganda breakthrough for the republican movement but would also save his life motivated the party activists, who flooded into the constituency from all corners of Ireland to fight the campaign. On 9 April the results were announced. Sands topped the poll with 30,492 votes, beating the Unionist candidate, Harry West, by over a thousand votes. On the fortieth day of his hunger strike, Bobby Sands, the convicted IRA gunman and bomber, had become a Westminster MP. The government's attempts to criminalize the republican movement had given it the kind of political recognition it had not enjoyed since 1955, the last time one of its members was elected to Westminster.

Adams, who had been campaigning hard for Sands in the constituency, heard the news on a car radio. 'I was ecstatic,' he said.[44] Many assumed that Thatcher would now concede – after all, the Provisionals had proved that they were not a bunch of isolated gunmen who held sway through terror, that they did represent a considerable body of opinion within the nationalist community. But the fact that Britain's criminalization policy was actually achieving the opposite to its intentions did not penetrate the Prime Minister's obduracy. Nor did the spread of the campaign in support of the hunger strikers – marches and protests mushroomed in New York, Boston, Chicago and San Francisco, and as far away as Australia. Thatcher continued to say no to the five demands.

Sands grew weaker. On 5 May at 1.17 a.m. Robert Sands, MP died. Sixty-six days without food had reduced him to a shriveled, waxen corpse.

When news of his death emerged, there was a brief but profound silence in the Catholic areas of Belfast. Then came the insistent clang of dust-bin lids on the pavement – a sort of bush telegraph spreading the news. Gangs of Catholic youths took to the streets, hijacking, burning, hurling rocks and petrol bombs at the soldiers and police sent to contain them. A Protestant milkman and his son died when their milk van crashed after a mob hurled rocks at it in a Catholic district of North Belfast. The Provisionals struck at policemen and soldiers in an effort to show the government that the dying men inside the prison had a military organization outside able to avenge their sufferings. Five soldiers died in one land-mine blast in South Armagh on 19 May. But by then another hunger striker, Francis Hughes, had died, and two more, Patsy O'Hara and Ray McCreesh, were on the verge of death. The crisis deepened, then levelled out on the dull plateau of repetition as another six hunger strikers died throughout the summer. As the futility of the protest became more and more apparent, relatives often under pressure from the Catholic Church started to intervene, taking their loved ones off the protest as soon as they lapsed into unconsciousness.

The hunger strike had begun in spring. The last hunger striker died on 20 August as the autumn closed in. On 3 October, the six remaining hunger strikers ended their fast and the following day spokesmen for the prisoners declared that the hunger strike had ended.[45] Within three days, the new Northern Ireland Secretary of State, James Prior, announced that prisoners would be allowed to wear their own clothes at all times, and that 50 per cent of lost remission would be restored. Eventually, everything the prisoners asked for was granted. That leg of the criminalization policy had collapsed. The consequences of this failure would resound for years to come.

The protest offered two contrasting lessons. The first was that republicans and their supporters could be contained – at a security level. The H-Block and hunger strike riots were almost entirely confined to West Belfast and other nationalist areas, so that even at the height of the protests life went on undisturbed in most of Belfast and throughout the rest of the province. The Provisionals' military campaign, though stepped up, still could not reach the level it was at through most of the 1970s. During the entire seven-month crisis (March to October) the Provisional IRA and the INLA combined managed to kill thirty members of the army, UDR and RUC – no more than they had been able to kill during the first seven months of 1977, at a time when the armed campaign was going into decline. However, the second lesson showed that the political impact of the hunger strike could not be so easily contained. In the May local elections, twenty-one members of the nationalist Irish Independence Party won seats along with two IRSP members. Adams concluded that it was a grave mistake for Sinn Fein not to have contested them. It was a mistake the party would not make again. In June, two IRA prisoners were elected to the Irish parliament. In August, when a by-election was held to replace Sands, Sinn Fein's Owen Carron, who had been his election agent, won his seat with an increased majority. Soon afterwards, Sinn Fein announced that in future it would contest all Northern Ireland elections.

At the Sinn Fein *ard fheis* in November the political wing of the movement was accorded unaccustomed respect. Danny Morrison, the editor of *An Phoblacht/Republican News*, and later a prominent member of CAT (the IRA's informer-hunting squad), closed his speech by asking: 'Who really believes that we can win the war through the ballot box? But will anyone here object if with a ballot paper in this hand and an Armalite in this hand, we take power in Ireland?'

Treating republicans like common criminals had turned them into politicians.

CHAPTER FIVE

Bullets and Ballots: 1981–85

1

The ballot box energized the Provisionals, and left the moderate nationalists dismayed and afraid. John Hume observed that after the hunger strikes 'there was no disguising the bleakness of the scene that confronted us in Northern Ireland'.[1]

With the rise of Sinn Fein in 1981, the Irish political establishment confronted a political threat that it did not expect. For the moderate nationalists of the Social Democratic and Labour Party it could not have come at a worse moment. In Belfast, where Sinn Fein was at its greatest strength, the SDLP was at its weakest. Four years before the hunger strike crisis, in 1977, one of the SDLP's founding members, Paddy Devlin, was forced out of the party for denouncing what he saw as its departure from socialist politics. In those days, Devlin, a feisty working-class Belfast man, had a large following in the Falls area. Gerry Fitt, the party leader, was also unhappy. After ten years of relentless violence, he believed the conflict was more intractable than ever, and was unhappy with the direction the SDLP was taking. His despair came to crisis point in September 1979, during the first papal visit to

Ireland. Pope John Paul II preached in Drogheda on 30 September, attracting a crowd of a quarter of a million. In an emotional moment the Pope got down on his knees and appealed to the IRA to halt its campaign. The IRA rejected the plea, convincing the volatile and unpredictable Fitt that the situation was hopeless.

His dissatisfaction with the SDLP came to a head shortly afterwards when the government proposed a conference to discuss the future of Northern Ireland, but one that would exclude from consideration the Irish dimension, or Northern Ireland's constitutional status. Fitt advocated that the party should join the conference regardless. However, Hume, who earlier in 1979 had won a massive vote in the elections to the European parliament, had already formulated the way forward as he saw it – any solution had to go outside the parameters of Northern Ireland itself. Fitt resigned, accusing the party of espousing the same politics as the IRA.

Like Devlin, he came from a trade union, labour background, very much rooted in the traditions of British working-class politics. The bright new world of European politics, where Hume felt most comfortable, was alien to him. He was bitter towards his former colleagues, whom he accused of turning the SDLP into another Nationalist Party. 'The others were nationalists,' he said. 'While it was in my blood to be a Labour man – it was in their blood to be Nationalists. There is no Labour standing within the SDLP. It is not a Labour party and never was.'[2] Hume replaced him. In fact, Hume had been the guiding force behind the party for some time. But Fitt's departure meant that there was no one in the SDLP with the kind of grit needed to survive in Belfast's two-fisted street politics. The majority of the party's councillors in the city were well-meaning middle-class Catholics too polite to spit in public.

The fact that Margaret Thatcher was Prime Minister did

not help matters as far as constitutional nationalists were concerned. Hume reflected ruefully:

> Politics, our hope, were never bleaker. The British government was dominated by someone who seemed to care little about the problem of Northern Ireland. Northern Ireland, Mrs Thatcher said, was as British as Finchley. We hoped, at least for the sake of Finchley, that she was wrong . . . We were again, what we have so often been for British politicians: either an embarrassing nuisance to be concealed from view if possible or a political football in which our fortunes were usually neglected.[3]

However, in spite of this grim assessment, the Irish Taoiseach Charles Haughey met with Thatcher for an Anglo-Irish summit in late 1980, encouraging Hume to believe that at last there might be some movement out of the stagnating swamp of political inertia that was Ulster.

At this summit, the two leaders commissioned a series of studies to look at, among other things, the possibility of new institutional structures, economic measures, and ways of building mutual understanding between the two nations. This dovetailed well with Hume's belief that going outside Ulster and dealing with the relations between Britain and the Irish Republic that underlay the crisis was the only way to solve it. But the hunger strike crisis followed, and that 'derailed the Anglo-Irish process', in the words of one SDLP member.[4] A year later came the war over the Malvinas, during which Haughey withdrew his government's support for European Union sanctions against Argentina, outraging the British. This chilled Anglo-Irish relations for some time to come.

In the meantime, dire economic developments deepened the political gloom in Ulster. Unemployment reached levels not experienced since the 1930s. In January 1982, figures showed that 113,000 people were out of work – representing 19.7 per cent of the total adult population, the highest rate of unemployment in the United Kingdom. A month later, Harland and Wolff shipyards, traditionally one of Belfast's major employers which in the 1950s could boast 22,000 workers on its books, announced that 1,000 of the remaining 7,000 workers were to lose their jobs. On 1 March, British Enkalon closed its plant in Antrim, throwing nearly 1,000 people out of work. The company had been in Northern Ireland for decades, and as part of the artificial fibres industry was one of the 'star performers' (in the words of one economist) in the reindustrialization of the Ulster economy that had commenced under Terence O'Neill in the early 1960s. Unemployment climbed relentlessly throughout the year until 25 per cent of the adult male population were registered as out of work in September 1982.

It was not only the political violence which was affecting the province's economic fortunes. As a marginal economy, Ulster was disproportionately hurt by the international recessions of 1973 and 1979. Its traditional industries, shipbuilding and linen, were already weak, and by the early 1980s had virtually collapsed. In 1981, only 30 per cent of the workforce was employed in industry, compared to 62 in the service industries.[5] By 1985, there were more people out of work than were employed in the entire industrial sector. The only bright spot in the economy was the development of the security industry. Because of the political violence, there was a huge increase in the number of people employed in defence-related services and in the public administration needed to support them. In 1985, it was estimated that some 59,000 people, the vast majority of them Protestants, were employed in this sector (not including those in the UDR and RUC). That is, by the 1980s the Provisional IRA was, at least indirectly, keeping more Protestants in jobs than Harland and Wolff.

While Ulster's economy continued to sink, it looked as if the British government was spending its time rearranging the political deckchairs. James Prior, who became Secretary of State for the province in September 1981, launched his 'rolling devolution' plans in early 1982. These envisioned the setting up of an assembly to which powers would be gradually devolved. The SDLP showed no enthusiasm for the plan. It was, in Hume's thinking, a purely internal solution, which took no account of the broader context of the problem, involving London and Dublin. Elections for the proposed seventy-eight seat assembly took place in October 1982, and though the party ran candidates, it said they would not take their seats if elected. It meant, in effect, that Prior's plan was rolling nowhere. But the elections were notable in Northern Ireland's history as the first in which Sinn Fein put up candidates on a province-wide basis. The results stunned the Irish and British political establishments.

Sinn Fein won five seats and just over 10 per cent of the vote; the SDLP won fourteen seats, representing 18.8 per cent of the vote. In West Belfast, Gerry Adams was elected – well ahead of his SDLP rival Dr Joe Hendron, an ominous sign for the party's organization in that area. Martin McGuinness, former Chief of Staff of the Provisionals, was elected in Derry. The Ulster Unionists began to beat back Paisley's challenge for the first time in years and took almost 30 per cent of the vote and twenty-six seats – leaving Paisley's DUP with 23 per cent and twenty-one seats. But this resurgence of 'moderate' Unionism was largely ignored as the spotlight rested on the drama within the nationalist community. In a panic, some predicted that Sinn Fein was poised to overtake the SDLP. Others consoled themselves by affirming that the Provisional IRA's political wing was still exploiting a sympathy vote for the hunger strikers, which would soon fade.

The events of the following year made this explanation look less tenable. In March 1983, Sinn Fein contested local elections in Northern Ireland for the first time in fifty years and won a seat on Omagh district council in Co. Tyrone. Three months later, in the British general election, Gerry Adams was elected as MP for West Belfast, defeating veteran Gerry Fitt, who ran as an independent candidate. In Mid-Ulster, Danny Morrison, the editor of *An Phoblacht* and coiner of the 'ballot-paper in one hand and the Armalite in the other' phrase, came within seventy-eight votes of giving Sinn Fein a second seat. Had Morrison won, the IRA's political wing would have had two MPs to the SDLP's single success, John Hume. It would have scored a devastating propaganda victory, allowing it to claim to have overthrown the SDLP in only its second full-scale electoral campaign. As it was, Sinn Fein took 42 per cent of the nationalist vote. Overall, the party increased its share of the vote to 13.4 per cent (102,701 votes) from 10.1 per cent, while the SDLP's share declined to 17.9 per cent from 18.8 per cent in the previous year, though its actual vote rose somewhat compared to 1982.

Margaret Thatcher's obstinacy during the 1981 hunger strikes undoubtedly helped Sinn Fein in their electoral campaigns in the following two years. So did her insistence on removing references to closer Anglo-Irish relations in the proposals of her Secretary of State for Northern Ireland, James Prior.[6] Prior himself did not help matters when he said that his plans for the new assembly would tie Northern Ireland more closely to the United Kingdom. Thatcher would write in her autobiography, *The Downing Street Years*: 'My instincts are profoundly Unionist.' In part, the Sinn Fein vote was in reaction to this sentiment. The question was, how high would electoral support for Sinn Fein go? Neither the SDLP nor the Irish government felt that they could afford to wait around passively to find out.

2

A political machine and a killing machine were now running in tandem. The most powerful weapon in the armoury of the

Provisional IRA was surprise. It was the single advantage that compensated for the Provisionals' actual military weakness when compared to the might of the British state. And the police had only one way to counteract it – through the gathering of intelligence. If they knew what the Provisional IRA and other groups were planning to do, they could prevent it. Whoever has intelligence about an operation can control it – at least in theory. During the early years of the twilight war, when the RUC Special Branch was honing its intelligence-gathering skills, it became clear that in practice this was not so easy. There were problems in interpreting intelligence, in mounting effective responses to anticipated terrorist actions, and difficulties co-ordinating the different arms of the security forces. But results showed an overall decline in the levels of violence.

The year of the hunger strike, 1981, was a turning point in more ways than one in the Ulster conflict. It was the last year in which more than a hundred people lost their lives as a result of the political violence (101 died that year, including the 10 hunger strikers). In 1982, the figure was 97. The following year, it fell to 77. In 1984 and 1985 it stood at 64 and 54 respectively. That is, between 1981 and 1985, the yearly average was 78.6 deaths, compared to an average of 270.8 between 1971 and 1975. A marked feature of the Northern Ireland violence has always been the disparity between the numbers of military personnel killed and the number of civilians, with the latter far outnumbering the former. This disparity became even greater in the early to mid-1980s. In 1983, for example, of the 77 victims of the violence only five were serving members of the British Army, and of those the Belfast IRA, which in the early 1970s had been the most active and dangerous part of the organization, accounted for only two. The statistics were also affected by a sharp decline in the number of killings carried out by loyalists. In 1981 there were nine, in 1982 eight, in 1983 and 1984 six, and in 1985 only two.

While there were several reasons for the decline in violence, intelligence operations played a key role in bringing about this reduction, especially in Belfast, the cockpit of the conflict. The city was in the grip of the hunger strike crisis and the Provisionals and the INLA were doing all in their power to wreak havoc. But by early 1981, the RUC Special Branch had identified some of the city's top republican gunmen and operators – part of a new generation of activists who had grown up since the civil rights movement and whose childhood was overshadowed by the conflict. Among them were young men in their twenties like Bobby Storey, Dermot Finucane and Danny McCann, Provisional IRA members, and Gerard Steenson, who took over control of the INLA after the murder of the organization's Belfast O/C, Ronnie Bunting, in 1980. Finucane came from a West Belfast republican family. Two of his brothers were also active Provisionals and another, Patrick, was a well-known Belfast lawyer who specialized in defending IRA suspects. Storey had been active in the IRA since his teens, and though a suspect in several killings and bombings from 1973 onwards, always managed to slip through the police net. McCann, like Storey, already had a history of IRA involvement by the mid-1970s, when he served several periods of imprisonment. He was convicted of possession of explosives in 1983, but on his release quickly became active again, both as a gunman and as the Belfast brigades Explosives Officer.

Often the key to catching the gunman was locating the arms dump where the guns were kept. An E4A surveillance operation in the spring of 1981 had uncovered a dump used by an Active Service Unit whose leading members were Finucane and Storey. The ASU had killed a police officer in February 1981. Finucane was held and questioned about the murder but released in May. Later, police learned that he and his colleagues were planning to ambush an army patrol. By monitoring the arms dump over a period of weeks, they were able to keep track of the weapons when they were moved, and then intercept the gunmen as they tried to escape following an attempted ambush on 20 August. Storey, Finucane and a third man were arrested near the scene of the attack, in which a soldier was slightly wounded. All three were sentenced to eighteen years in jail. The removal of Storey and Finucane was a severe blow to the Belfast brigade's operations in the west of the city. (Both men later escaped. See below.)

The police enjoyed another important breakthrough which crippled several major Provisional operations in Belfast in 1981. Thanks to 'DJ' – the informer recruited in late 1979 – they had identified the route that the IRA used to get resupplies of explosives into Belfast. It ran from Co. Tyrone northeast through Antrim town – a mainly Protestant town near Lough Neagh, about thirty miles from the city. The Special Branch located the house in the town which was used as a staging post. In July 1981, they tracked a large haul of explosives from Antrim to Belfast, where they swooped, netting three top members of the Belfast Provisional IRA and five hundred pounds of explosives. In September, another attempt to resupply the Belfast units was frustrated when the police arrested a leading member of the Belfast brigade, Anthony Cahill, and more bomb-making material was found.

However, forewarned was not always forearmed, as became apparent when the police tried to counter the rising threat from the Belfast INLA. In the emotional climate of the hunger strikes, INLA attracted more recruits, teenagers and young men from the Catholic ghettoes who found its left-wing rhetoric attractive. They also found the less stable INLA afforded them more opportunities to carry out operations than the more hierarchical Provisionals. As for Steenson, a fastidious young man with a murderous streak, the most important thing was the willingness to do the job.

'He looked like an off-duty policeman,' as one RUC Special Branch officer described him. Behind the well-groomed good manners, which he invariably displayed when stopped at checkpoints, lay a ruthless operator who was not only willing to take risks himself but could inspire others to follow him. Steenson had first come to police attention when he was a teenager in 1975. He murdered the Official IRA Belfast commander Liam McMillen, and then spent four years in jail on an arms charge. He was released in April 1980.

He began killing again in December 1980, claiming two victims, one an off-duty UDR man and the other a member of the Territorial Army. By January 1981, the Special Branch had intelligence about Steenson coming from within the INLA. Yet, although E4A commanders knew in advance about INLA 'hits', they failed to prevent a whole series of attacks, which claimed the lives of several members of the security forces.[7]

One frustrating operation followed another. Meanwhile, the INLA struck again and again, sometimes rivalling the Provisionals in the number of attacks mounted in Belfast. The most embarrassing failure of all came in September 1981. Information allowed the RUC to identify the next INLA target as a twenty-year-old off-duty UDR man called Mark Stockman, who worked in Mackies, a predominantly Protestant engineering factory in West Belfast. Stockman was warned of the impending attack, but agreed to follow his normal routine, safe in the knowledge that E4A and Specialist Support Units (police officers trained in SAS-style tactics) were primed to pounce in the streets surrounding the factory. At lunch-time, Stockman was playing a game of football outside the factory, as he did every day. Steenson and several other INLA members were spotted in a nearby street and the police went after them. As they were pursuing Steenson, two gunmen walked up to Stockman and shot him dead. Two other RUC officers in a side street heard the shots and gave chase, opening fire on the gunmen. They missed and the assassins escaped.[8] Several of Steenson's unit were arrested, but he got away. He had used himself as a decoy to distract the RUC, who were covering Stockman. The repeated failure of the police to intercept Steenson led some high-ranking RUC officers to advocate the use of the more highly trained SAS in such situations. But the authorities remained reluctant to employ the fire-power of the Troop in built-up areas.

Steenson was not arrested until one of his colleagues turned 'supergrass' and began naming names, in February 1982 (see below).

Though the security forces managed to contain the upsurge in republican violence during 1981, the Provisionals still remained capable of brutal surprises. From 1981 they carried out a series of attacks on prominent people, varying their targets from politicians to paramilitaries to leading legal figures.

South Belfast Unionist MP the Rev. Robert Bradford had vehemently opposed giving any concessions to the hunger strikers. On 14 November 1981, two unknown IRA gunmen murdered him, along with Kenneth Campbell, the caretaker of the community centre where the MP held constituency meetings. The police arrived just as the gunmen escaped, almost capturing them. The fact that the republican movement was now involved in the electoral process did not stop them from attacking its very basis.

Thanks to a surveillance operation code-named Furlong, which targeted the Provisionals' intelligence-gathering cell in Belfast, police identified the next high-profile IRA target as Lenny Murphy, the most notorious loyalist killer in the history of the Troubles. Murphy, the head of the Shankill Butchers gang (see Chapter 4), had been released from prison in 1982 after serving six years for an arms offence. He quickly started up where had he left off, torturing and murdering a forty-eight-year-old Catholic, Joseph Donnegan, on 24 October 1982. The RUC learned that the Provisionals were planning to shoot him on the evening of 11 November.

Undercover officers tracked the IRA ASU into the Shankill Road, ready to strike as soon as the gunmen made their attempt, but owing to British Army activity in the area the Provisionals pulled out and the operation was abandoned. A decision was made to lift surveillance on the UVF leader. Five days later, Murphy was visiting his girlfriend when Provisional IRA gunmen shot him dead. It was another frustrating setback in the shadowy war against the paramilitaries, this time caused by poor co-ordination between undercover operations and those of the regular security forces.

Operation Furlong, however, produced results. It had uncovered a strange alliance between the Provisional IRA and certain UDA men who were passing information to republicans about fellow loyalists. The O/C of the Belfast brigade was meeting regularly with two well-known UDA men, Tommy McCreery and James Pratt Craig, in bars in downtown Belfast. Both McCreery and Craig had abandoned any pretence of being involved in paramilitary activities for anything other than personal gain. McCreery had been a close associate of UDA Vice-Chairman Tommy Herron, and may well have been involved in his murder in September 1973 (see Chapter 3). Craig, a former boxer turned UDA thug, had been released from jail in 1981 after serving a sentence for hijacking. He was a high-living criminal with a taste for leather and furs who had set up many lucrative rackets in Belfast. In return for money and other favours, McCreery and Craig gave information to the Provisionals about fellow loyalists whom they regarded as underworld rivals. McCreery became involved in an attempt to murder an IRA informer in prison in 1983 by poisoning him with arsenic, which the Provisionals' Belfast O/C provided. However, he was arrested before the plot could be executed.[9]

Operation Furlong was also crucial in uncovering a series of IRA plots against prominent legal figures in Northern Ireland between 1982 and 1983. In March 1982, gunmen tried to kill the Lord Chief Justice, Lord Lowry, as he was visiting Queen's University in South Belfast. The university, located near the city's wealthy Malone Road district, was outside the normal area of operations of republican gunmen. But following the attack on Lowry it became evident that the Provisionals had a cell operating in the university itself. Thanks to Furlong, police learned about an assassination plot against a Catholic judge, fifty-five-year-old William Doyle. The Provisionals particularly targeted Catholic members of the judiciary, believing them to be traitors to the nationalist cause. Unfortunately, the information led the police to conclude that the killers would strike as the judge left his home. On Sunday, 16 January 1983, Judge Doyle went to Mass as usual at a chapel not far from the university, having refused a police escort. He was shot dead as he left the service.[10]

The RUC believed that a university lecturer and two students were passing information to the head of the Belfast IRA, who was also the Intelligence Officer for the Northern Command. The lecturer allowed Doyle's killers use of a house on the elegant Malone Road, a few blocks from the scene of the shooting.

For their next prominent victim, the Provisionals hatched a plot as brutal as it was elaborate. Their target was another Catholic judge, Judge Kelly. A milk float would deliver a bomb to Kelly's home early in the morning. If the judge survived the blast, an ambulance coming behind the float and driven by IRA men would arrive to 'aid' the unfortunate man, but instead take him away to be finished off. One of the most prominent players in this grotesque scheme was Daniel McCann, the Belfast IRA's chief bomb-maker. The Provisionals' plans unfolded over the summer of 1983. In June two IRA members, one of them a woman, Evelyn Glenholmes, rented an apartment in a village near the judge's home. Glenholmes was a suspect in several major PIRA operations in Ireland and England. The RUC got ready to launch a counter-operation. However, the Provisionals did not strike for another two months. But when they did, the RUC had the trap ready.

As the unlikely convoy of milk float, ambulance and back-up car made its way to the target on the morning of 4 August, it 'just happened' to run into a police checkpoint. The police stopped the milk float to express their concern as to the stability of the milk crates. Much to the relief of the IRA man in the float, after a cursory glance the police waved the vehicle on, only to stop it a second time to inspect it more carefully. When the officers tired of this little jest, they seized the bomb. Two of the Belfast IRA's top gunmen, Alex Murphy and Harry Fitzsimmons, were arrested in the ambulance, disguised as medics. McCann, meanwhile, was arrested at the home of the milk float owner.[11]

The interception of the ASU had been aided by the fact that the RUC had uncovered and bugged a major Provisional explosives dump in a building at the rear of a housing development in West Belfast. A device (named after a flower) had been installed, which detected movement and alerted the police that bomb-making materials were being shifted. This in turn led the police to uncover the Provisionals' major bomb-making factory, located in a nearby glass-making works. The factory was raided and four hundred pounds of explosives recovered, packed into cylinders, apparently intended for an attack on a South Belfast RUC station. Although this was another RUC success, subsequent events demonstrated some of the difficulties of fighting a twilight war in which the need for secrecy was paramount. Three men were arrested on the premises, two of them known to the police as active Provisionals who had been frequently observed in the factory and at the explosives dump. However, the courts later freed them. The problem for the police was that the twilight war was waged mostly in secret, its participants rarely if ever identified, and its connections to other events hardly ever made public. In the case of the bomb factory, this meant that the police could not reveal in court much of the evidence they possessed without exposing a valuable on-going surveillance operation. Instead, they chose to keep that secret and continue monitoring the hide. Further successes and arrests throughout 1983 compensated them for the fact that culprits walked free.

The RUC's military role, while increasingly effective against terrorism, frequently clashed with efforts to 'normalize' its relations with the community. In 1982 a series of incidents highlighted this problem dramatically. The task of running the RUC had fallen to Jack Hermon, a burly, tough-minded fifty-year-old Ulsterman whose puritanical streak was alleviated only slightly by an appreciation of Bushmills whiskey. In January 1980 he replaced Sir Kenneth Newman as Chief Constable. Hermon, as one of the architects of the 'Ulsterization' policy, could be relied upon to see it implemented. He also boasted that he was keen to see the day dawn when the RUC could patrol the streets without needing flak jackets or weapons or a patrol of soldiers in tow. But the 'Ulsterization' policy with which Hermon was so closely identified continued to frustrate that ambition. In 1982, it led to accusations that the RUC was little better than an Ulsterized version of the SAS, as well as exposing features of the twilight war that the police would rather have kept secret.

Two separate events were involved, which nationalists claimed proved that the police was pursuing a 'shoot-to-kill' policy. The first had its genesis in a surveillance operation on a Provisional IRA explosives dump in a hay shed near Lurgan, Co. Armagh. In spite of it being covered, the Provisional IRA managed to retrieve the explosives and use them for a land-mine that killed three RUC men on 27 October 1982. Fifteen days later, three unarmed members of the IRA, Eugene Toman, Sean Burns and Gervaise McKerr, were shot dead. A Special Support Unit – a squad of heavily armed RUC men used to back up surveillance operations – was responsible. They claimed that they had fired at the IRA men's car after it had crashed through a checkpoint. But forensic tests indicated that the victims had been shot after their car came to a halt.

On 24 November, undercover RUC men opened fire on the hut from which the explosives had been taken, killing a seventeen-year-old Catholic, Michael Tighe, who it soon emerged had no connection with the Provisional IRA. Along with a friend who survived the shooting, he had stumbled haplessly on a covert operation.

The next sequence of events involved the INLA. As one of the organization's most dangerous activists, Gerard Steenson, was going behind bars in February 1982, Dominic McGlinchey was being freed. McGlinchey had been a member of the Provisional IRA but switched to the INLA while in jail in the Irish Republic. He was a volatile character, cunning, manipulative and violent, who had operated with such figures as Martin McGuinness and Francis Hughes, the South Derry IRA man who died on hunger strike shortly after Bobby Sands. He once boasted to an Irish reporter that he had murdered at least thirty people. The press nicknamed him 'Mad Dog'. In 1982, he became Operations Officer on INLA's GHQ Staff. On 6 December that year, an INLA bomb, consisting of ten pounds of Frangex explosive stolen from a silver mine in the Irish Republic, exploded at a pub and disco frequented by off-duty British soldiers from an army base in Ballykelly, Co. Derry. It killed seventeen people, eleven of them soldiers, and four of them young women whom the INLA in a follow-up statement contemptuously referred to as 'consorts'. McGlinchey became the most wanted man in Ireland.

An informer told the RUC that McGlinchey was in Armagh in the company of Seamus Grew and Roddy Carroll, both active INLA members. Carroll had been involved in several operations with Steenson in 1981, and Grew came from a family of republican activists.[12] Grew and Carroll were shot dead after passing a checkpoint near Armagh on 12 December. They were unarmed. Officers of the same Special Support Unit were involved, and again they advanced similar claims to those made after the shooting of McKerr, Toman and Burns. They asserted that the suspects had run through a checkpoint. And yet again forensic evidence contradicted important aspects of the police version of events. Grew was shot four times from a distance of between thirty and thirty-five inches as he lay outside the car.

The three incidents provoked an outcry in the Catholic community, prompting allegations that the RUC was pursuing a 'shoot-to-kill' policy and was involved in an elaborate cover-up to hide the truth of what had happened. Pressure mounted on the Chief Constable, Jack Hermon, to have the officers involved prosecuted on murder charges. An internal RUC investigation into the incidents led to a recommendation that one of the officers be charged with murder. Hermon firmly rejected it. He secretly argued that such a hearing would expose vital aspects of police undercover operations, and put informers at risk. Meanwhile, the Northern Ireland Director of Public Prosecutions ignored Hermon's objections. Four RUC men were charged with murder. Their acquittal, in the spring of 1984, provoked another outcry and a demand for an outside investigation.[13] To the dismay and disgust of the Special Branch, the demand was met. John Stalker, Deputy Chief Constable of Greater Manchester, was appointed to head the investigation.

Stalker arrived in Belfast in May 1984. Though he had spent most of his police life as a detective, he was despised within Special Branch circles because he did not have the kind of operational experience they thought would be needed to comprehend the nature of the problem the RUC faced. One high-ranking Special Branch officer, when asked what he would do if he met Stalker, said: 'I'd punch him.' Jack

Hermon was alleged to have said to him: 'Remember, Mr Stalker, you are in a jungle now.'[14]

Their fears that Stalker would expose too much were borne out when very early on his inquiry disclosed that MI5 had bugged the hay shed in which explosives were hidden and Michael Tighe shot dead. This was the first time that such details about MI5's role in Northern Ireland were made public. RUC resistance to the inquiry mounted. Stalker complained that files he wanted went missing or were handed over late. Nationalists saw this as evidence that the Special Branch were concealing evidence of a 'shoot-to-kill' policy. In fact, the police reaction stemmed largely from the inherent reluctance of the Special Branch – a closely knit élite within the force – to share information with anyone, including other police departments and MI5.

Stalker was removed from the inquiry in May 1986 to face disciplinary charges relating to his relationship with a Manchester businessman – charges of which he was later acquitted. It was taken over by Colin Sampson, Chief Constable of the West Yorkshire police force, who was also put in charge of the investigation into Stalker. The report of the Sampson–Stalker investigation was never made public for reasons of 'national security', but two high-ranking Special Branch officers involved in the 1982 shootings were suspended from duty, pending further enquiries.

Stalker had some harsh words for the RUC, especially in connection with the shooting of Tighe and the attempt to cover it up, which he described as the act of a 'police force out of control'.[15] But he also said that he had found no evidence of a 'shoot-to-kill' policy. Some RUC officers undoubtedly thought that there should have been. One Special Branch Superintendent who played a leading role in the undercover war in the 1990s, when confronted with allegations that there was a shoot-to-kill policy, used to joke: 'I wish.' The truth was that in the vast majority of cases, during which the police surveillance teams had paramilitary activists under prolonged observation or when police antiterrorist units intercepted paramilitary operations, there were no fatalities. As evidence, the statistics show that the RUC was responsible for only fifty-three deaths between 1969 and 1999 – by far the lowest total attributed to any of the different organizations involved in the conflict, and a tiny minority of the well over three thousand violent deaths that occurred during that period. Eighteen of those fifty-three were acknowledged as members of the IRA, INLA, UDA or UVF.[16] The 1982 incidents were the exception to this rule. Had there been a shoot-to-kill policy then there surely would have been far more deaths at police hands.

Because of the controversy surrounding the shootings and the inquiry, a decision was taken to reduce the role of the police antiterrorist units in situations where they were forced to confront the IRA; instead, the SAS's role was to be increased a role which provoked its own bitter allegations about a 'shoot-to-kill' policy. Some RUC officers had advocated this move all along. Not only is SAS training superior to that of the police, but soldiers do not have to live in the community where they are stationed and are returned to Britain after their tour of duty is finished. Any police officer, exposed during a trial because of incidents like those that occurred in late 1982, is placed in a grave situation, and might become the target of paramilitaries thirsting for revenge.

There were other consequences of the 'Stalker Affair', as it became known. The INLA's Dominic 'Mad Dog' McGlinchey went on a tout hunt to find the informer that had attempted to set him up in late 1982. Suspicion fell on Eric Dale, a forty-three-year-old republican who lived across the border in Co. Monaghan. On the night that Drew and Carroll were shot dead, Dale had been detailed to provide a car for them to ferry McGlinchey from the Irish Republic into Northern Ireland. Dale failed to show up, getting drunk instead with a well-known republican, George Poyntz, who owned a pub in

Castleblayney. The pub was a haunt for both the Provisional IRA and the INLA. On 3 May 1983 Dale was taken from his home and tortured for several days, during which a hot poker was thrust under his armpit. It was hardly surprising that he 'confessed' to being an informer. He was 'executed', his body dumped in South Armagh. It was after this that George Poyntz suddenly disappeared, showing up later in Northern Ireland, where it was revealed that he had been working for the police for many years. Republicans, including Bernadette McAliskey, were stunned. McAliskey had long known him and had stayed at his home on occasion.[17]

Shortly after the hunger strike ended, the Provisionals resumed their bombing campaign in Britain, killing a bomb disposal expert in Oxford Street, London, on 26 October. In July 1982, a double bomb attack in Hyde Park killed eleven soldiers, including six bandsmen and five members of the regimental cavalry, along with their horses. One of the IRA's biggest propaganda coups came a year later. On Friday, 23 September 1983, the Special Branch learned that a jail break was 'imminent'. Unfortunately for them, the information was not precise enough to enable them to launch a counter-operation. Under the leadership of Bobby Storey and six others – Gerry Kelly, serving life for bombing London in 1973, Brendan 'Bik' McFarlane, Gerry McDonnell, Padraig McKearney, Kieran Fleming and Tony McAllister – the prisoners planned to take over an entire block of the supposedly escape-proof prison H-7, which held 125 men.[18] The original break-out had been scheduled for 18 September, but was postponed for one week. Thirty-eight Provisionals were chosen. Twenty-five of those picked were Belfast activists and twenty-eight were serving life sentences for murder. Plans had been under way for a year, masterminded by Larry Marley, an Ardoyne IRA man nicknamed the Wee Devil. He had broken out of different jails on two occasions and had a reputation as an escape artist. Because of his escape attempts he earned another nickname – Papillon. But when the time came for Marley's most grandiose escape plan to be put into action, he stayed behind, having only two years left to serve in prison.

The thirty-eight Provisionals took command of H-7 on late Sunday afternoon, 25 September. Some disguised themselves as prison officers and hijacked a food truck which took them to the main gate.[19] There, things went wrong, however, and nineteen were recaptured almost immediately. The others got away after a chaotic chase. The Army Council regarded it as a great success – it was the biggest break-out in the IRA's history. Many of those who remained free were among the organization's most valuable operators. They included Dermot Finucane, Gerry Kelly and Gerry McDonnell from Belfast, Padraig McKearney and Seamus McElwaine from Counties Tyrone and Monaghan.[20]

The Provisionals came close to effecting an even more stunning propaganda blow against the state the following year. The hunger strikes had made Thatcher into the figure the republican movement hated most. In 1988, Gerry Adams said of her: 'She will be remembered when even some of the names of the hunger strikers are forgotten. All the six- and seven-year-olds have the memory of Thatcher in their heads.'[21] In 1984, the Provisionals evolved a plot to kill her.

On 15 September 1984, a man called Roy Walsh checked into the Grand Hotel in Brighton, on England's south coast. He stayed for three days in Room 629 and was not much noticed – nor did anyone realize that the name he signed in under was that of a Provisional IRA man arrested and jailed in England in connection with the 1973 London bombings. Patrick Magee, the man's real name, was playing a little joke. Magee was a thirty-three-year-old Belfast IRA man who had taken part in one bombing campaign in England in 1978. He was wanted in connection with an arms find there in 1983, along with another prominent IRA activist, Evelyn Glenholmes.

When Magee checked out on 18 September, he left behind a bomb thickly wrapped in cellophane, weighing between twenty and thirty pounds, in the wall of the bathroom of Room 629. It had a long-delay timer like those used in video recorders; it was set to explode at 2.54 a.m on Friday, 12 October. That day, Thatcher would be in the hotel along with most of her Cabinet, attending the Conservative Party's annual conference.

On the morning of 12 October, Jennifer Taylor, who was staying at the Grand Hotel with her husband Eric, was falling asleep at around 2 a.m. 'The next thing I remember is a loud bang. I was lifted upwards and then had the sensation of falling and falling. When I finished falling I opened my eyes believing I had been dreaming but I couldn't see anything. My eyes slowly cleared and I found myself sitting on the ground. I saw a wall and a light to my left about four feet away. There was debris all around me – a stainless-steel sink, girders, bricks and water, and lots of smoke and dust.'[22] Her husband was killed in his sleep, along with four others, including an MP, Sir Anthony Berry. One woman who died, Mrs Jeanne Shattock, was preparing to take a bath in Room 628, and was cut to pieces with shards of tile. The blast brought a massive chimney crashing through the twenty-eight rooms below, narrowly missing Mrs Thatcher, who emerged shaken but uninjured.

The Provisionals quickly claimed responsibility for the attempted assassination. They ended their statement with a warning: 'Today, we were unlucky, but remember, we only have to be lucky once – you will have to be lucky always. Give Ireland peace and there will be no war.'[23]

The RUC's top priority was to catch the Brighton bomber. A fingerprint found on the hotel registration card identified Magee as the man who had checked into Room 629 on 15 September. The problem was finding him.

In May 1985, RUC Special Branch in Belfast learned two

things – one, that the IRA was planning another series of bomb attacks in Britain, and two, that it wanted to smuggle someone, identity unknown, into Britain. A leading member of the Belfast IRA was involved in making the arrangements. After some confusion the police identified the unknown as Peter Sherry from Dungannon – a prominent member of Sinn Fein and the commander of the East Tyrone Provisional IRA, one of the most violent of the IRA's brigades. Sherry was known as a marksman and was suspected of involvement in many murders and attempted murders.

Sherry was eventually tracked to Carlisle railway station, where the police watched as a man approached him. They recognized him as Patrick Magee, the Brighton bomber. Sherry and Magee took the train to Glasgow. The Brighton bomber was later trapped in a house by twenty-two police officers, most of them armed. When it was raided, they found Magee, Sherry and Gerry McDonnell, the Maze escapee, who was commander of the IRA's bombing operation in England. Along with him were two young women, Martina Anderson, a former beauty queen from Derry, and Ella O'Dwyer, a middle-class student from Dublin. McDonnell was found with a set of plans to bomb eleven seaside resorts and the Hotel Rubens near Buckingham Palace in London. As with the Grand Hotel bomb, the devices had long-delay timers. The first was due to explode in over a month on 29 July at 1300 hours.

All were convicted of conspiring to cause explosions, and Magee was also convicted of the murders of five people at the Grand Hotel. He was sentenced to eight life sentences. The judge commented: 'You intended to wipe out a large part of the government and you very nearly did.'[24] The Provisionals took that as an unintended compliment. But the arrest of Magee, Sherry and McDonnell was a demoralizing blow and a bad setback for the IRA's bombing campaign in England.

The occasional 'spectacular' operation, like the 'great escape' or Brighton bombing, could not disguise the fact that many crucial operations were being intercepted and as a result the level of violence was dropping considerably. Sectarian attacks by the UDA and UVF fell considerably between 1981 and 1985, and the nature of their targets changed somewhat. While the majority of the victims were still ordinary Catholics, often picked at random, the UDA and UVF began to have some success in targeting members of the republican movement. One of the most notable attacks came in February 1981, when a lone UVF gunman broke into the home of IRA man James Burns and shot him dead. Burns, a close ally of Adams, had been the quartermaster for the Northern Command. As Sinn Fein became more active, it provided loyalists with ready targets. Two members of the party were shot dead in 1982 and another in 1984. Loyalists almost pulled off their own 'spectacular' on 14 March 1984. As Gerry Adams and several colleagues drove through central Belfast, three UDA gunmen pulled alongside their vehicle and sprayed it with bullets. The Provisional leader was in the front passenger seat. He felt the thumps as four of the twenty rounds that smashed into the car hit him. 'So this is what it's like,' he thought. Everyone in the car was wounded. Adams was surprised to find he was still alive when the shooting stopped.[25] Undercover RUC men chased the gunmen, who ran into another car driven by an off-duty UDR man.[26] All three were arrested. One of them had been accidentally shot by a colleague and was bleeding badly.

Between 1982 and 1986 violence went into a sharp decline. The successes of undercover police operations were not the only cause. Police began to 'turn' paramilitaries, who after their arrests agreed to give evidence against their former colleagues. They were known as 'supergrasses', who in return for leniency and financial rewards named names. Though paramilitaries had been 'turned' before, it was not until 1982 that this became an important weapon in the war against terrorism.[27] For the next few years it became the main weapon. Altogether, there were some thirty supergrasses between 1981 and 1983, leading to the arrests of three hundred people, most of them from Belfast. It was as many as were held after the first internment swoops. A special wing of Crumlin Road prison, where suspects were incarcerated pending trial, was set aside to accommodate the supergrasses. Rumours spread about the privileges they enjoyed, including access to drink, drugs and women. The defendants appeared *en masse* in the dock, which led to civil rights and pro-republican groups denouncing the trials as 'show trials'. There were several mass convictions. The most successful supergrasses, in terms of sheer numbers of arrests, were Christopher Black, a member of the North Belfast Provisional IRA, and Harry Kirkpatrick, a petty criminal and henchman of Gerard Steenson, the INLA leader. Black's testimony led to the conviction of thirty-eight people, and Kirkpatrick's convicted twenty-four including Steenson, who received a life sentence after the judge declared him an 'enemy of society'.[28] According to police, thanks to Black's confessions only four active IRA men were left in North Belfast. The statements of two loyalist supergrasses, Joseph Bennett and William 'Budgie' Allen, led to the arrests of many UVF men.

Thirteen supergrasses retracted their evidence before trial. Meanwhile, there was genuine disquiet among civil rights groups and lawyers about convictions obtained solely on the word of a convicted criminal, without any corroborating evidence. The judgments handed down thanks to the evidence of the other supergrasses did not hold. By December 1986 nearly all the convictions, including those in the Black and Kirkpatrick cases, had been overturned on appeal.

Though the use of such evidence gave genuine cause for unease, its crippling impact on the paramilitary organizations was undeniable, as the decline in violence indicates.

As the twilight war was being waged behind the scenes, the

political struggle for the hearts and minds of the nationalist voters took on a sudden urgency. Sinn Fein's challenge to the SDLP would prove more of a spur to the Irish and British governments than the IRA's faltering campaign. It convinced them to launch the most daring political initiative that Northern Ireland had seen in over a decade.

3

Following the assembly elections in 1982, the SDLP sought support in the Irish Republic for establishing a Council of Ireland in which all parties – barring those committed to violence – could discuss the issue of Ulster, and how to find a way of incorporating Unionist identity into a new Ireland. This idea soon blossomed into the New Ireland Forum, with the backing of the recently elected Irish Taoiseach, Dr Garrett Fitzgerald. The aim was to produce proposals to encourage the British to reopen the Anglo-Irish process, which Hume held was the key to resolving the conflict. It was in reality an attempt to counteract the growth of Sinn Fein, as Fitzgerald admits. 'I had come to the conclusion', he wrote in his autobiography *All in a Life*, 'that I must now give priority to heading off the growth of support for the IRA in Northern Ireland by seeking a new understanding with the British government . . .' In the aftermath of Adams's victory in the June 1983 general election, Fitzgerald went to Thatcher to impress upon her the urgency of the situation.

'I had a meeting with Dr Fitzgerald at the European Council at Stuttgart in June 1983,' wrote the British Prime Minister. 'I shared the worry he expressed about the erosion of SDLP support by Sinn Fein. However uninspiring SDLP politicians might be – at least since the departure of the courageous Gerry Fitt – they were the minority's main representative and an alternative to the IRA. They had to be wooed.'[29] It would prove to be a very stormy courtship, with the SDLP often playing the role of the scorned suitor. But because it was a courtship based on political expediency, it would have a happy outcome.

The Unionists refused to take part in the proceedings of the New Ireland Forum, though two party members of the younger generation, Chris and Michael McGimpsey, with a more liberal, intellectual background, did make the journey south to give the Northern Protestant angle, and later claimed that what they said was ignored.[30] Protestants were, as ever, sceptical about the participants' claims to be forging a new, 'pluralist' Ireland, where their identity and traditions would have a place. Their scepticism was heightened due to the fact that the Forum's deliberations were going on against the background of the Irish Republic's abortion referendum, which brought to the surface the deeply conservative strain of Catholicism in Irish life. An overwhelming majority voted in September 1983 to enshrine the state's anti-abortion law as part of the Constitution, reinforcing Protestant fears that south of the border Rome still ruled.

The New Ireland Forum produced a series of study papers and a report in May 1984. It criticized British government policy in Northern Ireland as being one merely of 'crisis management' and sounded a note of desperation: 'The situation is daily growing more dangerous. Constitutional politics are on trial and unless there is action soon to create a framework in which constitutional politics can work, the drift into more extensive civil conflict is in danger of becoming irreversible . . .'[31]

Its conclusions were for the most part unsurprising. They posed three different solutions to the Ulster crisis: a unitary state, joint rule from Dublin and London, and a federal/confederal structure. The preferred option was, of course, the first. But the report's emphasis upon it tended to distract attention from the fact that constitutional nationalists were prepared to accept joint authority – a compromise of their historic aim. However, Thatcher's response made the matter academic. The report was presented to her at the Anglo-Irish conference in November 1984. The timing was, to say the least, unpropitious, being just over a month since the Provisional IRA, also in pursuit of a unitary state, had almost murdered her and her entire Cabinet. At a press conference with Fitzgerald, the Iron Lady lived up to her reputation as she responded to the three options: 'A united Ireland was one solution. That is out. A second solution was confederation of the two states. That is out. A third solution was joint authority. That is out. That is a derogation from sovereignty.' Fitzgerald called her reaction 'gratuitously offensive'.[32] It would not have helped matters had he been aware that at the time Thatcher was privately discussing the possibility of another solution – repartition, and the moving of hundreds of thousands of Catholics from Northern Ireland to the South, which has been called a form of 'ethnic cleansing without the bloodshed'.[33] It was one more indication of her alarmingly uncertain grasp of Ulster realities.

Thatcher's reaction to the New Ireland Forum report became known as the 'out, out, out' speech. It was a humiliating blow to the efforts of the constitutional nationalists to offer a convincing response to Sinn Fein. However, because of John Hume and the Irish government's patient cultivation of American support, other resources were at hand to set Anglo-Irish relations back on course. Thatcher was due to visit Washington in the wake of her 'out, out, out' remarks. She was scheduled to speak before the joint houses of Congress in February 1985. Hume's congressional watchdog, the Speaker 'Tip' O'Neill, forewarned Thatcher that her reaction to the Forum report made it difficult for him to offer her such a platform. At the same time, the Irish utilized an even more powerful channel.

President Ronald Reagan was a close ally of Thatcher's and emulated her brand of free-market economics. In return for her practical and ideological support, Reagan relentlessly hounded IRA supporters in the US and initiated a series of extradition hearings against IRA men who had fled to the US.[34] In early 1985, he was persuaded to step into the Anglo-Irish dispute by one of his advisers, Bill Clark, who was a close friend of the former Irish ambassador to Washington, Sean Donlon. Donlon had returned to Ireland in 1981 to become the Secretary of the Department of Foreign Affairs, but had kept up contacts with his friends in the administration to make sure they were informed of developments in the Irish question. Reagan called Thatcher about the matter and later praised the Forum's work as 'courageous and forthright'. When Thatcher came to Washington in December, Reagan raised the Northern Ireland issue and 'stressed the need for progress and the need for all parties concerned to take steps which will contribute to a peaceful resolution of the existing problems'.[35] From then on, Thatcher sounded a much more conciliatory note, and when speaking before Congress was fulsome in her praise for Garrett Fitzgerald and his efforts to reach a settlement.

Within months, the British and Irish governments were locked in secret negotiations as rumours spread about a new Ulster initiative. Just what shape it would take was a matter of wild speculation throughout the summer of 1985. Joint authority was the favourite guess, and indeed was in line with the Irish government's own expectations. Though it fell far short of this, when it was revealed in November 1985 the Anglo-Irish Agreement proved to be a landmark in Ulster's history.

It accommodated many of the ideas that Hume had long been seeking to establish as working principles in the search for a solution. There was a formal recognition of the right of the majority to remain part of the UK as long as they wished. The agreement set up an intergovernmental conference to meet on a regular basis and deal with a range of matters relating to politics, security and the administration of justice. It gave the Irish government a direct role in Northern Ireland for the first time as guarantor for Northern Irish nationalists' rights. To exercise this function, an Irish Secretariat was to be set up in Maryfield just outside Belfast, staffed by Irish civil servants. It established parity of esteem between Protestant and Catholic traditions. And it provided for a devolved government on the basis of 'widespread agreement within Northern Ireland' – which was shorthand for power-sharing. It contained as well a transatlantic dimension with President Reagan and 'Tip' O'Neill issuing a joint statement on the day the agreement was signed, promising US financial support for the areas most affected by the violence.

When the Anglo-Irish Agreement was signed on 15 November 1985, the SDLP and the Irish government regarded it as a triumph. According to Hume it was not a solution to the Ulster crisis, but the framework within which such a solution could be worked out. He wrote later. 'When history is written, the Anglo-Irish Agreement will be seen to have been the first major step in the current peace process.'[36]

The agreement presented problems for both Unionists and republicans. The Unionists had not taken part in the negotiations that led up to the 15 November accord and were deeply perturbed at what they saw as a weakening of the British parliament's claim to sovereignty over Northern Ireland. Britain's link now depended on the will of the majority within the Northern Irish state, not on any active desire on the part of Britain as a sovereign power to maintain that link. However, it was simply making explicit what had been the case for a long time. Over the years, British politicians would occasionally let the truth slip out, as the first Labour Party Northern Ireland Secretary of State, Merlyn Rees, did when he once said 'we have not the faintest desire to stay in Ireland and the quicker we are out the better'.[37] Now an international agreement formalized that position.

During a two-day debate on the agreement in the House of Commons at the end of November, Ulster Unionist Party leader James Molyneaux predicted: 'The agreement will not bring peace, but a sword . . . I have to say honestly and truthfully that in 40 years in public life I have never known what I can only describe as a universal cold fury which some of us have thus far managed to contain.'[38] Unionists launched an 'Ulster Says No' campaign to try to overturn the agreement, as they had the Sunningdale Agreement in 1974, holding massive protest rallies.

The republican response was more uncertain. They denounced the agreement as 'copper-fastening partition' and emphasized its security aspect, which promised greater co-operation between the RUC and the Irish police. Yet they realized that the recognition of the Irish government's relation to Northern Irish nationalists was a real step forward. Sinn Fein began to claim that if any benefits accrued from the agreement it was because of the IRA and Sinn Fein, since fear of republican militancy had forced Britain to make this concession. But the agreement's assertion that the link between Northern Ireland and Britain depended on the popular will was as much anathema to Sinn Fein as it was to Unionists. It contradicted the republican claim that British imperialism maintained Ulster. On this rested the whole justification for their armed campaign.

Adams had been elected President of Sinn Fein in 1983, in the euphoria surrounding the party's electoral success, ousting the old guard of O Bradaigh and O Conaill. Both the military and political wings were now in the hands of Northerners. But by the time the Anglo-Irish Agreement was signed, in November 1985, that euphoria was fast disappearing. The party received a setback in 1984, during the European parliamentary elections, when its candidate, Danny Morrison, came in far behind John Hume, receiving 91,476 votes to Hume's 151,399. The next year, Ruairi O Bradaigh's prediction that Sinn Fein would overtake the SDLP at the local level proved to be over-optimistic when the party won

59 seats on local councils to the SDLP's 101. Republican leaders were beginning to accept that as long as the Provisionals were engaged in a violent campaign then there was going to be a limit to the amount of political support their party could expect. For the first time, Sinn Fein leaders began to criticize, at least obliquely, IRA actions, calling for a 'controlled' and 'disciplined' use of force. Following the setbacks of 1984 and 1985, the criticisms became more frequent. Warned Adams: 'There is [sic] a number of people who while they voted for us in June 1983, may not have been able to tolerate some aspects of IRA operations in which civilians were killed or injured.'

In August 1985, at the very moment that Republican leaders were revaluing their attitude toward political violence, a huge shipment of arms arrived from Libya. It was the first, but it would not be the last. The Provisional IRA was now better armed than at any time in its history.

CHAPTER SIX

Gaddafi's Gift: 1985–90

1

International events are not usually seen as helping to shape the Ulster crisis, which of all the world's trouble spots is usually regarded as among the most local and immune from outside influence. The right-wing rhetoric of the Thatcher–Reagan era, with its talk of international terrorist conspiracies, was singularly inappropriate when viewed from the market towns of East Tyrone or the alleyways of Belfast, where people needed to go no further than the next field or street to explain the sources of their conflict. However, the Cold War and the situation in the Middle East had a direct impact on what happened in Ulster, most profoundly in 1985, when the Libyan dictator Colonel Gaddafi's intervention may well have changed the course of the crisis.

The Middle East and Eastern bloc were already playing a role in the conflict. The INLA had received many of its weapons and explosives from the A1 Fatah wing of the PLO. PLO officers trained INLA activists in the Bekka Valley in Lebanon, as they did members of the Provisional IRA. In the 1980s, PLO safe houses in Prague and East Berlin were made available to the INLA as it arranged for arms shipments via eastern Europe through Paris to Ireland.[1]

In 1972, Libya supplied the Provisionals with a shipment of RPG-7 rockets, a deal that Joe Cahill helped arrange (see Chapter 3). A subsequent attempt to ship arms from Tripoli in March 1973 failed, with Cahill, then Chief of Staff, caught red-handed on board the ship with a huge arms haul. Another effort failed four years later.

As relations between the US, Great Britain and Libya deteriorated throughout the mid-1980s, an offer came from Gaddafi that would dwarf all previous Arab contributions to Irish republicans. A Libyan contact approached a member of the INLA Army Council, arranging to meet him in Malta. When the INLA leader arrived, the Libyan said he had an arms offer to make. 'How much?' the Irishman asked. 'How big a ship do you have?' the contact replied. He was talking in tons. There was so much being offered that the INLA had to refuse – it simply could not have absorbed it all.

In the meantime, Libya was spreading its largesse elsewhere.

Between August 1985 and September 1986, Gaddafi shipped approximately 150 tons of weapons and explosives to the Provisional IRA in Ireland. There were four shipments. The first arrived in August 1985, the second in October that year. Following the US bombing of Tripoli in April 1986, there were two more – one in July, and the other in September. The US used British airbases to launch its strikes, so Gaddafi decided to punish Thatcher, Reagan's closest ally. 'The Arabs were ready to give you anything. You could have gotten anything you wanted then,' according to a high-ranking INLA member.

Another shipment comprising 150 tons on the *Eksund* was dispatched in October 1987. But this one was intercepted by French authorities off the coast of Brittany on 1 November.[2]

The police estimated that the Provisionals received more than a thousand AK-47 rifles, a million rounds of ammunition, a dozen surface-to-air missiles, large quantities of handguns, Russian-made heavy machineguns, and four tons of Semtex plastic explosive. Colourless, odourless and malleable, Semtex can be moulded into almost any shape, from a bar of soap to a box of chocolates; it would soon figure prominently in the IRA's bombing campaign. A piece of republican graffiti that appeared on a wall near the Falls Road declared with hate-filled Belfast humour: '*IRA Recent Survey Shows Semtex Is Killing More Germs Than Vortex . . . Ha Ha*'. (Vortex is a well-known household drain cleaner.)

When the size of the shipment became known, a frightened Irish government minister said that the IRA now threatened 'the very existence of the state'.

The huge influx of weapons, the largest the IRA had ever received, affected the organization at every level. According to one Belfast Provisional IRA man: 'After the Libyan arms came in, volunteers were handed an AK-47 for a job which usually required only a pistol and told they could have 100 lbs. of Semtex for bombs.'[3] At a political level, it prolonged the dual strategy of ballot and bullet, and led the Army Council to believe that the IRA could score a significant military breakthrough that would end the political deadlock. At this time, a new Chief of Staff took over – Kevin McKenna, from Tyrone. The RUC claimed he had been active in the border areas from the 1970s, and they linked him to twenty murders. According to a senior republican, McKenna was given a 'carte blanche' to conduct the war.[4]

The Provisionals were not only better equipped than ever, thanks to Gaddafi, but they had also developed their own do-it-yourself terrorist technology. In the mid-1980s they constructed a mortar capable of hurling a forty-pound bomb over the protective walls of security bases and RUC stations. On 28 February 1985, a mortar attack on Newry police station in South Down struck a busy canteen and killed nine constables, two of them women, the largest loss of life the RUC ever suffered in one incident. One of the ASUs involved came from

South Armagh, which had a reputation for harbouring the IRA's most effective units.

The well-armed ASUs launched a series of attacks on small, isolated RUC stations, in a campaign mainly concentrated in East Tyrone. They hoped thus to duplicate the IRA's successes in the 1919–21 War of Independence, when they forced the police to abandon their garrisons in nationalist areas of the Irish countryside. East Tyrone seems an unlikely setting for a brutal conflict that was part civil war, part political terrorism. It is a rural patchwork of Catholic and Protestant districts, mostly small farms and dull market towns, a featureless landscape bounded on its northern side by the Sperrin Mountains and to the east by the flat expanse of Lough Neagh, the biggest lake in the British Isles.

In December 1985, Provisionals killed two RUC men at a base in Ballygawley, Co. Tyrone. They then left a bomb which devastated the building. An ASU consisting of up to thirty-five men demolished another at the Birches, near Portadown, using a mechanical digger loaded with a bomb to crash through the building's defences. It was one of sixteen bases hit in a period of just over a year, at a cost to the British government of £150 million. Only one was ever reopened. As part of this campaign, the Provisionals murdered building contractors who repaired the damaged buildings. Seamus McAvoy, a successful Co. Tyrone businessman who lived in a middle-class area of Dublin, was the first to be targeted. He was shot dead outside his home on 20 August 1985. His crime: he supplied Portakabins to the police.[5] On 21 November, six days after the Anglo-Irish Agreement was signed, the Provisionals shot dead Kurt Konig, a German building contractor, at his home in Derry. Within days of his death, it was revealed that some three hundred building workers had been laid off work because their firms were refusing to carry out jobs on behalf of the security forces owing to threats made against them. In East Tyrone, the campaign against building contractors took on a particularly vicious character. Late on the night of 21 April 1987, IRA gunmen burst into the home of Harold Henry, who with his brother James ran a building firm that specialized in doing repair work for the police and army. Five IRA men dragged him outside in his stockinged feet, put him up against a wall and shot him in the head.[6]

A few days later, the South Armagh Provisionals exploded a huge bomb near the main road across the border as seventy-four-year-old Chief Justice Maurice Gibson and his sixty-seven-year-old wife Cecily drove past on their way from Dublin to Belfast. (It was Gibson who had congratulated an RUC officer involved in a controversial shoot-to-kill incident in 1982 on his marksmanship. See Chapter 5.) The assassination put further pressure on the RUC to do something to counter the upsurge in Provisional IRA violence.

An opportunity came when police received information from a complex surveillance operation to the effect that the Provisionals were planning another 'spectacular' like that which destroyed the Ballygawley and Birches RUC bases. Their target was a small RUC station in Loughgall, just across the Armagh border. The information came from a surveillance operation directed at Jim Lynagh. Lynagh, at thirty-one years old, was the Provisional IRA's commander in charge of all cross-border operations in the Monaghan–Armagh region. A former Sinn Fein councillor, he was known to the local Irish police as the 'Executioner'.[7] The RUC connected him with about a dozen murders. Loughgall had little or no security significance, but in terms of loyalist mythology it was the holiest of holies. In 1795 the Orange Order was founded there to counter rising republican militancy. Loyalists would view a successful IRA attack in Loughgall as a desecration. To counter it, a complex operation code-named Judy was mounted involving undercover soldiers, surveillance police, UDR and heavily armed RUC Headquarters Mobile Support Units (HMSUs).

Four cut-off groups of SAS men were placed outside the station, hidden in the hedges, and one group inside, along with three policemen who had volunteered to man the station to make it look normal. There were other observation groups and surveillance units covering all approaches to the area. HMSU patrols were hiding in hedgerows in a lane just outside the village to block any attempted escape by the ASU. Amazingly, the Provisionals failed to detect any of the considerable amount of security force activity in the area throughout that day.

It was a well-laid trap, and at around 7.20 p.m. on the evening of 8 May the Provisionals' eight-man ASU clad in blue boiler suits and Balaclavas drove right into it.

The ASU arrived in a blue Hiace van, which scouted the village before coming to a halt near the entrance to the station. Two gunmen got out, walked up the road a little and began firing at the target. A mechanical digger with a bomb in the bucket came rumbling down the road, turned and crashed through the high wire fence surrounding the station. One of the two Provisionals in the digger's cabin lit the bomb's fuse. The device, of between three and four hundred pounds, exploded, turning one side of the station into a pile of rubble and lifting off the roof. Other members of the ASU began scrambling out of the van, intending to rake the damaged building with automatic fire. Jim Lynagh was accompanied by Paddy Kelly, the O/C of the East Tyrone Provisionals, Paddy McKearney, who had escaped from the Maze in 1983, Declan Arthurs and Eugene Kelly, all of whom had been in the back of the vehicle. Suddenly, they were enfiladed with heavy fire. In the words of one officer who was there, they were 'totally shocked at such a reception'.[8] The SAS emitted a sustained fusillade from two general-purpose machineguns, Heckler and Koch high-velocity rifles and Browning pistols. Fire came from the side of the road, the station itself, and a nearby wood.

The machineguns hit the driver of the van, Seamus Donnelly, and blew off his head. Kelly returned fire, and was into his second magazine before he was riddled, near the door of the van. Lynagh and McKearney climbed back into the van for cover, but it was futile as its walls were perforated with bullets from all sides. When one of them moved suddenly, wounded and dying, an SAS soldier finished him off with a final shot (though at the inquest, not held until May 1995, the soldier described it as a 'warning shot'). Arthurs and Eugene Kelly were killed trying to find cover at the side of the van. Tony Gormley, one of the two men in the digger, shouted 'I'm a Special Branch source'. But this did not save him. He died alongside the others, still holding what appeared to be a detonator in his hand. Not far away, two brothers, Anthony and Oliver Hughes, also dressed in overalls, drove into the ambush. Anthony was killed and his brother seriously wounded. Another innocent bystander, a Guinness sales representative, stumbled into the jaws of death and found himself being chased towards a nearby house where the SAS trooper was about to shoot him, before hesitating because the suspect was respectably dressed. His suit saved his life.

The exact number of shots fired in the few minutes of hell that was Loughgall has never been satisfactorily established – the official figure of 678, 78 of which were from IRA guns, seems rather conservative seeing that one soldier alone used up 125 rounds from a belt-fed machinegun.[9] A police officer who was at the scene noted that the bodies looked like sieves. The weapons recovered from the dead men were forensically tested and shown to have been used in a string of seven murders, including that of Harold Henry a few weeks earlier, and twelve attempted murders.

It was the single biggest loss that the IRA had suffered since the 1919–22 period, and the RUC's most successful blow against the Provisionals. Three of their top operators – Kelly,

Lynagh and McKearney – were dead, and an entire ASU annihilated. At the funerals of the dead men, who soon became known as the Loughgall Martyrs, Gerry Adams delivered an oration, using the rhetorical trick of turning defeats into victories: 'Loughgall will become a tombstone for British policy in Ireland and a bloody milestone in the struggle for freedom, justice and peace.'

The battle for East Tyrone was far from over, and the Provisionals would take bloody reprisals. In August 1988, a British Army bus carrying soldiers back to their base took a route through Ballygawley to Omagh, nicknamed by the SAS 'Bomb Alley'. The RUC warned the Ministry of Defence never to allow the security forces to use it. SAS units avoided it, even if it meant crossing the Irish border – an illegality that the authorities ignored. On 20 August, the coach full of troops was blown to bits just outside Ballygawley, and eight men killed. Ten days later, the SAS struck back, killing two brothers, Gerard and Martin Harte, and Brian Mullin, as they tried to murder an off-duty UDR man near Carrickmore in Co Tyrone.[10] One of the IRA men had the top of his head blown off, a phenomenon the SAS refer to with grisly wit as a 'flip-top terrorist'. Mullin had been reportedly questioned about the British Army coach bombing, as had Martin Harte. His brother Gerard was believed to be the O/C of the local Provisionals.

Between 1983 and 1992, the Provisionals in East Tyrone lost thirty-four men, of whom the SAS killed twenty-five. The UVF, which was also active in the area, killed four in two separate shootings in 1989 and 1991. In the end, the East Tyrone Provisional IRA was, in the words of one of its activists, effectively 'wiped out'.

For the Provisionals, the 'final push' was off to a bad start. It was not only their own members who paid the price. On 8 November 1987, a remote-controlled bomb exploded prematurely at a Memorial Day service in Enniskillen, Co.

Fermanagh. Eleven people were killed. The IRA's explanation that a British Army radio signal detonated the device only gave comfort to its hard-core supporters. Most people, Catholic and Protestant, were appalled. For Sinn Fein, and its President, Gerry Adams, it was an especially bitter blow, effectively nullifying their efforts to build some electoral base in the twenty-six counties. The leadership was beginning to realize the cost that the bullet was exacting from the ballot as the dual strategy started to break down. The republican cause had not been helped either by a bloodbath earlier in the year, when feuding factions of the INLA turned their guns on each other, leaving twelve people dead within a few weeks, including Gerard Steenson, the organization's foremost gunman.[11] Much of this internecine violence took place south of the border, further alienating the Southern electorate from Ulster and its problems. The Enniskillen massacre only confirmed the growing feeling that the Ulster crisis was intractable.

2

Long before the Enniskillen massacre, Gerry Adams believed that the Provisionals must broaden their base of support if their struggle was to succeed. By the mid-1980s, the former barman was the dominant figure in the organization, both in Belfast and nationwide. While a member of the Army Council, Adams by this stage was probably not involved directly in the operational side of the movement. Perhaps it is for this reason that Special Branch surveillance on him was less than might have been expected, given his stature. At any rate, he was in a position to impose his vision on the course the Provisionals should take. He had already helped guide the organization through a whole series of transformations, honed down its terrorist structure and built up its political machine. In 1986, he and his supporters asked the Provisionals to take a major step away from traditional republican thinking and recognize the Irish parliament.

The non-recognition policy dated back to the 1921 Treaty, which partitioned Ireland. Republicans rejected the Treaty and the institutions that flowed from it, and barred any of their members from taking their seats if elected to either the Stormont parliament near Belfast or the Dail. Unhappiness with such a strict line led Eamon De Valera to resign from Sinn Fein, of which he was President, in 1926 and establish a new party, Fianna Fail. It was a dispute about the same matter which had led the IRA to split in 1969 into Official and Provisional wings. In the mid-1980s the issue re-emerged yet again. Adams and his supporters were arguing that Sinn Fein's refusal to recognize the Dail meant that it would be permanently isolated in the twenty-six counties, unable to tap into the hidden reserves of nationalism that he believed existed there, especially among Fianna Fail supporters. In effect, Adams was following the line Seamus Costello expounded in the late 1960s, that abstentionism was a tactic, not a principle. (Indeed, Adams later maintained that even though he opted to go with the Provisional wing in 1969 his decision was not based on the new group's attitude to abstentionism.) Traditionalists like O Bradaigh countered that to recognize the legitimacy of the Irish state was to go down the road to constitutional nationalism; the Provisionals would end up like De Valera and the Official IRA before them – just another moderately radical political party.

The IRA held an army convention in September – the first in over a decade – and voted to endorse the change of course. In November, Sinn Fein followed suit at its *ard fheis*. Martin McGuinness gave the keynote speech. He was blunt. 'We must accept the reality that sixty-five years of republican struggle, republican sacrifice and rhetoric have signally failed to convince the majority of people in the twenty-six counties that the Republican Movement has any relevance to them,' he said. 'By ignoring that reality we remain alone and isolated on the high altar of abstentionism, divorced from the people.' McGuinness appealed to the traditionalists: 'If you allow yourselves to be led out of this hall today, the only place you will be going is home. Don't go my friends, we will lead you to the Republic.' A bitter debate ensued which ended in a reprise of the 1970 *ard fheis*. O Bradaigh and O Conaill walked out with about a hundred supporters – whom one commentator has described as a 'geriatric minority'[12] – and founded their own party, Republican Sinn Fein.

The split did not greatly affect the Provisionals. The founding members of PIRA, most of whom were strong advocates of abstentionism, were nearly all gone by then. MacStiofain never attained any status within the movement after his failed hunger strike in 1972. O Conaill and O Bradaigh had lost credibility years earlier because of their handling of the 1974/75 ceasefire. The Provisionals' longest-serving Chief of Staff, Seamus Twomey, on his release from prison in 1982, worked on Sinn Fein's electoral efforts in the South, but eventually became disillusioned and left the movement before his death. Billy McKee, the former Belfast leader who was in favour of abstentionism, had already resigned from the IRA because of a dispute over the kidnapping of a prominent Irish businessman.[13] Only Joe Cahill remained of the old guard, still playing a key role on the Provisional Army Council. But he was ready and willing to adapt to the new outlook of the younger generation. Crucially, the Adams–McGuinness line had strong support north of the border, where the traditional republican quarrel about the status of the Dail had less resonance than among republicans in the South. It was also a recognition that regardless of what republicans might say about a 'British-imposed' Dail, the people of the twenty-six counties accepted the Dail as their parliament, and showed they did in election after election. Any party that did not take account of this was doomed to political irrelevancy. Recognition of the Dail also represented an admission on the leadership's part that the republican struggle was about the Northern state, and was not aimed at the Republic of Ireland. It that sense, the ending of the policy of abstentionism was the last stage in the Ulsterization of the republican movement and its struggle.

Behind the scenes, the Provisional IRA warned O Conaill and O Bradaigh that if they tried to split the IRA by daring to set up another republican 'army', they would be shot. In spite of this threat, within a few years O Conaill was at the head of a new Army Council, recognized by republican purists as the legitimate inheritor of the 1916 revolutionaries. It would take eight years for it to emerge under the name Continuity IRA and challenge the Provisional IRA for the mantle of violent republicanism (see Chapter 8).

In New York, the new group won the support of the old IRA gunrunner, George Harrison, who along with another member of his network, Tom Falvey, issued a statement denouncing the Provisionals' change of course. 'We reaffirm our support to those who stand solidly behind the traditional Republican policy of abstention or boycott of all British-imposed institutions of servility and replace, not reform them, with Republican institutions of liberty and freedom.'

Some saw the change as a harbinger of things to come. If abstentionism can be sacrificed to political expediency, using the argument that it was blocking Sinn Fein's progress, why not that other previously untouchable principle, the 'right' of the IRA to use violence to achieve a united Ireland? It was not long after the 1986 decision that one leading Provisional, Danny Morrison, admitted publicly that if indeed it could be demonstrated that the armed campaign was standing in the way of political progress, and there was a viable alternative, the IRA would halt its violence.[14]

3

Belfast remained the key to the Provisionals' armed campaign. If that campaign was to continue to pose a threat to British rule, it was essential that the IRA demonstrate its ability to operate in the capital, either against so-called economic targets or members of the security forces. But from the mid-1980s, operational problems mounted. Attacks against on-duty members of the army and police fell drastically. The RUC, having uncovered the route from Tyrone that was used to ferry explosives into the city (see Chapter 4), successfully contained the Provisionals' bombing campaign. Over a period of two years, until June 1985, the IRA managed to detonate only one large bomb in the city centre. Occasionally they succeeded only because of police ineptitude. The most outstanding example of this occurred in December 1986 and led to the complete destruction of a police station.

The episode began when the RUC discovered that the Provisionals were using a rather unconventional place in which to store explosives: a mortuary. An army surveillance unit (known as Det.) was dispatched to cover it. However, a senior officer in charge of the operation concluded that the explosives were unlikely to be moved soon. No plans were made to set up checkpoints as a precaution should the IRA decide it needed the material. Shortly afterwards, the army surveillance team watched helplessly as the IRA moved the explosives from the dump and drove off to a safe house where the bomb was constructed. Two hours later, bombers forced the driver of a school bus to park it, packed with the explosives, outside Lisburn Road RUC station in South Belfast. The bomb exploded with a thud that was heard for ten miles, igniting a gas main that burned for two days, consuming what remained of the shattered station. Seven hundred homes in the nearby streets were damaged in the blast, which caused millions of pounds' worth of damage. 'It couldn't be our explosives,' a senior officer stated. He was told it was. Another lamented that the failure was 'one of the biggest acts of incompetence by Belfast TCG'. No explosives were ever recovered from the mortuary.

However, the Provisionals could not always rely on police mistakes. Another major bombing blitz against Belfast was planned for the summer of 1987. The bomb-making material was being brought from a farm near Omagh in Tyrone via the organization's usual route but this time in a horse box with a false bottom. When the police stopped it, they discovered 2,700 lbs of explosives hidden there. It was one of the largest finds ever made, and it thwarted the IRA's summer offensive.

Both the UVF and the UDA were facing their own difficulties by the mid-1980s. Unionism was facing a grave crisis as a result of the Anglo-Irish Agreement. Thousands of Protestants demonstrated in protest in Belfast and elsewhere as part of an 'Ulster Says No' campaign. There were co-ordinated attacks on the RUC and their families in Protestant areas. By the summer of 1986, over five hundred RUC homes had been attacked, and Sir John Hermon, the Chief Constable, was making plans to evacuate thousands of policemen and their families to England. For Protestants, it was the most serious crisis since 1974. But unlike then, neither the UDA nor the UVF was playing a leading role in the attempts to frustrate Britain's plans. As a result, their support declined.

When looked at closely, the Troubles dissolve into a series of local conflicts in areas where, as in East Tyrone, the distribution of Catholic and Protestant is a kind of patchwork. North Belfast is another. At the beginning of 1986, a mini-war erupted there which was a continuation of the old and bloody battle between North Belfast republicans and local loyalists that had been going on since 1969.

Beginning in January 1986, the UVF carried out a series of sectarian murders of Catholics in the area, bringing an end to the period of inactivity that had lasted throughout most of the previous year. John Bingham, the UVF's North Belfast commander, was the man responsible. He had a long history of involvement in the UVF, going back to the early 1970s. For a while he was associated with Lenny Murphy, the leader of the Shankill Butchers gang, a man whom Bingham admired greatly. On the night of 14 September, 1986, an IRA ASU sledgehammered its way into his home, shot the lock off the security gate that barred the way to the bedrooms, dragged him from where he was cowering and shot him in front of his wife and child.

The Provisionals killed him at home in a calculated display of bravado, showing loyalists that they could penetrate the very heart of Protestant areas. In the days following Bingham's death, two Catholics were murdered at random. But the UVF plotted a more deliberate revenge.

Larry Marley, the man behind the IRA escape in 1983, was released from prison in November 1985. Soon, he was ferrying explosives from Tyrone, working on the Toomebridge to Belfast stretch, sometimes driving up to three hundred pounds at a time to a dump in Ardoyne. Though watched, he managed to avoid arrest over a period of some eighteen months, during which he was also linked to a garage where the Provisionals were making mortars. But on 2 April 1987 two UVF men shot him dead at his home, settling the score for the loss of Bingham. Marley's death was a severe blow to the Provisionals in Belfast, and the turn-out at his funeral (around six thousand people) was the largest seen since the deaths of the hunger strikers.[15] More shootings followed as the Provisionals took their revenge, killing William Marchand, a lesser UVF figure.

However, this time the tit-for-tat threatened to take a more serious turn when the UVF targeted Gerry Adams. At the time, Adams was fighting to retain his West Belfast parliamentary seat in the 1987 British general election. The UVF planned to assassinate him on 20 May. Police surveillance teams were forewarned and ready. But for reasons unknown the UVF called off the attack at the last moment. If it had succeeded it would have provoked a bloodbath.

The other main loyalist organization, the UDA, emerged from the doldrums of the mid-1980s with its own political programme in a document called *Common Sense*. It emerged out of a rethink the UDA had undertaken in the late 1970s involving principally Andy Tyrie, Glenn Barr, who was a UDA spokesman during the 1974 action against the power-sharing executive, and John McMichael. In 1986 McMichael took over the running of the UFF. Somewhat paradoxically, given his links to sectarian violence, McMichael recognized that there was a need to accord a role to Ulster Catholics in any settlement. *Common Sense* advocated a new constitution for Northern Ireland, with protection for human rights, and a system of devolved government that would include power-sharing. The fact that McMichael could organize a campaign of sectarian violence and at the same time advocate closer co-operation with the SDLP was symptomatic of the confusion within loyalist ranks.

Common Sense impressed Hume as a sign that ten years after being largely responsible for bringing down the first power-sharing government, the most militant wing of loyalism now accepted the need for power-sharing. The UDA's efforts, however, did not impress the Provisionals. They hatched plans to murder one of the document's authors. The first plan was to shoot McMichael in the carpark near the bar he ran in central Lisburn, a small town south of Belfast. That scheme came to nothing. But the Provisionals did not give up. Three days before Christmas 1987, the year *Common Sense* was published, the Belfast brigade's Explosives Officer, Danny McCann, booby-trapped McMichael's car. The Semtex bomb killed the UDA chief as he left home. He was thirty-eight years old. His son Gary would later take up his father's political ambitions and become a major figure in the peace process.

The murder of McMichael shook up the UDA, and helped bring about the end of the long career of its Supreme Chairman, Andy Tyrie. Tyrie had run the organization since 1973, his reputation resting on the pivotal role he had played as the man who brought down the power-sharing government in 1974. After the UDA's 1977 'strike' failed disastrously (see Chapter 3), Tyrie said: 'As far as loyalist paramilitary organizations are concerned, they will never be the same again – until there's a crisis situation. All we can do is hold on to a good nucleus of men and build an organization, wait for the opportunity and ride the waves again.'[16] The opportunity came in 1985, with Unionist outrage at the Anglo-Irish Agreement. But the UDA failed to 'ride the waves again'.

In the meantime, corruption and racketeering were flourishing. The most prominent racketeer was Jim Craig, McCreery's associate and a close friend of Tyrie. Craig was burly, flamboyant and ruthless. By 1984 he was running seventy-two protection rackets.[17] When asked how he disciplined his men he replied: 'I've got this big fuckin' hammer and I've told them that if anybody gives me trouble I'll break their fuckin' fingers.'[18] After McMichael's murder, McCreery and Craig came under suspicion when someone noticed that their loyalist rivals had a tendency to get murdered by republicans – beginning with Lenny Murphy. A younger generation of UDA men were getting impatient with the old guard. Tyrie's relationship with Craig damaged his credibility with them. Following McMichael's murder, Tyrie's standing was weakened even more by another blow in January 1988. A Lebanese-South African connection had provided loyalist organizations with a large arms shipment. Davy Payne, a close colleague of Tyrie's from the 1970s, was put in charge of delivering the UDA's share of the weapons. E4A had Payne and one of his colleagues under close watch. The

UDA's arms smugglers met with Tyrie on 7 January to discuss their plans. The following day, as Payne drove the weapons to the city, he was stopped and arrested at a checkpoint, along with the arms haul – 50 AK-47 rifles, 50 nine-millimetre pistols, 150 Russian grenades, plus 11,000 rounds of ammunition.[19] The police uncovered a second arms supply on 3 February, destined for the UVF, which included rocket-launchers. However, a third supply got through, and was eventually divided up between the UDA and the UVF.

One morning not long thereafter Tyrie found a retirement present from his UDA colleagues in the form not of a gold watch and chain but of a bomb attached to the underside of his car. It did not explode, but it meant that the vote of no-confidence taken by the organization's ruling Inner Council was a formality, and he resigned in March 1988. Seven months later the UDA murdered Craig as he played pool in a bar in East Belfast. His fellow conspirator McCreery disappeared from Northern Ireland.

Under Tyrie, the UDA declined from around 26,000 members to 'well under 10,000'.[20] With his departure, younger activists soon took control, eager for it to return to its violent habits of the early 1970s. They had their way. The UDA would increase the level of its violence until it was killing more people than the Provisionals.

4

In early 1988, as Sinn Fein sought a way out of the political impasse, a series of meetings began between John Hume and Gerry Adams. The two were brought together by Father Alex Reid, a West Belfast priest whom Sinn Fein trusted, in spite of his opposition to violence. Adams and Hume first met in January 1988. They were later joined in their deliberations by other representatives of their parties. Hume's aim was to impress upon Adams his view that Britain's role in Northern

Ireland had fundamentally changed, and that there was no justification for the armed campaign. The Anglo-Irish Agreement hinged on consent, and the British government had accepted that if the majority wanted a united Ireland then it would effect the legislation necessary to bring it about. In other words, Britain was now 'neutral' on the question of a united Ireland. He argued that the task was to persuade the Unionists that a united Ireland was to their benefit. This could not be achieved through terrorism. Hume envisaged a process that would include representatives from all parties with a mandate, convened under the auspices of the British and Irish governments. But it could only take place if violence ended. He told Adams that if the IRA called a ceasefire, it would change the situation drastically and open up all sorts of political opportunities for nationalists.

Dishearteningly for Hume, Adams replied that there was no chance of a ceasefire. His arguments were based on the standard republican analysis that the Anglo-Irish Agreement's primary function was to consolidate British rule in Ireland by co-opting the Irish government to help it maintain control. Britain, republicans still insisted, was the problem. It had strategic concerns about preventing 'another Cuba' from appearing. However, no one other than the extreme right wing of the Conservative Party took seriously Sinn Fein's aspirations for a Cuban-style revolutionary socialist republic. The party's subsequent development showed that not even Sinn Fein took them seriously.

In the exchange, republicans found it more and more difficult to explain their view that somehow Britain was strengthening its hold over Northern Ireland by diluting its sovereign claims, which was one of the effects of the agreement.

The broad political establishment did not welcome the first Hume–Adams dialogue. Within the SDLP itself there were some members who feared that in the aftermath of the

Enniskillen massacre the dialogue was helping the republican movement repair its public image. Sinn Fein would benefit politically because Hume was seen to take them seriously. The Unionists were outraged, and accused the SDLP leader of throwing a political lifeline to terrorists. The Irish government too was uneasy. But for Hume it was of paramount importance to find a way of bringing the republican movement into the political process. He knew there could be no settlement with the IRA still active.

As their talks progressed, the two developed a level of trust. 'When I first started talking to Adams,' Hume recalled, 'I found him to be totally straightforward in what he said to me, and we built a strong personal trust in one another, even though we had different opinions on many matters. It was this mutual regard and trust that was crucial to our success.'[21] The first Hume–Adams initiative was stillborn. The 'success' would not come for another six years.

5

The Provisional IRA, more and more restricted in its ability to carry out operations in Belfast and throughout Ulster generally, constantly sought other fronts on which to extend its campaign. It carried out a handful of attacks in Europe from the late 1970s, claiming several lives, including that of the British ambassador to the Netherlands, Sir Richard Sykes, and his nineteen-year-old Dutch valet, Krel Straub. But European operations did not seriously get under way until the late 1980s. In 1987, a bomb exploded outside a British Army base in West Germany. The following year, the Provisionals planned a major operation in Gibraltar – using its new supplies of Semtex. The bomb-maker in charge of the operation was Danny McCann, the Belfast brigade's Explosives Officer.

It was a foolish choice. McCann was well known to the

Special Branch as an active republican and under steady surveillance (See Chapter 5). In July 1987, he was involved in a scheme to blow up a boat that was used by off-duty British soldiers in the seaside town of Bangor, Co. Down, but it fell through. A month later, McCann, along with Sean Savage, gave E4A surveillance teams the slip long enough to murder two Special Branch officers in a bar in the docks area of Belfast. In December, he assassinated UDA chief John McMichael. But surveillance was stepped up and it led to the revelation of the Provisionals' Gibraltar plans, which also involved Savage and two women, Mairead Farrell, who had served time for a bombing attack in the 1970s, and a woman who is currently a prominent member of Sinn Fein. The ASU moved south, to a safe house in the west of Ireland, before leaving to carry out their operation in Gibraltar.

The quartet wanted to plant a huge car bomb not far from a changing-of-the-guard ceremony. On 5 March, SAS men followed the second woman as she did a 'recce' of the target area, before going into a nearby chapel to light a candle. The next day, as Farrell, Savage and McCann walked away from a parked car, near where the ceremony was due to take place, the SAS struck, shooting dead all three. The fourth – the woman who was seen in the chapel – escaped.

The killings outraged many people. Catholics condemned them as cold-blooded murder and argued that the three could have been arrested. Anger increased when it was discovered that the parked car did not contain any explosives. However, on 8 March, two days after the shootings, a car linked to the ASU was found in a lock-up garage in Marbella, just across the Spanish border, containing detonating equipment and 140 pounds of Semtex – the biggest Semtex bomb ever uncovered in the history of the Troubles. Had it exploded, it would have caused horrendous casualties.

McCann, Savage and Farrell all came from West Belfast, where thousands gathered as a mark of respect when their bodies were returned. Their deaths set off a chain reaction of violence. At the funeral on 15 March, Michael Stone, a UDA gunman, attacked the mourners in the cemetery, hurling grenades and firing wildly, creating pandemonium in an assault that killed three people. Four days later, at the funeral of one of Stone's victims, two off-duty British officers drove into the funeral cortège and in panic mounted the pavement, then reversed. The mob quickly surrounded their car, thinking another loyalist or SAS attack was imminent, and dragged the men away to a nearby football field, where they were stripped and brutally beaten. The bloodied and almost naked captives were bundled into a taxi, then driven to waste ground where they were dragged out and shot in the head. A British Army helicopter videoed the whole horrifying spectacle from between 1,500 and 500 feet above, including the final scene: the dark form of a priest standing over the corpse of one of the dead, who lay stretched out, stripped and blood-covered on the grimy, rubble-strewn ground.[22] There was almost universal disgust at the mob killings, and West Belfast became for some the heart of darkness. But for the community itself, the response of the mob was the visceral reaction of an embattled community driven to desperation by decades of violence.

In 1988 the Provisional IRA leadership gave itself a time-table of about two years to show whether or not the armed campaign was capable of breaking the stalemate.[23] A bombing in June, which killed six soldiers, and another that August, which claimed the lives of eight, prompted Thatcher to consider the reintroduction of internment without trial, which the IRA would have regarded as a propaganda victory, whatever its military ramifications. The Prime Minister was only with some effort dissuaded from taking this retrograde step. There were attacks in the Netherlands, in which three off-duty members of the RAF were killed. And on 1 August, for the first time in almost five years, an IRA bomb went off in

Britain, killing a soldier and wounding nine in an attack on a barracks in North London.

Instead of internment, the government banned Sinn Fein representatives from being interviewed on radio and television. The ban also applied to spokespersons for the UDA and Republican Sinn Fein. The government also announced that it was curtailing the right to silence. The Northern Ireland Secretary of State, Tom King, said that the courts would now be allowed to give 'whatever weight they think proper' to a suspect's refusal to answer questions.[24] Civil liberties groups were outraged at this erosion of the judicial principle of innocent until proven guilty. It was actually unpopular even with the government ministers who took the measure in order to 'divert' Thatcher from reintroducing internment.[25] The army also launched a massive sweep through Catholic areas of the province, searching 700,000 vehicles and 1,100 buildings, on occasions using pneumatic drills to dig up the floors of houses as they tried to unearth the Libyan arms shipments.[26]

The Provisionals saw these and other measures as proof of growing British desperation. Danny Morrison, the Sinn Fein spokesman and editor of *An Phoblacht*, was in a seemingly confident mood when he claimed:

> There is a recognition that we can break the will of the British government to remain in Ireland. There's a tremendous sense of confidence within the nationalist community and particularly that section of it which owes its allegiance to the republican movement . . . Next year, August 1989, will be the 20th anniversary of the open deployment of British troops on the streets here . . . that represents twenty years of British military and political failures to stabilize the North in British interests.

When asked if he still thought that the IRA had a hope of defeating the British he answered: 'I know there is. I wouldn't be involved in a struggle if there was nothing but the prospect of a glorious failure . . . the struggle goes on. And we sniff in our nostrils the smell of success.'[27]

Morrison, a self-confident and shrewd propagandist, was aware of the obverse of his argument – that almost twenty years of IRA violence had failed to dislodge Britain, which seemed in fact to have regained enough control of the situation to restore a sense of normality. This was noticeable to a visitor to Belfast in late 1988. The downtown area was bustling, the shops were brightly lit and busy with shoppers, and traffic poured down the roads, where army checkpoints were just another irritation for rush-hour commuters. Of course, the more normal the city seemed, the greater the propaganda benefits the Provisionals could derive from disruptive bombings which 'proved' that this normality was a sham.

Their campaign was being waged at an increasing political cost, which in the cold calculations of the propaganda war were measured in civilian lives lost, most of them Catholic. In a period of nine months in 1988, the IRA killed eighteen in botched operations. It wiped out an entire family – Robin Hanna, aged forty-four, his wife Maureen, also forty-four, and their six-year-old son David – in a huge bomb blast, which disintegrated them and their car not far from where Chief Justice Gibson and his wife were murdered in 1987. The car they had been driving was mistaken for that of the actual target, another high-ranking judge. On the Falls Road itself a sixty-year-old woman, Elizabeth Hamill, and a twenty-four-year old man, Eamon Gilroy, were killed when an IRA bomb went off prematurely near the public baths. Adams was spending more and more of his time fending off questions about what the Provisionals chose to call 'mistakes' and trying to give a rationale for continuing a campaign that was taking such a toll. He called the sequence of civilian deaths an 'unfortunate coincidence of tragic accidents', reiterating an 'appeal' to the IRA 'to pursue the armed struggle in such a way that it helps either to broaden the base or doesn't obstruct the broader aims of the movement'. He said it would have to 'put its house in order'. But the 'accidents' continued, and claimed the lives of three Derry Catholics, who triggered a booby-trap bomb placed in a neighbour's apartment in an elaborate plot to lure troops or RUC men to their deaths.

The political toll on Sinn Fein was more obvious in the Irish Republic. In a general election in February 1989 the party's vote collapsed. It polled a derisory 1.2 per cent of the vote.[28] It was a bitter blow to the leadership's hopes of breaking out of the political ghetto. The strategy of the Provisionals of building a broad nationalist front, as evolved under Adams, was unable to overcome the reluctance of Southern Irish voters to put their trust in a movement responsible for atrocities such as the Enniskillen massacre. The conclusion was obvious: the armed campaign was the chief obstacle blocking the road to political success in the Irish Republic. To analyse the obvious is difficult enough, but to face up to the consequences of that analysis – that the armed campaign would have to end sooner rather than later – was something that in 1989 the Provisional Army Council was unable to do.

That year, 1989, provided lots of opportunity for reflection on these and other matters relating to the Troubles as the twentieth anniversary of the introduction of British troops on to the streets of Derry and Belfast approached. It marked the longest uninterrupted period of conflict Ulster – and Ireland – had sustained in centuries. In September, the Northern Ireland political magazine *Fortnight* marked the anniversary with a front cover that reflected the general mood of deep pessimism. *AND NOW FOR THE NEXT TWENTY YEARS*, it proclaimed, illustrating the sentiment with a photograph of a boy wearing a Balaclava and carrying an automatic rifle almost as large as himself. His proud parents were political inertia and political murder, and he was striding into the future with alarming confidence.

The issue contained an open letter from Adams to Margaret Thatcher, a 'wee 20-years-on note', as he described it with a rather self-conscious attempt at folksy bravado. It proclaimed the mood of West Belfast as being as defiant as ever as it entered 'the 21st year of this phase of British military rule'. He wrote of the 'happy and confident aura' among local nationalists as they celebrated the annual West Belfast Festival with poetry, music and dancing. 'In a way I think we were like marathon runners who hit and cleared the wall and discovered to our surprise that we have lots of stamina left. It was fitting therefore that we celebrate 20 years of resistance with such joy and good humour.' The letter ended: 'Until then, take care. You'll be hearing from us again', a somewhat sinister note considering that Adams's organization had tried to murder her.

The British had already heard from the Provisionals during the anniversary year, but it was not a message set to the refrain of an Irish tune. In March, they claimed the lives of the two highest-ranking RUC officers to die in the Troubles; in July they detonated a thousand-pound car bomb outside the High Court in central Belfast; and at the end of September, a time bomb killed eleven soldiers in a barracks in Deal, Kent – the worst loss of life for the army since 1979.

An even more drastic lapse in British security occurred when the Provisional IRA were given an unprecedented opportunity to assassinate members of the Royal Family, including Her Majesty the Queen, Prince Philip and Prince Charles. In the summer of 1990, a member of the IRA working in England was hired as a food supervisor in Green Park, near the Mall in London, a banqueting hall often used as a venue by the Royal Family. He got the job after going through two MI5 security checks. Though active in the IRA for several years, he had never been arrested, nor had any member of his family.

Before important events, Scotland Yard gave the staff security briefings. Police officers instructed the bemused IRA man in how to detect bombs and recognize a detonator. Since he had already been involved in several bombing operations himself it was quite unnecessary. The four-man ASU to which he belonged had been operating in England for about a year, where it had carried out a series of attacks, including an attempt on the life of Sir Anthony Farrar-Hockley, Commander of Land Forces in Northern Ireland between 1970 and 1972. It would later bomb Victoria railway station in London, killing a passer-by.

Part of his job was to help set up the tables for the banquet. He was able to look at the schedule of upcoming events for the summer, complete with lists of those attending, which included Her Majesty the Queen and Prince Philip. Prince Charles was being honoured on another occasion, and there were events involving leading members of the British government, including Michael Portillo, a cabinet minister. In September, there was to be a conference on international terrorism.

Realizing the potential to strike a terrible blow at the heart of the British state, he travelled to Northern Ireland on a weekend, pretending he was returning for a sister's birthday. He took with him a list of possible targets, at the top of which was the Queen and Prince Philip. The Provisionals' intelligence chief on Northern Command told him it was 'too hot' for them to handle. He would have to cross the border to speak directly to the GHQ staff. A meeting was arranged in Dundalk. After showing the GHQ representative the target list, he was promptly told that the Royal Family was a 'no-no'. They were not regarded as legitimate targets.[29] But the Provisional leadership were interested in the conference on international terrorism scheduled for 27 September, because it would involve among others Professor Paul Wilkinson. Professor Wilkinson had acted at times as an adviser to the

Thatcher government. Also attending would be high-ranking officers from Italian, French and German police forces, as well as the RUC, Scotland Yard and the London Metropolitan Police. The bomb – consisting of four pounds of Semtex – was smuggled into the banquet hall in a lunch box, and placed under the lectern. It was timed to go off at 10.30 a.m. when Wilkinson was due to speak. However, it was located and defused.[30] But it was a propaganda victory for the Provisionals and a tremendous political embarrassment for the government, who put half a million pounds' ransom on the head of the former Green Park table-setter.

Not long after *Fortnight* carried Adams's jokey and defiant epistle to Mrs Thatcher, a very different view emerged of the republican position and its prospects from a source within the Belfast IRA. It was contained in a secret 'comm.' smuggled out of Crumlin Road prison in early 1990. The comm. was written on a tiny piece of cigarette paper two and a half inches wide by four inches long and directed to a veteran republican, requesting assistance for an escape attempt, a previous one having failed. The sender, a high-ranking member of the Provisionals' Belfast brigade, approached the veteran rather than go through the Belfast brigade (BB) itself because of a 'number of significant RUC "successes" in Belfast and elsewhere recently i.e. the abortive Crum prison break, the arrest of Morrison & co plus a number of abortive op[s] like ours. Our conclusion is the BB may well be compromised . . .'[31] The comm. went on to ask for stun guns, wigs and a simple means of making a facial disguise. But it is the closing words that are interesting. The sender wrote:

Hoping that this talk of bringing the armed struggle to a conclusion that McGuinness and co. are talking about bears fruit as I've thrown the hands up on at least two occasions. But I've an awful feeling this war is set for at least another decade. Whether we have the ability to break out of the containment the Brits are imposing on the war I think is crucial to the ultimate success/failure of the conflict. At the present I'm not optimistic of our ability to do so. You would not believe the change in attitude and resolve of the Northern nationalist community regarding their commitment to the war . . .

The 'comm.' contains none of the hollow bravado of Adams's letter, a pose for public consumption. The reality was that after twenty years the Provisionals were being contained and their support base was wearying of the endless violence. An especially vicious series of operations in late October using human car bombs suggested the desperate lengths to which the Provisionals were prepared to go to break out of the containment being imposed upon them. On three different occasions, the IRA strapped men into bomb-laden vehicles. One of them, Patrick Gillespie, a forty-two-year-old Catholic who worked in the canteen of a British Army base in Derry, was forced to drive to a checkpoint on the Donegal border a few miles from the city. As Gillespie neared the checkpoint in the early hours of 24 October, the Provisionals armed the bomb by remote control. Four minutes later, as the soldiers approached, the thousand-pound device exploded, blowing him to bits along with five soldiers. His body was never found. Another soldier died in a similar attack in South Down, but the driver managed to escape with a broken leg. In a third attack, the bomb failed to explode. Even in a society where the language of condemnation was by now exhausted, and horror grown monotonous, the manner of Mr Gillespie's death made decent people shudder.

The fact that the Derry Provisionals were responsible for this atrocity did not discourage the British government from secretly opening up direct contacts with Martin McGuinness, their overall commander, at around the very time it took place. They used a line of communication that dated back to the ceasefire negotiations of 1974/75 and was used during the hunger strikes in 1980/81. When the approaches were made, beginning in mid-1990, McGuinness was a member of the Provisional Army Council and head of the IRA's Northern Command. 'We thought that this was only an opening approach aimed at picking up on the bad situation between us since the hunger strikes and we received some general and occasional oral briefings on the British position during this time,' wrote McGuinness.[32] However, the contacts would prove to be the opening moves in a complex endgame, soon involving Adams, Hume, the Irish government and the US administration, which would eventually bring a halt to the twenty-five-year-old IRA campaign, setting the stage for the most ambitious attempt so far to settle the Ulster crisis.

PART THREE

The Perilous Path to Peace

CHAPTER SEVEN

The Twilight of the Armed
Campaign: 1990–94

1

F ew guessed as the new decade dawned that the end of
the Provisional IRA's long war against Ulster was in
sight. The tradition of physical force which had endured for two centuries within Irish republicanism was in its
last days. But if anything, the opposite seemed to be happening. With a dramatic series of bombings, the Provisionals
broke out of the containment the British were imposing on
them.

Bombing Britain, the IRA believed, was the key to keeping
pressure on the British government. The Army Council gave
Kevin McKenna, the Provisionals' Chief of Staff, the go-ahead
to put all the resources he could command into English
operations and create 'mayhem', according to a veteran
republican activist.[1]

In the 1990s, all operations in Britain were under the
control of the South Armagh Provisionals. South Armagh
was regarded as a safe base, so far impervious to penetration
from the intelligence services, which were making inroads

elsewhere, especially in Belfast. Materiel was supplied from South Armagh, and all volunteers involved in the British campaign, whether from Derry or Belfast or Dublin, were placed under the authority of the O/C of the South Armagh IRA. Those chosen to join the overseas ASUs were usually Provisionals with no security trace on them, such as the volunteer involved in the Green Park plot (see Chapter 6).[2] When their period of 'active service' in Britain was finished, they were brought back to South Armagh or its environs (often Dundalk or Co. Monaghan) for debriefing.

In February 1991, an IRA mortar landed in the back garden of 10 Downing Street during a Cabinet meeting to discuss the Gulf War. The unit that was responsible for this affront to British security was also involved in a fire-bomb campaign on the London Underground system which caused massive disruptions in the weeks leading up to Christmas. But the most massive strike came over a year later, on 10 April 1992. A bomb consisting of one ton of explosives constructed in South Armagh and smuggled into England exploded in the Baltic Exchange, the financial heart of London, killing three people and causing £750 million worth of damage. A second bomb went off the same day next to a flyover in the north of the city. A report in the *Belfast Telegraph* later revealed that the Baltic Exchange bomb cost more in insurance claims than all the bombs that had exploded – some ten thousand of them – in Northern Ireland between 1969 and 1992.

The Provisionals' renewed bombing campaign in Northern Ireland was also proving costly to the government. In 1991, a series of large car bombs in Banbridge, Co. Down, Kilrea, Co. Derry, Craigavon, Co. Armagh, and Belfast – where two went off within two weeks in the city centre in December – forced the government to freeze public spending in certain areas in order to drain off sufficient funds to pay the two million pounds required for repairs to the damage the IRA's attacks had inflicted on housing. But the bombing that caused the most outrage occurred on 2 November, when the Provisionals left a twenty-pound Semtex device inside the military wing of Musgrave Park hospital in South Belfast, killing two army medics and injuring several children in a nearby civilian ward. Demands for the reintroduction of internment grew louder, coming mainly from the Unionist Party. But there was also some support from within the army for the measure. An unnamed high-ranking security source told the London *Independent on Sunday* that without the reintroduction of internment the police and army had no hope of beating the IRA.[3]

The government did not give in to internment demands, partly because not long after the gloomy prognosis was being aired in the *Independent on Sunday* the Special Branch in Belfast recruited a major source within the IRA leadership. Internment was not needed. But the government was also reluctant to use it because it feared the political backlash. Chiefly, it did not want to upset the delicate, preliminary approaches being made in secret towards the IRA. So the public response to the rising wave of violence was to dispatch several hundred extra troops to patrol Northern Ireland's increasingly edgy capital and put 1,400 members of the UDR on full-time duty.

The hospital incident highlighted the increasingly contradictory position in which Adams was finding himself as he struggled to marry the armed campaign with ordinary politics as West Belfast's MP. The day after the IRA bombed the hospital, Adams made two statements. In the first, he refused to condemn the bomb attack, saying that the hospital was a 'British military installation'. In the second, he criticized a proposal to take Belfast's leading hospital, the Royal Victoria, which was in his constituency, out of Britain's National Health scheme and turn it into a trust-funded institution. He said such a move 'would be bad for the hospital, bad for workers, but particularly bad for patients'. He claimed that 'patient care will be severely affected'. He made this statement just after television news viewers witnessed pictures of rescue workers digging children from the rubble of the devastated ward; even as he spoke, doctors from Musgrave Park hospital were forced to cancel operations because of the bomb. The juxtaposition was a study in contradictions so startling as to make an observer wonder if the republican movement had lost its grip on reality. There is no more serious way of affecting patient care at a hospital than by planting a bomb in it. But the political absurdity, and cost, of the armed campaign were already obvious to the apparatchiks of Sinn Fein. The party no longer celebrated the IRA's terrorism with an Armalite in one hand and a ballot paper in the other; now, its spokesmen more often than not said they could neither 'condone nor condemn' it. Increasingly cornered as apologists, they employed the evasive vocabulary of people who realize they are defending the indefensible. 'Understanding' the reasons for the violence was often the best they could do.

A prominent Sinn Fein spokesman in Belfast, Richard McAuley, was unusually direct about the party's and the republican movement's dilemma: 'We're not going to realize our full potential as long as the war is going on in the North and as long as Sinn Fein is presented the way it is with regard to armed struggle and violence. I think that is a reality that perhaps we weren't conscious or aware of back in the early 80s when we first got involved in electoral politics.'[4]

The winter of 1991 was a gloomy one for Ulster. Headlines in the local papers screamed of a return to the dark days of the early 1970s, when death squads stalked the streets, killing at random. There was good reason for this fear. The murder rate began to climb again, mainly thanks to a resurgence in loyalist assassinations. In the space of a few days in mid-November a forty-year-old Catholic woman and her sixteen-year-old daughter were burned alive after loyalist petrol bombers attacked their home in a Protestant district, the Provisionals shot dead four Protestants, and the UVF killed three workers (two Catholics and by accident one Protestant, for which they apologized) as they left a factory near Lurgan, Co. Armagh. The UDA was also active again under the control of Joe English, a little pit-bull terrier of a man. Behind him a pack of young bloods growled menacingly, hot to avenge republican attacks.

This, 1991, was the first year in which loyalist groups ran neck and neck with republicans in the grim race of death known as the Troubles. Of the ninety-eight political murders in Northern Ireland, loyalists were responsible for forty-one – almost 50 per cent. During the late 1980s loyalists groups had been responsible for about 25 per cent of the deaths. But from 1992 to 1994 loyalists established themselves as Ulster's most prolific killers. Sinn Fein councillors and party members were increasingly targeted; between May and September, the UDA murdered four leading members of the party. On one of the rare occasions when loyalists managed successfully to target an actual republican operator, a UVF hit squad murdered Martin O'Prey, an ex-INLA gunman. (O'Prey was once active with Gerard Steenson but had since joined another splinter group.)

The safest thing to be in Ulster in the 1990s was a member of the security forces, as fewer and fewer of them fell victim to republican groups. Only eleven soldiers and policemen died violently in Ulster in 1992 – representing just over 10 per cent of all victims.[5]

The re-emergence of the loyalist threat was linked to several developments. The old leadership of Tyrie was overthrown at the same time as a resupply of weapons and explosives fell into the hands of the UDA and UVF (see Chapter 6). Behind the scenes another factor came into play. One of the British Army's top agents within the UDA, a forty-four-year-old former British soldier called Brian Nelson, had been exposed and brought to trial.

Nelson's arrest in 1990 was the result of another inquiry into the RUC after allegations that the police force was colluding with loyalist groups. Police files on suspected republicans had gone missing, turning up in the hands of loyalist killers. When the UDA murdered Loughlin Maginn on 25 August 1989 they justified it by producing an RUC file identifying him as a republican. The crisis occurred just as Sir John Hermon, who successfully brought the RUC through the Stalker affair, was retiring and his replacement Sir Hugh Annesley was taking up his post. Annesley, a Dublin-born Protestant, was a quiet-spoken, cautious and low-key diplomat, in contrast to his predecessor. When an investigation into the leaks was announced the new Chief Constable was determined to make sure it did not get bogged down in controversy as had the Stalker inquiry. An English police officer, John Stevens, selected by Annesley himself, was put in charge of the inquiry.

The Special Branch was not happy that for the second time in five years its most sensitive area of operations – the compilation and handling of intelligence – would be exposed to an outsider. Stalker's investigation had made public vital aspects of how the RUC fought the twilight war (see Chapter 5). The Special Branch were afraid of a repeat performance. Their fears were not misplaced. Stevens's inquiry cleared the police of charges of collusion. For the most part, the files that were leaked had passed through the hands of UDR members, many of whom were found to have loyalist associations. The inquiry undoubtedly helped convince the government to dissolve the UDR, which it did in 1992, merging it with the Royal Irish Rangers.[6]

Police fears about damage to intelligence operations were heightened when in early 1992 Nelson was brought to trial on charges of murder and conspiracy to murder, as a result of the Stevens inquiry. Most sensationally, it was revealed that Nelson's handlers in British Army intelligence did not act on information he gave them concerning three murder plots. One of those who was killed as a result was Patrick Finucane, a well-known Belfast lawyer from a prominent republican family. (His brother Dermot, who escaped from the Maze in 1983, was head of the Provisionals' Southern Command.) Finucane routinely defended paramilitaries, especially republicans. It was alleged that while the RUC were interrogating loyalist suspects the detectives would say things like 'Now that Finucane, he's a real IRA man', with the clear suggestion that he should be shot.

During Nelson's trial it was claimed that he had been involved in gathering intelligence about Finucane for the UDA. On 12 February 1989, UDA gunmen broke into the Finucane home and shot him dead in his kitchen in front of his family.

Cover-up and collusion allegations once more hit the intelligence community. The RUC defended itself, insisting that the army did not pass on the information needed to prevent the planned murder. In spite of the setting up of the TCGs, rivalry between the various intelligence-gathering wings of the security forces was still endemic. It is feasible that army intelligence officers deliberately kept back information from the RUC Special Branch in order to protect their agent. The RUC itself has frequently withheld information from other agencies including BOX if it thought that it might compromise one of its operations or agents. (In fact, this rivalry would lead to a crisis between the Branch and MI5 in 1994.)

Murder charges against Nelson were dropped and he was sentenced to ten years on conspiracy to murder. But the case has left a cloud hanging over both the RUC and army intelligence concerning the handling of information and the relationship that its agents have with the terrorists they are supposed to be thwarting.[7] As with cases involving IRA informers, it exposed the uncomfortable fact that in order to maintain their cover within paramilitary groups, people working for the security forces often have to commit crimes.

The exposure of Nelson severed the flow of information from one important source about UDA activities, and as loyalist killings increased Ken Maginnis, the UUP spokesman on security, blamed the British government. In a speech at the party's 1991 conference, he accused the government of 'being responsible for a great deal of the terrorism in Northern Ireland'. He alleged that the Stevens inquiry 'blew the identity of people who were providing the Royal Ulster Constabulary with information' about loyalist gangs.[8] Maginnis, who was himself the target of several IRA assassination plots, was a former UDR man with close contacts in the security forces; no doubt he was reflecting the feeling of police and army officers that once more politics was allowed to take priority over security concerns.

Recruitment to both the UDA and UVF increased. Continued anger at the Anglo-Irish Agreement, frustration at the security forces' failure to defeat the IRA, and a rise in Protestant working-class unemployment in Belfast contributed to what some were calling Protestant 'alienation' from the state that they once saw as their own. The UDA became active again in areas such as East and South Belfast, where it had been relatively quiet since the 1970s.

On 17 January 1992, near a crossroads called Teebane in East Tyrone, the Provisional IRA bombed a coachload of Protestant building workers, employed by the Henry Brothers company to work on security force bases (see Chapter 6). The six hundred pounds of explosive killed eight workers (aged between twenty-two and sixty-one), scattering body parts over several fields, where the mutilated lay screaming in pain in the winter darkness. The young turks of the UDA swore revenge. Just after lunch-time on 5 February, a small crowd had gathered in a betting shop on the Lower Ormeau Road in South Belfast – a once Protestant district that was now Catholic. It was the scene of many sectarian killings, including the bombing of the Rose and Crown pub, next door to the betting shop, which left six Catholics dead on 2 May 1974. As the punters were watching a race, two UDA gunmen walked into the shop armed with a rifle and handgun, and opened fire. In the small space the dead and wounded fell on top of each other. 'It was horrifying,' said an ambulance driver who arrived at the scene shortly after the shooting. 'There were bodies all over . . . it was so bad we could hardly get into the place.' Another witness said tersely, 'It was like a butcher's shop.' Five people lay dead and nine seriously wounded. The dead ranged in age from fifteen to sixty-six. When the RUC arrived to cordon off the area, the grieving and sometimes hysterical relatives greeted them with hostility. 'Bastards,' one screamed, and another shouted, 'I hope one hundred of you are blown to bits by the IRA tonight.'[9]

The UDA issued a claim of responsibility under its *nom de guerre*, UFF, and said 'Remember Teebane', threatening more to come. By 16 February, thirty-one people had been killed, compared with three for the same period in 1991. An off-duty RUC man went berserk and shot dead three people in the Sinn Fein headquarters in West Belfast, and the SAS ambushed and wiped out a four-man IRA ASU near Coal-island, Co. Tyrone, after it attacked the local RUC station. Little did anyone realize at the time, when civil war seemed on the horizon, that these four would be the last victims of the SAS in Ulster.

For the first time since 1976 the British government called a security conference with the heads of the four major parties in Northern Ireland, but this produced nothing other than the perennial demands from Unionists for more security and from nationalists that the UDA, still legal, should be outlawed. Six hundred extra troops were sent to the province.

The government, however, finally took the step that many nationalists had been calling for for over twenty years, and banned the UDA on 10 August 1992. By this stage, the group had killed around five hundred people (the exact figure is impossible to estimate) and over a hundred of its members were in jail serving life sentences for murder. Yet as late as 1988 a Northern Ireland Office briefing paper, prepared for foreign correspondents, could say of the UDA: 'There is no evidence that it is engaged in organizing terrorist attacks.'[10] The government's reluctance to acknowledge the real nature of the UDA may have been the result of its wish to keep the world's attention focused on the Provisional IRA as the cause of the conflict. Or it may have thought that, as a legal organization, the UDA could be more easily persuaded to move in a political direction, which it at times gave hints of doing. There was also a fear that driving the UDA underground would remove the more 'moderate' leaders and replace them with young hotheads. By 1992, this had already happened and the authorities perhaps concluded they had nothing to lose.

Ban or no ban, the killings continued until by the year's end ninety-one new names (including six victims in England) had been added to the Ulster Troubles death list – seventy-nine of them civilians.

After almost a quarter of a century of violence, despair had turned the face of Ulster into a mask of resignation contorted at times by rage.

2

However, politics had not gone away. Both behind the scenes and in public, minds were focused as never before on finding a way to end the political stalemate.

In 1989 Peter Brooke became Secretary of State for Northern Ireland. Brooke, an affable upper-class sort with a slight speech defect, seemed far too good-natured to make an impression on the calloused hide of Ulster politics. He was a lover of cricket; and whatever might be said about Ulster politics, it was definitely *not* cricket. He soon provoked a reaction from the Unionists, who suspected that he was a typical English softy, bland and gutless. In November 1989, one hundred days after he took office, he declared during a television interview that the IRA could not be beaten. 'The first factor is that I would recognize', he said, 'that in terms of the late twentieth-century terrorist, organized as well as the Provisional IRA have become, that it is difficult to envisage the defeat of such a force . . .' A policy of containment allows normal life to go on, he mused, and meanwhile it might spark off among the terrorists a debate as to whether or not 'the game had ceased to be worth the candle . . .' He added that if violence did end, then the government would be 'flexible and imaginative' in its response.[11] Brooke was reiterating what many of his predecessors had come to accept as a given fact of life about the Ulster situation – the policy of 'an acceptable level of violence', as Reginald Maudling had put it almost twenty years earlier. Predictably, Brooke's broad hint about what would follow if the IRA gave up the Armalite entirely and embraced the ballot box exclusively provoked outrage from the Unionist community. But among the republicans it aroused cautious curiosity.

The British had reopened its secret channel of communication with the Provisional leadership, and in October 1990 the government's contact with the republican movement met with Martin McGuinness to tell him that a new contact would reactivate the 'long-standing line of communication'.[12] Just over a month later, after a leadership challenge, John Major replaced the Provisionals' old nemesis, Margaret Thatcher, as leader of the Conservative Party and Prime Minister of the government.

Thatcher had been Conservative leader since 1975 and Prime Minister since 1979. In that time she managed to alienate both communities – the Unionists because of the Anglo-Irish Agreement, and the nationalists because of the hunger strikes, thus achieving a rare status in Ulster: Unionists hated her almost as much as nationalists.

With the arrival of the more mild-mannered Englishmen, Major and Brooke, on the political scene, two separate political processes were initiated. In public, Brooke began a series of meetings with the four main parties, the SDLP, the UUP, the DUP and the Alliance Party, in what most thought was a hopeless effort to reach a new constitutional settlement for Ulster. In secret, the government stepped up its contacts with the Provisional IRA. The aim of these contacts was to convince the Provisionals to end their armed campaign. A few days before Brooke was to make an important speech – indeed, it has since been seen as a watershed – the British secretly forwarded a copy of it to Sinn Fein. In the speech, given on 9 November 1990, Brooke declared that partition was 'an acknowledgment of reality not an assertion of national self-interest'. Britain had no 'selfish strategic or economic interest in Northern Ireland, our role is to help, enable and encourage'. The British would not stand in the way of Irish unity if it came about with the consent of the people of Northern Ireland. Hume had long argued that the Anglo-Irish Agreement of 1985 showed that Britain was now 'neutral' on the question of Irish unity. In discussions with Hume in 1988, Adams had demanded 'proof'. Brooke's speech, which was written after consultation with Hume, was an attempt to meet that demand.

The Provisionals wanted more than words. They demanded that Britain abandon its support for what they called the Unionist 'veto' over a united Ireland and begin the task of persuading Ulster's recalcitrant Protestants that unity was to their benefit. In Sinn Fein's view, it was unacceptable that the Unionists, whom it referred to as a 'minority' within the island of Ireland, should be allowed to hold such power over the country's future. The very fact that republicans engaged with the British at this level suggested that they were starting to accept Hume's analysis – that Britain was no longer an imperial power aggressively defending its last colony but was in fact stuck there, and willing to disentangle itself if circumstances were right. In itself this represented a significant change in Sinn Fein's position. As significant as Brooke's speech and the republican response to it was the fact that the British had secretly shown it to Sinn Fein in advance. This was a gesture of trust, made at a time when official statements from the government continued to denounce Sinn Fein and the IRA as terrorists.

Hume's influence was seen not only in Brooke's 'no selfish interest' speech, but within the structure of the Brooke talks themselves. The SDLP leader had long argued that the Northern Ireland problem could only be dealt with by taking into account three different strands or sets of relationships: the relationship between Catholics and Protestants, the relationship between Dublin and Belfast, and the relationship between Ireland and Britain. The crisis was a product of all three. If the Gordian knot of Ulster was to be untied then it had to be picked apart one strand at a time. So Brooke's approach was three-stranded: strand one would deal with relations between Northern Ireland's two communities, strand two relations between Belfast and Dublin, and strand three relations between Dublin, Belfast and London.

Between April 1991 and April 1992, the talks stumbled along. There were problems right from the start. The Unionists were going into the talks in the hope of finding a replacement for the hated Anglo-Irish Agreement, which their years of protest and boycott had failed to remove. The SDLP were taking part in the talks to strengthen the agreement, especially its Irish, cross-border dimension. In the end, only strand one made any headway, with the four main parties discussing the form of any new devolved government for Northern Ireland.

As the process went on it became apparent that Hume did

not seem to be fully engaged in the negotiations. He disliked the emphasis on strand one, fearing that it would push the talks towards an internal, Northern Ireland-only settlement, anathema to his thinking since the early 1970s. He was also afraid that the British would try to appease the Unionists by building up strand one at the expense of the other relationships. But underlying this was a deeper and more fundamental concern about the viability of the whole process. The talks lacked a key player – the republican movement. Hume believed that unless Sinn Fein, the Provisionals' representatives, were included, then the process could not succeed in bringing peace and stability. The Unionists were prepared to offer considerable concessions to the SDLP – a power-sharing government, a Bill of Rights, and recognition of the Irish dimension. But Hume stalled, even though others in the SDLP were willing to cut a deal. As a result the process collapsed in November 1992. The UUP has ever since remained bitter about what they saw as Hume's undermining of the Brooke talks. But for Hume the stakes were much higher than just finding a way of accommodating constitutional nationalism and Unionism. By late 1992, he had already begun in secret a new round of contacts with Sinn Fein in the hope of ending the historical conflict for ever.

While Sinn Fein was not part of the 1991/92 talks, they were engaged in their own talks with the British – a sort of strand four, which London kept secret. The government made sure that the republican movement was kept abreast of developments. Its representative told Sinn Fein in April 1991 that the loyalist groups were about to call a temporary ceasefire to coincide with the beginning of the Brooke talks. He forewarned republicans of an upcoming Brooke speech in October that year, and in early 1992 promised them a copy of the British Prime Minister's scheduled address to Scottish Conservatives. In a long (undated) message from the government it was recommended to the Secretary of State that if the

Provisionals decided to declare a Christmas ceasefire then 'we should prepare to respond very quickly'. It spoke of the possibility of the need to take a 'far-reaching political decision' in such an event.[13] The British kept the Provisionals fully informed as to the progress or lack of it that the Brooke talks were making throughout 1992, their representative usually expressing pessimism.

On 26 October 1992, the government allowed Sinn Fein to preview a speech that the new Secretary of State, Sir Patrick Mayhew, was not to make until 16 December. In it he said that if there was an end to the IRA campaign then troops would be withdrawn and Sinn Fein would be included in the talks process. Republicanism would be able to 'seek a role in the peaceful political life of the community'. Communications between London and the Provisionals were stepped up in early 1993. On 12 January the government's representative assured the Provisionals that given the political risks the government was taking in contacting them 'they should be in no doubt that this indicates their seriousness in the whole thing. The conflict had been going on for too long. He said that the British government were not serious in 1974/75 but they were now.'[14] For the Provisional leadership this admission about the events surrounding the previous, failed ceasefire was hardly news, since Adams and McGuinness had come to that conclusion seventeen years earlier. But it seemed significant that the British government's representative was ready to admit it.

He also stressed that 'there was a conviction by senior civil servants that talks had to start . . . It could not be done without a major gesture from republicans. They realized that an IRA ceasefire was a non-starter. He voiced his view that a suspension – an easing off – would start the ball rolling in a significant way. That republicans would be convinced in that time that armed struggle was not necessary any longer.' On 19 March 1993, the British sent a nine-paragraph document to the Provisionals which outlined the conditions for their involvement in an 'inclusive' peace process. When it spoke of the need for a 'healing process' and the recognition that 'no one has a monopoly of suffering' it actually used the same language as Hume and Adams. Paragraph four stated: 'If violence had been genuinely brought to an end, whether or not the fact had been announced, then progressive entry into dialogue could take place.' Such a process would not have a predetermined outcome, but if a united Ireland was agreed on, with the consent of the people of Northern Ireland, then the British government would 'bring forward legislation to implement the will of the people here'.[15]

A growing sense of urgency marks the subsequent communications. The Brooke talk's three-strand format had by then collapsed, and the new Secretary of State, Sir Patrick Mayhew, was planning to meet with the parties bilaterally – a means that would allow Sinn Fein to enter the process more easily. The British representative told the Provisionals on 23 March that a recent speech by McGuinness

> had triggered government action. Mayhew had tried marginalization, defeating the IRA, etc. That's gone . . . Mayhew is now determined. He wants Sinn Fein to play a part not because he likes Sinn Fein but because it cannot work without them. Any settlement not involving all of the people North and South won't work. A North/South settlement that won't frighten unionists. The final solution is union. It's going to happen anyway. The historical train – Europe – determines that. We are committed to Europe. Unionists will have to change. This island will be as one.[16]

The government sought to reassure the Provisionals that there would be 'no cheating involved' and referred again to the 1974/75 cessation and the failed negotiations between the IRA and the British during which he admitted that the government had deliberately set out to 'con' the republicans, and succeeded. He said that the government had authorized him to tell Sinn Fein that if agreement on ending the violence was reached at 'six o'clock' then 'clearance for meetings at the level of delegations would be forthcoming by one minute past six'.

In spite of what they were hearing from the government's secret representative, who at times sounded like John Hume, the Provisionals moved cautiously. There was a noticeable decline in Provisional IRA activity in Ulster, but on 24 April 1993 they successfully exploded another huge bomb in the centre of London, killing a press photographer who entered the evacuated area after it was cleared. The explosion caused hundreds of millions of pounds' worth of damage. At the beginning of May the Army Council sanctioned a two-week cessation of violence.[17] It was a gesture of goodwill to the British. And it gave them an opportunity to follow through on their previous statement that in the event of violence ending, they would respond rapidly.

The secret notification of the May stoppage was accompanied by an outline of Sinn Fein's basis for entering into dialogue with the British. It recognized 'the concerns and perceived concerns' of the Unionists about an 'Irish national democracy' but resorted to the traditional republican analysis that the cause of the continued instability in Ireland was Britain's defence of partition. Before there would be any hope of peace, 'this must be addressed', the notification stated. Paragraph nine recognized that 'the most urgent issue facing the people of Ireland and Britain' was

> the need for a genuine peace process which sets equality, justice and political stability as its objectives and has as its means dialogue and all-embracing negotiations in the context of democratic principles. In attempting to progress towards that position we are prepared to be as reasonable and flexible as possible.

In this context, we are willing to seriously consider any proposal which genuinely aims to set such a process in train and to take the accompanying political risks involved.[18]

Accordingly, the armed campaign was brought to a halt on 11 May for two weeks – one of the longest cessations in the history of the conflict. But despite the promise of immediate clearance for further talks, it wasn't until five days later that the Provisionals were told that the 'May 10 position' had been accepted and that 'a new draft British paper had been formulated' which would be put to Major 'at a special meeting on Tuesday 18 May in Downing Street'. The British were becoming much less open with their documents at this stage and refused to hand over a draft of the new position to Sinn Fein. Meanwhile, the British contact man went off on a walking holiday. When he returned on 24 May he told the Provisionals that he was 'absolutely disgusted' at the government's lack of action.

At the 18 May government meeting, there was consternation among some ministers at the prospect of entering into dialogue with the Provisionals. Kenneth Clarke, Major's Chancellor of the Exchequer, said it was 'much too risky at the present time with the government under siege and if republicans were sincere about their intentions then the Prime Minister should hasten slowly to adopt such a radical departure from their previous publicly successful anti-terrorist line'.[18] Mayhew also expressed 'reservations' and wobbled between accepting the two-week cessation as sufficient and calling for a longer ceasefire. Major dithered, and began working on a new plan which demanded that the Provisionals call a longer cessation. On 3 June, a message to the Provisionals said that the government was working on another plan which because it was 'radical . . . needed careful crafting'. It was a greatly different response to the promised 'one minute past six' clearance for delegate meetings that the British had pledged in their 23 March communication.

The British representative expressed his 'depression and anger . . . at our failure to respond to your brave and straightforward offer' of 10 May. Further communications continued throughout the summer, but the secret peace process was now mortally wounded, mainly thanks to Major's prevarications. During the summer, his government was clinging to power and became more and more dependent on the support of Ulster Unionists in Westminster, which made it even harder for him to risk any daring initiative such as opening talks with the Provisionals. At the same time, the revelation that John Hume and Gerry Adams had reached an accord in an 'Irish peace initiative' began to eclipse other efforts – overt and covert – to launch a peace process. The prospect that the two wings of Irish nationalism, representing the constitutional and physical-force traditions, were after seventy years on the verge of reconciliation appeared now as the best hope that history's dead weight would finally be thrown off and progress made towards a lasting peace.[20]

The secret communications between Sinn Fein and the British government from 1992 onwards occasionally refer to the 'Irish initiative', without elaboration. In fact, by late 1992 there were effectively four sets of exploratory talks going on in Ulster, only one of which – the Brooke–Mayhew talks – was being held in the open. The other three involving Sinn Fein and the British government, Sinn Fein and Hume, and Martin Mansergh, an envoy from Fianna Fail leader Albert Reynolds, who met with Sinn Fein leaders from 1988 to 1994, were all secret.[21]

From the autumn of 1992 Hume was in contact with Mitchel McLaughlin, a high-ranking member of Sinn Fein in Derry, exploring the possibility of more thoroughgoing talks with the aim of reaching an understanding between the two parties. It was an ambitious goal – the republican movement had long castigated the SDLP as the 'Stoop Down Low

Party'. In Derry, Hume's home was regularly daubed with slogans proclaiming 'TRAITOR HUME'. In 1987, young members of the Provisionals fired shotguns at the windows, attempting to smash the glass to enable them to hurl petrol bombs into the downstairs rooms. The reinforced glass withstood the shots, but the attackers hurled their bombs anyway. The house went up in flames and John Hume's wife Pat and her youngest daughter Maureen were lucky to escape with their lives. Hume himself was at a conference at the time.[22]

The historical roots of the animosity between them were deep. Republicans regarded the SDLP the way they did Fianna Fail in the Irish Republic – as collaborators who had come to terms with British imperialism in order to forward their own selfish interests. As long as Sinn Fein saw itself as a revolutionary socialist party, whose 'cutting edge' was the Provisional IRA, able to take power in Ireland, then this attitude would remain. But from the late 1980s onwards, Sinn Fein spokesmen moderated their criticisms of the SDLP. Sinn Fein's view of the republican movement's prospects began to change, thanks to continuing difficulties with the armed campaign and a sense of the party's growing isolation.

This sense was heightened in April 1992 when Adams lost his West Belfast seat to Dr Joe Hendron of the SDLP in a British general election. Following a bitter campaign, Adams lost by a margin of just 589 votes. Hendron, a persevering but not very inspiring candidate, won the support of some Shankill Road Protestants among whom he canvassed. This, apparently, proved crucial to the outcome. The Sinn Fein President and his supporters were outraged. Their reaction revealed not only anger but a feeling almost of persecution. Richard McAuley, Sinn Fein spokesman, declared: 'Joe Hendron went to the electorate with a ballot paper in one hand and a loyalist death squad in the other.' Adams himself reacted with anger and said that 'the seat has been stolen from the people of West Belfast. I am sure it will not be long until they get it back.'[23] The implications of this go beyond the usual terms of electoral politics to identify the supporters of Sinn Fein as 'the people' of the constituency – as if SDLP supporters who live there are somehow not really part of West Belfast. It is also a reflection of Sinn Fein's increasing anxiety that the electoral tide was decisively turning against it. In other constituencies there was a swing against Sinn Fein and towards the SDLP. Sinn Fein's overall share of the vote was reduced to 10 per cent, compared to the SDLP's 23.5 per cent. In Fermanagh-South Tyrone – a shrine of republican mythology as the seat formerly held by hunger striker Bobby Sands – the SDLP overtook Sinn Fein and became the largest nationalist party.

By ending its policy of abstentionism in the South, Sinn Fein had changed its attitude towards Fianna Fail's role in the settlement of the conflict; from 1988 it had begun to modify its approach to the SDLP. After the 1992 loss, it accelerated this change of course. Contacts with Hume were resumed, in secret, so that by late 1992 Sinn Fein could refer confidently to an 'Irish' peace initiative in its secret communications with the British government.

The Mitchel McLaughlin–Hume talks came to the attention of the RUC when they were investigating a Sinn Fein wiretap on Hume's telephone in December 1992. They were of sufficient interest to the authorities that the RUC Special Branch got permission from the government to tap Hume's telephone in January 1993. A report was drawn up and presented to Mayhew about the developing contacts between the SDLP leader and high-ranking Sinn Fein officials. Its contents led Mayhew to ask if Hume's antipathy to the Provisionals was sincere.[24]

Hume's contacts with Sinn Fein were finally revealed on 10 April 1993, when Adams was seen visiting his house in Derry, walking in through the door that six years earlier the Provisional IRA had fire-bombed. On 24 April, the two issued a joint statement. It recognized the need for 'national reconciliation' based on the

> peaceful accommodation of the differences between the people of Britain and Ireland and the Irish people themselves.
>
> In striving for that end, we accept that an internal settlement is not a solution because it obviously does not deal with all the relationships at the heart of the problem.
>
> We accept that the Irish people as a whole have a right to national self-determination. This is a view shared by a majority of the people of this island, though not by all its people.
>
> The exercise of self-determination is a matter for agreement between the people of Ireland. It is the search for that agreement and the means of achieving it on which we will be concentrating.
>
> We are mindful that not all the people of Ireland share that view or agree on how to give meaningful expression to it. Indeed, we do not disguise the different views held by our own parties . . . we have told each other that we see the task of reaching agreement on a peaceful and democratic accord for all on this island as our primary challenge.[25]

The statement's language is more Hume than Adams, more SDLP than Sinn Fein. Its thesis accepts that a section of the Irish people – the Protestants – do not share the goals of Irish nationalists and that agreement has to be achieved on how to reach reconciliation with them. There is no hint of the traditional republican analysis of the role Britain has played in Irish history, nor of the demand that Britain declare its intention to withdraw, which the IRA and its spokesmen insisted over the years was the key to bringing the armed campaign to an end.

The joint statement was the most dramatic indication so far of the tremendous transformation that was taking place within the Provisional movement – or at least within its upper echelons. It represents not only the beginning of the reconciliation of the two wings of Irish nationalism, constitutional and physical force, but effectively marks the ideological defeat of Provisional republicanism – the last significant exponents of the physical-force tradition – and the beginning of its absorption into the wider spectrum of constitutional nationalist tradition that had marginalized the IRA and Sinn Fein in the Southern Irish state in the 1920s and 1930s.

A signal of the changing status of Sinn Fein was given in June 1993 when the Irish President, Mary Robinson, shook hands with Adams during a visit to West Belfast.

Hume and Adams continued to meet throughout the summer of 1993. On 25 September, they issued a second statement, claiming that

> our discussions, aimed at the creation of a peace process which would involve all parties, have made considerable progress. We agreed to forward a report on the position reached to date to Dublin for consideration . . . We are convinced from our discussions that a process can be designed to lead to agreement among the divided people of this island, which will provide a solid basis for peace. Such a process would obviously also be designed to ensure that any new agreement that might emerge respects the diversity of our different traditions and earns their allegiance and respect.

Just over a week later, the Provisional Army Council announced that it welcomed the Hume–Adams initiative. 'If the political will exists or can be created,' the IRA statement said, 'it could provide the basis for peace. We, our volunteers and our supporters, have a vested interest in seeking a just and lasting peace in Ireland. Our objectives which include the right of the Irish people to national self-determination are well known. Our commitment remains steadfast.'[26]

This was the most conciliatory statement from the IRA to date. Four days later, on 7 October, Hume briefed the Irish government on his meetings and discussions with Adams and Sinn Fein. He reiterated his belief that the principles that he and the Sinn Fein leader had agreed to – contained in their April statement – could provide the basis for a peaceful settlement to the Ulster crisis. Later, the results of the Hume–Adams discussions were presented to John Major. But efforts to get both the Irish and British governments to endorse them failed throughout the autumn of 1993.

The British told Dublin that 'as long as Adams' fingerprints were on it' they couldn't touch the Irish peace initiative. With consummate hypocrisy, the London government was rejecting the initiative on the grounds that it involved negotiating with terrorists while it itself was still involved in secret talks with the Provisional IRA's leadership.

'I don't think they are going to run,' Major commented at one point when asked about the Hume–Adams proposals. Albert Reynolds, whose shrewdness was born of years working as a provincial entrepreneur, now led the Irish government. Alarmed, he told Hume to stop 'playing up' the Hume–Adams proposals. The Irish were engaged with the British in trying to devise their own and found Hume's constant reiteration of what he declared was a recipe for peace embarrassing and unhelpful. In the meantime, both Dublin and London put pressure on the Provisional IRA to end its campaign. 'We want to hear from the Provisional IRA that they are going to repudiate violence,' said Major. 'By that I don't mean a short term cease-fire to be casually tossed away at the first opportunity. I mean the clearest possible indication that they have decided . . . to give up violence for good.'[27]

The Provisionals' campaign produced another crisis in the peace process when on 23 October a bomb attack aimed at the UDA headquarters above a fish shop on the Shankill Road went wrong. The bomb exploded prematurely inside the shop, killing the bomber and nine Protestants, including four women and two children, and injuring hundreds. It was a Saturday afternoon, the busiest time on the road.

There was a wave of loyalist retaliatory killings. Hume, who had staked his whole career on convincing the Provisionals to give up violence, had a nervous collapse and was hospitalized suffering from exhaustion. It was perhaps the bleakest moment of the peace process and one of the grimmest since the conflict began. A week after the bombing, on a grey, sunless afternoon, one of the victims, seven-year-old Leanne Murray, was being buried. The bomber, Thomas Begley, a semi-literate twenty-three-year-old from Ardoyne in North Belfast, had grown up a short distance from the street where Leanne lived. As her small white coffin came slowly along the Shankill Road, Begley's funeral cortège crossed its path less than a hundred yards further down. Gangs of youths who were following the Begley procession jeered and shouted obscenities at the Protestant mourners. How could the delicate hope for peace survive such hatreds? It seemed to have been buried in the rubble of the Shankill bomb, never to be exhumed. However, it would prove a hardier flower than most expected.

Oddly enough, it was nourished by the revelations, which appeared not long after the Shankill bombing, that for years the British government had been in secret contact with the IRA. Unionists were appalled, of course, but the reaction in the British parliament was less critical than many had predicted. The tale of secret IRA–British government diplomacy allowed the Dublin and London governments to address the Hume–Adams proposals more directly. Irish civil servants 'rejigged' them, incorporating some of the proposals and jettisoning others. One of the civil servants, Fergus Finlay, brought them North, where he showed them to the Rev. Roy Magee, who had been trying to persuade the UDA and UVF to call a ceasefire, and Gusty Spence, the former UVF leader. Spence served over seventeen years for the murder of Peter

Ward (see Chapter 1) and had been released in 1984. During his prison years, he had been transformed from a sectarian thug into a thoughtful, tolerant man, anxious to find a way out of the endless cycle of violence. Magee and Spence suggested some additions to the draft. After a further period of intense working and reworking, it was presented to an expectant public on 15 December 1993 as the Downing Street Declaration.

It stated: 'The ending of divisions can come about only through the agreement and co-operation of the people, North and South, representing both traditions in Ireland.' The declaration committed both governments to 'foster agreement and reconciliation, leading to a new political framework founded on consent and encompassing arrangements within Northern Ireland, for the whole island, and between these islands'. Once more, Britain reiterated that it had 'no selfish strategic or economic interest in Northern Ireland'. The statement declared that Britain's 'primary interest' was 'to see peace, stability and reconciliation established by agreement among all the people who inhabit the island, and they will work together with the Irish government to achieve such an agreement, which will embrace the totality of relationships'. Further, Britain acknowledged that 'it is for the people of the island of Ireland alone, by agreement between the two parts respectively, to exercise their right of self-determination on the basis of consent, freely and concurrently given, North and South, to bring about a united Ireland, if that is their wish'.[28]

The declaration qualified the Hume–Adams reference to Irish self-determination by including the provision that the people of the North and the South were to exercise it separately, thus protecting the current wish of the Northern Ireland majority to remain within the UK; and it ditched the Sinn Fein demand that Britain act in the role of a 'persuader' of the Unionists to join a unitary state. To further placate Protestants, it included paragraphs (at the suggestion of Spence and Magee) committing the Irish government – 'in the event of an overall settlement' – to change the Irish Constitution, removing territorial claims over Northern Ireland, and to removing any 'elements in the democratic life and organization of the Irish state' that could be viewed as a 'real and substantial threat' to the Protestant way of life. There was also a provision for the setting up of an institution that would give recognition to the 'links between the people of Britain and Ireland as part of the totality of relationships'. It opened the door to negotiation with all democratically mandated parties 'which establish a commitment to exclusively peaceful methods and which have shown that they abide by the democratic process'.

It was immediately clear to Unionists of all shades that this would include Sinn Fein. Coming so soon after the Shankill bombing it outraged some Protestants, especially as Adams had been seen carrying the coffin of Begley, the IRA bomber, as it left his Ardoyne home. Yet the mainstream Ulster Unionist Party was restrained in its response, and greeted the declaration with guarded acceptance. Others did not. 'You have sold Ulster to buy off the fiendish republican scum and you are prepared to do this notorious deed with such speed that time is not even given for the Christian burial of their latest victim,' Paisley wrote to Major after the declaration was published.[29] After thirty years of such fulminations, no one was surprised at Paisley's reaction. People were far more interested in seeing how Sinn Fein and the Provisional IRA would respond.

The Provisionals had rejected the Sunningdale Agreement outright in 1973. They had condemned – sometimes stridently – the Anglo-Irish Agreement twelve years later, but with some qualifications that left room for recognition that indeed it contained progressive elements. When confronted with the Downing Street Declaration, the Provisionals hesitated. The

IRA had endorsed the Hume–Adams proposals as providing a basis for peace, but the declaration abandoned important parts of that initiative. Six days after the declaration, Adams held a press conference at which he criticized the Irish–British initiative for 'its lack of mechanisms' and 'its lack of a clear process'. He said 'it needs to be clarified'. Major rejected his appeal and said he would not enter into a dialogue with the republican movement about the declaration.

The Provisionals were trapped. The Downing Street Declaration was clearly insufficient for them to declare a cease-fire. But they could not reject it out of hand unless they were prepared to risk alienating their new-found constitutional nationalist allies in the SDLP and the Irish government. They continued to press for 'clarification' while at the same time muting criticism of it. 'More significantly, they did not encourage community groups or prominent personalities, such as Bernadette McAliskey, to identify the declaration for what in fact it was'[30] – an historic compromise of traditional republican goals, or, some would say, an abandonment of those goals.

Among the political figures who supported the declaration as providing the basis for a permanent settlement of the Ulster conflict was America's new Democratic President, Bill Clinton, in office just less than a year. While trying to win the Democratic nomination, Clinton attended a forum on Irish issues held in New York City in April 1992. During the discussion with Irish American journalists and activists, who included Martin Galvin, the prominent NORAID spokesman, Clinton more or less committed himself, if elected President, to appointing a peace envoy to Northern Ireland and granting Gerry Adams a visa to go to the US. Cynics dismissed Clinton's avowals as being no more reliable than the promises of a drunk man. When Adams's application for a visa was rejected in May 1993, and talk about the peace envoy shelved, many British reporters in the US chortled that once more the 'special relationship' between the UK and the US had triumphed over the gang of sentimental Irish Americans – the Irish lobby – which was pressing Clinton to put Ulster high on his administration's agenda. They declared victory too soon. The battle to place Northern Ireland on the US agenda had hardly begun, as became clear that autumn.

In September 1993 Bruce Morrison, a former Congressman and Clinton confidant, led a delegation of Irish Americans to Belfast on a fact-finding mission. They were followed in late November by a New Jersey lawyer, Edmund Lynch, who was campaigning to have the visa ban on Adams lifted. On 14 December, back in Washington, Lynch had a 'confidential' meeting with Jane Holl, the Director of European Affairs on the National Security Council.[31] Holl told Lynch that Clinton would reconsider the visa ban if Adams was invited to the US, which he was in January 1994. In spite of fierce British government opposition, Clinton lifted the ban, and let Adams into the US, where he received a rapturous reception during a weekend visit to New York. For Adams, it was an impressive display of Irish American power. In conjunction with the Irish government and the SDLP it would constitute a powerful pan-nationalist front, able to wrest concessions from Britain. But before it could be fully harnessed, he knew the armed campaign would have to be brought to a close.

3

By early 1994, two factors were pushing the Provisionals to end the armed campaign. The first was internal, the dynamic of their engagement in the peace process, which created expectations within the broad nationalist community that were becoming ever more difficult to disappoint. The second was external – the pressure from the security forces' intelligence services that was crippling the ability of the IRA to conduct its operations, especially in Belfast. The truth was that by 1994 the RUC Special Branch and its allies in BOX were winning the twilight war.

Accurate intelligence built up through both human and technical sources allowed the RUC to acquire a detailed knowledge of the membership and structure of the Provisional IRA leadership. The organization's upper echelons were gradually penetrated. The seven-man Army Council was known, and included one old hand, Joe Cahill, a founding member of the organization, along with Gerry Adams, Martin McGuinness, Gerry Kelly, Thomas 'Slab' Murphy, Kevin McKenna, and Paddy Doherty. Belfast men (Kelly, Adams, Cahill) dominated the governing body.

Under the Army Council was ranged the PIRA's General Head Quarters, headed by Kevin McKenna as Chief of Staff. His two deputy Chiefs of Staff were Adams and McGuinness. The GHQ had ten departments – operations, intelligence, adjutant general, quartermaster general, training, finance, overseas operations, overseas liaison, engineering, and GHQ staff officers. Among the most important of these were the post of quartermaster general, held by Micky McKevitt, which controlled the arms dumps; intelligence, headed by Belfast man Martin Lynch; operations, controlled by 'Slab' Murphy; engineering, where new terrorist technology was developed, headed by Patrick 'Val' Lynch and another man; and finance, with three officers, including Joe Cahill and a Belfast woman. Altogether, the GHQ staff consisted of around fifteen members as of 1994.

There were two separate commands, Northern and Southern. By late 1993, Martin McGuinness headed the first and Dermot Finucane (the Maze escapee) the second. Among Northern Command's officers were 'Big John' Magee, a former British soldier from Belfast who was head of the Civil Administration Team (the tout-hunters), and Sean 'Spike' Murray, a member of the Belfast brigade and a cousin of Danny McCann, who was shot dead in Gibraltar.

Successful surveillance and intelligence-gathering cost the Belfast brigade two of its chief bomb-makers within a few months of each other. The first was arrested on 11 January 1992, with 1,500 pounds of explosives, and the second on 23 July while holding a bomb-making class. After that, the IRA's campaign using large car bombs against so-called commercial targets in the city centre went into decline. (There were only two such explosions between July 1992 and May 1993.) A source, cited as 'senior Special Branch', told a Belfast newspaper that 'the IRA in Belfast is now facing operational difficulties because of a shortage of skilled activists in bomb making and other areas'.[32] Meanwhile, sniping attacks against the security forces were rare in Belfast. When on 2 August, twenty-four-year-old Damian Shackleton was shot dead in North Belfast, he was the first British soldier to die at the hands of an IRA sniper in the city in four years.[33] As of August 1992, the IRA had managed to kill only two soldiers and a policewoman. According to *The Irish Times* of 13 August 1992 this reflected 'the lowest level of activity since the IRA campaign began in 1971'.

The Provisionals were relying more and more on the do-it-yourself technology of small bombs made out of explosives packed into coffee jars and hurled like improvised grenades over the walls of RUC stations or at passing patrols. They inflicted injuries but hardly ever caused fatalities among the security forces.[34] The GHQ's engineering department developed a potentially more devastating weapon, the so-called Mark 15 mortar or 'barracks buster'. It was unveiled in early 1993. It was sixteen inches in diameter, and capable of hurling between 300 and 400 pounds of explosives over a 60-foot fence or wall at a range of 150 yards. It was used in February 1993 to severely damage Bessbrook RUC base in South Armagh, after several earlier attacks on other security installations failed. A subsequent attack on the Crossmaglen security base injured several soldiers. A civilian worker died when the 'barracks buster' struck the RUC/army base in Keady, Co. Armagh, on 5 March 1993. But the device, though menacing, was not enough to enable the Provisionals to regain the military initiative. It was never used in Belfast, the cockpit of the conflict.

If the Provisionals saw Belfast as the key to continuing the war, then they still saw London as the key to winning it – that is, instrumental in wearing down the British government's commitment to Ulster. For a long time, the police had little or no success in stopping IRA attacks in Britain. In 1992 the RUC Chief Constable, Hugh Annesley, warned that there was a 'void that is yet to be filled' concerning information on the IRA 'mainland' ASUs.[35] But shortly after the Baltic Exchange bomb, in April, the police arrested James Canning, a thirty-seven-year-old Scot, and uncovered a substantial arms and explosives dump in a garage in West London. He was linked to twelve bombings and sentenced later to thirty years' imprisonment. But small bombs continued to explode in London throughout the rest of 1992. There were five attacks between June and October. Between 7 and 12 October there were eight, one of which killed a man in a pub in Covent Garden. However, shortly afterwards a haul of Semtex weighing seventy pounds was found in a tea chest in a shop in East London. In November, police thwarted two attempts to explode thousand-pound car bombs near the centre of London. One of the targets was London's tallest building at Canary Wharf in the docklands area of the city.

The Provisional IRA remained defiant. In an interview with the *Guardian* on 12 February 1993, an IRA spokesman said that only 'fortuitous luck' had been behind the success of the British police. The statistics he trotted out seemed to support him. In 1992 the organization exploded forty-six bombs in Britain, 'causing 1,200 million pounds' worth of damage, the collapse of insurance cover and the introduction of armed roadblocks in London. There were 1,000 occasions when commuter traffic and businesses ground to a halt' creating a 'crisis in the heart of the British capital which has demonstrated that so long as interference in Irish affairs continues, then the consequences of that conflict will spill over and be visited on the national territory of the occupier'. He also denied that there was any debate going on within the leadership about the continuation of the armed campaign. 'Our discussions revolve around the best means of prosecuting the war,' he said.

Luck was undoubtedly involved in many arrests. But the police were also helped by the fact that, beginning in 1992, the Provisionals departed from their precaution of using for the English operations only 'lily-white' volunteers. In June 1992, English police arrested Paul 'Dingus' Magee after he shot two constables who stopped him and another IRA man at a routine road check. One of the constables died. Magee was a well-known Provisional from the Ballymurphy area of West Belfast who was first jailed in 1971 for possessing explosives. He was arrested again in 1980 after a gun battle in which an SAS captain was killed in North Belfast.[36] He escaped a year later from the Crumlin Road jail and went on the run in the Irish Republic before heading for England.

In 1993 another two well-known 'players', Rab Fryers and Phelim Hamill, became involved in the English operations. Fryers had already been arrested in connection with a mortar-making factory in Belfast in the mid-1980s, and was known for his republican sympathies, which he did little to keep secret in pubs and clubs. Thanks to telephone taps, the Special Branch were able to keep track of Fryers' movements around Britain. He was finally arrested in London on 14 July 1993 after the surveillance unit thought he was about to plant a bomb. Hamill was a different character entirely. He was an academic, but the police had had him under suspicion since 1983 for links with an IRA ASU that was involved in a series of killings and attempted killings of legal figures near Queen's

University, Belfast (see Chapter 5). Six months after Fryers' arrest, Hamill accepted a university job in Britain – a posting that some suspect was deliberately arranged in order to lure him to England, where it was hoped he would lead the police to other IRA ASUs. However, though this part of the plot failed – perhaps owing to premature action on the part of the English police – when he was lifted he had in his possession a small arsenal, including Semtex, plus a list of 274 names of possible targets.

The Provisionals' main command centre in South Armagh for English bombing attacks still continued to function. In April 1993 it successfully organized the huge bomb attack in Bishopsgate, London. At the beginning of 1994, shortly after Adams returned from his triumphant trip to New York, it was behind a series of mortar bomb attacks on Heathrow airport. None of the mortars was armed, however, and the incidents were regarded as more of a demonstration of the IRA's continued ability to carry out such operations than a serious attempt to do damage. As it turned out, it was the last time in this phase of the struggle that they would succeed in demonstrating that ability. The RUC Special Branch pre-empted their next major bombing attempt on 12 July 1994, when the police intercepted a lorry as it came off a boat from Warrenpoint, Co. Down, at Southport on the English coast. It possessed a secret compartment packed with nearly a ton of explosives. The lorry originated in South Armagh. The ceasefire was only a matter of weeks away and the Provisionals had intended this huge bomb as their way of showing that they were quitting the battlefield from a position of strength, not weakness. Its interception was another demoralizing blow to the Army Council.

The eight months before the Southport bust had been bad ones for the Provisionals in Belfast. The UDA and UVF were on the rampage, especially in the north of the city, traditionally their favourite hunting ground. Three Catholics were

Top The political rise of
Sinn Fein in the early
1980s frightened the Irish
political establishment.
The SDLP, along with the
three main political parties
in the Irish Republic,
created the New Ireland
Forum to examine
constitutional Irish
nationalism and its
relationship to Northern
Ireland. It restated
nationalist goals and
ideals. Though its findings
were rejected outright by
British Prime Minister
Margaret Thatcher, they
helped inspire the
beginning of negotiations
which led to the Anglo-
Irish Agreement. Seen
here is the forum's first
meeting in 1984. (Eamonn
Farrell/Photocall Ireland)

Middle Loyalists protest
the Anglo-Irish
Agreement, signed in
November 1985, which
gave the Irish government
a say in the running of
Northern Ireland for the
first time. The agreement
was the first major British
initiative since 1973, and
though it was never
accepted by Unionists,
some believe it laid the
groundwork for future
progress in Northern
Ireland and the beginning
of the peace process.
(Eamonn Farrell/
Photocall Ireland)

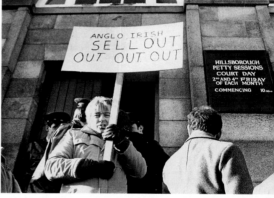

Below In the 1980s,
after the break up of the
Harrison network,
republicans turned to the
Middle East for arms
supplies. Pictured is the
villa owned by the PLO
where the INLA's quarter-
master often stayed while
arranging arms shipments
back to Ireland.
(Private collection)

A Chara: It must be crisis time again as its the only time you hear from me. Firstly I should explain why I'm seeking assistance from you rather than going through the RA. As I am sure you are aware there have been a number of significant R.U.C. 'successes' in Belfast & elsewhere recently i.e. the abortive Crum prison break, the arrest of Morrison & co plus a number of abortive op like ours. Our conclusion is that the B.B. may well be compromised. Therefore we are seeking as much as possible to minimise our reliance on the O.O. Secondly as a former IRSP you can understand its a question of who you know rather than what you know that guarantees the degree of cooperation you ultimately receive. Of course we are in contact with some volunteers outside and before we make any move we will be informing the O.O. outside. However before this we intend our plans to be finalised & our resources in place to avoid being given the run around by outside. Therefore we have decided to rely on friends wherever possible. Now I realise this may put you in a predicament on a personal basis, but two things I guarantee is (A) your total anonymity – no one outside of myself & our R.O. knows your I.D., and (B) there will be no kick back from the RA as re a Northern Command brief its just we are reluctant to chance possibly compromised channels. So down to what I require & to discover if you can assist. So you recall having one of those stun gun devices, I think that're an anti rape/mugging device that women carry, I remember you mentioned having at least one, well if you can still get your hands on one or preferably two, I would ask you to supply them to me. If thats not possible could you put me in contact with someone who could. Now the type of thing I am talking about would have to be easily concealable. I also would need a full rundown on how they effect work. For example, is it possible to put down more than one person at a time with one of these efforts, or is it that after using it once you must wait it recharging before its possible to use again. How long, is it possible to immobilise a full grown man for using one of these, and anything else you feel I should know about the use of one of these things. I've also asked our kid to ask you about stun/gas grenades, hell they're not that important as I may be going overboard on that. What I'm looking really is means of immobilizing a number of screws/cops, so if you can suggest anything. Also could you suggest good methods of disguise. I mean I know about wigs etc but do you have any ideas on good wigs, facial disguise etc. Now we won't have the opportunity to sit down in front of a mirror so I mean a means of disguising oneself quickly & simply that would allow one to walk out past guards who may or maynot ... if you know of any or have access to good disguise they too would be useful. As this scheme develops and if you are willing to cooperate I may require your opinion on a few aspects of the plan, I know it wouldn't be easy for you to put yourself in our shoes but maybe some hints you could

about stun/gas grenades, hell they're not that important as I may be going overboard on that. What I'm looking really is means of immobilizing a number of screws/cops, so if you can suggest anything. Also could you suggest good methods of disguise. I mean I know about wigs etc but do you have any ideas on good wigs, facial disguise etc. Now we won't have the opportunity to sit down in front of a mirror so I mean a means of disguising oneself quickly & simply that would allow one to walk out past guards who may or maynot ... if you know of any or have access to good disguise they too would be useful. As this scheme develops and if you are willing to cooperate I may require your opinion on a few aspects of the plan, I know it wouldn't be easy for you to put yourself in our shoes but maybe some hints you could
offer based on your past ability to get out of tricky situations. Well Cara I think this is about it for now. If you agree with what I'm asking I'll be in touch. I see ... is getting himself in trouble again smashing up diners. Tell him I was asking, hows Elish & the family I hope all is well with yours. I'm hoping that this talk of 'bringing the armed struggle' to a conclusion that McGuinness & co are talking about bears fruit as I've thrown the hands up on at least two occasions, but I've an awful feeling this war is set for at least another decade whether we have the ability to break out of the containment the Brits are imposing on the war I think is crucial to the ultimate success/failure of the conflict. At the present I'm not optimistic of our ability to do so. You would not believe the change in attitude – resolve of the Northern Nationalist Community regarding their commitment to the war. Slán do Chara Scout.

A 'comm.' written on cigarette paper and smuggled out of Crumlin jail. It contains one of the first indications of peace moves developing within the Provisional leadership.

Paddy Hill, one of the Birmingham Six, on his release in March 1991. The six Irishmen were convicted of killing 21 people in bomb attacks on two Birmingham pubs in November 1974. They alleged they were beaten and forced into signing confessions of guilt. After a long campaign to prove their innocence they were released when the second appeal against their convictions was upheld. The Birmingham Six case was one of three in which miscarriages of justice against Irish men and women in Britain in the 1970s were found to have taken place. *(Photocall Ireland)*

Below Peter Brooke, who became Secretary of State for Northern Ireland in 1989. During his tenure, secret contacts were reopened with the IRA leadership, beginning in 1990. Brooke stated on 9 November of that year that Britain had 'no selfish strategic or economic interest' in staying in Northern Ireland. It was an appeal to the IRA to end its campaign. Secret contacts continued until 1993 and helped prepare the way for the broader peace initiatives. Brooke was replaced by Sir Patrick Mayhew in April 1992. *(Eamonn Farrell/Photocall Ireland)*

Below right Martin McGuinness former Chief of Staff of the Provisional IRA, head of Northern Command and a member of the Army Council, played a key role in the secret moves within the IRA to bring about an end to the armed campaign, beginning in 1990, when he was in contact with a British government representative. *(Eamonn Farrell/Photocall Ireland)*

Above left Mitchel McLaughlin, a leading member of Sinn Fein from Derry. Police wire-taps on the telephone of John Hume revealed discussions between McLaughlin and the SDLP leader from January 1993 onwards. *(Eamonn Farrell/Photocall Ireland)*

Above right Martin Mansergh, an Irish official who acted as a special envoy to Northern Ireland for the Fianna Fail leader Albert Reynolds. Reynolds later became Taoiseach (Irish Prime Minister) and was instrumental in bringing about the IRA ceasefire in 1994. Mansergh engaged in secret talks with members of the Provisional IRA from 1988 to 1994. *(Eamonn Farrell/Photocall Ireland)*

US President Bill Clinton, Taoiseach Albert Reynolds and US Ambassador to Ireland Jean Kennedy Smith. Kennedy Smith and Reynolds convinced Clinton to grant a visa waiver to the Sinn Fein President Gerry Adams to allow him to visit New York in late January 1994. This helped persuade Adams that a pan-nationalist front was viable. The IRA ceasefire followed eight months later. *(Photocall Ireland)*

Left above Sean O hUiginn, a high-ranking official in the Irish Government who played an important role in the negotiations in the wake of the IRA ceasefire of 31 August 1994. He helped draft the Irish government's contribution to the major statements and documents on the peace process that followed. He argued that it was crucial never to mislead the IRA and proved such a trenchant negotiator that the British dubbed him 'The Dark Prince'. He later became Irish Ambassador to the US. *(Eamonn Farrell/Photocall Ireland)*

Left below President William Jefferson Clinton, the first US president to put Northern Ireland firmly on the US agenda. The photograph was taken at the White House on 11 September 1998, just hours after the Kenneth Starr report was published. But the Irish American audience gave the President – who was receiving the Paul O'Dwyer Peace and Justice Award – a five-minute standing ovation in thanks for his part in the peace process. *(Courtesy of the Irish Echo)*

Below Gusty Spence, who founded the UVF in 1966 and launched the first sectarian murder campaign of the Troubles. Jailed in 1966 he served 18 years during which he learned Irish and for a long time grew close to the Official IRA. He became a loyalist icon. Spence was an important influence on the loyalists' decision to call a ceasefire on 13 October 1994 and helped draft their statement halting the long campaign of terror. *(Kelvin Boyes)*

Above left David Ervine, leader of the Progressive Unionist Party, the political wing of the UVF, founded in 1979. Ervine, a former UVF prisoner, became a vocal supporter of the peace process, and showed a willingness to break loyalist taboos. Here he is seen after a meeting with John Bruton, the Irish Taoiseach in Dublin in September 1995. Ervine won a seat in the new assembly in 1998. *(Eamonn Farrell/Photocall Ireland)*

Above right Former US Senator George Mitchell. President Clinton made Mitchell his economic envoy to Northern Ireland, and then asked him to chair a commission to look at the paramilitary disarmament issue. In 1997 Mitchell became chairman of the all-party talks, and is credited by all sides with helping to shepherd the talks to a successful conclusion in April 1998 with the signing of the Good Friday Agreement.
(Eamonn Farrell/Photocall Ireland)

Below left David Trimble, Unionist Party leader, seen on 18 April 1998 after he won a two-to-one vote in support of his signing the Good Friday Agreement. In subsequent elections, only a narrow majority of pro-Agreement Unionist members won seats to the new assembly. Trimble was a joint winner along with John Hume of the Nobel Peace Prize in 1998. He was elected First Minister of the new assembly. By the summer of 1999 a dispute over disarmament was still preventing the new government from taking office.
(Leon Farrell/Photocall Ireland)

Below right Northern Ireland Secretary of State Mo Mowlam, who on her appointment under Labour Prime Minister Tony Blair in 1997 helped bring about another IRA ceasefire leading to the Good Friday Peace Agreement. *(Courtesy of the Irish Echo)*

erry Adams, leading his platform in voting in favour of the Good Friday Agreement on
May 1998. Adams also helped convince the republican movement to abandon a long-
anding Sinn Fein policy and allow all candidates to take their seats in the new assembly
d power-sharing executive which were envisioned as part of that agreement. *(Eamonn
rrell/Photocall Ireland)*

elow left Seamus Mallon, deputy leader of the SDLP and Deputy First Minister of the
w assembly. Mallon, MP for Armagh, has been a consistent critic of the IRA and
pressed concern at times that his party leader John Hume's political engagement with
rry Adams might bolster Sinn Fein support. He was also widely trusted by Unionists.
amonn Farrell/Photocall Ireland)*

elow right The beginning of all-party talks in Stormont in September 1997 for the first
e brought together Sinn Fein and the Unionists in an attempt to resolve the long-
anding conflict. *(Photocall Ireland)*

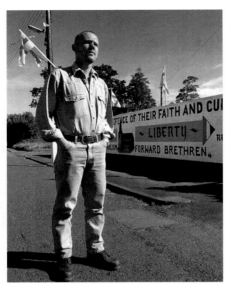

Billy Wright, a former leader of the UVF in North Armagh. He was jailed for paramilitary offences as teenager. During the 1980s and 1990s he was believed to have been involved in dozens of sectarian killings. In 1996, Wright broke with the UVF in disagreement over its ceasefire to form the Loyalist Volunteer Force which launched a campaign of sectarian violence that lasted two years. Wright was assassinated by the INLA in December 1997 while serving a prison sentence in The Maze. *(Kelvin Boyes)*

A member of the Orange Order preparing to march in Portadown, Co. Armagh. The Order was founded in North Armagh in 1795. Many of its marches remain a provocation for Catholics and continue to threaten widespread violence, in spite of the peace process and the euphoria over the Good Friday Agreement. To date, the controversy over the parades in Drumcree near Portadown, remained unresolved. *(Eamonn Farrell/Photocall Ireland)*

murdered in August, including Sean Lavery, the son of a popular Sinn Fein councillor. Of the ten murders that occurred over the following days, only two were the responsibility of the Provisionals. The killings were largely the work of the Shankill Road UDA, 'C' company, which in the early 1970s John White had helped mould into a feared murder machine. In 1993, it was under the command of Johnny Adair, a twenty-nine-year-old killer who when asked once by a Catholic reporter if he had ever had a Catholic in his car before replied 'only a dead one'.[37] The blundered bombing attack on the Shankill Road fish shop was a desperate attempt to strike back at Adair, who the IRA thought was attending a meeting in a room above the shop. Loyalists went on the rampage and murdered another thirteen people, seven in one attack on a pub in Co. Derry, between 24 and 31 October.

Adams was angry that the Shankill massacre had ruined his peace strategy. Under stress, he blew up, something of a rare event, shouting abuse at several high-ranking members of the Belfast brigade.

In February 1994, the Provisionals suffered a further setback in Belfast when the RUC, disguised as building workers, intercepted one of their top ASUs as it made ready to assassinate Superintendent Derek Martindale, who had been in charge of the RUC's anti-fraud squad, C-13. Among the three IRA men arrested was David Adams, a cousin of the Sinn Fein leader, and a high-ranking member of the Belfast brigade, who was badly beaten during the arrest and had his leg broken.

The failure of this assassination, which had been planned for almost six months, was a severe blow to the Provisionals. It caused a row between the Belfast brigade and GHQ, which was convinced that a high-ranking informer had penetrated the Belfast organization, thoroughly compromising it. A tout hunt began. What the Provisionals did not realize was that the plot to assassinate Martindale was uncovered by a small unit in the Special Branch known as E9. Set up in 1988, it had only fifty members. It was under the command of Superintendent Ian Phoenix, a fifty-one-year-old veteran of the RUC who had been in the force since 1970. In 1971, he was a young constable serving in Springfield Road RUC station when the Provisionals hurled a fifty-pound bomb into it. Phoenix was blown off his feet by the explosion, which killed an army sergeant. A Special Branch officer since 1979, he had reorganized E4A surveillance units, served on TCG South, and then at RUC headquarters in Belfast. From September 1992, his team was responsible for many breakthroughs against Protestant paramilitaries and the Provisionals, including the interception of Hamill and Fryers' bombing mission in England and the seizure of the one-ton blockbuster bomb destined for London and intended to allow the Provisionals to go out with a bang.[38]

It is certain that these setbacks, coupled with the mounting political pressure on Sinn Fein, pushed the Provisional IRA to end the armed campaign. The Army Council discussed the idea of a permanent halt in November 1993 but decided on a Christmas ceasefire lasting seventy-two hours and 'not a second more'. The resistance to halting the armed campaign was immense. It meant going against the most deeply embedded republican belief – the necessity of armed force to break the British link with Ireland. Even as the IRA leadership debated the issue Martin McGuinness declared in January 1994 that the IRA would not halt its campaign short of the British giving a commitment to withdrawal. In countless assertions over the years, the IRA leadership made it absolutely clear that the campaign would go on until there was such a declaration. Among the more notable expressions of undying devotion to physical force was McGuinness's emotional speech during the 1986 debate on whether or not to recognize the Dail. He forcefully emphasized the movement's commitment to violence. 'Our position is clear and it will never, never, never change,' he declared. 'The war against British rule must continue until freedom is achieved.'[39] He shouted 'shame, shame, shame' at the O Bradaigh faction, who were opposed to granting recognition to the Dail, for suggesting – correctly, as it turned out – that this would eventually lead the Provisionals down the path to revisionism and constitutionalism, as it did the Officials.

The same year (1986) Adams stated that 'if at anytime Sinn Fein decide to disown armed struggle they won't have me as a member'.[40] As late as 1993, the IRA leadership was still sounding bellicose, as the interview granted to the *Guardian* in February that year showed. The spokesman boasted of the group's new terrorist technology, and asserted that the war would go on until Britain declared its intention to withdraw. 'Unfortunately for us, the British are slow learners. But we are patient teachers,' he concluded menacingly.

A year later, things changed drastically. The situation the Army Council confronted in 1994 was critical. After twenty-five years of guerrilla war, in East Tyrone the Provisionals were effectively wiped out, Derry was more or less inactive, and the campaign in Britain broken. And now Belfast was compromised. By the summer of 1994, according to Special Branch sources, 80 per cent of all IRA operations in the city were either intercepted or aborted. Meanwhile loyalist death squads were butchering Catholics with renewed ferocity. Though the Provisionals managed to carry out several successful revenge attacks against the UDA, they knew that this was but a temporary respite.[41] Though South Armagh still remained defiant, the IRA leadership realized that the twilight war could not be won through occasional sniper attacks or bombing ambushes along the border.

On 31 August 1994 it issued a statement: 'In order to enhance the democratic peace process and underline our definitive commitment to its success the leadership of Oglaigh na hEireann [Irish Republican Army] have decided that as of midnight 31 August, there will be a complete cessation of military operations. All our units have been instructed accordingly.'[42]

On 13 October the loyalist paramilitaries followed in their wake. Gusty Spence, the founding member of the UVF (see Chapter 1), twenty-eight years later helped pen the loyalists ceasefire announcement of 13 October 1994. The Provisionals' statement was dry and formal, giving no hint that they felt they had been wrong. But Spence infused the loyalists' declaration with something of his own sadness and regret for the suffering he and others like him had inflicted in the decades of violence. Part of it read:

> In the genuine hope that this peace will be permanent, we take the opportunity to pay homage to all our fighters, commandos and volunteers who have paid the supreme sacrifice. They did not die in vain. The union is safe ... In all sincerity, we offer to the loved ones of all innocent victims over the past 25 years, abject and true remorse. No words of ours will compensate for the intolerable suffering they have undergone during this conflict.
>
> Let us firmly resolve to respect our differing views of freedom, culture, and aspiration, and never again permit our political circumstances to degenerate into bloody warfare.

In 1966 Gusty brought the gun back into Ulster politics; 3,351 deaths later, hope triumphed over history.[43]

CHAPTER EIGHT

To Forsake Arms: 1994–98

1

The Northern Ireland peace process was based on the failure of violent republicanism to achieve its aims. The Provisional IRA never admitted defeat; nor did the authorities ever utter that word, preferring the evasive language of conflict resolution studies in which there are no winners and no losers. But all the euphemisms in the dictionary could not mask the fact that the IRA's violence failed to drive the British from Northern Ireland. Nor did it even secure a declaration of intent to withdraw.

Among most nationalists it was not interpreted as a defeat for republicanism. On the contrary, in West Belfast the mood was celebratory. Many assumed that the Provisionals must have secured some major concession from Britain for them to have halted a campaign that their leaders swore over and over again would not end until their goals were achieved. Many in the Protestant community assumed the same thing. Even after the loyalist groups declared their own ceasefires, there was no rush to embrace the new situation. Instead, Protestants remained cautious and mistrustful, their free-floating paranoia ready to crystallize around any particle of suspicion that the perfidious English were once more doing a deal behind their backs. 'The rank and file unionists are still wondering what the hell the IRA have been given,' commented James Molyneaux, the UUP leader. Change always made the Unionists insecure. For twenty-five years, IRA violence gave them justification for their intransigence and meant that their own moral and political position was not scrutinized too closely. At times, their spokesmen almost seemed to regret the passing of the Troubles, when the menace was easy to identify. For them, the new terrain of peace was full of potential traps. Britain, too, reacted warily. The British Prime Minister expressed scepticism and asked why if the IRA was serious about ending its violence it had not included the word 'permanent' in its ceasefire declaration.

However, in Dublin and Washington things moved swiftly. On 6 September 1994, the Irish Taoiseach, Albert Reynolds, John Hume and Gerry Adams met on the steps of Government House in Dublin. The three shook hands in public, a gesture of reconciliation between constitutional nationalism and violent republicanism that had taken seventy years to achieve. A month later, on a tour of the US, Adams took a telephone call from Vice-President Gore. Anthony Lake, Clinton's National Security Adviser, wrote to inform Adams that the administration was lifting its ban on meetings with Sinn Fein. An invitation to the White House was just months away. Within weeks of being declared, the Provisionals' ceasefire reunited the different wings of nationalism and secured the backing of the most powerful nation in the world. That was the easy part.

There was still the matter of Northern Ireland's 900,000 or so Protestants. Between them and the IRA lay a sea of blood. Those who had waded in it already seemed more willing to undertake the journey across than the conventional politicians of Unionism. At the end of October, Gusty Spence, the founder of the modern UVF and the man whose gunfire raised the curtain on the modern Troubles, led a delegation of loyalist paramilitary spokesmen to America. They followed in the footsteps of Sinn Fein as guests of the National Committee on American Foreign Policy. Among the delegation was Gary McMichael, whose father John McMichael the IRA murdered in late 1987 (see Chapter 5), and Billy Hutchinson, a former UVF member who served time in jail for his part in the murder of two Catholics in 1974. Spence, Hutchinson and Davy Ervine represented the UVF-linked Progressive Unionist Party, McMichael and David Adams the Ulster Democratic Party, which spoke for the UDA. The loyalists were not accorded anything like the reception Adams had received on his first visit to the city eight months earlier. As far as Irish Americans were concerned, they were an unknown quantity. For most, the Rev. Ian Paisley represented loyalism. If anything filtered through the almost complete absence of US media coverage of loyalist actions it was Sinn Fein propaganda, which portrayed them as the puppets of the British government and its security forces.

'Loyalist opinion can now be heard in the United States,' McMichael declared on arrival in New York. The delegation soon made clear where they stood politically. 'I am just going to talk from the heart,' said Ervine, throwing away his notes. 'Nationality is a state of mind. I am British. I will always be British. And I have always been British.'[1] The UDA and UVF representatives insisted that the only reason their organizations had called a ceasefire was that they were convinced that a deal had not been done with the IRA behind the scenes and that, as they put it, 'the Union with Great Britain was safe'. This was the polar opposite to the line that Sinn Fein was expounding. It was trying to reassure its supporters that the IRA had ended its armed struggle because conditions were ripe to make political progress towards a united Ireland. However, there were two things both loyalists and republicans agreed upon, and which Ervine stressed: the first was the need to free the 'political' prisoners; the second was that there would be no paramilitary disarmament until a political settlement was reached upon which all sides could agree.

To cement this agreement, Belfast IRA leaders met with UDA and UVF representatives in a South Belfast hotel three days before Christmas. An informal pact was made. The paramilitaries would present a united front on the release of their prisoners, disarmament and the need for 'inclusive talks'. They vowed to oppose any attempt to make disarmament – or decommissioning, as it soon came to be known – a precondition for the entry of their political representatives into negotiations.

Christmas 1994 was the first in twenty-five years during which Ulster people dared to look to the future with hope. The clamp of security that held Belfast and other towns in its grip began to ease. The shops thronged with customers, traffic poured into the city centre; people stayed out late, and did not rush home before darkness fell. Along the roads of North Belfast, for decades the favourite hunting ground of sectarian assassins, a more casual mood now prevailed – people did not scrutinize every car that approached, looking for some telltale sign of imminent danger. Soldiers patrolled without helmets, and police officers shed their bulletproof vests. A few streets that ran through the Peace Line between the Shankill and the Falls, sealed off from each other for a generation, were now opened. Soon civilian searchers were no longer to be seen at the main department stores, and cars were allowed to park close to the city centre. The Europa Hotel, the most bombed hotel in western Europe, was renovated with a brave new front that bulged out towards the sidewalk, and had all barricades and security checks lifted for the first time since 1971. In mid-January 1995, all daytime army foot patrols in Belfast ceased. At the end of that month, border patrols were also drastically reduced. The Irish government announced that nine IRA prisoners released on parole for Christmas were free.

The British government, however, continued to move cautiously. There were no big gestures. Paramilitary prisoners would for the time being stay behind bars. Twelve weeks were to pass after the IRA ceasefire before Major allowed even a preliminary meeting between his government and Sinn Fein officials. He began speaking about the need for the decommissioning of IRA weapons before Sinn Fein could get into fully fledged talks. Among nationalists, impatience and unease were growing. There were suspicions that Major was afraid to do anything that might jeopardize the support of the nine Ulster Unionist MPs at Westminster, which was helping to keep him in power. Irish officials in particular were concerned that the IRA would become restless at the delays, and interpret them as a deliberate attempt by the British to undermine its military capacity. To add to the uncertainties, Reynolds, one of the chief architects of the IRA ceasefire, had been replaced as Taoiseach by John Bruton, whom republicans viewed as being much less sympathetic to their position. Meanwhile, behind the scenes civil servants from the two governments were working hard to come up with a political programme that would appeal to nationalists without frightening Unionists and keep the ceasefires on track. The result was the Framework Document, the first political fruit of the peace process, which the two governments revealed in February 1995.

It was a complex set of proposals, but they repeated three themes familiar since the 1973 Sunningdale Agreement: the maintenance of the Union as long as the majority wished it, the establishment of a devolved assembly in Northern Ireland, and the creation of a 'North–South body' with a potential for 'dynamic' development. The concept of 'power-sharing' was there but not the term; instead the Framework Document spoke of institutions for local government that respected both traditions; the 1973 Sunningdale provisions for a Council of Ireland became a 'North-South body' but its functions remained the same. It was all set within the context of Britain's oft-repeated assertion that it no longer had a 'selfish strategic or economic interest in Northern Ireland'.

The Framework Document was not what republicans wanted. It did not contain plans for a British withdrawal or even a promise to persuade Unionists of the benefits of a united Ireland. But it was not what Unionists wanted to hear either. The proposals were an emphatic reminder that Northern Ireland's membership of the United Kingdom was dependent on the consent of the people of Northern Ireland, not on the sovereign claims of a confident imperial power. That kind of union was no longer on offer. Britain in effect was telling the Unionists, 'Yes, you can stay as long as the majority of you want to but you are free to leave whenever you like. And in the meantime, you are going to have to accommodate the political aspirations of your nationalist neighbours.'

The sun had long ago set on the British Empire; it was now setting on the union between Great Britain and Northern Ireland.

The Ulster Unionist Party rejected the Framework Document in its entirety. But the proposals had a major advantage over the Sunningdale Agreement and indeed every other Northern Ireland initiative that came before them. The only ones to have been born in a time of peace, they were not greeted with strikes, arson, bombs or bullets. While republicans and Unionists found much to dislike about the document, there was no concerted campaign to thwart or destroy it. The only problem was that the document was not itself a settlement – only the outline of what a settlement might look like. It remained to be enacted. It the meantime much could go wrong, and it did.

During the secret talks between Britain and the Provisional IRA, decommissioning was rarely if ever referred to as a demand needing to be met before the republican movement could be 'sanitized' and brought fully into the peace process.

Nor was it on the agenda during the months before the Provisionals called their ceasefire, when the Irish government and Hume sought to persuade republicans that armed force was counterproductive. But now Major and his deputy in Northern Ireland, Sir Patrick Mayhew, were raising it with increasing frequency. On 7 March 1995 in Washington, Mayhew announced three steps the IRA must take before Sinn Fein would be allowed into the conference room. It must agree in principle to disarm; there must be agreement on how to go about it; and there must be a 'confidence-building' measure, a token gesture of disarmament to begin the process.

It did not take long for republicans to reply. Martin McGuinness said he wanted to remind the British, 'just in case reality had escaped them', that 'the British army had not defeated the IRA – that the IRA had not surrendered – and that the British government could not even remotely expect Sinn Fein to deliver that surrender to them'. Decommissioning, he said, must be 'seen for what it is, an excuse to delay the all-party peace talks . . . All-party peace talks are the inevitable next step in the peace process.'[2] But the British argued that unless there was a 'token gesture' from the IRA they could never persuade the Unionists to take part in any peace talks with Sinn Fein present. Decommissioning soon became the major issue of the whole peace process and threatened to destabilize it.

In June 1995 Adams replied to the continued demands from Britain. He told *The Irish Times* that '. . . the surrender of IRA weapons as a precondition to negotiation was never mentioned by the British government before August 31 1994 . . . In my view, had a surrender of IRA weapons been imposed as a precondition to peace negotiations prior to the cessation, it is possible there would have been no cessation . . . The British government is not simply interested in a gesture. It is, in reality, demanding the start of a surrender process as a precondition to all-party talks.'[3]

The first summer of 'peace' was fraught with political and sectarian tension, which erupted in mob violence. A paratrooper convicted of murdering a Catholic teenage girl was freed in early July after serving only four years of a life sentence. (His murder conviction was later overturned.) Catholic neighbourhoods, where tension was high because of the deadlock over disarmament, exploded. At the same time, Orange marchers at Drumcree, near Portadown, Co. Armagh, were blocked from parading along Garvaghy Road, which skirted a Catholic district. A thousand RUC men confronted ten thousand Orangemen. Loyalists rioted in protest throughout Northern Ireland. Though the violence (at least at an organized level) had ended, the underlying conflict between Catholic and Protestant, nationalist and Unionist, remained unresolved. By September, and the first anniversary of the IRA ceasefire, Sinn Fein was still barred from entering talks, and the peace process was crumbling, thanks to the issue of decommissioning. The IRA repeated its rejection of what it termed the 'ludicrous' demand, and insisted there would be no surrender of weapons. 'There is no possibility of disarmament except as part of a negotiated settlement,' it said. Republicans pointed out that decommissioning was never an issue when earlier IRA campaigns had ended. The Official IRA called a ceasefire in May 1972, and its political wing, the Workers' Party, entered the Dail nine years later, without any demands ever being made for the organization to hand over weapons or explosives, of which it was believed to possess three tons – enough to arm about three hundred volunteers. Leading Unionists felt comfortable enough negotiating with Workers' Party representatives, regardless of the fact that the Official IRA was still armed. Indeed, John Taylor, whom the Officials tried to assassinate, later praised them for their commitment to the political process.[4] But such arguments moved neither the Unionists nor the Major government. They quoted RUC sources as claiming that the IRA had murdered a drug dealer in Belfast in April 1995, and was still involved in scouting for potential targets and planning operations.

The Irish government turned to the Clinton administration for assistance in finding a way around the disarmament dispute. Clinton helped maintain the momentum throughout 1994 and 1995, often doing so at the cost of angering the British. In December 1994, when the British declared that Sinn Fein would be barred from an investment conference it was holding in Belfast, Clinton threatened to withhold his representative, Ron Brown. The British relented. In March, in the face of British protests, Clinton gave Adams permission to raise money in the US. He shook hands with the Sinn Fein leader (but not in public) later that month during the St Patrick's Day festivities in Washington, again defying British protests.[5] May saw Clinton host a Northern Ireland investment conference in Washington. In July, at the height of the turmoil on the streets, the President announced that he would be visiting Northern Ireland, beginning on 30 November. Neither the British nor the Irish governments wanted a stalled peace process and an unseemly row over decommissioning to tarnish the prestige of an American presidential visit.

As the 30 November visit drew closer, the Irish and British strove desperately to get around the obstacle of decommissioning which Major had planted firmly on the path to peace. Eleven hours before Clinton was due to arrive in London on the first leg of his trip, the British agreed to adopt a twin-track approach, as the Irish had been advocating for some months. Former Democratic Senator George Mitchell, Clinton's economic 'envoy' to Northern Ireland, was appointed to chair an international committee to report on the decommissioning issue by mid-January 1996. Meanwhile the two Prime Ministers stated that their aim was to achieve all-party talks by February. No untidy policy issues would be left lying around when the President arrived. The place would be presentable.

Behind the scenes it was a very different story. Unknown to Clinton, Bruton and Major, a decision was taken at a meeting of the Provisional Army Council in Donegal in October that unless Britain abandoned its demand for the IRA to disarm, it would end the ceasefire. The aim was not to relaunch the armed struggle, but to carry out a limited bombing campaign concentrated in Britain. It was shortly after this meeting that Adams stated that the peace process no longer existed, having been 'subverted' by the British government. Sinn Fein leaders chose not to tell the world about the decision of the IRA leadership, even though several of their most high-ranking members were at the meeting when the decision was taken.

Innocent of these machinations, Bill Clinton and the First Lady arrived to celebrate the peace that was about to collapse. Apart from that small matter, the first visit of a US President to Northern Ireland was a spectacular success. Even the weather, for once, co-operated. It was bright and cold when they arrived in Belfast on the morning of 30 November. The President's first stop was on the Shankill Road, where he converted the suspicious Protestants into Clinton enthusiasts with a brief walkabout and some flesh-pressing. From then on, it was one huge welcome after another, with thousands upon thousands showing up along the Falls, where he shook Adams's hand again, this time in public, and in Derry, where he shared a platform with John Hume. It was erected in Guildhall Square, near the city centre, not far from the spot where, in 1972, the Provisional IRA exploded its first car bomb. That evening, he lit the Christmas tree in front of Belfast's City Hall while some fifty thousand people cheered and applauded. The city was not used to crowds of that size assembling for a happy purpose. Many onlookers contrasted the positive, enthusiastic mood of the Clintons when they spoke of peace with the reluctant, cautious and sometimes downright suspicious reaction of Major and the Unionists. It was refreshing for a city to find that the President also wanted to celebrate the change, not pick it to pieces with doubts and prevarications. 'Hillary and I thank you from the bottom of our hearts for making us so welcome,' the President said. 'I will remember this day for as long as I live with great gratitude.'[6]

Even as the lights went on for Belfast's first Christmas at peace, in a small house in the middle of West Belfast the IRA was holding a meeting with a group of Irish Americans, some of whom had been active on the 1992 Clinton election campaign. They were told that unless the disarmament demand was dropped, the ceasefire would crumble. And it would be sooner rather than later. The Irish Americans left in a depressed frame of mind, but tried to console themselves with the thought that republicans had been crying crisis now for months, yet the ceasefire still held.[7]

2

On 24 January, 1996 George Mitchell's international body published its recommendations. It advised that the disposal of weapons should not be a precondition for entry into all-party talks but that the two should take place along parallel tracks. Major effectively rejected the report, and then added what the IRA saw as a new precondition. Before the all-party talks began, elections would be held in Northern Ireland so that those parties who wanted to take part in them could secure a 'democratic mandate'. Sinn Fein, with a solid electoral base, saw this as simply another delaying tactic intended to prevent those talks from taking place for as long as possible. Mayhew rejected an appeal from Adams to abandon plans for elections. Meanwhile, there was a series of murders of alleged drug dealers in Belfast. A group calling itself Direct Action Against Drugs claimed responsibility. It was a thinly disguised front for the IRA.

It was now clear that the promise of all-party talks by the

end of February would not be met. Sean O'hUiginn, a high-ranking Irish government official who played a key role in the negotiations, commented in early 1996: 'I'd be very nervous about saying anything that sounds like a self-fulfilling prophecy. But from last August or so the political graph has been dipping. The question is at what point will it intersect with the killing graph?'[8] It was a prescient remark.

At 5.40 p.m. on 9 February, Scotland Yard received a telephone call warning that the Provisional IRA ceasefire was about to end. A short time later, an IRA statement followed which read:

> It is with great reluctance that the leadership of Oglaigh na hEireann announces that the complete cessation of military operations will end at 6 p.m. . . . The cessation presented an historic challenge for everyone, and Oglaigh na hEireann commend the leadership of Nationalist Ireland at home and abroad. They rose to meet the challenge. The British prime minister did not. Instead of embracing the peace process, the British government acted in bad faith, with Mr Major and the Unionists leaders squandering this unprecedented opportunity to resolve the conflict. . . . selfish party political and sectional interests in the London parliament have been placed before the rights of the people of Ireland . . . The resolution of this conflict in our country demands justice. It demands an inclusive negotiated settlement. That is not possible unless and until the British government lives up to its responsibilities. The blame for the failure thus far of the Irish peace process lies squarely with John Major and his government.

At one minute after seven that evening a huge bomb exploded in an underground carpark in an office building near Canary Wharf (the object of an earlier IRA bombing attempt in 1992) in East London. It killed two men, injured a hundred and inflicted about seventy million pounds' worth of damage. The blast created a crater fourteen feet wide and twenty feet deep. There was dismay, anger and outrage, but among many nationalists, who were frustrated by Britain's response to the IRA's ceasefire, the bombing did not come as a complete surprise. Nor was it unexpected among the Irish government's advisers and civil servants, who had been working for months to defuse the decommissioning crisis. Privately they too blamed the Major government for mishandling events since the ceasefire. One Irish official commented that 'the British government didn't know why the violence stopped. And they didn't know why it started again.' Some among them suspected, as did the IRA, that it was a deliberate policy, not just ineptitude, that led the British to delay and prevaricate, in an effort to debilitate the IRA, the theory being that the longer the organization remained inactive, the more difficult it would be for it to resume its terrorist activities, so that by holding back on concessions, the British had nothing to lose and everything to gain. But in public, the British and Irish governments adapted a united front and announced that they were breaking off any further meetings with Sinn Fein. However, the Clinton administration said that it would maintain contact with Adams as 'it is hard to imagine a process making progress without him'. Hume also rejected calls, some from within his own party, to turn away from Adams.

As usual in Northern Ireland, the two communities interpreted the return to violence in diametrically opposed ways. For nationalists, it was final proof of what they had been arguing all along, that the demand for decommissioning would destroy the ceasefire; for Unionists, it was proof that decommissioning was necessary and Major correct in refusing to allow Sinn Fein into talks until it took place. But the vast majority of both Catholics and Protestants were vehemently opposed to a renewal of the killing. At a peace rally in Belfast just days after the London bombing, 6,000 people gathered.

In less than a week, 150,000 people telephoned Belfast's two morning papers demanding that the ceasefire be restored.

In his response to the IRA's statement that he was to blame for the failure of the peace process, Major replied that in spite of the ceasefire the IRA had never really abandoned violence but had been preparing for a renewal of operations for some time. The Prime Minister's assertion was based on accurate intelligence. The IRA's Northern Command had set up a special intelligence-gathering unit, the aim of which was to penetrate middle-class areas where high-profile targets such as judges and senior policemen lived. The organization's return to violence was intended to be spectacular. MI5 warned the government a full month before the Canary Wharf attack that violence would restart. When it came, the RUC's E9 counter-surveillance unit was ready. Three days after the bombing, the RUC intercepted an eight-man IRA ASU as it attempted to pull off a major robbery at a warehouse in South Belfast. Among those arrested was one of the Belfast brigade's top gunmen. (He had escaped arrest in February 1994 when the police seized the IRA squad planning to assassinate Superintendent Martindale. See Chapter 7.)

It was the first of a series of setbacks for the IRA. On 18 February, a premature explosion killed an IRA volunteer as he transported a bomb on a London bus. Hundreds were injured in a bomb attack in a shopping centre in Manchester in June. But at the end of that month the Irish police raided an IRA bomb factory in Co. Laois and arrested six leading members of the organization. On 15 July, a police raid in London netted eight IRA men and led to the discovery of another bomb-making factory. Another London bombing team was seized on 23 September along with ten tons of home-made explosives, Semtex and weapons; during the arrest operation, an IRA volunteer was shot dead and five others held. By the autumn of 1996, seven months after the ending of the ceasefire, the IRA's strategy of confining its campaign to bombing attacks in Britain was abandoned. The RUC realized that it was only a matter of time before the armed campaign would be resumed in Northern Ireland. The police feared that this would lead to a backlash from the loyalist paramilitaries, who so far had maintained their cease-fires.

The IRA resumed operations in Northern Ireland on 7 October with a double car bomb attack inside the British Army headquarters in Lisburn, near Belfast, which by some miracle killed only one soldier. It was a 'spectacular' – proof that the IRA could still carry out headline-grabbing operations and embarrass the security forces. However, whatever satisfaction the IRA derived from this success was short-lived. Within weeks, the RUC swooped on the special intelligence unit they believed responsible for this operation and arrested Bobby Storey, a high-ranking IRA veteran not long out of prison. Police claimed that Storey was the Northern Command's Intelligence Officer.[9]

The IRA's strategy of going for high-profile targets collapsed, as had its bombing campaign in Britain. Within a period of a few months, it had lost around thirty of its most seasoned operators in police raids; two were dead. It now attempted to relaunch its campaign in Belfast with attacks on the security forces. However, the IRA's weakness was more apparent than ever, as one bungled effort followed another, and more men were arrested. A senior RUC officer commented that it was a 'pathetic, grubby little war'.[10] The Belfast IRA was now thoroughly compromised, thanks mainly to RUC intelligence operations, but the 'pathetic, grubby little war' struggled on into the new year. Among the units most keen to end the ceasefire were those in South Armagh, where doubts about the peace process were prevalent. An Armagh man, Thomas 'Slab' Murphy, was now the Chief of Staff. It was from South Armagh that the bomb attack on Canary Wharf was launched, like so many others before it. On 13

February 1997 an IRA sniper shot and killed a British soldier as he chatted to a woman at a vehicle checkpoint near the town of Forkhill. The police believed the same sniping unit was involved in a whole series of attacks, using a Barrett 'Light Fifty', a powerful American-made weapon with a range of up to six thousand feet. Bullet-proof clothing was no defence against it. Ten soldiers and a police officer were shot dead between 1992 and 1997, victims of the same or a similar gun, the majority of them in the South Armagh area. In April, the sniping tactic was repeated in Derry, where a police-woman was seriously wounded during an attack in the city centre. But as ever, South Armagh was the most dangerous zone. And as long as it was a safe haven for IRA militants, it would remain so.

Over the years the security forces enjoyed few successes there. But finally, on 13 April, a surveillance operation involving the SAS, MI5 and the RUC produced results. SAS men burst into a disused farm just as the sniper was getting ready to begin an operation. He was caught in a mask, gloves and boiler suit, along with five other members of the unit, reading a newspaper and relaxing before going out to kill. Two rifles were recovered as well as an armour-plated car that was used as a sniping platform. For the police, it was a major coup. They were convinced they now had the South Armagh's 'A' team of IRA operators. It was, at any rate, another demoralizing blow to the IRA. For the first time, their safe haven had been penetrated.

The IRA leadership would never admit it publicly, but the attempt to resume the armed campaign was proving a dis-aster. In just over a year it had claimed the lives of two soldiers and two civilians. But at a high cost. Aside from the deaths of two of its volunteers, the IRA saw its bombing teams in Britain broken, a major intelligence-gathering unit of its Northern Command seized, a series of ASUs in Belfast inter-cepted, and a team of top operators in South Armagh under arrest. It strengthened the hand of those who, like Adams, were arguing that the physical-force option was no longer viable. Outside events also helped him and those of his supporters who were seeking to resume the political process.

In May 1997, the Labour Party won a crushing and historic victory over the Conservatives, who were ousted from power for the first time in eighteen years. Tony Blair became the new Prime Minister, and Mo Mowlam was made his Secretary of State for Northern Ireland. In the province, Adams recovered his West Belfast seat and Martin McGuinness won a second seat for Sinn Fein when he took the Mid-Ulster constituency from Paisley's DUP. Sinn Fein scored its highest percentage of the vote ever. The party's electoral successes stood out in sharp contrast to the IRA's military failures.

Most interpreted the increased votes for Sinn Fein as an expression of the nationalist desire to see another ceasefire, since bolstering the party, they believed, would strengthen those in the republican movement in favour of such a move. The question now was not if but when it would happen. Unfortunately, two more lives were lost in the meantime. The North Armagh IRA shot dead two community policemen on patrol in the centre of Lurgan on 16 June. It was a provocative act. North Armagh was seething with Protestant discontent over the continued crisis at Drumcree, where every summer Orangemen confronted Catholic residents who wanted to prevent them from marching near their neighbourhood. The previous two summers had seen serious violence. It was feared that the killing of the two officers would provoke worse. However, the army sealed off the Catholic area, and created a secure corridor of troops, armoured vehicles and barricades through which the Orangemen were quickly marched. It infuriated local Catholics, but a new Chief Constable, Ronnie Flanagan, responded that the alternative would have been a province-wide breakdown of law and order.

The new government quickly put out feelers to the republican leaders about the prospects for another ceasefire. In their response they said that the British would have to set a date for when Sinn Fein could join the talks following any new ceasefire, that those talks must have a deadline, and that constitutional issues would be matters for negotiation.

Blair was eager to restart the peace process as soon as possible, and involve Sinn Fein, not because he liked the party but because he knew that without it there could be no meaningful settlement in Northern Ireland. He met Sinn Fein's conditions. His new Secretary of State said that if the IRA renewed its ceasefire, Sinn Fein would be included in the talks within six weeks, and that the deadline for reaching a settlement would be 9 April 1998 – the day before Good Friday and the Easter weekend. Constitutional issues would be on the negotiating table. It was also confirmed that former US Senator George Mitchell would chair the negotiations, giving the US administration a direct role in them – a reassuring factor for the Provisionals. Pressure on the Provisional IRA to call a halt was now irresistible. On 20 July, it announced it was ending its campaign of terror. After criticizing the British government and the Unionists for blocking 'any possibility of real or inclusive negotiations' during the last ceasefire, the statement went on:

> The IRA is committed to ending British rule in Ireland. It is the root cause of divisions and conflict in our country. We want a permanent peace and therefore we are prepared to enhance the search for a democratic peace settlement through real and inclusive negotiations. So having assessed the current political situation, the leadership of Oglaigh na hEireann are announcing a complete cessation of military operations from 12 midday on Sunday 20 July 1997. We have ordered the unequivocal restoration of the ceasefire of August 1994. All IRA units have been instructed accordingly.

This time, there were no quibbles from the British government about the wording of the announcement. The government was as good as its word and, on 15 September, Sinn Fein joined the peace negotiations in Belfast. For the first time since 1921, when Michael Collins went to London to meet with Lloyd George, IRA representatives engaged in direct negotiations with the British government. Seventy-six years earlier, Collins had come away with a measure of freedom for twenty-six of Ireland's thirty-two countries. The question was now being raised as to what Adams could get as a result of the talks that he and other Sinn Fein leaders seemed so keen to enter. Among some republicans there was a growing disillusion – even the most positive outcome from their point of view would still fall far short of what the republican movement was seeking. Anthony McIntyre, a former IRA prisoner turned academic, wrote that

> To claim . . . that the IRA did not win but had not lost either is demonstrably wrong. The political objective of the Provisional IRA was to secure a British declaration of intent to withdraw. It failed.
>
> The objective of the British state was to force the Provisional IRA to accept – and to respond with a new strategic logic to – the position that it would not leave Ireland until a majority in the North consented to such a move. It succeeded.[11]

Other republican groups such as the INLA and its political wing, the IRSP, were more and more critical of the Sinn Fein strategy, as was Republican Sinn Fein, which had broken with the mainstream organization in 1986 (See Chapter 6). They viewed the IRA and Sinn Fein involvement in the peace process as a sell-out, and made an increasingly bellicose statement to the effect that they at least would continue what they termed 'the fight for Irish freedom'. The INLA received a shipment of explosives from New Zealand in 1994, and possessed a supply of AK-47 and hand grenades. But as usual it proved more deadly to its own members than to its declared enemies. Another vicious feud debilitated the organization in 1996, claiming the lives of two of its leaders, Hugh 'Cueball' Torney and Gino Gallagher, and four others.[12] But the INLA still remained a threat to peace.

Concern was also focused on Republican Sinn Fein and its alleged links to an armed faction calling itself the Continuity IRA. One of the founding members of the Provisionals, Daithi O Conaill, formed CIRA in 1986 at the same time as Republican Sinn Fein split from the mainstream republican movement. He was its first Chief of Staff. The organization lay dormant until 1994 and the first Provisional IRA ceasefire. In December that year it planted a small Semtex bomb in Enniskillen and some weeks later another in Newry. The first public statement appeared in its name on 6 January 1996 when it declared that

> The Irish Republican Army under the leadership of the Continuity Army Council renews its allegiance to the All-Ireland Republic of Easter 1916 and the First (32-county) Dail. It is the final custodian of that Republic and is the absolute guarantor of continued resistance to British rule in Ireland.
>
> We wish to clarify our position to the people of Ireland. We are neither Official nor Provisional and rejecting reformism we remain revolutionary as the true Oglaigh na hEireann, Irish Republican Army.

The statement pledged 'unremitting hostility to the British forces of occupation' and vowed that 'action will be taken in the future at an appropriate time to further this objective'.

In July 1996, CIRA bombed a hotel in Enniskillen, and subsequently carried out a series of bombings and attempted bombings in Belfast and provincial towns near the border. On 16 September 1997, the day after Sinn Fein joined the talks, CIRA exploded a huge bomb in the mainly Protestant town of

Markethill, Co. Armagh, sending a signal to both governments and the Provisionals that there were still militant republicans ready to use terror. Just how many it was difficult to estimate, but probably CIRA could count on no more than forty or fifty activists. They possessed few weapons – some hand grenades, shotguns and AK-47s. So it is not surprising that one of CIRA's leaders appealed to the Provisionals not to surrender any weapons to the authorities but to hand them over to 'true republicans'. It is known that CIRA received a small cache of MAC-10 machineguns from supporters in New York in 1997.[13] However, intense police surveillance in the Irish Republic frustrated many of its operations and limited its capacity to strike.

As the Provisionals were drawn more deeply into the peace process and actual negotiations got under way, a more serious threat emerged. It came from within the Provisional IRA itself. In order for Sinn Fein to take part in the talks, the party was asked to sign up to six principles devised by the chairman of the talks George Mitchell. These principles committed the talks, participants to forswear the use of violence and to dissociate themselves from any organization that employed violence to achieve its ends. This was a dramatic challenge to the traditional republican claim that as the legitimate 'army' of the Irish Republic the IRA possessed the right to wage war. It was a claim that went back to 1919, when the Sinn Fein government in Dublin (outlawed by the British) devolved that right to the IRA, and was one of the moral foundation stones on which the republican movement rested. In order for those Sinn Fein delegates who were also members of the IRA, including McGuinness, Adams and Gerry Kelly, to accept the principles, a special army convention would have to be held to give them 'special dispensation' to do so. When it took place in October 1997, it was acrimonious. Several leading members walked out in protest, including Mickey McKevitt, the former quartermaster general of the Provisionals' GHQ staff and for a brief period a member of the Provisional Army Council. McKevitt was married to Bernadette Sands, a sister of Bobby Sands, the 1981 hunger striker who became a republican icon. He commanded a considerable following in the Co. Louth area of the border, and in South Armagh. It was alleged that as many as twenty other high-ranking Provisionals went with him, and that the South Armagh IRA suffered a large number of defections. Sinn Fein, especially in the Louth area, was also shaken with reports of many resignations.

The republican leadership denounced these stories as mostly fictions. *The Irish Times* quoted a veteran republican who compared the dispute to the split of 1969, when the Provisional IRA was born. 'It was all claim and counterclaim,' he said. 'Things were happening on the ground but they were denied. Both sides manipulated the facts. Sometimes it took months, even years, for the whole truth to emerge.'

It was clear, however, that Adams and his supporters emerged with the vast majority of republicans still in line, supporting their course. The kind of split that divided the republican movement in 1969 did not take place. Most importantly, the Belfast organization remained overwhelmingly committed to Adams's leadership.

Still, the security forces could not be complacent. Louth was an important staging area for republicans moving weapons and explosives across the border into Northern Ireland. Whichever faction controlled it possessed the capacity to cause trouble. As well, McKevitt knew the locations of the organization's major arms dumps. There was much speculation about whether or not the dissidents had access to supplies of Semtex and weapons or would dare to seize them from their former colleagues. (Such a move would certainly have provoked a bloody feud.) Equally disturbing for the peace process was the revelation that one of the heads of the IRA's bomb-making department joined the dissidents.[14] As 1997 came to a close, just as people's hopes were brightening the prospect of a new campaign of terror cast a shadow over the future.

The dissident republicans went public and formed the 32-County Sovereignty Committee, with Bernadette Sands-McKevitt as its vice-president. At its first press conference in Dublin on 7 December the committee spelt out its aims. Its primary goal was to bring about 'total British disengagement from Ireland and to oppose any internal settlement in the 6 Occupied Counties or any settlement which provides for continued British Rule in any form'. The committee said it would oppose 'all groups who call for such internal settlements'. That now included Sinn Fein, which according to the committee's view was part of a process that guaranteed a 'unionist veto' and prohibited 'an end of partition'. The new group reaffirmed 'the right of the Irish people to armed struggle in pursuit of national sovereignty'. At the same time, it denied that it was anything other than a pressure group or possessed an armed wing. Sinn Fein acted rapidly against any party members who were also involved with the 32-County Committee and expelled them.

The peace process was threatened on other fronts. Much to the disgust of a few militant loyalists, the ceasefires of the UDA and UVF had remained intact, even after the IRA resumed its bombing campaign in February 1996. They were further angered as the authorities rerouted some Orange parades away from Catholic areas or blocked others, seeing this as the appeasement of republicans. In July 1996, under the leadership of a local gunman, Billy Wright, whose nickname was 'King Rat', a section of the UVF in North Armagh split away from the organization. North Armagh loyalists were among the most violent and sectarian killers in Ulster; in the mid-1970s the area where they operated became known as the Murder Triangle. As the police and army blocked

Orange marchers at Drumcree on 6 July 1996, loyalist gunmen murdered a Catholic taxi driver. The former UVF men soon began using the name the Loyalist Volunteer Force. Like the dissident republicans, they viewed their leadership's commitment to the peace process as a sell-out. LVF victims included a teenage Catholic girl, murdered as she slept in her Protestant boyfriend's home, and a teenage boy, who was tortured before being shot and dumped in a slurry pit. The group's support was mainly confined to rural areas. The Belfast UVF and UDA suffered only a handful of defections.

Not longer after forming the LVF, Wright was jailed on charges of intimidating a witness. On 27 December 1997, two INLA prisoners, using guns smuggled into the Maze prison, shot Wright dead as he was being moved from his cell block to the visiting area. It was the most sensational assassination the organization had carried out since its booby-trap bombing of Conservative Party chairman, Airey Neave, in March 1979.

Wright's murder was avenged in the traditional loyalist fashion – through indiscriminate attacks on Catholics. Within days, two were murdered and eight seriously wounded as LVF gunmen struck in Tyrone and North Belfast. There were concerns that the Belfast UDA was behind some of the incidents, which could mean that the loyalist ceasefire was about to unravel. By the end of January 1998, twelve people were dead as a result mainly of LVF violence. Ominously, imprisoned UDA men stated that they were withdrawing their support for the peace process, claiming it was a 'one-way street' of concessions to republicans. Once more, Ulster's hopes for peace seemed doomed to disappointment.

Pessimism deepened when the IRA retaliated and killed a UDA member in February 1998. It also took responsibility for the murder of an alleged drug dealer. Sinn Fein was temporarily suspended from the talks.[15] It returned after two weeks, and the peace talks struggled on. With only two months to go before the 9 April deadline for a settlement, few believed that it could be achieved. Violence from dissident republicans and angry loyalists was not the only difficulty. Throughout the negotiations, the Ulster Unionist Party delegates refused to speak with Sinn Fein, even after an appeal from President Clinton. But David Trimble, the party leader, pledged that Unionists would not meet with republicans until the IRA disarmed.

Both dissident republicans and disaffected loyalists hoped that their attacks would bring the talks crashing down. As Easter approached they tried to apply more pressure on the beleaguered negotiations. During the last week in March, republicans fired mortars at an RUC base in South Armagh and attempted to set off a huge bomb consisting of 1,300 pounds of explosive. But it was intercepted near Dundalk in a lock-up garage. Two men linked to the Sands-McKevitt committee were arrested. The bomb was a sophisticated device with Semtex stuffed into booster tubes to enhance its power; it resembled those the Provisional IRA had once manufactured that caused such devastation in London. The dissident republicans' attempts to disrupt continued throughout March and April. A week before the settlement deadline, the Irish police seized another large bomb at a ferry port near Dublin as it was on its way to England. LVF gunmen, meanwhile, murdered two young friends, one Catholic and one Protestant, as they chatted in a pub in Poyntzpass, Co. Down.

The talks became a race against the gunmen, as the politicians strove for a settlement before some awful act of violence could set off a chain reaction of killings and draw in the Provisionals and the major loyalist paramilitary organizations.

The eight parties involved were sequestered near the site of the old Northern Ireland parliament at Stormont, just outside Belfast.[16] All the skills that chairman George Mitchell honed as majority leader of the US Senate were tested as he sought to

287

find common ground between Unionist and nationalist, loyalist and republican. Sinn Fein and the UUP proved the most implacable opponents. Since the UUP refused face-to-face meetings with the republicans, Mitchell was the go-between. Sinn Fein was pushing for maximum, the Unionists for minimum change. The fiercest battles took place over the issues of the number and scope of any cross-border bodies, the powers of the new assembly, the fate of paramilitary prisoners, and the future of the RUC. During the first week in April, Mitchell worked feverishly on a document outlining what the agreement would look like. On 7 April, two days before the talks deadline, he delivered it. The outline's most important proposals were for between five and eight cross-border bodies to handle such matters as tourism, agriculture and railway links, set up by legislation in the British and Irish parliaments, a North–South council of ministers to select membership of those bodies, a commission to look at how the RUC might be made more amenable to Catholics, and a commitment from the British to speed up the release of prisoners.

Within twelve hours, Unionist leader David Trimble rejected it as a 'Sinn Fein wish list' and a 'charter for a United Ireland'. His deputy, John Taylor, proclaimed that he 'wouldn't touch it with a forty-foot pole'. The Unionists stormed out of the negotiations and demanded that the sixty-five-page document be rewritten. Trimble wrote to British Prime Minister Tony Blair that 'it is now 25 years from the failed Sunningdale Agreement and it now appears that the Irish government has learned nothing from the reasons for its failure'.[17]

The deal seemed about to collapse. Clinton rang Bertie Ahern, the Irish Taoiseach, from Air Force One, offering to 'do anything we can' to help. British Prime Minister Blair flew into Belfast and held talks with Trimble. An air of crisis prevailed as television crews and reporters from all over the world gathered around Stormont. It began to seem foolishly optimistic for anyone to have dared to declare that a problem which some traced back to 1169 could be resolved by a specific date, i.e. 9 April 1998. Yet Blair insisted he was sticking to his deadline. The Unionists saw the cross-border bodies established under government decree as too independent; they wanted them demoted, and to come under the assembly's control. They wanted the proposed 108-seat assembly to be restricted in its powers, more like a county council than a real government. Ironically, the Ulster Unionists, who for many years had lamented the loss of their parliament at Stormont, were now pressing for weak, not strong, devolved government. They were worried that under the new dispensation, a strong assembly, with a large number of nationalist deputies and powerful links to the Irish Republic, would slip out of their control. Most problematic of all, they were demanding that the paramilitaries disarm before their political representatives be allowed into any new government. Sinn Fein, meanwhile, warned that any such concessions would not be acceptable to republicans and nationalists.

As 9 April dawned, Blair was still arguing with Trimble, at one point blocking the doorway to prevent him from walking out again. Would the Unionists, who had rejected so many initiatives designed to settle the Irish conflict, play the wreckers' role yet again? Irish officials who were involved in the negotiations were less pessimistic. The threat to walk-out to them seemed more of a negotiating stunt than a real rejection. After all, where would Trimble go? Paisley already occupied Ulster's political wilderness.

At 11 p.m. (US East Coast time), the British Prime Minister called Clinton in Washington asking for his help in persuading the Unionists and republicans to accept a compromise on their core issues, including weaker cross-border bodies, and no immediate disarmament. Clinton manned the telephones into the early hours of Friday morning, cajoling Trimble and

Adams to reach an agreement. Trimble was assured that disarmament would not be ignored, and Adams that the North–South arrangements would be meaningful, that police reforms would be sought and the prisoners not forgotten. On Good Friday, 10 April, at 4.30 p.m., after a series of last-minute doubts, Trimble said to his still uneasy Unionist Party colleagues: 'I'm going for it. Who's with me?'

One of those closest to him, Jeffrey Donaldson, walked out, angry that disarmament of the paramilitary groups was being shunted aside. But what seemed impossible only a few days before occurred: agreement was reached.

Clinton's intervention was judged crucial. Commented George Mitchell: 'I was there from the first day to the last. There would not have been a peace agreement in Northern Ireland without the efforts of Bill Clinton.'[18]

The governments moved swiftly to shore up the agreement. At the end of May referenda were held simultaneously in Northern Ireland and the Irish Republic on the Good Friday Agreement. As part of the agreement the Irish government was asking its citizens to dilute the state's claims to jurisdiction over Northern Ireland, contained in articles two and three of the Irish Constitution. They were to be changed to express an aspiration for unity, based on consent. Rewriting the Constitution was aimed at placating Unionists who for years had cited the articles as an obstacle to any agreement between the two states. Militant republicans attacked the proposed changes as an abandonment of the last vestiges of Ireland's claims to sovereign status on a thirty-two-county basis. In the North, Paisley ran a 'No' campaign against the agreement. He argued that it was an IRA ruse to get its prisoners out of jail. Paisley's claims gained emotional credence when a group of IRA bombers serving long sentences for a string of murders in Britain were released on bail and went to a Sinn Fein pro-agreement conference where they received a thunderous welcome. Many ordinary Protestants were disgusted, as they were a few days later when a UDA killer also on parole was accorded a similar reception at a loyalist conference in Belfast. Undoubtedly, the spectacle reduced the 'Yes' vote in the North, especially among Protestants. But the Good Friday Agreement still received an enormous endorsement: 94.4 per cent voted in favour of it in the Republic, and 71.1 per cent in Northern Ireland. The accord laid foundations for a settlement; the referenda strengthened them. Anyone who set out to oppose the Good Friday Agreement, republican or loyalist, could now be accused of defying the will of the Irish people, democratically expressed, North and South, in the referenda.

However, amid the optimism the overwhelming 'Yes' vote created, there was a cause for concern. While Northern nationalists overwhelmingly supported the agreement, around 95 per cent voting in favour, only 55 per cent of Unionists agreed with them. Paisley and the others in the 'No' campaign claimed a moral victory. The uncertain response to the agreement among Protestants invigorated the rejectionists' campaign for places in the new 108-seat assembly, for which elections were held at the end of June. Once more the pro-agreement parties won a majority, with Sinn Fein securing eighteen seats and 17.65 per cent of the vote, its biggest ever. It was now just six seats behind its nationalist rival, the SDLP.

Once more there was a marked difference between the two communities in how they responded to the new arrangements. Within the nationalist community, there was in effect no serious electoral opposition to the agreement. But within the Protestant community, Paisley and other dissident Unionists who ran against it translated the 45 per cent 'No' vote they achieved in the referendum into twenty-five seats in the assembly. While Trimble's mainstream UUP took twenty-eight seats, it left the pro-agreement Unionists with only a narrow majority. However, the loyalist PUP, which was pro-agreement and could be expected to support Trimble, took two seats. But in the months of negotiations that lay ahead for the setting up of the assembly executive and the cross-border bodies, the UUP leader was forced to move slowly to avoid desertions to the anti-agreement camp. After the election, Trimble was elected to be First Minister in the new government, with SDLP member Seamus Mallon as his deputy. It was due to take office in February 1999. Some expressed surprise that Hume, the man who more than any other was responsible for creating the peace process that led to the agreement, did not become deputy leader of the new assembly. But for Hume the Northern Ireland political arena was too narrow. Its still-divisive sectarian squabbling held little interest for him, as did the more august corridors of Westminster. It was thought that he would not defend his seat there in the next British general election. The man who in 1959 as a university debater advocated Ireland's membership of the Common Market, as the European Union was then known, was happiest in the Brussels parliament, dealing with issues that were on a scale more commensurate with his vision.

3

Throughout May and June 1998, it was apparent that Ulster was entering a new stage of its history when a former RUC Chief Constable, Jack Hermon, and a Sinn Fein President and IRA leader, Gerry Adams, were seen canvassing support for the same agreement. In spite of many difficulties and dangers, a remarkable consensus was being built, one that even a few years earlier would have been unimaginable.

In May, Sinn Fein announced that it would allow its members to sit in the new Northern Ireland assembly – the first time in the party's history that it agreed to take part in the government of a state it had previously tried to violently overthrow. Sinn Fein's goal was still a united Ireland. But the party now believed that this could be better achieved by working within the new institutions of government, especially the cross-border bodies, than by attempting to destroy them from the outside through violence.

On the loyalist side, the referendum and election campaigns revealed an equally startling change. During the entire period, Paisley, once the voice of loyalism, did not appear on the Shankill Road, for fear, it was said, of being heckled. The Shankill, the heartland of Ulster loyalism, was where in 1966 Paisley's rhetoric inspired UVF men like Gusty Spence to take up the bomb and the gun. When the referendum result in favour of the agreement was announced in Belfast's King's Hall, a group of UVF men and their political spokesmen chanted like fans at a soccer match, 'Cheerio, cheerio, cheerio', as a flushed and angry Paisley strode from the scene of the count. His son, Ian junior, who was following his father's political path, accompanied him. 'Where are you going to lead us now?' one of the UVF men asked, running after him. 'We're not going to prison for you any more,' another shouted.

'Try to smile,' said Paisley's son.

It was wasted advice. Paisley stalked from the hall scowling.

'The people have spoken. The modern world awaits,' commented Davy Ervine, a spokesman for the UVF which thirty-two years earlier had begun the killing.

4

The Troubles were over, but the killing continued. Some of the heirs to Ireland's violent traditions refused to give up their inheritance.

As the Irish people were getting ready to vote in the referenda, a group calling itself the 'Real' IRA emerged. On 8 May, 1998, it announced its existence, claiming to represent 'true' republicans. It stated that Sinn Fein had no right to enter the new assembly which was 'a complete betrayal of the claim of Irish self-determination for which volunteers gave their lives . . . The cease-fire as called by the old leadership is over and our war machine will once again be directed against the British.' The 'Real' IRA was made up of about thirty or more former Provisionals who had left the organization late in 1997 (see above). They were associated politically with the 32-County Sovereignty Committee. Their leader was former Provisional IRA Army Council member and Quartermaster General Micky McKevitt. One of its members was shot dead during a bungled raid on a security van a few miles outside Dublin at the beginning of May. During the summer of 1998, the group bombed Banbridge in Co. Down and tried and failed to launch several bombing attacks in Britain.

On Saturday afternoon, 15 August 1998, the market town of Omagh in Co. Tyrone was swarming with shoppers. Several days of mist and rain had given way to sunshine, drawing more people to the town's main shopping area around Market Street. Among the shoppers were many women with their children, getting ready for the new school year, which was only a couple of weeks away.

The population of Omagh was mainly Catholic. But for many years, long before the Troubles, the town had been the home of a British Army garrison. Over the years Omagh had experienced its share of political and sectarian killings, but it was never regarded as an especially dangerous place. Indeed, it was quieter, more well-integrated than most towns and villages in Tyrone. With the peace process firmly in place, and the ceasefires in force, there was even less reason for those milling about in the streets that August afternoon to worry about violence.

Shortly before 3 p.m. newspapers received a warning that there was a car bomb parked between three and four hundred yards from the courthouse, not far from the town centre. The

RUC was informed and began moving the crowds away from the suspect area towards the already bustling Market Street, where a fatal Vauxhall Cavalier was parked. For whatever reason – stupidity, confusion or sheer ruthlessness – the person who called in the warning had misled people. The bomb was not close to the courthouse but ticking away in the Cavalier in the middle of the crowd of shoppers, now swollen by those fleeing into what they thought was the safe zone. At 3.10 p.m. the five-hundred-pound device exploded, killing twenty-eight people. Fourteen were women. Seven children died. Three generations of one family were wiped out – Mary Grimes, aged sixty-five, her daughter Avril Monaghan, aged thirty, and her granddaughter Maura of eighteen months. Mrs Monaghan was pregnant with twins.

Another victim died two months later, bringing the total to twenty-nine, and making the Omagh bombing the single worst atrocity in the history of the Ulster conflict.

The 'Real' IRA claimed responsibility and apologized to the victims' loved ones. It said that it did not intend to kill civilians but that its warning had not been acted upon properly. As ex-Provisionals, this excuse came easily to them. However, the resignation with which such excuses were once accepted was no longer in evidence. By 1998 hope had replaced it.

Shock quickly turned to anger and disgust. Protesters picketed the home of Bernadette Sands-McKevitt and her husband Micky McKevitt – the two most public figures associated with the new organization. It became obvious that what was left of the tradition of violent republicanism was completely discredited. Sinn Fein, past master in the art of evasive language thanks to decades of IRA 'mistakes', now joined the chorus of unequivocal condemnations. The time for waffling about violence was over. The INLA too issued a statement saying that 'there was now no basis for the continuation of armed struggle by republicans'. For the first time in its history, it called a ceasefire. Not long afterwards, the 'Real' IRA announced that it also was calling a ceasefire. Violent republicanism was drowning in the blood of ordinary Catholics and Protestants, the very people for whom it claimed to be waging its war.

A similar fate befell extreme loyalism. In July 1998, during the annual Drumcree crisis, the Orange marchers tried yet again to force their way past the Catholics on Garvaghy Road. But this time the police and army blocked their path. As the stand-off continued, Protestant petrol bombers set fire to the home of a Catholic woman who lived in a loyalist district with three of her sons. The three young boys, who were ironically enough being raised as Protestants, were burned to death. The Drumcree protest effectively collapsed.[19] Within weeks the Loyalist Volunteer Force, the last of the Protestant paramilitary groups still defying the peace process, said it was ending its campaign.

On 1 September 1998, two weeks after the Omagh massacre, Gerry Adams made a momentous statement in which he said that 'violence must be a thing of the past – over, done with . . .' Though 'must' implied a moral imperative, not a statement of fact, it was the closest the republican movement had come to saying that the armed campaign was ended for ever. It was sufficiently close to allow Trimble to do what he said he would not do until the IRA disarmed: meet with Adams. The two held face-to-face negotiations on 10 September. This was the first meeting between a leader of the republican movement and a leader of Ulster Unionism since 1922, when Michael Collins held talks with James Craig, the Prime Minister of the new state of Northern Ireland, in an effort to halt the sectarian violence then sweeping Belfast. In 1922, the talks failed. The killings continued. And when they stopped, the two communities were hunkered down behind the barricades from which they had viewed each other with hatred and suspicion over the long, dark decades.

In 1998, the problems the two leaders discussed concerned that distrust, fear and insecurity, immeasurably deepened now thanks to the years of killing. Trimble's demand for paramilitary disarmament was still the chief obstacle to accommodation between the two communities. The refusal, principally of the IRA, to concede to the demand was blocking progress on the setting up of the power-sharing executive, which was supposed to take place in 'shadow' form by the end of October, with departments and their ministers nominated, and decisions reached on the number and scope of the cross-border bodies. Failure to resolve these matters would delay the moment when the assembly formally assumed power as the new government of Northern Ireland, which was supposed to occur in February 1999.

Agreement between Trimble and his deputy, Mallon, was not reached until 18 December, following another round of long and tortured negotiations. The First Minister announced that there would be ten ministerial departments in the new power-sharing executive, and six cross-border bodies to deal with matters such as inland waterways, trade and business development and special European Union projects. Most significantly of all, perhaps, was the breakdown in the distribution of the ministerial departments, which were apportioned out to different parties according to the number of seats they held in the assembly. Of the ten departments, three would go the Ulster Unionist Party, two to the Democratic Unionist Party, three to the SDLP, and two to Sinn Fein. That is, there would be five Unionist-controlled departments and five controlled by nationalists.

For the first time in Northern Ireland's history, nationalists, though still a minority, had achieved political parity with Unionists.

Another 'first' occurred the same day. The LVF, under police escort, brought a small cache of weapons to a workshop in East Belfast, used by the International Body on

Decommissioning. It consisted of nine guns, 350 rounds of ammunition, two dozen shotgun shells, six detonators, and two pipe bombs. Shortly after 10 a.m., before a small group of reporters, disarmament made a modest beginning as two guns were chopped to pieces in a metal-slicing machine, their fragments dumped in a waste bin. The LVF became the first paramilitary group in Ireland's long history of illegal militias and secret brotherhoods voluntarily to disarm.

The bigger paramilitary organizations like the Provisional IRA and the UVF shrugged this off as a publicity stunt, knowing full well that if the settlement was to survive they too would eventually have to do the same.

CHAPTER NINE

In Conclusion: Time Past and Time Present

History is often made in unlikely places. A drab building, a dreary market town, a street corner, a field, an alleyway, a dingy pub. In Northern Ireland, the scale is small, the location precise. St Comgall's, Belfast, is one such spot, a nondescript redbrick building that has served as a primary school to the Falls community since the 1920s. Centuries before that, local legend has it that a fairy thorn grew on the spot. Though the Troubles did not begin there, it was there that they assumed the form they were to retain for thirty violent years. In the early hours of 15 August 1969, a small group of IRA men fired on Protestant mobs threatening their neighbourhood, drove them off, and in doing so to all intents and purposes created the Provisionals. Almost thirty years later, St Comgall's was a polling station for the referendum on the Good Friday Agreement, the aim of which was to take the gun out of Irish politics for ever.

A few streets away, Billy McKee, ex-leader of the Belfast Provisionals, and one of the small band who in August 1969 had occupied the school, sat in his parlour reflecting on the past and present. 'You can see it all like a picture,' said the spry seventy-six-year-old of the events of August 1969, 'the flames everywhere.' Except for a few years in Dublin, and various spells in jail for IRA activities, McKee has lived in this neighbourhood all his life. But the old Falls is gone – the maze of narrow streets of tiny redbrick homes with black slate roofs has been completely remodelled. The neighbourhood is greener now, the homes have gardens. 'It's strange to see the trees,' he mused, 'there's trees in every garden.' Outside, a British patrol edged along the hedgerow, in what was once a sniper's alley but is now a wide leafy street with no gunmen lurking at the windows of its pleasant houses.

McKee spent time in jail with Gerry Adams's father and also with Adams himself, but has no kind words for the son. 'He was never a republican of our type,' according to McKee. He greets with anger and disbelief the prospect of Sinn Fein entering a Northern Ireland government. 'I don't know how anyone who calls himself a republican can build it up . . . Back to Stormont is back to the status quo.'

'I still follow the old line,' he said, expressing his disgust at the Provisional IRA's change of policy. But he has no illusions that there's much support for his line. 'There's despondency among good republicans,' he admits. 'They're actually broken.'

On the day Ireland said 'Yes' to the agreement, up and down the Falls Road black flags on lampposts flapped in the mild May breeze. They commemorated the seventeenth anniversary of the hunger strike that began the transformation of the republican movement into a political party ready to take its place in the new government as part of the settlement reached on Good Friday, 1998.

In the wake of the IRA ceasefire, a settlement became possible. A majority of Unionists recognized that their goal of an 'Ulster' that incorporated and protected only a Protestant sense of identity was no longer viable. The new Northern Ireland that hopefully will emerge from the Good Friday

Agreement has to express the messy reality of two conflicting aspirations, nationalist and Unionist, that for better or worse constitute the nature of the state. 'To see what is in front of one's nose requires a constant struggle,' George Orwell wrote in 1946.[1]

In the 1960s, it was believed that the clashing aspirations of Catholics and Protestants, nationalists and Unionists, could be resolved through raising Catholics up to the same economic level as Protestants and removing at the same time the various obstacles to their full integration within the state. This remedy encountered a simple problem. It was impossible to integrate Catholics into Northern Ireland without radically changing the nature of the state. From the early days of Spence's UVF to Paisley's 'No' campaign against the 1998 agreement, some Protestants resisted that prospect because they viewed it as a threat to Northern Ireland's very existence.

Johnny White had been one of those, and in August 1969, as a nineteen-year old vigilante, was in the Protestant mob that was throwing petrol bombs at Catholic homes only a few streets away from where Billy McKee and his men were crouching, guns in hand. In the summer of 1998, White's face adorned election posters that hung from walls and lampposts along the Shankill Road and the streets of North Belfast, a reminder of his failed attempt to win a seat in the new Stormont assembly as a member of the UDA-linked Ulster Democratic Party. As leader of the UDA's most dangerous assassination squad in 1973, he prowled those same streets looking for Catholics to murder. Now the bespectacled face of candidate White beamed a reassuring smile at all who passed. He was not long back from a cruise that took him to, among other places, Rome, where he visited the Vatican. Michelangelo's Sistine Chapel ceiling deeply impressed him.

On a trip up the Shankill he paused at a new mural depicting the history of the UDA. Had he won a seat in the new assembly, his portrait would have been part of the mural. Near election time, however, the local BBC television station did a profile of him and described his role in the murder of SDLP councillor Paddy Wilson and Wilson's companion Irene Andrews, both of whom were stabbed to death in a quarry on the outskirts of North Belfast (see Chapter 3). 'They showed the funerals,' White said. 'It was very emotive.' He shrugged off the disappointment of his defeat and inspected the unfinished mural from various angles. 'It isn't just the way we wanted it,' he said.

Ultimately Protestant resistance failed, as did the IRA's armed campaign. And it failed mainly because Northern Ireland was not 'Ulster'. Ulster was a Unionist vision, the secure homeland the Protestant planters sought to establish. Northern Ireland was the complex reality, a 'Little Ulster', six counties carved out of nine, securing them a majority but one that was brittle and subject to change. Census figures published in 1991 showed that Catholics were an increasingly large minority, around 43 per cent of the population. Over the years, that change was most noticeable west of the River Bann in the counties Derry, Tyrone and Fermanagh, where Catholics were in fact in an overall majority. Were Unionists to attempt through a new partition to carve out a 'safer,' more homogenous homeland today, they would be constrained to draw the border down the east bank of the Bann, with a salient around the Protestant enclave of Coleraine. But even within that new, even littler 'Ulster', there would be areas where Catholics were in a large majority, such as South Armagh and South Down.

Meanwhile, in the state's capital, Belfast, once a 'jewel' of the British Empire, Catholics have been growing in numbers since the 1960s, as evidenced by the abandoned Protestant churches and Orange Halls engulfed in the demographic shift. Some have fallen to ruin. One Orange Hall in West Belfast has become a well-appointed republican drinking club, and a Protestant church in the same area is now a cultural centre where the Irish language is taught and Irish events held. The population of the Shankill Road, the working-class heart of loyalist Belfast, fell from 76,000 in the late 1960s to 27,000 in the early 1990s. In North Belfast, in the decade between 1982 and 1992, the Protestant population dropped from 112,000 to 56,000.[2] In the prosperous Malone Road district of South Belfast, once a bastion of middle- and upper-middle-class Protestants, there is one Catholic church. It was originally erected for the servants who worked in the surrounding redbrick mansions owned by wealthy businessmen. Now it has undergone a major expansion in order to accommodate the drastic rise in the number of its parishioners. They are no longer servants. They now own the mansions.

Catholic students are in a majority at Belfast's oldest university, Queen's.

In 1997, after over one hundred years, Unionists' political domination of the city was broken when the first Catholic Lord Mayor of Belfast, SDLP member Alban Maginness, took office. The Ulster homeland proved an unrealizable dream, just as the Provisional IRA's thirty-two-county socialist republic did.

Almost as dramatic were the political changes within Belfast's expanding Catholic community. By the mid-1990s Sinn Fein was the biggest nationalist party in the city, with thirteen council seats, almost twice as many as the SDLP and the same number as the Ulster Unionist Party. It is only a matter of time before there is a Sinn Fein Lord Mayor of Belfast.

The changing demographics and the rise of a new Catholic middle class have attenuated the long-prevailing sense of grievance in the Catholic community. The explosion of violence in August 1969 was mainly a working-class phenomenon, but it was originally set off because of frustration as upwardly mobile, well-educated Catholics ran into the old barriers of discrimination. With the rise of the Provisional IRA, who sought not the reform of the Northern Ireland state but its destruction, civil rights concerns soon became second-ary to the violent pursuit of a united socialist Ireland, the holy grail of republicanism.

Direct rule brought about the dismantling of the Unionist structures from 1972 onwards, and the barriers to social and economic progress for middle-class Catholics gradually came down. However, working-class Catholics still suffered dis-proportionately from unemployment and other forms of disadvantage. Additionally, they bore the brunt of the security forces' response to republican violence which was launched mainly from working-class Catholic districts. Their sense of grievance remained, and spurred the rise of Sinn Fein as a political power. But within the working-class Catholic com-munity, changes were also apparent.

The kind of poverty and bad housing typical of the 1960s was all but eradicated in the 1980s and 1990s. While un-employment remained high, a black economy flourished (usually controlled by the republican paramilitary groups) with people collecting welfare and working at part-time jobs. A tour of even the poorest housing developments of West Belfast in the mid-1990s shows a remarkable transformation from the way things were in the 1960s – streets of well-kept houses with neat gardens, cars parked at the gate, and satellite dishes on nearly every home have replaced the Victorian slums. Large shopping malls flourish, their carparks nearly always full. What sense of grievance remains has become more focused on specific issues – such as the police and the need to reform it to make it more acceptable to nationalists. Demands for reform of those aspects of Northern Ireland that most offended Catholics, including the handful of Orange marches that their organizers insist on forcing through na-tionalist areas, have gradually replaced the old, generalized hostility against the state. As the millennium approached and Catholics got ready to take their share of responsibility for running Northern Ireland's government, a new self-confidence characterized their community, replacing the deep sense of alienation that had felt for almost a century.

How much 'credit' the Provisional IRA can claim for this transformation is a matter of debate. Undoubtedly, the fall of Stormont in 1972 was at least in part due to the IRA. But ultimately it was not the IRA that determined the nature of the changes which overtook Northern Ireland. More than anything it was the failure of Unionism to create a moderate centre able to accommodate Catholic demands which forced the British to rethink, and then restructure, the 1920 settlement. That failure dated back to the mid-1960s and the Unionist government's inability or refusal to advance the reforms Prime Minister Terence O'Neill sought. At the same time, the progress of Paisleyism helped open and then exploit the first crack in the Unionist monolith. The rise of the Provisionals made it harder for any moderate centre to develop later. But the chief obstacle to its development always lay within Unionism itself. Even after the peace process was in place, the IRA's campaign had ended and Sinn Fein was ready to take part in the new institutions of government, Unionist leaders were still wavering over the Good Friday Agreement, uncertain about their ability to deliver a majority of their party in favour of the new reforms.

The rise of confidence within the nationalist community has been accompanied by a corresponding decline in the morale of Unionists. In Protestant working-class communities throughout the 1990s there were echoes of the kind of complaints that once were typical of poor Catholics. They expressed a sense of alienation from the state made still more bitter because, unlike Catholics, they once identified with it and saw it as 'theirs'. This was partly explained by the rise of unemployment in Protestant areas where before jobs were once virtually guaranteed. Working-class alienation from the predominantly middle-class Ulster Unionist Party took the form of growing support for 'fringe' loyalist parties like the

UVF-linked PUP. A deep sense of betrayal characterized the feeling many loyalists harboured towards the Protestant middle class who, they believed, reaped most of the benefits of the state while condemning and dissociating themselves from the Protestant paramilitaries who 'defended' it. Middle-class Protestants, meanwhile, regarded loyalist paramilitaries as mere criminals. There was no equivalent sympathy for them as is found for IRA prisoners in virtually all sections of the Catholic community. 'Respectable' Protestants of all classes were angry at the sight of convicted gunmen and bombers being released in a steady stream from the Maze Prison until by the end of 1998 it was almost empty. To them, the Good Friday Agreement was simply rewarding the wicked. By the 1990s, increasing numbers of the sons and daughters of the Protestant middle classes, rather than finishing their education at Queen's University or the University of Ulster, were choosing instead to go to universities in England and Scotland. Many would settle there, leaving Northern Ireland for ever.

Protestants were clearly more uncomfortable with the new Northern Ireland than their Catholic counterparts. However, in late 1998, when it was announced that the Nobel Peace Prize was to be awarded to John Hume and David Trimble, it was thought that this international recognition of the role Protestants had played in the peace process might help them adjust more easily to some of its consequences. In fact, it highlighted their continued defensiveness and suspicion. Many of them scoffed at the award as an attempt by the outside world to 'bribe' them through flattering Trimble, claiming (as did many nationalists) that is was given for purely political reasons in order to shore up his commitment to implementing the accords; a few, even in his own party, could hardly disguise their hostility to the honour. Their reactions made obvious the isolated nature of Unionism as an ideology, and the self-referential narrowness of its vision.[3]

The honouring of Hume was, in contrast, welcomed in the nationalist community and beyond almost without reservations. There was no problem in recognizing Hume's role in the peace process (after all, without him it would not have happened); nor was the world's attention viewed suspiciously as containing some kind of threat or bribe. Quite the opposite was the case: Ulster's nationalist community has always welcomed, indeed sought, outside attention, perhaps because they were convinced that the world could not but see things their way.

Until fairly recently, it appeared extremely unlikely that it would ever be possible to write a 'conclusion' to the story of the Ulster Troubles. Few dared predict that a conflict involving such irreconcilable demands could be brought to an end. Indeed, some doubt that it is as yet possible. As there is a dispute about when the Troubles actually began, it is fitting that there should be controversy over if and when they came to an end.

However, the conflict known as the Troubles was never a continuous, unchanging struggle. As is argued in these pages, the 'classic' period of the Troubles ended more than twenty years ago, in 1977. Loyalist paramilitary organizations drastically reduced their level of activity, as did the Provisional IRA. But organized violence remained, in the form of terrorism linked to a developing political organization that attempted to articulate the republican movement's aims but ended up spending most of the time justifying its methods. By the early 1990s, it was clear to some of those involved in that campaign that it would not achieve its aims, thanks mainly to the successes of the security forces and the RUC's counter-terrorism measures. Within the republican movement there was a growing feeling that violence was counterproductive and was limiting the capacity of Sinn Fein (who had tasted electoral success) to make further political progress. It was the ending of the armed campaign which allowed the moderate political centre to develop into a public sphere where compromise would eventually replace the clash of contending absolutes, the dogmas of Unionism and republicanism.

For too long those dogmas proved deadly, as the burnt-out shell of a house where three young brothers died and the devastated shopping street of a quiet market town, where twenty-nine men, women and children were slaughtered, mutely testify. But hope too is found in unlikely places.

POSTSCRIPT

Transitions

Since the signing of the Good Friday Agreement, Northern Ireland has enjoyed its longest period of peace in over a generation. But the political transitions that the agreement entails have proven difficult to make. While the Provisionals' armed campaign – and loyalism's violent response to it – became things of the past, the sense of crisis remained. The British and Irish governments' attempts to implement the accords have driven a wedge through the Ulster Unionist Party, dividing it uneasily between the pro- and anti-agreement factions, and have threatened to split the republican movement. Old political positions have been shaken and transformed, and deep-seated anxieties exposed by the shifting ground.

Crisis long ago became a part of the ritual of life in Northern Ireland. As the province entered the new millennium, that had not changed. In spite of the Good Friday Agreement of April 1998, the conflict remained in many ways unresolved, punctuated by acts of brutal violence that harked back to the worst days of the Troubles. At the beginning of 1999, Provisional IRA men murdered one of the organisation's former intelligence officers turned author, Eamon Collins, repeatedly stabbing him in the body and head and battering his face so badly as to leave him unrecognisable. Collins' checkered history with the organisation, which he recounted in telling detail in his 1997 book, *Killing Rage*, had included a four year period when the information he gathered partly thanks to his job as a Customs officer had led to a series of IRA assassinations of off-duty UDR and RUC officers. In 1985 during interrogation he had made statements to the police which led to the arrest of many of his IRA colleagues. He later retracted them. Eventually in a remarkable trial, the judge ruled that Collins' confessions to the police were unreliable and he was acquitted of all charges.

After his acquittal, Collins left Northern Ireland for a period but then had defied local Provisionals by returning to live in the Newry area near where he was raised. More dangerously he defied them again when he appeared as a witness on behalf of the *Sunday Times* in a libel trial. He testified in court that Tom 'Slab' Murphy was, as the paper had alleged, a high-ranking member of the IRA. (Murphy had lost an original judgment against the paper and was appealing it. In fact, 'Slab', from South Armagh, had been a member of the IRA's ruling body, the Army Council, for many years and police say became its chief of staff with the resignation of Kevin McKenna in late 1996.)

The brutality of Collins' death provoked little outrage, nor did the fact that he was the first writer to be singled out and killed in the recent history of the conflict. The human rights activists and nationalists in general reserved their outrage for the murder that took place two months later. On 15 March, Rosemary Nelson, an Armagh solicitor who like Patrick Finucane before her frequently represented IRA suspects and like Finucane was allegedly threatened by the police, died when a booby-trap bomb exploded under her car as she drove from her Lurgan home. A loyalist organisation, the Red Hand Defenders, said they killed her. The group had emerged the year before, claiming responsibility for a series of bomb attacks on Catholic homes mainly in the South Antrim area. However, the organisation was almost certainly a front for dissident members of the UDA and Red Hand Commandos.

As in the Finucane case, there were cries of collusion. The RUC came under tremendous pressure to resolve the murder. To meet with objections from human rights activists and local Catholics who did not trust the RUC, the case was put in the hands of Colin Port, an English policeman. As well, the FBI agreed to become involved. Four agents were dispatched to give 'technical assistance'. However, its agents were able to achieve little and left by the middle of April.

Every under-car booby-trap bombing that had ever occurred in Northern Ireland was painstakingly reconstructed and computer models made of each in what to date has proved to be an expensive and futile search for the murderers. But the investigation did reveal that like the IRA ceasefire, that of the major loyalist groups the UDA and the UVF was conditional. It was almost certainly a UDA bomb-maker from Belfast who made the bomb, though it was ex-members of the UVF and LVF who were actually involved in the planting of the device.

Privately, RUC officers compared somewhat bitterly the extraordinary effort and expense invested in the Nelson murder with the relative paucity of attention paid to similar crimes against policemen over the years. Many of them, especially in the North Armagh area, had little time for Nelson. The fact that they believed that she had become close to a high-ranking IRA man who was her client made them even more hostile to her. Nationalists angrily rejected the allegations as ugly rumours designed to discredit her.

There were less publicised murders as the peace process became bogged down in the decommissioning dispute. Following the killing of Collins, the IRA targeted several alleged drug dealers and 'criminal elements' in the border area around Armagh and Down. Loyalists in Portadown murdered a Catholic grandmother who was married to a local Protestant. In parts of south and east Antrim and north Armagh a small-scale but vicious campaign of ethnic cleansing Ulster-style to drive Catholics out of Protestant neighbourhoods through fire-bomb attacks continued. An incipient feud was threatened between dissident loyalists and the UVF Supporters of the LVF and other loyalist splinter groups were unhappy with the UVF's attempt to reclaim lost influence in areas of North Armagh where they had once reigned unchallenged.

Dissident republicans in the Real IRA and the Continuity IRA, along with the INLA, had faded into the background after the Omagh atrocity of August 1998. However, the struggle to implement the Good Friday Agreement in full, which meant increasing pressure on the mainstream IRA to begin decommissioning, opened up new and dangerous opportunities for traditional republicans to accuse the Provisionals of selling out. It provided a temptation for dissident activists to demonstrate that there was still a republican threat to the Northern Ireland state, and thus, they hoped, win over more recruits from disillusioned Provisionals. At least one major meeting occurred in 1998 which brought together CIRA, the Real IRA and the INLA in an effort to coordinate their activities. But the attempts to relaunch a campaign of violence were frustrated by police surveillance north and south of the Irish border. The few attacks that did succeed, in which a small hotel was bombed in Fermanagh and slight damage done to an army barracks near Derry, were pathetic. They served only to highlight the unreality of the politics that lay behind them. However, they did remind everyone of the potential dangers when sophisticated weaponry was recovered by the police in February 2000. After a dissident IRA attack on a security forces base was aborted a new type of rocket launcher was found near the base, primed and ready for use. It had originated in Eastern Europe. It was known that the leader of the Real IRA had paid a visit to Prague in the months following the Omagh massacre. The former Quartermaster General of the Provisional IRA was thought to have been attempting to open up arms supply sources. The rocket find indicated that he might have succeeded. The Real IRA was also known to have a certain amount of Semtex at its disposal. Police suspected that the Provisionals in South Armagh were helping the dissident group to carry out operations.

It was imperative then that the promise contained within the Good Friday Agreement be realised. By the summer of 1999 the British and Irish governments were anxious to implement the political structures outlined in the agreement. They were far behind schedule. The deadline for the 'shadow form' of the executive, October 1998, by which time ministers were supposed to have been nominated to their posts, had long passed. Unionists had summed up their position as regards Sinn Fein's participation in the envisioned power-sharing arrangements as 'No Guns, No Government'. It was the latest in the long line of pithy slogans, such as 'No Surrender', 'Ulster Says No' and 'Not An Inch', which have defined Ulster politics for generations. In their laconic negativity they defy ambiguity. They are a challenge to the studied euphemisms in which so much of the language of the peace process is couched. They cannot be misinterpreted. They are verbal barricades which have to be breached.

In July 1999, over a year after the agreement had been signed, and endorsed overwhelmingly in referendums north and south of the border, Dublin, London and Washington launched a full frontal assault on the Unionists' 'No Guns, No Government' position.

There was actually nothing in the agreement, Sinn Fein argued, that stated when the decommissioning of weapons must begin, just that all parties will do everything in their power to see that it is completed by 22 May 2000. Republicans said they were striving to fulfil that commitment. Unionist leader David Trimble countered that while there was no commencement date mentioned in the agreement for the release of prisoners, that process had started; meanwhile, the Patten Commission to look into the reform of the RUC was preparing its report, and human rights reforms were underway. So, the Unionist argument ran, it was incumbent upon the IRA to demonstrate its willingness to support the new settlement by beginning to disarm. Otherwise the fact that republicans continued to cling to an illegal arsenal was proof for Unionists that the IRA was engaged in a deceptive exercise, and remained ready to resume political terrorism if things did not go according to its plan. Unionists were strengthened in their arguments when in July 1999 the FBI disrupted a republican arms smuggling operation in Florida and took four into custody. The IRA admitted those arrested were members of the organisation but claimed that the operation had not been sanctioned by the Army Council.

Regardless of Unionist objections, Blair said that the British government would ask Trimble as First Minister elect to go ahead and trigger the mechanism for the nomination of ministers for the devolved assembly on 15 July. Included among them would be two Sinn Fein members. He made a dramatic announcement that though the IRA had not yet begun to disarm, the organisation had undergone a 'seismic shift' in its position which convinced him that it was serious about meeting the terms of the agreement. The IRA had agreed to appoint a representative to meet with General John de Chastelain, the chairman of the decommissioning body set up under the agreement's auspices. The move was the first time that the group had acknowledged, formally, that the sensitive issue of arms must be dealt with. This was not enough for Trimble. Unionists did not want words but weapons.

On the day the new government was supposed to be nominated, the UUP did not show up at Stormont but Sinn Fein did. Historic roles were thus reversed. Unionists were now boycotting Stormont while Sinn Fein's nominees for ministerial seats Martin McGuinness and Barbara De Bruin arrived eager to start work. Without Unionist participation, the executive quickly folded, followed by the resignation of Seamus Mallon, the SDLP's deputy leader who was also Deputy First Minister. The agreement was then put under review. George Mitchell, the former US senator who chaired the talks in 1997–1998 that led to the Good Friday settlement, agreed to chair the review, scheduled to begin in September.

There were those, including Martin McGuinness, who predicted that by then there would be nothing left to review. Right from the start it has been among Unionists that support for the agreement was most qualified. Pro-agreement Unionists had won the June 1998 elections to the proposed assembly by a fragile majority. Now, among republicans, a feeling of frustration with what they saw as Unionist intransigence was corroding the enthusiasm that had helped win the agreement such overwhelming nationalist backing in May 1998. They saw Unionist insistence on getting IRA guns before Sinn Fein got into government as a means of derailing the whole political process. Adams and McGuinness had secured backing for their policy on the basis that the republican movement would see political results within a short time. Instead, over one year had passed, and neither the cross-border bodies nor the power sharing government had been established, and the whole agreement was 'parked'. There were also growing doubts in Irish government circles about Trimble's leadership. Privately, Irish officials expressed fears that his anxiety to appease the anti-agreement forces within his party was making it impossible for him to carry out the mandate of implementing the agreement. There was a malign interpretation of Unionist policy as being a deliberate tactic aimed at delaying implementation until May 2000, by which date, under the agreement's terms decommissioning was supposed to be completed. Failure to achieve that completion would force the governments to suspend it and place it under review. Though the wording of the agreement was purely aspirational, and contained no reference for punitive measures against Sinn Fein or the other paramilitary-linked parties in the event of such failure, it was possible that some Unionists believed that under those circumstances the British and Irish governments would be forced to consider a renegotiating of the terms that would exclude Sinn Fein from government and allow the establishment of a SDLP–UUP coalition to take power. Unionists, however, deny that there ever was such a master plan.

Few gave Senator Mitchell much chance of success when he returned to Northern Ireland in September 1999. Nationalists wanted the review to be short, sharp and focused on the one issue – the decommissioning problem. However, Mitchell's proceedings were immediately suspended because of the publication of the Patten Commission's report on policing, which came out on 9 September. Its 175 recommendations for reform were more thorough-going than many, especially Unionists, expected. Most upsetting for Unionists, and the majority of Ulster Protestants, was the report's finding that the name of the force should be changed to something more politically neutral and that the requirement to take an oath of loyalty to the Crown be dropped. They could accept the need to increase recruitment of Catholics or to incorporate a human rights agenda into police training or even a reduction of manpower by almost 50% over a period of time. But to abandon the name Royal Ulster Constabulary was too explicit an attack on the identity of the force. To Unionists, the RUC was Ulster in uniform, an Ulster with which they could identify where loyalty was the key to security. The proposed new name, 'Northern Ireland Police Service', cut the links to the 'Ulster' homeland they had fought to create, and replaced them with something which had no resonance for them.

There was a furious reaction from Protestants, though it came nowhere near the explosion of anger and violence that followed the publication of the Hunt Report almost exactly 30 years earlier (See Chapter 1). Trimble was attacked for not defending the RUC more vigorously. It mattered little that the Good Friday Agreement, to which Unionists had signed up, explicitly outlined the need to reform the police in a way that would make it more acceptable to Nationalists. The only way, the Patten commission concluded, to achieve this goal was to depoliticise the police, which meant getting rid of any symbols identifying it with the political culture of Unionism.

Among Nationalists, the report was generally welcomed. The SDLP praised it, human rights activists welcomed it. However, Sinn Fein stayed mute. For years, the party had been engaged in a demonisation campaign against the RUC, a campaign which was in effect the political and by extension moral justification for the murder of police officers. Since the party's involvement in the peace process, republicans had been calling for the RUC's disbandment. The report's recommendations, while bringing a real overhaul, would leave many of the former RUC officers in place in the new structures, so it fell far short of republican demands. However, Sinn Fein could not condemn it outright for fear of encouraging the anti-agreement elements within their own constituency who would see the report as yet more proof that the British would never grant the kinds of changes republicans needed. Nor of course could Sinn Fein accept it, for fear of those same elements who would see that as proof that the Provisionals had sold out much the way the Official IRA had done in the 1970s. In its ceasefire announcement of May 1972 the Official IRA had demanded the disbandment of the police. Within three years, Official republicans representatives were welcoming RUC officers into its drinking clubs to inspect the premises when application was made for license to sell alcohol. Critics of the Provisional leadership were predicting a similar 'sell-out'.

The Pattern report put further pressure on Trimble not to bend over the demand 'No guns, no government'; pessimism therefore deepened about the likelihood of a successful outcome of the Mitchell review which resumed a week or so after its publication. In the meantime, UUP deputy leader John Taylor announced he was withdrawing from the party's talks team, adding to apprehensions about Mitchell's chances. As Unionists protested against the Patten report it was feared that Unionism as a whole would turn against the agreement, thus depriving Trimble of the small advantage in support he held over his opponents.

'It is hugely depressing,' commented an Irish government official who for many years had been involved in the process as he surveyed the scene in the Autumn of 1999.

At first it was thought the review would last a few weeks at the most. The Irish Prime Minister Bertie Ahern had asked Mitchell if he thought he could stick it out until 30 September.

Almost a month passed. Mitchell issued an uncharacteristically gloomy prognosis that progress would have to come soon. There was speculation that the middle of October was his deadline for significant progress to be made or else he would go home. Other interruptions occurred, such as the Ulster Unionist Party conference, which meant that the party leader could not take political risks until it was safely behind him.

In the middle of October, as pessimism deepened, Mitchell imposed a media black-out and moved the talks to the residence of the US ambassador in London. For the first time, positive indications began to emerge that a deal was in the making. Trimble, it seemed, was ready. Mitchell had succeeded in getting the UUP leadership and the Sinn Fein leadership to talk directly to each other (something they had not done during the negotiations that led to the Good Friday Agreement), and, more importantly, to socialise in the less fraught atmosphere of the residence. The Sinn Fein and UUP negotiators, along with Mitchell, even shared an evening meal together. Contact was creating trust. Amazingly, by mid-November 1999, the review had concluded with an accord on how the agreement would be implemented. By then, according to a BBC reporter's estimate, over 1,000 hours had been spent on talks about decommissioning during a period of just 18 months.

There was actually little or nothing original in what emerged about the solution – the paramilitaries would appoint representatives to meet with General John de Chastelain, the chairman of the decommissioning commission, to focus on when and how disarmament would begin, while the political institutions – including the power-sharing government and the cross-border bodies – would be set up. It was more or less what had been on offer in July. There was speculation that this time it had worked because both sides trusted Mitchell as a detached and objective arbitrator, something lacking in the previous summer when the two governments had tried to cajole Unionist and Republican into an acceptable compromise.

A series of statements followed, from Mitchell, Adams, Trimble, and the IRA which gave its backing to its party's pursuit of goals by peaceful means. The IRA announced that it was appointing a representative to meet with the decommissioning body. The other main paramilitary groups, the UDA and UVF, then named their representatives. There followed a statement from de Chastelain welcoming the liaison with the paramilitary organisations as an important step towards decommissioning.

It was also widely assumed – especially by Unionists – that at some point, there would be the actual destruction or giving up of weapons. But like so much in the agreement as in the talks, couched as they were in the euphemisms of conflict-resolution speak, this was not made explicit in any of the statements.

Euphemisms are not part of the political rhetoric of Ulster Unionism. This was made clear almost immediately the review was concluded, as Northern Ireland heaved a sigh of relief and plaudits rained down on the head of George Mitchell. On 27 November, Trimble went to a meeting of the Ulster Unionist Council, the party's 860-strong governing body, to report on what had happened and try and quell the unease among its members at the fact that he had seemingly abandoned the 'No Guns, No Government' barricade. Trimble was not sure of a majority in favour of his move. In order to swing the council behind him, he agreed to write a post-dated letter of resignation to take effect by the next council meeting, 12 February 2000, if the IRA had not begun to disarm by then. Even with this proviso, he managed only a narrow majority – 58% – in favour of setting up the new government.

Unfortunately, Trimble's commitment to the UUC effectively doomed any hope of the new government enduring. The republican movement saw it as an artificial deadline outside the terms of the Good Friday Agreement and outside the remit of the Mitchell review's conclusions. Once more the Unionists were testing them, demanding what the IRA saw as a gesture of surrender. Both Pat Doherty, Sinn Fein vice President, and Martin Ferris called the threat to close down the new government over the arms issue as lunacy and unthinkable – an indication of just how ignorant they were of Unionists' feelings. Republican thinking seemed to be that once Trimble and his fellow Unionists had their jobs in the government, and the institutions were functioning, then they would never relinquish them because of a dispute over decommissioning. Once again, republicans' limited grasp of Unionist realities led them to underestimate the depth of the UUP's anxiety over decommissioning. A certain sectarian stereotyping of Protestants as being fundamentally only concerned with money and prosperity, also seemed to play a part in the blithe assumption that once in power, Unionists would drop their demand.

Meanwhile, the government was formed, powers were devolved from Westminster, the various bodies were set up. At the beginning of December 1999, powers were transferred to the new assembly. It had been twenty-five years since the last power-sharing experiment under the Sunningdale Agreement had been tried and had failed. This time, there were reasons to be more sanguine.

The armed groups were on cease-fire and indeed were now (with a few unimportant exceptions) supporting the initiative. Mainstream Unionism, and even Paisley's DUP, appeared ready to accept power-sharing. As part of the new deal, the Irish government passed legislation changing Articles 2 and 3 of the Irish constitution, claiming jurisdiction over the North of Ireland; they now expressed an aspiration for unity rather than an imperative, thus meeting Unionist demands. The new arrangements superseded all previous constitutional provisions put into force by Westminster including the Government of Ireland Act of 1920 which was the basis for the partition of the island. For the first time in its history, Sinn Fein entered a Northern Ireland government, taking their place next to Unionists and SDLP members in the new Stormont parliament, the very place that they had dedicated themselves to destroying. In the dying days of the century which had witnessed the birth of the IRA, one of its former chiefs of staff, Martin McGuinness, became Minister of Education, and his colleague, Barbara De Bruin, Minister of Health. When George Harrison, the old IRA gunrunner in New York, was asked to comment on the new Minister, he said that the only lesson he thought it worthwhile to teach was

'Brits Out'. It was a lesson he claimed the IRA now seemed to have forgotten.

The preparation for this extraordinary reversal of traditional republican policy had begun in early 1995, when Adams asked the party leadership to approve of a measure allowing elected republicans to enter a Northern regime as long as it was deemed 'transitional' and not part of an 'internal' settlement. He had achieved that aim in a remarkably short period and, even more strikingly, without splitting the republican movement. He and his supporters within the IRA were able to sell the Good Friday Agreement as such a transitional stage, much the way, years earlier, Michael Collins had sold the treaty to a majority within the republican movement as a 'stepping stone' to their goal of a united Ireland. (A more sinister parallel was drawn between the two republican leaders. Graffiti appeared on the Falls Road which warned Adams 'Remember Michael Collins'. Collins was shot dead in August 1922 shortly after the outbreak of the Irish civil war.)

Unfortunately for Adams, the new government would prove more transitional than expected.

On 13 December, the first meeting of the North-South Council took place in Armagh without protests from Unionist hard-liners or Paisleyites. Its importance to the Irish government was evidenced by the cavalcade of government limousines which swept across the border to attend the great event. Since 1922, Dublin had been trying to establish some institution which would express, however weakly, the nationalist goal of one nation. The North-South Council went no further than accepting that there were common areas of economic and cultural concern between the two Irish states. It was not like the Council of Ireland as envisioned in the 1920 act which the British at the time saw as an all-Ireland government in embryo; nor was it as all-embracing as the version contained in the Sunningdale Agreement.

Over the years nationalism, even in its more militant forms, had learned to be more modest and take an incremental approach to changing relationships between North and South. Of course, Sinn Fein, even more than Fianna Fail and the SDLP, had to make as much as they could of the new cross-border body in their continuing effort to sell the settlement as significant progress in their struggle for a unitary state. But they found it hard to deflect the sour, cynical remarks from some quarters where it was being asked if Bobby Sands had starved to death for a cross-border fisheries body.

The government was up and running, the new councils with their bureaucratic paraphernalia were in place by the middle of December. McGuinness as the new Education Minister was the object of some protests in Protestant schools and the butt of a few droll remarks in the new assembly ('The new Minister of Education's three "Rs",' commented one DUP member: 'Reading, Writing and Armalites'.) But he got down to work, impressing most with his assiduousness. However, the crucial question of what the IRA was going to do as its former Chief of Staff was making the rounds of school visits and shaking hands with bemused Protestant schoolboys, remained unanswered.

So the new millennium dawned in Ireland, with the old republican traditions and shibboleths overthrown and replaced, all except one, that is. An Irish government official commented at the beginning of January that there was an 'ominous silence' from the IRA on the matter of decommissioning. In the IRA's New Year statement, decommissioning was noticeable by its absence. Instead it said that it supported the search for a 'a just and lasting peace' and attacked Ulster Unionists for setting another 'precondition' – the UUC deadline that was 'outside the agreement'.

Unease began to grow. Rumours in the press that decommissioning was to begin in January were quickly proven to be untrue. There was talk about an IRA commitment to de Chastelain to 'putting weapons beyond use' (the preferred republican euphemism for decommissioning) by sealing off arms dumps. People waited for de Chastelain to prepare his next report due at the end of January on what progress was being made – if any. Even so, among liberal Unionists who supported the agreement, there was optimism that the IRA would do something to ensure that Trimble would not have to act on his post-dated resignation letter which was lying in the safe of Sir Josias Cunningham, the chairman of the Ulster Unionist Council.

A new factor had entered into the Ulster equation a few months earlier. In mid-October, the British Prime Minister Tony Blair had replaced 'Mo' Mowlam as Northern Ireland Secretary of State with his confidante Peter Mandelson. The shift had been planned since the previous summer, but for internal party reasons took longer to be effected than expected. There were several reasons why Blair made the change. After two years on the job, Mowlam had become increasingly unpopular with Unionists. They viewed her as being much too friendly with republicans, addressing Adams and McGuinness, for example, by their first names. But the problem was as much cultural as it was political. For Ulster Unionism the world of New Labour, and New Britain, was an alien one. Women had never played much of a role in what was still very much a male-dominated culture. At Unionist party conferences, their main role seems to be to butter the scones for the tea-breaks. Coming from such a world, not surprisingly, many Ulster Unionists could not comfortably adjust to Ms Mowlam, a product of a world which they did not understand or like. She was an affront to their image of womankind as prim, domesticated and unobtrusive house-wives.

Mowlam's relationship with Unionists became so bad that the party leader at one point accused her of trying to drive the

UUP from the talks process. Increasingly Trimble had by-passed her and gone straight to Blair when important issues were being discussed. It meant, in fact, the Prime minister was being drawn into day-to-day disputes that he would rather have left to the Secretary of State.

There were, of course, broader, political reasons for the move. Mandelson, the mastermind of Blair's landslide victory in 1997, had been asked to leave the cabinet in December 1998 when it was revealed that he had borrowed money from one of his cabinet colleagues in order to buy a house. Blair was keen to reinstate him, with the eventual aim, it was presumed, of using Northern Ireland as a springboard into a higher government post. Being much closer to Blair, it was understood that he would be seen as acting with the PM's authority at all times, avoiding the confusions that sometimes marred Mowlam's final months in the office.

The new Northern Ireland proconsul arrived in Ulster with the reputation of a Mandarin – a rather clever, somewhat haughty architect of New Labour and its policies. Mandelson was the grandson of Herbert Morrison, and had begun his political life on the left of the party before moving to the middle. As much as Mowlam, though in a very different way, he was a creature of the new social and political alignments that were changing the face of Labour and of Britain. The blurring of ideologies was accompanied by a sort of melting of class markers, apparent in Mandelson's aura of social self-confidence as well as his elegance of manner, one that in times past would not have been associated with a Labour Party member. It seemed to many to be more appropriate to a Tory grandee. It antagonised some, while it charmed others.

How much of an advantage these attributes would actually give the new Secretary of State in Northern Ireland was not at all clear. The Ulster mentality, especially the Protestant variety, is deeply suspicious of 'cleverness' which it tends to equate with dubious moral tendencies. As one rather jaundiced Irish government official put it with some foreboding: 'Ulster eats clever people for breakfast'.

As the deadline of the next Ulster Unionist Council loomed, Mandelson went to work. He outraged Unionists by announcing that he intended to implement almost in full the recommendations of the Pattern report; within 18 months, the RUC would be history and the first recruits to the new Police Service of Northern Ireland as it was now christened (rather than the 'Northern Ireland Police Service' – to avoid the embarrassing acronym NIPS) would be appearing from the training centre to plod the streets and laneways of Ulster, mindful of the civil rights of its citizens and respectful of their 'traditions'. Many police officers viewed this as inevitable. One Special Branch veteran said it was the government's 'last card' to get the IRA to begin decommissioning, the thinking being, 'We've started decommissioning our people, now you decommission yours'. It had no effect. Sinn Fein spokesmen dryly (but correctly) observed that there was no 'linkage' in the Good Friday Agreement between reform of the police and decommissioning. Amid growing anxiety, the new Secretary of State said that David Trimble would not be left alone. If by the end of January, de Chastelain could not report that significant progress had been made towards disarmament, Mandelson threatened he would suspend the new government and reimpose direct rule. Saving David Trimble was his chief concern.

If forced to resign, Trimble as First Minister would be vulnerable to challenges from anti-agreement members of his own party. He would need to be re-elected to the post of First Minister in the event of the power-sharing government being reformed and would almost certainly be unable to garner enough Unionist votes to win. Britain looked at the Unionist landscape and saw no one other than Trimble who had a hope of leading the Unionist Party in the direction in which it wanted the party to go. Better direct rule than face those prospects.

However, logic said that it would not come to that. The IRA would do something. After all, the republican movement had dedicated its energies for the best part of five years to the peace process, its political wing had signed up to an agreement obligating it to helping to achieve the completion of decommissioning by 22 May 2000 – by January only a few months away – Sinn Fein ministers were busily (and happily) engaged in their governmental departments, the IRA had been on ceasefire for almost three years, the Maze Prison was almost empty, police reforms were in hand; it was reasoned that the IRA and Sinn Fein could not run the risk of alienating its new friends in Dublin, London and Washington who clearly wanted a 'gesture' to resolve the arms controversy once and for all. Yes, the logic was impeccable. The problem was that the Northern Ireland conflict has never been logical. Had logic been applied then it never would have arisen in the first place. An effort was made before Christmas 1999 to test opinion within the IRA at local level about decommissioning. But emissaries from the army council received a ferocious rejection of any such move.

By the end of January, de Chastelain's report was ready. Publication was delayed, however, at the request of the Irish government. Those government officials who had seen it said it was frighteningly negative, disclosing that the paramilitaries had done nothing, and had not even indicated their intention to do anything about decommissioning weapons. Dublin feared that publication would precipitate a crisis and force Trimble to resign, or the British to suspend the new government forthwith. The report was kept under wraps.

The Irish government launched a desperate mission to the IRA in an attempt to get some concession from them that Trimble would be able to take to his council meeting and say to them: 'This is good enough. It enables us to continue in government'. What form such a concession would take, short of actual 'product' as the Unionists called it, was the subject of much speculation. A 'form of words' was suggested, with the IRA declaring that the war was over, accompanied by a time-table for decommissioning. Talk of 'putting weapons beyond use' began to replace 'decommissioning'. Blair was said to be willing to extend the May deadline for a year to allow the paramilitaries time to meet their obligations.

The feverish activity persuaded Mandelson to postpone the imposition of suspension for another week. A week before the 12 February UUC meeting, the IRA issued a statement. It rejected accusations that it had betrayed the peace process and pointed out that it 'never entered into any agreement, under-taking or understanding at any time with anyone on any aspect of decommissioning . . . Those who have once again made the political process conditional on the decommission-ing of silenced IRA arms are responsible for creating the current difficulties and for keeping the peace process in a state of perpetual crisis. The IRA believes that this crisis can be averted and the issue of arms resolved.

'This will not be on British or Unionist terms, nor will it be advanced by British legislative threats.

'We recognise that the issue of arms needs to be dealt with and in an acceptable way and this is a necessary objective of a genuine peace process. For that reason we are engaged with the IICD (Independent International Commission on Decom-missioning).

'We have supported and will continue to support efforts to secure the resolution of the arms issue.

'The peace process is under no threat from the IRA.

Though the Irish and British tried in public to put a positive spin on the statement, both knew that if Trimble went to the Ulster Unionist Council armed only with that he would be torn apart.

Another attempt was launched as 11 February approached

– the day when it was believed Trimble would activate his resignation letter. Early that morning, the Irish Prime Minister Bertie Ahern spoke with the IRA who informed him that it had prepared a new statement. Later that day, it was given to the de Chastelain commission. It declared that the IRA accepted that the arms issue had to be dealt with in a way that would inspire maximum confidence on all sides, and reiterated that the IRA was no threat to the peace process. It was an implicit recognition that the IRA's war was over.

Adams declared it was a 'major breakthrough'. However, the UUC chairman Josias Cunningham contacted Mandelson at around 5 pm, warning him that Trimble would be forced to resign unless the government was suspended. At that point, Mandelson said he had received nothing from de Chastelain to indicate any change of position by the IRA. Sinn Fein alleges that he was aware of the contents of the new IRA statement by noon. (A BBC report supported the contention that the Secretary of State had the new statement.) At any rate, Mandelson said later that though significant, the IRA's new submission to de Chastelain would not have been enough to allow Trimble to face down his opponents and continue in office. The British government announced that from midnight Friday 11 February, the power-sharing government of Northern Ireland was suspended and direct rule reimposed. For the second time in twenty-five years the experiment in cross-community government for Northern Ireland had failed.

Ironically, Nationalists and republicans were angrier than Unionists at the loss of local government. There was no comparable sense of outrage in the Unionist community. It was Sinn Fein and the SDLP leaders who immediately went on the offensive demanding the new institutions be reinstated. Sinn Fein spokesmen were particularly bitter, accusing the British government in general and Peter Mandelson in particular, of allowing the Unionists to exercise a veto over progress once again. More ominously, Adams remarked during a press conference a few days later that the events of 11 February (dubbed 'Frantic Friday') showed that 'politics had failed'.

Since the early 1990s, the strategy of the IRA and Sinn Fein leadership had been predicated upon the belief that violence was no longer useful and that progress towards republican goals could be made through a political strategy. It was on this basis that the IRA army council closed down the armed campaign. Did Adams' remarks indicate that the IRA would revert to its old tactics? Within three days of direct rule's reimposition, the IRA announced it was withdrawing its representative from meetings with the de Chastelain commission. The offer it had put on the table on that fateful Friday was null and void. Once more Unionists' attempt to get the IRA to decommission had produced the exact opposite effect. A rash of reports appeared in the British press claiming that the movement had imported arms from the US during the summer of 1999 and had stepped up its surveillance operations on members of the security forces. However, security sources continued to insist that there was no sign of any imminent breakdown in the ceasefire.

Confusion also reigned in the political sphere, as accusations and recriminations flew fast and furious. Peter Mandelson went on the offensive, arguing that his actions were designed to save the Good Friday Agreement, not to wreck it. The alternative, he said, was to have 'staggered on in a mounting crisis until assembly elections would've been called. They'd have been the most divisive in Northern Ireland's history. It would have been a disaster'. While most agreed with him, nationalists argued that more should have been done with the new IRA offer. After all, de Chastelain had said in a statement that it did provide the opportunity for his commission to 'fulfil its mandate in full'. The charge from Nationalists was that Trimble and the Ulster Unionist Council had effectively usurped the function of de Chastelain's commission by deciding what was or was not acceptable in decommissioning, and they did so outside the terms of the Good Friday Agreement. Mandelson countered that the understanding at the end of the Mitchell review, to which Sinn Fein was a party, was that decommissioning could begin 'soon'. Trimble had risked going into government, defying his own party's policy, based on that understanding. And it was not fulfilled. By January, nothing had happened. The IRA offer should have come a lot earlier to give Trimble a chance to sell it to his supporters.

Irish government officials had privately concluded some time ago that the real problem was not with the IRA, but with Trimble. The débâcle of the power-sharing Government was yet another proof of their thesis that he was not in full control of his own party and was continually obliged to appease the anti-agreement faction within it. By doing so, he constantly went outside of the agreement's own terms, thus undermining the very process he was supposedly trying to move forward. A further, and perhaps ultimately fatal, demonstration of his weakness came six weeks after the suspension of government.

While in Washington for the annual St. Patrick's Day festivities at the White House, Trimble addressed the National Press Club during which he remarked that 'we are prepared to be involved in a fresh sequence which probably will not involve arms up front'. These words, suggesting he would be prepared to re-form the government without any decommissioning first, caused consternation among his supporters and delight among his enemies. Trimble quickly tried to qualify his words by arguing that they represented in fact a 'tightening' of his previous position. He said he had meant that 'we would not do it again unless we were certain that it would work. By that, of course, it means that the destruction of weapons would follow very soon thereafter.'

The reaction among anti-agreement Unionists was predictable. Trimble's supporters were also taken aback since they knew he must face another meeting of the Ulster Unionist Council on 25 March. There already was talk of a 'stalking horse' challenge being mounted. Trimble's Washington remarks gave his opponents the opportunity they needed.

Just before the meeting, the Rev. Martin Smyth, former Grand Master of the Orange Lodge, stepped forward as the challenger. Smyth, the party's MP at Westminster for South Belfast (to which he was elected after the Provisional IRA murdered the previous MP for the area, Rev. Robert Bradford in late 1981), was an unexpected opponent and regarded rather derisively, even by anti-Trimble Unionists. One referred to him as a 'cart horse rather than a stalking horse'.

It was in some ways an unfortunate analogy. A cart horse's heavy hooves can prove formidable weapons. After only a two-day campaign, Smyth secured just over 43% of the vote. While he did not succeed in trampling his opponent into the ground, he did leave footprints all over him, which may prove to be indelible. As the result was announced Jeffrey Donaldson, who decided Trimble in the closing stages of the negotiations for the Good Friday Agreement, was seen to punch the air in triumph. Donaldson is viewed by many as a future leader of the party.

'He smelt blood,' commented a government official. Smyth's unexpectedly strong showing will almost certainly mean a serious challenge to Trimble from Donaldson before too long, one he might not be able to turn back.

Perhaps even worse for the party leader was the UUC's vote to impose a new precondition on re-entering government with Sinn Fein. It overwhelmingly endorsed a motion saying that the UUP should not go into a power-sharing arrangement again unless the British government dropped their proposal to rename the RUC as part of the Patten commissions recommendations on police reform. Trimble now laboured under two obstacles to a return to devolved government. To the demand 'No Guns, No Government' had been added 'No RUC, No Government'.

As Easter 2000 loomed both the Irish and the British governments were still talking about an all-out effort to restore power-sharing in time for the second anniversary of the signing of the Good Friday Agreement or by the end of April at the latest. But no one seriously gave them any hope of succeeding.

Two years after the signing of the agreement, the political process had broken down. The peace process, however, remained intact. That depended on the ability of the paramilitary leaders to hold their cease-fires. The question loomed as to how long the peace process could continue without political progress?

As the second anniversary approached, without any sign of a political breakthrough, Sinn Fein's leaders began to utter more ominous warnings. To the suggestion that the IRA issue a statement that the campaign of violence was over, and thus help Trimble, Adams retorted: 'It isn't within the gift of any one group to guarantee that the war is over'. He added: 'The only guarantee is for all of us to come together and to make politics work'. A few weeks before Easter, he wrote in an Irish American newspaper that he detected 'a sense of extreme foreboding'. (Irish Voice, 12 April 2000.)

His colleague in the peace process and the party's chief negotiator, Martin McGuinness, said in answer to a similar suggestion that the IRA should declare its war was over: 'I don't think anybody can guarantee anything any more in this type of world we are living in'. In September 1995, McGuinness had given an equally gloomy assessment of the situation. Within a month, the IRA army council had met and decided in principle to end the first ceasefire and launch a short, sharp campaign in Britain. Could history repeat itself? Would Adams' despairing remarks about politics having failed, made just after the suspension of the power-sharing executive, be taken to their logical conclusion by the IRA? After all, if one of the chief architects of the republican movement's turn towards politics has admitted that the attempt has failed, does that not mean the alternative must be pursued again?

Certainly, the delays and frustrations republicans have experienced since 10 April 1998, culminating in the reimposition of direct rule, will confirm in the minds of many IRA members their deep-seated scepticism about politics and what they can achieve through purely constitutional means. For them, the return to direct rule represented yet again the triumph of the Unionist veto over any prospect for political change and proof that Northern Ireland political structures were basically 'irreformable'. They saw an analogy between what had happened on 11 February and what had happened in the early 1970s. During those years, British policy was aimed at saving Brian Faulkner, as the standard bearer of 'pragmatic' Unionism, in order to avoid having to impose direct rule. This meant in practice conceding to Faulkner's security demands, including the introduction of internment and Bloody Sunday, in an effort to placate his own right wing. Of course, these measures had the opposite effect and forced the British eventually to do the very thing they had sought to avoid – impose direct rule. Two years later, Britain allowed the first power-sharing government to collapse rather than confront the UWC. On 11 February 2000, they had, according to republicans, rather than stand up to the UUC allowed its demands to collapse the second power-sharing government. Republicans and other nationalists saw a pattern and many concluded that events proved that it was impossible to do a deal with Ulster Unionism of no matter what variety.

Adams was acutely aware of this and his warnings in the wake of the events of 11 February can be viewed as a reminder to the British government that David Trimble was not the only participant in the peace process whose leadership was threatened by its failure.

Disillusionment with politics is dangerous, especially in a movement with such a long tradition of hostility to constitutionalism and a fierce, puritanical contempt for people who 'sell-out' for the rewards of office. But the IRA now found itself in a contradictory position. Politics may have failed to deliver what republicans wanted. But the IRA leadership knew better than anyone that the alternative – political violence – had also failed to bring about their goals. The armed struggle was obsolete. That was one of the reasons why the political course had been adopted in the first place. Most importantly, even if there was a prospect of success, the IRA was also aware that it could hardly proclaim a return to violence following the suspension of Stormont which would make it seem that republicans were fighting so that Stormont be restored. At the first Sinn Fein ard fheis of the new millennium, reporters had been treated to the novelty of Sinn Fein's leading spokesmen calling for the restoration of Stormont. But the irony of the IRA fighting for a new Stormont against the opposition of Unionists would be so hilariously unthinkable for republicans that it would make it impossible for the leadership to justify. Any return to terrorism would only occur in reaction to a renewed campaign of loyalist sectarian killings. And it would have to be on the basis of a complete rejection of the political path, which would condemn republicans – and the people of Ireland – to further years of violence with no end in sight. It is hard to see how anyone in the republican movement, however bitter his or her rejection of the current peace process, could seriously contemplate offering that course as an alternative.

The strength of the current peace process lies in the overwhelming support for it among Nationalists, North and South of the border. There is no sentiment in any significant section of the Irish people for a return to violence. For the IRA leadership to ignore this fact would be political suicide, and it was Sinn Fein's political needs that were determining republican strategy. Sinn Fein has set its sights on two chief tasks. The first is to overtake the SDLP in the North as the dominant voice of Irish nationalism there. By 2000, John Hume was an ailing figure. His exit from the North's political stage was expected sooner rather than later. It would leave his party, which was never organisationally very strong, facing an uncertain future. Sinn Fein knew this and were determined to exploit it. The party's second major goal is winning enough seats in the Dublin parliament to present itself as a coalition partner in a future Fianna Fail led government, perhaps by the next Irish general election. A full-scale return to armed struggle would set back such plans for a decade or more.

However, many Unionists remained unconvinced by the IRA's new policies and Trimble erected new demands before agreeing to enter into another power-sharing government with Sinn Fein. The UUP asked for concessions on the proposed Pattern police reforms, principally that the RUC's name somehow be retained. Once more it seemed progress would be stalled. But with or without a devolved government in Northern Ireland, the British will be at pains to preserve the peace process, which means essentially ensuring that the IRA does not return to violence (the theory being that as long as republican guns are silent the mainstream loyalist paramilitary groups will also stay quiet). The way to achieve this is to push ahead and implement those aspects of the Good Friday Agreement which do not depend on local government. Reforming the police, restructuring legal procedures, introducing human rights safeguards, ensuring equality of opportunity in jobs, the continuing release of paramilitary prisoners, and reduction of the military presence, are all measures that have the potential to transform Northern Ireland, making it into a more normal society, and perhaps creating the conditions which would allow decommissioning in some form or other to be realized eventually.

It was always the case that the IRA would never hand over

weapons to the authorities under any circumstances. At best, the governments could expect the IRA to acknowledge that its campaign had ended and would not be resumed and that its volunteers had been told to 'dump arms'. This was the formula that brought the 1956–62 border campaign to a conclusion. It would be further enhanced if the IRA agreed to some sort of inspection and verification procedure, under the aegis of the de Chastelain commission, to confirm that the arms dumps were sealed. The weapons would be, in the words preferred by the IRA, 'put beyond use'.

On 6 May 2000, to the surprise of almost everyone, the IRA did just that. It issued a statement saying that the leadership 'will initiate a process that will completely and verifiably put the IRA arms beyond use. We will do it in such a way as to avoid risk to the public and misappropriation by others and ensure maximum public confidence.'

'We will resume contact with the Independent International Commission on Decommissioning and enter into further discussions with the commission on the basis of the IRA leadership's commitment to resolving the arms issue.'

The statement expressed confidence that the agreement, if fully implemented, would provide 'the potential to remove the causes of the conflict' and allow 'republicans and unionists as equals' to pursue their respective political objectives peacefully. Within weeks, the power-sharing government had been restored.

After the Good Friday Agreement was signed, Seamus Mallon, the SDLP's deputy leader, called it 'Sunningdale for slow learners' (referring to the 1973 power-sharing deal that was later brought down by loyalist opposition). The May 6 IRA statement might well be described as the final lesson in 'The War is Over' course, for slow learners.

It was simply a formal, public recognition of the existing state of affairs. The current leadership of the IRA has turned its back on the armed campaign. In any case, after a ceasefire which has lasted for more than three years, the Provisional IRA would find it extremely difficult to go back to war even if the leadership decided it was necessary. Guerrilla armies are not like regular armies. They cannot survive inactivity for very long. Unlike a regular army they cannot maintain themselves in a state of readiness through the kinds of discipline, exercises and going on manoeuvres or other activities that are part of regular military routine. The Provisionals were the product of a specific situation and when that situation changed, they adapted. This is one reason why the Unionist demands for decommissioning are, in the end, beside the point (as well as being politically counterproductive). There are some problems which time itself solves by simply making them irrelevant. Decommissioning is one of them.

The statement was the first public recognition from the IRA that the Unionist position within Northern Ireland was based on their desire to remain part of the UK and it implied the necessity of winning their consent if that arrangement was to change.

It was issued one day after the nineteenth anniversary of the death of Bobby Sands, the hunger striker whose election to parliament helped set the republican movement on the course that led ultimately to the abandoning of the armed struggle.

There are people in the republican movement who see this as a threat not a hope. Ireland in the new millennium still has armed, dissident republican groups, and fringe loyalist paramilitaries, still willing to resort to violence. The so-called 'Real' IRA (responsible for the Omagh atrocity in 1998) continues to recruit a handful of former Provisional activists and threaten attacks. Likewise, the Continuity IRA remains in the field. The INLA though on ceasefire since 1998, has formed operational alliances with the Real IRA and as its history has shown is always capable of nasty surprises. But all of these organisations are moving against the political tide. Irish history has taken a different course, and they are not strong enough to stop it. Nor do they have within their leadership the kind of influential or charismatic figure able to act as a catalyst. They represent no new course but simply a reversal to an old, and failed approach. That is not to say that further acts of violence will not threaten the peace process. They will. But the basis is no longer there for anything like the sustained campaign the Provisionals carried out for 25 years. Nor have any of the republican splinter groups shown any capability of being able to wage such a war even if circumstances were more propitious than they are.

In 1969, Northern Ireland moved on to a new and dangerous course. Twenty-five years later, it started out on a different track. At either time, no one could say for certain where it would lead. No one could have predicted that the small, ignored gang of old IRA men gathered in the school house in Belfast with a handful of guns would grow into the most dangerous and powerful armed guerrilla group in Europe, almost overnight, representing the physical force republican tradition in its most virulent form. By the mid-1990s that tradition was spent and had not achieved its aims. Nor could it, thanks to the successes of the security forces, mainly the RUC. The IRA leadership for the most part recognised this (though it would never be admitted publicly). Just as the leaders of the IRA in the early 1960s realised that the physical force tradition had failed and that a political alternative had to be found if their movement was to survive, so men like Gerry Adams, Mitchel McLaughlin and Martin McGuinness came to the conclusion that guerrilla days in Ireland were drawing to a close and another strategy had to be evolved. Nothing that has happened since has fundamentally changed that position. The peace process like the conflict fought before it will be a long and gruelling one, full of setbacks and frustrations and doubtless liable to be challenged by those who are unable to understand the nature of the transformation that has come over Ireland, north and south. The culture of deprivation and oppression that through the generations created so many recruits for violent republicanism, leading them to embrace martyrdom and defeat when victory eluded them, is gone. The dynamic for peace and political progress is far more powerful now than it was in 1962. Only if that is recognised openly will it be possible to persuade the hardliners within both the republican and loyalist dissident organisations that the pursuit of their aims through violence is as futile as it is doomed.

In areas of life which need not wait on politics catching up with reality, the new thrives of its own accord alongside the old. Two internet cafes operate now in Shaftsbury Square, near the heart of the modern, revitalised Belfast, with its Italian and French restaurants and new hotels hungry for tourists. The cafes are busy with visitors logging on to the World Wide Web, surfing the net, and sending e-mails around the Earth. A few blocks distant lies the old loyalist working-class district known as Sandy Row, one of the last remaining stretches of 19th-century working-class Belfast left standing. There, every July, youths still gather wood for the 12 July celebrations, the centre piece of which is an enormous bonfire. It covers most of a large waste ground. Planks, old chairs, gutted sofas, broken-legged tables, hundreds of crates and boxes were dumped to form a huge, growing ramshackle pyramid, waiting for the torch.

The Belfast Hilton now towers over the banks of the Lagan River helping to define the new post-industrial cityscape – unrecognisable in many ways to those who grew up there in the 1950s. The hotel had opened just a year before, part of an investment boom which was changing the face of the city. It looks down on the old nationalist Markets area of the city, once the stronghold of the Official IRA and later the INLA. Nearby, construction was already under way for a huge sports–leisure complex, covering 23 riverside acres, consisting of 100,000 square feet of bars, restaurants and other facilities, including a basketball court, a running track, an ice hockey arena and a science centre.

The old culture of conflict is now merging with the new culture of information technology and consumerism. One day, no doubt, the appropriate politics will emerge to suit it.

May 2000

Notes

Chapter One

1. The UVF took its name from a militia established in 1912 to oppose Home Rule for Ireland. The original UVF was 100,000 strong. Incorporated into the British army *en masse* during the Great War, it lost over 5,000 men in the first hour of the Battle of the Somme on 6 July 1916.
2. David McKittrick and Jack Holland, *The Assassins: A History of the Ulster Defence Association*, Unpublished.
3. A.T.Q. Steward, *The Narrow Ground: Aspects of Ulster 1609–1969*, Blackstaff Press, Belfast 1977.
4. Ibid.
5. Thomas Hennessy, *History of Northern Ireland 1920–1996*, St Martin's Press, New York 1977.
6. Hennessy, op. cit. In 1958, of the twenty full-time clerical staff working for Newry Urban District Council, all were Catholics; of the seventy outdoor full-time workers, all were Catholics; of the 765 houses belonging to the council, only 22 were occupied by Protestants, though Protestants represented one-fifth of the population.
7. Daniel O'Connell used the tactic of protest march and passive resistance in the mid-nineteenth century in his successful campaign to end the anti-Catholic Penal Laws. O'Connell was greatly admired by the black anti-slavery campaigner Frederick Douglas, who visited Ireland. When NICRA took up the same tactic from the black civil rights marchers, it had come full circle.
8. *Irish Times*, 20 June 1998.
9. Eamonn McCann, *War in an Irish Town*, Pluto Press, London 1980.
10. Gerry Adams, *Before the Dawn*, William Morrow, New York 1996.
11. Alexis de Tocqueville, *The Old Regime and the French Revolution*, Knopf, New York.

12. Michael Farrell, *Northern Ireland: The Orange State*, Pluto Press, London 1980.

13. Bernadette Devlin, *The Price of My Soul*, André Deutsch, London 1969.

14. A subsequent inquiry found the RUC guilty of 'misconduct which involved assault and battery'. *Disturbances in Northern Ireland (1969)*, The Lord Cameron Report.

15. McKittrick and Holland, op. cit.

16. Ibid.

17. Patrick Bishop and Eamonn Mallie, *The Provisional IRA*, Corgi Books, London 1988.

18. Interview, 1998.

19. Sean MacStiofain, *Memoirs of a Revolutionary*, Gordon Cremonesi, Edinburgh 1975.

20. Adams, op. cit.

21. MacStiofain, op. cit.

22. Adams, op. cit.

23. MacStiofain, op. cit.

24. Henry Patterson,*The Politics of Illusion: A Political History of the IRA*, Serif, London 1997. In fact O'Donnell was exaggerating the amount of sectarianism within the Belfast IRA. In late 1932 striking railway workers in Belfast, most of them Protestant, successfully enlisted the IRA's aid in trying to stop scabs from taking supplies by road into the city. During an attack on scabs, the IRA shot dead an RUC officer – the police force's first fatality. The Belfast IRA at one time even succeeded in recruiting a unit of Shankill Road Protestants.

25. Interview, July 1998.

26. Bishop and Mallie, op. cit.

27. McCabe, a Catholic, was home on leave at the time of his death. He joined the British Army in 1966, after refusing a job as a bartender at the International Hotel in Belfast. The position was filled instead by Peter Ward, whom the UVF murdered a few months later. An American television crew caught McCabe's death on camera.

28. During the disturbances of July and August, gunfire wounded 154 people and killed ten, eight of them in Belfast; 1,820 families in the city were forced to move home, 1,505 of them Catholic. Most of the damage and casualties occurred between 12 and 15 August. Protestants especially targeted Catholic-owned or managed pubs; 30 were destroyed and 46 damaged.

29. *Daughters of the Troubles: Belfast Stories*, a documentary produced by Marcia Rock, co-written by Jack Holland.

Chapter Two

1. McKittrick and Holland, op. cit. Interview with UDA leader, 1977.

2. Interview, 1998.

3. Adams, op. cit.

4. Paul Bew, Peter Gibson and Henry Patterson, *Northern Ireland, 1921–61, Political Forces and Social Classes*, London, Serif 1996.

5. On a visit to London in 1965 the author astonished his hosts – university students – by informing them that Northern Ireland was still part of the United Kingdom. They had assumed Britain had left Ireland in 1922.

6. Quoted in Bew, Gibson and Patterson, op. cit.

7. Paul Bew and Gordon Gillespie, *The Northern Ireland Peace Process 1993–1996: A Chronology*, Serif, London 1996.

8. Steward, op. cit. The Hunt Report was the latest in a long line of inquiries into Belfast's street disorders, and repeated familiar themes about the inefficiency and partiality of the police. In 1864, a report had observed that 'as regards the local police, the absolute necessity for change is universally acknowledged . . .' The Royal Irish Constabulary and the Royal Ulster Constabulary were each in turn 'criticized for allowing riots to develop, and failing to contain them when they did develop. If they were unarmed, it was recommended that they should be armed; if they used their arms, it was recommended that they should be disarmed. When Lord Hunt recommended in 1969 that the RUC be instantly disarmed, he was, whether he knew it or not, following a well-established precedent.'

9. For a time McKeague was associated with Paisley's UPV, the UVF and an obscure organization, Tara, which was run by Billy McGrath, also a homosexual and paedophile.

10. Henry Patterson, *The Politics of Illusion: A Political History of the IRA*, London, Serif 1997.

11. Ibid.

12. MacStiofain, op. cit.

13. Interview with Billy McKee, 1998.

14. Interview, 1998. Adams has stated that he did support certain aspects of the Goulding strategy, such as the building of a nationalist liberation front.

15. In contrast, the Provisionals used pins to affix their lilies and for a while were called 'Pinheads'. But this nickname did not last.

16. Interview, 1998.

17. Jack Holland, *The American Connection: US Guns, Money and Influence in Northern Ireland*, Roberts Rinehart, Colorado 1999.

18. A second Provisional IRA team was also trawling through the US with the approval of a member of the Irish government, which had made over £105,000 available to the Catholic 'defence committees' for the 'relief of distress in Northern Ireland'. The 1969 crisis had caught Dublin unaware and, in a desperate effort to do something, its agents linked up with a few leading Provisionals who were involved in Belfast's Catholic defence groups. Subsequently, controversy erupted, in which the Official IRA alleged that the Irish government was responsible for creating the Provisional IRA, with the intention of splitting the republican movement and weakening its socialist programme in the South. The Provisionals dismissed this conspiracy theory and countered that their organization would have come about anyway, thanks not to the Irish government but to the circumstances. Later, several high-ranking ministers in Dublin would stand trial for arms smuggling, including Charles Haughey, who later became Taoiseach (Prime Minister). They were acquitted after a sensational trial in 1970.

19. Adams, op. cit. Disapproval of local women who went out with soldiers gradually grew. From 1971 onwards, shaving the offender's hair, then tarring and feathering her became the punishment for women who violated this communal rule.

20. The residents accused the soldiers of stealing and abusive behaviour, which later led to several court cases.

21. McKittrick and Holland, op. cit. Members of the UDA later claimed to have started the whole episode. They said that a few of their members went to the fringes of the Falls district on 1 July and opened fire on troops in order to provoke the army, who blamed republicans, into raiding for weapons. The UDA used a similar tactic on several occasions in 1972 and 1973, intending to spark clashes between Catholics and soldiers.

22. Colonel Michael Dewar, *The British Army in Northern Ireland*, Arms and Armour Press, London 1977.

23. South Armagh had been the scene of the first fatality experienced by the Ulster Special Constabulary, which preceded the RUC, when in January 1921 the IRA shot and killed a Special Constable in the village of Crossmaglen. In 1985, Donaldson's brother Alexander, who was also in the RUC, died along with eight other constables in a mortar bomb attack on the police station in Newry, Co. Down.

24. *Ulster*, *Sunday Times* Insight Team, Penguin, London 1972.

25. Patricia McCluskey, quoted in Hennessey, op. cit.

26. Hennessy, op. cit.

27. Ibid.

28. *Fortnight*, 5 February 1971, quoted in Hennessy, op. cit.

29. Interview, 1998.

30. Dewar, op. cit. In late June 1970, an IRA sniper shot and seriously wounded a soldier in North Belfast during the riots between Protestants and Catholics. There were many other instances when troops were fired on.

31. MacStiofain, op. cit.

32. Bishop and Mallie, op. cit. Reid died three months later in a gun battle with soldiers. A popular ballad still celebrates his life and death.

33. Interview with Billy McKee, 1998.

34. These figures are taken from the European Commission of Human Rights report *Ireland against the United Kingdom of Gt Britain and Northern Ireland: Application No. 5310/71*.

35. Jack Holland and Susan Phoenix, *Phoenix: Policing the Shadows. The Secret War Against Terrorism in Northern Ireland*, Hodder and Stoughton 1996.

36. Jack Holland, *Too Long a Sacrifice: Life and Death in Northern Ireland since 1969*, Dodd Mead, New York 1981.

37. Chairman Lord Parker of Waddington, *Report of the Committee of Privy Counsellors appointed to consider authorized procedures for the interrogation of prisoners suspected of terrorism*.

38. MacStiofain, op. cit.

39. Adams, op. cit.

40. Ibid.

41. Holland, op. cit.

42. *Report of the Committee*, op. cit. Lord Gardiner also revealed that the techniques derived from KGB interrogation practices.

43. Holland, op. cit. Seven years later, the European Human Rights Court at Strasbourg, after a lengthy and exhaustive investigation, found Britain guilty of violating the European Human Rights Convention, to which it was a signatory. The European Human Rights Commission's inquiry was initiated by the Irish government. It uncovered the fact that contrary to what the British asserted, that the use of the 'so-called' five techniques was 'informal' and never authorized in any written document, there were written instructions concerning their application in the hands of British Army intelligence officers. An Irish psychiatrist, who appeared as an expert witness for the Irish government, produced the document during secret hearings into the allegations held by the commission. He had acquired it during a conference on the uses of sensory deprivation at a security services intelligence centre in England in 1969. Most embarrassingly, it showed that there were in fact six techniques – the sixth being the

use of beatings to force prisoners to their feet again when they collapsed at the wall. The document was subsequently suppressed.

44. The only Protestant arrested was a member of the Official IRA, Ronnie Bunting. His was an unusual political evolution. The son of a leading Paisleyite, Bunting joined the civil rights movement as a student and then became active in the Officials, eventually ending up as a leader of the Irish National Liberation Army.

45. In their accounts of the IRA MacStiofain and Adams ignore this attack, as they do the murders of the three Scottish soldiers. Likewise 'Freedom Struggle', the Provisionals' booklet which recounts the story of the organization's first four years, completely omits this and other sectarian attacks in claiming that in over 1,000 IRA operations between the beginning of 1971 and March 1972 civilian casualties 'were about nil'.

46. McKittrick and Holland, op. cit.

47. Ibid.

Chapter Three

1. *Bloody Sunday and the Report of the Widgery Tribunal: The Irish Government's Assessment of the New Material*, Dublin 1998.

2. This has led some experts to surmise that a dumdum bullet was used. *Irish Government*, op. cit.

3. The wounds of all three, experts claim, showed that the bullets that inflicted them were fired from above at a trajectory of 45 degrees. Evidence to this effect comes from Dr Raymond McClean, who was at the march on 30 January, attended to some of the victims and later was at the post mortems, and from the examination of the photographs, statements and inquest reports carried out twenty-five years later by Robert Breglio. Breglio was a detective in the New York Police Department's ballistics squad for a quarter of a century. In a report he concluded that 'the angles of trajectory of bullet wounds of three deceased named William Nash, John Young and Michael McDaid originated from an area in the vicinity of Derry Walls . . .'

4. *Irish Government*, op. cit.

5. Bew and Gillespie, op. cit.

6. Quoted in *Irish Government*, op. cit.

7. Ibid.

8. *Ireland against The United Kingdom*, op. cit.

9. Colm Keena, *A Biography of Gerry Adams*, Mercier, Cork 1990.

10. Ibid.

11. Quoted in Bew and Gillespie, op. cit.

12. Interview, 1998.

13. The Prime Minister, Edward Heath, later revealed in his account of those years that he had the Royal Navy and the RAF on stand-by near Derry in case his troops should encounter severe resistance when they moved in the Bogside and Creggan areas.

14. Interview, 1998.

15. W. D. Flackes, *Northern Ireland, A Political Directory, 1968–79*, Gill and Macmillan, Dublin 1980.

16. McKittrick and Holland, op. cit.

17. Interview, 1998.

18. Interview, Jackie Hutchinson, 1977. Hutchinson, who was an active member of the Shankill Road murder squad, said that before McCartney was killed there was talk of raping her so as not to let her 'go to waste'. But this was rejected in favour of a song. In July 1977, the UDA 'executed' Hutchinson as an informer.

19. There were several other torture killings in Belfast in 1972 for which the UDA was to blame. On 14 August, forty-eight-year-old Thomas Madden's body was found in a shop doorway in North Belfast with over 150 stab wounds. James McCartan was abducted from an East Belfast hotel on 3 October and his badly beaten body found the next day; he had been hung by the heels, stripped and beaten with bats. Two months later, the UDA team in South Belfast tortured and killed Patrick Benstead. He had been burned on his feet and fingers, and a cross and the number four branded on his back with a hot poker. His eyes were gouged out. His body was dumped in East Belfast to make the police think it was the responsibility of Herron's gang, much to Herron's annoyance.

20. The Provisional IRA denied responsibility for the Claudy bombings, as they did the deaths of the three Scots soldiers in March 1971. However, shortly before the bombs exploded, at 10.15 a.m., on the morning of 31 July, three youths were seen desperately trying to find a telephone that worked in the nearby village of Dungiven, in order to call the Claudy RUC station with a warning about the bombs. Unfortunately, they could not find a working telephone thanks to the fact that a few days earlier the IRA from Derry had knocked out the local telephone installation. The men involved in the operation were from Claudy. One was a priest. Another of those involved was working as a barman in New York City as of 1998.

21. *Ireland against The United Kingdom*, op. cit.

22. McKittrick and Holland, op. cit.

23. Interview, 1998.

24. Interview, 1977.

25. White said that Wilson and Andrews were murdered in reprisal for the

Official IRA's killing of a mentally retarded Protestant teenager, David Walker, on 21 June, whom the Officials mistakenly believed was involved in sectarian murders. He also said that the reason Wilson and Andrews were stabbed so many times was that the knife used, a common 'commando'-style knife available in any sports shop, had a short blade, and he wanted to make sure the couple were dead. But he admitted that the UDA also wanted to provoke another 'Jack the Ripper' scare such as had gripped Catholic areas in the summer of 1972. 'Murder is murder no matter what way you do it,' he added. (Interview, 1998.)

26. The detective who investigated the Herron assassination said it was one of the most puzzling he had ever encountered. Among the possibilities that the RUC considered was that an undercover army unit had killed him; then an RUC detective with whom Herron was known to have had a link was questioned. To no avail. Almost certainly, Herron was murdered by fellow UDA men who suspected he was stealing money from the UDA prisoners' funds.

27. Quoted in Bew and Gillespie, op. cit.

28. Farrell, op. cit.

29. Ibid.

30. *Belfast Newsletter*, 17 May 1974 quoted in Farrell, op. cit.

31. J. Bowyer Bell, *In Dubious Battle: The Dublin and Monaghan Bombings 1972–1974.*

32. Ibid.

33. Interview with family, 1994.

34. In 1977, the UDA claimed that one of its units from mid-Ulster had carried out the Monaghan bomb attack which was supposed to have taken place before the Dublin bombings. The aim was to lure Irish security forces away from the capital allowing the UVF men delivering the bomb a free run. But the Monaghan bomb had a faulty timer and exploded later than those in Dublin. McKittrick and Holland, op.cit. While no one was ever charged in connection with the Dublin and Monaghan bombings, most of the names of the twenty-six or so men allegedly involved have been made public. They include several who have since been killed – Billy Hanna, William 'Frenchie' Marchant, and Horace Boyle. Hanna was killed during an internal UVF dispute on 27 July 1975. Four days later, Boyle died when a bomb he was planting exploded prematurely. The Provisional IRA shot Robert McConnell, who was in the UDR, at his home on 5 April 1976. Marchant was standing outside the Shankill Road offices of the Progressive Unionist Party, the UVF's political wing, when the Provisionals shot him dead on 28 April 1987. The UVF did not claim responsibility for the bombings, perhaps because shortly before the

attacks the Northern Ireland Secretary of State, Merlyn Rees, had lifted the ban on the organization to encourage it to go into politics. Claims that undercover British agents were involved were denied by the organization in 1994.

35. Quoted in Bew and Gillespie, op. cit.

36. Ibid.

37. *Ireland against The United Kingdom*, op. cit.

38. Interview, 1998.

39. The unit was arrested attempting to return to Ireland. Among those apprehended were Dolours Price and her sister Marion. Dolours had been a student civil rights protester on the Burntollet march in early 1969. Along with them was Gerard Kelly, from Ballymurphy. He would later become a leading member of the Provisional Army Council.

40. Seven people were later arrested and charged in connection with these murders. Four of them, Paul Hill, Gerard Conlon, Patrick Armstrong and Carole Richardson, who became known as the 'Guildford Four', were convicted of the Guildford bombing itself. All later had their convictions overturned as they were found to be unsafe and unsatisfactory although not until after they had served long sentences. The experience of Gerard Conlon, whose father Giuseppe died while still imprisoned because of the bombings, became the basis of the successful movie, *In the Name of the Father*.

41. Chris Mullin, *Error of Judgment: The Truth about the Birmingham Bombs*, Poolbeg, Dublin 1989. One of the IRA men involved later claimed to Mullin that they had given thirty minutes' warning. Even if true, as Mullin points out, the warning was so vague as to be misleading.

42. Four of the six signed confessions. There was forensic evidence against two – traces of an explosive substance were found on their hands. But in October 1985 an investigative television programme, *World in Action*, showed that the original forensic tests were not sufficiently liable to substantiate the prosecution's case. After several appeals, all were released in January 1990.

43. Mullin, op. cit.

44. Quoted in Bew and Gillespie, op. cit.

45. McKittrick and Holland, op. cit.

46. In 1993, during secret talks between the British and the Provisionals, a British government representative would admit that in 1975 the Labour government had set out to 'con' the IRA and had succeeded. See Chapter 7.

47. By 1977, 1,800 people had died as a result of the conflict, which is more than half of the total number killed between 1969 and 1994.

Chapter Four

1. By 1976 unemployment in the majority nationalist counties, Derry, Tyrone and Fermanagh, had risen to 21.3 per cent – more than double what it had been five years earlier. In Belfast, during the same period, it had risen to 8.3 per cent from 4.6 per cent.

2. Chairman Lord Gardiner, *The Report to consider in the context of civil liberties and human rights, measures to deal with terrorism in Northern Ireland*.

3. Ibid.

4. The gang carried out a series of mass murders, beginning in October 1975, when they murdered four Catholics in a bottling plant. Included among the dead were two sisters. In February 1976, his gang murdered two Protestants, mistaking them for Catholics, in a gun attack on a lorry-load of workmen. In June the same year, they shot up a downtown bar, killing five customers, three of whom were Protestants – one of them a UVF man. Murphy and his men also killed at least three UDA men, one of whom, Noel Shaw, he tied to a chair and 'executed' on a stage in a loyalist drinking club in front of a crowd of drinkers.

5. Martin Dillon, *The Shankill Butchers: A Case Study of Mass Murder*, Hutchinson, London 1989.

6. Interview, 1998. In jail, White struck up friendships with members of the Official IRA, who impressed him with their socialist analysis of the Northern Ireland situation and helped convince him of the futility of sectarian violence. When released seventeen years later, he became active in the peace process.

7. Peter Taylor, *Beating the Terrorists? Interrogation In Omagh, Gough and Castlereagh*.

8. Drumm's wife, Maire, had been the firebrand vice-president of Sinn Fein. She once threatened in a speech to dismantle Belfast brick by brick. On 28 October 1976 a joint UDA–UVF hit squad murdered her in the Mater Hospital, Belfast, where she was a patient.

9. Soon afterwards, McKee was sent to New York to look into fund-raising problems. A former IRA man and ex-paratrooper, Pete 'the para' McMullen, who had been extorting money from Irish American bar-owners in the city, supposedly on the IRA's behalf, assumed he was the target of McKee's enquiry and fled to San Francisco where he handed himself over to the police and became the subject of a long-running extradition battle with the British government, which he eventually lost. Interview, 1998.

10. Taylor, op. cit.

11. Ibid.

12. This pattern persisted over the decades. In the small Protestant border community of West Tyrone, Victoria Bridge, the IRA murdered fourteen men between 1983 and 1991. David McKittrick. (*Endgame: The Search for Peace in Northern Ireland*), Blackstaff Press, Belfast 1995.

13. Chris Ryder, *The RUC, 1922–1997: A Force under Fire*, Mandarin paperbacks, London 1997.

14. Interview, 1979. Only eight Catholics were killed during 1978, the lowest number since 1970. Of those eight only one, 29-year-old Thomas Trainor, was a member of a republican group. Trainor was O/C of the INLA in Armagh when he and a friend were shot to death by the UVF on 8 March. Jack Holland and Henry McDonald. (*INLA: Deadly Divisions*, Poolbeg, Dublin 1994.)

15. The other sections were E1, administration, E2, training, E7, TCG work, and E9, specialized surveillance, which was established in 1988. (See Chapter 8.)

16. Holland and Phoenix, op. cit.

17. Mark Urban, *Big Boys' Rules: The SAS and the Secret War against the IRA*, Faber & Faber, London 1992.

18. On 12 December 1977, an SAS unit in Derry shot dead an 18-year-old member of the INLA, Colm McNutt, as he tried to hijack a car. McNutt was unarmed at the time. On 26 February 1978, the SAS struck again, killing Provisional IRA member Paul Duffy, aged 23, at an IRA arms dump in an unoccupied farmhouse in Co. Tyrone. Denis Heaney was shot dead in Derry on 10 June by SAS men who said he had tried to hijack their car. Witnesses claim he was shot without warning as he walked along the street. Another Derry member of the Provisional IRA, 50-year-old Patrick Duffy, was shot dead on 24 November in a house that was being used as an arms dump. SAS soldiers said he had taken a gun from a wardrobe when they opened fire. This was disputed by the dead man's widow. As well, between July and September, the SAS killed two innocent civilians, John Boyle and James Taylor. Boyle, aged 16, was shot dead at an IRA arms dump, which he had discovered earlier and which had been reported to the police. Two SAS men were charged with his murder and acquitted. Taylor was out wildfowling when he became caught up in an undercover operation and was shot.

19. Holland and Phoenix, op. cit.

20. Ignorance about groups like the UDA was common among Irish Americans, partly as a result of the fact that the US media virtually ignored loyalist terrorism, but also because it served the interests of republican propaganda not to play it up except when Sinn Fein could present

Protestant paramilitaries as British-controlled. They were only able to do so because of widespread ignorance as to the nature of the UDA and UVF.

21. The Irish government compiled a document showing links between the Caucus and the Provisional IRA. However, by 1979 the INC and the Provisionals had parted company following an acrimonious dispute.

22. Holland, op. cit.

23. Ibid.

24. Ibid.

25. In 1979, however, Biaggi succeeded in getting Congress to block the sale of weapons from a US company to the RUC, citing a law that prohibits US companies from selling guns to any group that has violated civil rights. The vote banning the sale could not have been taken on a more provocative date: 12 July.

26. Connors was later murdered by the Mafia in a gangland dispute.

27. Holland, op. cit.

28. By that time, all but one of the original six M-60s from Harrison had been captured, after claiming the lives of 12 soldiers and RUC men. An M-60 was recovered on 2 May 1980 after a gun battle in which an SAS officer, Herbert Westmacott, was killed. One of those arrested at the scene was Joe Doherty, who later escaped prison and fled to the United States, where he became the subject of a celebrated extradition battle. Among his most prominent defenders was George Harrison.

29. Harrison believed that McLogan, who was found dead with a bullet wound in the head, had been murdered on the orders of the IRA leadership because of his opposition to the course of reform being undertaken at the time. An inquiry was promised but never undertaken.

30. Interviews, 1985, 1998. In a later account, *The IRA and Sinn Fein*, by Peter Taylor, Bloomsbury, London 1997, it was claimed that the IRA told Harrison he was being replaced. According to Harrison, the claim is untrue. In fact, he says he came under increasing pressure from the leadership to supply more weapons in 1980 and 1981.

31. Interview, 1985.

32. All five men were eventually acquitted in 1982 after a trial notable for the ingenuity of its defence. The defence convinced the Brooklyn jury that De Meo had all along been working with the CIA. Since the CIA is authorized to export weapons without a licence, none of the five IRA supporters was in fact breaking the law, as unknown to them, they were under CIA supervision. Official sources dismissed the allegations about De Meo as absurd. However, there was proof that at some point De Meo worked for government agents. In 1969, gunrunning charges were dropped against him to protect a source.

354

Wisely, the defence did not ask Harrison, a convinced leftist, to take the stand.

33. Tim Pat Coogan, *The Troubles: Ireland's Ordeal 1966–1995*, Hutchinson, London 1995.

34. Adams, op. cit.

35. The INLA had enjoyed something of a resurgence in the late 1970s, even though its founder, Seamus Costello, had been assassinated in 1977 by the Official IRA. It had linked up with Al Fatah shortly afterwards, and began receiving regular arms and explosives supplies from them. It had originally targeted Sir Robert Haydon, the British Ambassador to Ireland, who had replaced Sir Christopher Ewart-Biggs, assassinated by the Provisionals in July 1976. On Remembrance Day, in November 1978, a remote-controlled bomb planted under his prayer stool in Christchurch Cathedral in Dublin failed to explode, thanks to the fact that the ancient cathedral walls were too stout for the radio signal to penetrate. They then launched an elaborate plot to murder Roy Mason, sending a sniper team to his Barnsley constituency to stalk him. But this plot was aborted when it became clear that Labour was going to lose the election. Jack Holland and Henry McDonald, (*INLA: Deadly Divisions*.)

36. Dewar, op. cit.

37. Ryder, op. cit.

38. Thatcher did, however, appoint a security co-ordinator to liaise between the army and the RUC. He was Sir Maurice Oldfield, former head of MI5 – made famous in the James Bond thrillers as 'Uncle'. Oldfield, a homosexual, was forced to leave his post within six months after a compromising incident in a pub. He died shortly afterwards of stomach cancer.

39. Adams, ibid.

40. Holland and McDonald, op. cit.

41. The attack on McAliskey was different from the other three incidents not only in that the assailants failed and were caught. McAliskey described later how they had burst into her home screaming and shouting – a far different demeanour from that of the calm, self-possessed assassins who Suzanne Bunting had confronted in her bedroom a few months earlier. The fact also that the murderers of Daly and Bunting carried out their killings in the very heart of West Belfast, which they entered and left without a trace – not even a getaway car was ever recovered linked to either incident – has suggested to some the involvement of the security forces. But the most likely culprits remain the UDA, which later did claim responsibility for the murders. They might well have acted on information from sympathetic UDR or RUC men. In July 1994, the Provisional IRA murdered Ray

Smallwoods, who had been one of the three UDA men charged and convicted with the attempted murder of Mr and Mrs McAliskey.

42. The titles of some of the poems, ballads and meditations will give an idea of their nature: 'The Lark and the Freedom Fighter', Weeping Winds, The Windows of My Mind, The Rhythm of Time, Flowers, My Friend, Flowers, The Rose of Rathfarham, Stars of Freedom, etc.

43. Adams, op. cit.

44. Ibid.

45. The ten who died were Bobby Sands (5 May), Francis Hughes (May 12), Ray McCreesh and Patsy O'Hara (May 21), Joe McDonnell (July 8), Martin Hurson (July 13), Kevin Lynch (August 1), Kieran Doherty (August 2), Thomas McElwee (August 8) and Michael Devine (August 20). Doherty endured the longest, going 73 days without food. Hurson died after only 46 days. O'Hara, Lynch and Devine were members of the INLA, the others of the Provisional IRA.

Chapter Five

1. John Hume, A New Ireland: Politics, Peace, and Reconciliation, Boulder, Colorado, Roberts Rinehart, 1996.

2. Gerard Murray, John Hume and the SDLP, Dublin, Irish Academic Press, 1998.

3. Hume, ibid; op. cit.

4. Murray, op. cit.

5. Ronnie Munck, The Irish Economy: Results and Prospects, Pluto Press, London 1993.

6. Murray, op. cit.

7. Holland and Phoenix, op. cit.

8. At a trial in 1985 involving Steenson, one of the police officers admitted that though he had been in the next street he had 'been taking a rest' when the gunmen murdered Stockman.

9. McCreery later fled to London, where his name was mentioned in a murder trial in 1993. He was believed to have been involved in providing ex-paramilitaries for London underworld figures who hired them as hit-men. By then he had disappeared. Craig's name was linked to a series of murders of loyalist figures by the Provisionals and the INLA. In October 1988, the UDA shot him dead in a pub in East Belfast.

10. During the course of the Ulster conflict republicans murdered eight members of the judiciary: three judges, four magistrates and an official who worked in the office of the Director of Public Prosecutions.

11. Fitzsimmons and Murphy were acquitted and released to continue

their violent careers. McCann was also returned to active service with the Provisionals. In March 1988, the SAS killed him and two other IRA volunteers in Gibraltar (see Chapter 6). Murphy was later convicted in connection with the death of an IRA man killed during a Loyalist attack on the funerals of those killed in Gibraltar.

12. His brother Dessie had been involved in a series of INLA murders in the Armagh area, including that of a prison officer, killed with an under-car booby-trap in December 1978, and a female prison officer, shot dead as she left the Armagh women's prison in April 1979. He would later join the Provisional IRA and become the O/C of IRA operations in continental Europe. The SAS shot him dead along with another IRA man at an arms dump near Loughgall, Co. Armagh, in October 1990. Because of his expertise with UCBTs, Grew was one of the few INLA members ever questioned about the assassination of Airey Neave, in which he was not involved.

13. The judge at one of the trials, Lord Chief Justice Maurice Gibson, congratulated the accused officer for his marksmanship and for dispatching the terrorists to 'the final court of justice'. These remarks did not endear him to the Provisional IRA. An IRA bomb killed him and his wife in April 1987.

14. John Stalker, *The Stalker Affair*, Harrap, London 1988.

15. Ibid.

16. When it is borne in mind that the RUC was subjected to a prolonged and organized campaign of violence which targeted its members both on and off duty, claiming the lives of 199 full-time constables and 101 reservists, its record in this regard stands up well when compared to that of other forces. For example, according to figures published in *The New York Times* (9 April 1997), the New York City police killed more than one hundred civilians between 1992 and 1997.

17. In his career, McGlinchey antagonized many fellow republicans. Two months after Dale's murder, he murdered two South Armagh republicans, Eamon McMahon and Patrick Mackin, accusing them of cheating him of money from a robbery. His wife, Mary McGlinchey, was also involved, luring them to their deaths. McMahon came from a powerful South Armagh republican family. In February 1987, a gang associated with Mackin and McMahon murdered Mrs McGlinchey at home as she bathed her two sons. By this time, McGlinchey himself was behind bars. In February 1994, eleven months after he was released, he was gunned down on a street in Drogheda, Co. Louth, in front of his son Dominic, who seven years earlier had witnessed his mother's murder. It is believed 'Mad Dog' was murdered by the same killers who had claimed his wife.

18. Derek Dunne, *Out of the Maze: The True Story of the Biggest Jail Escape since the War*, Gill and Macmillan, Dublin 1988.

19. Previously, the biggest escape had occurred on 5 May 1976, when nine INLA members dug a tunnel from Long Kesh. Two, including Gerard Steenson, were recaptured shortly afterwards, but the others got safely south of the border in spite of an SAS attempt to stop them.

20. As of August 1992, five of the 19 had been recaptured, three were dead at the hands of the SAS, and eleven were still at large. (Bew and Gillespie, op. cit.). Four of the eleven were in the United States – Kevin Barry McArt, Pol Brennan, Jimmy Smyth and Terence Kirby – and later fought extradition battles to avoiding returning to Northern Ireland.

21. Patrick Bishop and Eamonn Mallie, *The Provisional IRA*, London, Corgi, 1988.

22. Holland and Phoenix, op. cit.

23. Ibid.

24. W.D. Flackes and Sydney Elliott, *Northern Ireland: A Political Discovery, 1968–1993*, Belfast, Blackstaff Press, 1994.

25. Keena, op. cit.

26. Adams claimed that British intelligence was involved in the assassination attempt, citing as evidence the presence of undercover RUC operatives. However, given his prominence, their presence is hardly surprising. Had there been no RUC men present, Sinn Fein no doubt would have pointed to that as proof of collusion between loyalists and the security forces.

27. The first 'supergrass' came to light in 1974 when UDA hit-man Albert 'Ginger' Baker gave evidence leading to the arrests of many leading UDA men in East Belfast.

28. Steenson was by now known as 'Dr Death'. When he emerged from prison the INLA split and during the subsequent feud he was shot dead on 14 March 1987.

29. Margaret Thatcher, *The Downing Street Years*, New York, Harper Collins, 1993.

30. Murray, op. cit.

31. *The New Ireland Forum Report*.

32. Bew and Gillespie, op. cit.

33. *The Sunday Times*, 20 September 1998.

34. His administration pressed cases against IRA fugitives Peter McMullan, Dessie Mackin, William Quinn and Joe Doherty. The courts found that all but Quinn were protected by the law's political offence provision, and could not be extradited. It was a politically embarrassing setback, since it recognized that the IRA's violence was politically motivated, not

criminal as Reagan and Thatcher's propaganda claimed. Undeterred by the court's decisions, Reagan pressed ahead. In July 1985 he got the Senate to pass a redrafted version of the extradition treaty between the US and Britain, diluting the political offence clause. All but Mackin ended up back in British jails. (Holland, op. cit.)

35. Holland, op. cit.

36. Hume, op.cit.

37. Robert Fisk, *The Point of No Return: The Strike which Broke the British in Ulster*, André Deutsch, London 1975.

38. Bew and Gillespie, op. cit.

Chapter Six

1. Holland and McDonald, op. cit.

2. In June 1992, the Libyans offered to reveal details to the British government of arms shipped to Ireland. But it was not until late 1995 that they actually handed over such information to the British authorities. The UN acted as an intermediary when a breakdown of the arms supplies was made available in a series of exchanges between 31 October and 20 November. (*Irish Echo*, 20–26 December 1995.) Though Britain found some gaps in the information, it acknowledged that it was comprehensive. Libya agreed to the arrangement as part of its efforts to have UN sanctions against it lifted.

3. Interview, 1998.

4. Interview, 1995.

5. Portakabins – huts made of lightweight material – were in fact used to house Special Branch, MI5, SAS and army intelligence officers assigned to the Tasking Co-ordination Groups. Whether the IRA realized this, and targeted McAvoy as a result, is not known.

6. The local Provisionals later justified this callous murder to a journalist. According to one: 'The Henry brothers are collaborating in the oppression of the nationalist people by taking part in that work, just as the British crown is forcing those workers to prostitute themselves because of the huge money involved. They are corrupting the people. They have been warned countless times to stop.' (Kevin, Toolis, *Rebel Hearts: Journeys within the IRA's Soul*, New York, Picador, 1995.)

7. Brendan O'Brien, *The Long War: The IRA and Sinn Fein*, O'Brien Press, Dublin 1993.

8. Holland and Phoenix, op. cit.

9. *Just News, Bulletin of the Committee on the Administration of Justice*, June 1995.

10. At an inquest into the shootings in 1993, a coroner described the scenes-of-crime photographs as 'quite horrifying'.

11. The feud started over a dispute as to whether or not the INLA should disband. Steenson and his men believed that it was so badly corrupted that it had to be replaced. The leaders of the opposite faction, including its Chief of Staff, John O'Reilly, were invited to meet with Steenson to discuss the matter. The venue was a hotel outside Drogheda, about 30 miles north of Dublin. O'Reilly and three others were waiting for Steenson to arrive when he burst in disguised in a wig and, along with another gunman, opened fire on the delegation. O'Reilly and Thomas Power (an INLA activist from Belfast) were killed, and a third man was wounded. A fourth, Hugh 'Cueball' Torney, escaped, and later became Chief of Staff. There followed a series of revenge killings which only effectively ceased when Steenson himself was gunned down in West Belfast on 14 March, aged 29.

12. Toolis, op. cit.

13. Interview, 1998.

14. Interview, 1988.

15. Marley's funeral produced a tense stand-off between the Provisionals, who wanted a paramilitary display, and the RUC, who wanted to prevent it. The funeral was postponed twice, and clashes broke out between the police and the mourners. The result was a public relations disaster for the RUC, according to Hermon, the Chief Constable.

16. McKittrick and Holland, op. cit.

17. David McKittrick. *Dispatches from Belfast*, Belfast: Blackstaff Press, 1989.

18. Ibid.

19. Payne was sentenced to 19 years in prison on 1 November 1988.

20. David McKittrick, *Dispatches from Belfast*, op.cit.

21. Hume, op. cit.

22. Forty-one people were later charged in connection with the soldiers' deaths. Three were convicted under a law based on South African legislation which allowed serious charges, including murder, to be brought against the accused even though he or she might not have been present when the crime was committed, as long as 'common purpose' could be established. Patrick Kane, Michael Timmons and Sean Kelly were not even present when the soldiers met their deaths, but were nonetheless found guilty of murder and other, lesser charges. The case gave rise to controversy, especially after it was revealed that Kane was mentally retarded and had not fully comprehended the charges brought against him. The convictions were eventually overturned. Another of those convicted in connection with the killings was Alex Murphy, an

IRA gunman who had been involved in the plot to murder Judge Kelly in 1983. (See Chapter 5.)

23. Anthony McIntyre, *Modern Irish Republicanism: The Product of British State Strategies*, Queen's University, Belfast. Unpublished.

24. Bew and Gillespie, op. cit.

25. *Sunday Times*, 20 September 1998. Douglas Hurd was Home Secretary at the time and according to Mark Stewart was ashamed of the measures barring Sinn Fein from the media which he had introduced.

26. It had taken a year for the security services to realize the size of Gaddafi's contribution to the Provisionals' war chest. When they did, a British official described their failure to detect the shipments as Britain's biggest intelligence failure since World War II.

27. *Irish Echo*, 31 December 1988.

28. In the same election the Workers' Party, which descended from Official Sinn Fein, won seven seats in the Dail. To Sinn Fein, the example of the Workers' Party was both a temptation and a dire warning. It was achieving political success but the cost (as Sinn Fein saw it) was the complete dilution of its republicanism to the point of its becoming one of the Provisionals' harshest critics.

29. Interview, 1998. An IRA source came forward with this information in order to refute claims made by Sean O'Callaghan, a former member of the Provisionals who became a police agent. O'Callaghan attracted a lot of publicity in 1997 with claims that he was involved in an IRA plot to murder Princess Diana, which he says he deliberately botched in order to save her life. According to the IRA source, who was active in Britain in the 1980s and early 1990s, the Royal Family was not considered a 'legitimate target' and no such plot was ever hatched.

30. Professor Wilkinson had also earned the Provisionals' enmity when he testified in an extradition hearing against Joe Doherty in New York in December 1984. Doherty, who escaped from a Belfast jail in 1981, was wanted in connection with the murder of an SAS captain. The attempt on Wilkinson's life did not deter the terrorism expert. After the conference, he went to Germany to testify at the extradition hearing of Donna Maguire, an IRA member believed to have been involved in a series of attacks on British targets in Europe. Initial reports about the Green Park incident said that a minister in the Thatcher Cabinet, William Waldegrave, was the target. These were incorrect and seem to have been part of a deliberate IRA plan to mislead.

31. Danny Morrison was arrested on 7 January 1990, next door to a house where the Provisionals were interrogating a suspected informer, Sandy Lynch. The RUC believed that Morrison was a prominent member

of the so-called Civil Administration Team – the IRA's informer-hunting unit. He was later sentenced to eight years on charges in connection with the incident. Lynch had been a member of the INLA and was involved in many crimes, including the murder of Gerard Steenson, during the feud of early 1987. (See footnote, Chapter 5.) At the Special Branch's request, he infiltrated the Provisionals after some INLA members became suspicious of him. They kept their suspicions about Lynch to themselves and did not warn the IRA.

32. *Setting the Record Straight: A record of communications between Sinn Fein and the British government October 1990–November 1993*, Sinn Fein.

Chapter Seven

1. Interview, 1995.

2. For instance, Frank Ryan, aged 25, and Patricia Black, aged 18, who blew themselves up while carrying out a Provisional bombing operation in St Albans, England, on 15 November 1991, were described by the police as 'lily white', without any previously known links to the republican movement. But the Special Branch later identified Black, who was buried on her 19th birthday, as perhaps having been the unknown female involved in an assassination attempt in South Belfast in August 1991.

3. He was quoted as saying: 'The IRA terrorists are better equipped, better resourced, better led, bolder and more secure against our penetration than at any time before . . . If we don't intern, it's a long haul.' *Independent on Sunday*, 17 November 1991.

4. Patterson, op. cit.

5. In 1992, the Provisional IRA killed almost as many of its own members – six – as suspected informers as it did soldiers and policemen.

6. The Stevens inquiry led to the arrest and conviction of three UDR members on serious charges. Seventeen others had minor charges brought against them, some of which resulted in fines. In his report, published in 1990, Stevens said he found no evidence of institutionalized collusion within the RUC or the UDR. By then, however, the UDR had long been disgraced in the eyes of Ulster nationalists. By 1975, five years after it was formed, over 80 of its members or ex-members were charged with terrorist offences. This figure increased to almost 200 in 1990, prompting an Irish government minister to say that the UDR had 'no role to play in Northern Ireland'. Between 1970 and 1992 197 UDR members were murdered.

7. The two other Catholics who died as a result of the alleged failure to act on Nelson's information were Terence McDaid, whose brother Declan, a

known republican, had been the target, and Gerard Slane, who had no paramilitary links. According to Nelson's handler, who appeared as a witness for him in court, he had uncovered threats to the lives of 217 people, only four of whom died violently, including the three the UDA murdered. The fourth was the Belfast IRA's explosive expert, Daniel McCann, who seems to have been saved by the RUC only to be left to the SAS (see Chapter 6). There were UDA threats against the life of two other prominent nationalist lawyers, Patrick McGrory and Mary McAleese, head of the Legal Institute at Queen's University, who became President of Ireland in 1997.

8. *Irish Echo*, 30 October–5 November 1991.

9. *Irish Echo*, 12–18 February 1992.

10. *Independent*, 11 August 1992.

11. Patterson, op. cit.

12. Sinn Fein, op. cit.

13. Ibid.

14. Ibid.

15. Ibid.

16. Ibid.

17. The IRA had called shorter cessations every Christmas since 1990, which was the first in fifteen years.

18. Sinn Fein, op. cit.

19. Ibid.

20. In November 1993, leaks to the press about negotiations between Sinn Fein and the British government prompted the Northern Ireland Secretary of State, Sir Patrick Mayhew, to categorically deny such meetings had taken place. On BBC Television he stated: 'There has been no negotiating with Sinn Fein; no official, as I see it, is alleged to have been talking to Sinn Fein on behalf of the British government.' Subsequently, the Prime Minister's office also denied that there had been 'protracted contact and dialogue' with the republican movement. These denials were repeated and on 20 November John Major told the House of Commons that the prospect of talks with Gerry Adams would 'turn his stomach'. A week later, Mayhew was forced to recant and admit there were contacts with Sinn Fein, but even then he attempted to limit the damage by claiming they had only begun in February 1993. In order to refute what it described as lies, Sinn Fein published some of the documents relating to its contacts with the government in December and a fuller account in January 1994. A number of documents were withheld, the party said, due to their 'sensitivity'. Some of these related to the so-called Irish peace process involving Hume, Adams and others.

21. Mansergh's contacts with Adams, Mitchel McLaughlin and Martin McGuinness came through a Catholic priest in West Belfast, Fr Alec Reid. When Reynolds became Taoiseach they were subsumed into the general Irish peace initiative.

22. Interview, 1998.

23. *Irish Echo*, 15–21 April 1992.

24. This was apparently because during the talks Hume allegedly avoided condemning recent IRA bomb attacks, enhancing the easy familiarity that seemed to exist between the SDLP leader and Sinn Fein officials such as McLaughlin. Among the subjects they discussed was the IRA's choice of targets and the shift of Northern Ireland's Protestant population to such areas as North Down.

25. Bew and Gillespie, op. cit.

26. Ibid.

27. Ibid.

28. Ibid.

29. Ibid.

30. McIntyre, op. cit.

31. In fact, the RUC Special Branch was kept fully informed as to what transpired and was provided with Lynch's arguments in favour of lifting the ban in advance of the meeting with Holl.

32. *Sunday Life*, 26 July 1992.

33. The last was 21-year-old Alexander Bannister, who died on 8 August 1988 after being shot by a sniper three weeks earlier while on foot patrol in Ballymurphy, West Belfast.

34. Coffee-jar bombs claimed the lives of one soldier in May 1991 and a civilian the following August. A soldier wounded in the May attack lost both his legs and pleaded to his colleagues, 'Shoot me, shoot me.' He survived.

35. *Independent*, 11 November 1992.

36. Joe Doherty and two other IRA men were also arrested and charged with the murder. Doherty escaped along with Magee, Angelo Fusco and Robert Campbell, and later made his way to New York where he became the centre of a long-running extradition case. He was finally deported to Belfast in February 1992 to serve a murder sentence.

37. In murals around the Shankill Road 'C' company's exploits are celebrated under the slogan 'SIMPLY THE BEST', taken from a famous song by the American rock singer Tina Turner. The song is played whenever its members appear on political platforms. No doubt Ms Turner would be surprised at the use to which her lyrics have been put.

38. Phoenix, along with twenty-four other leading intelligence officers

and four crew members, died in a helicopter crash in Scotland on 2 June 1994.

39. McIntyre, op. cit.

40. Ibid.

41. On 29 July, an ASU murdered UDA activists Joe Bratty and Ray Elder on the Ormeau Road in South Belfast, not far from the betting shop where two years before five Catholics were shot dead in an attack that the IRA blamed on Bratty and Elder.

42. 31 August 1994 was the twenty-first anniversary of the death of Provisional IRA volunteer Paddy Mulvenna, who was married to one of Gerry Adams's sisters. Mulvenna was shot dead along with Jim Bryson in Ballymurphy after an encounter with British troops. It has been suggested that it was not a coincidence that the ceasefire was announced on that date. But Adams claims he was only reminded of it on the day itself when he was speaking before a crowd on the Falls Road.

43. This figure includes the three UVF murders in 1966, as well as 101 deaths in the Irish republic, 117 in Britain, and 18 on mainland Europe. However, the estimate is not exact. It does not include a number of people who died at the hands of the IRA or other paramilitary groups after being kidnapped and whose bodies have never been recovered.

Chapter Eight

1. *Irish Echo*, 1 November, 1994.

2. *Irish Echo*, 1–7 March 1995.

3. Quoted in Bew and Gillespie, op. cit.

4. In December 1994, the Democratic Left, a breakaway from the Workers' Party, entered into coalition government in the South with the Irish Labour Party and Fine Gael, their links to the violent past all but forgotten. The party merged with the Labour Party in 1999.

5. When told of Clinton's intention to shake hands with Adams, Sir Patrick Mayhew said that '50,000,000 British people would not be pleased'. The point was that among the 50,000,000 British people there was not one vote for Clinton, but among the 20,000,000 Irish Americans there was.

6. Clinton liked nothing more than to recount the story of his first trip to Ireland, as he did to this author at a White House party in June 1998. He must be one of the few people for whom the mention of Belfast evokes a broad smile.

7. *When the President Calls*, Trevor Birney and Julian O'Neill, Guildhall Press, Demy 1997.

8. *Irish Echo*, 7–13 February 1996.

9. Arrested in the same sweep was a 26-year-old schoolteacher who lived in Bangor in North Down. When the police placed her picture in several police stations in the area seeking information about her, a number of different RUC officers came forward. Each said he was having an affair with her. It appears she was on an intelligence-gathering operation. Also part of the same unit was Charles Tumelty, a 35-year-old law graduate who worked in a legal firm and had access to information on leading judges and police officers.

10. Quoted by Anthony McIntyre, *Sunday Tribune*, 25 January 1998.

11. *Guardian*, 22 May 1998.

12. Until the feud, the INLA had been quiet since 1994. Its last significant action was the assassination of three loyalists on the Shankill Road on 16 June that year. Two of the dead were leading members of the UVF. Hugh Torney was INLA Chief of Staff until 1995, when he and three others were arrested with an arms consignment near Dublin. After he was jailed he was replaced by Gallagher. Released on bail, Torney ordered Gallagher's murder, which sparked the feud. Torney, a republican since 1970, had survived at least two other assassination attempts. Fate caught up with him on 3 September 1996, in Lurgan, Co. Armagh, where he was gunned down on the street.

13. *Irish Echo*, 12–28 November 1997.

14. *Irish Echo*, 18–24 March 1998.

15. Both governments argued that it was linked to an organization that was still using violence and therefore the party was in violation of the Mitchell principles. The Ulster Democratic Party suffered a similar suspension because the UDA had been connected to several murders.

16. Locked in the negotiations were the Ulster Unionist Party – still the most powerful Protestant party – and the paramilitary-linked Ulster Democratic Party and Progressive Unionist Party. On the nationalist side were the SDLP and Sinn Fein. The remaining three parties were the Alliance Party, the tiny Northern Ireland Labour Party and a newcomer on the Ulster political scene, the Northern Ireland Women's Coalition. In fact, they were as much a cultural phenomenon as a political one. The Women's Coalition was formed in 1996. A handful of women, Protestant and Catholic, middle-class and working-class, decided they were sick of the male-dominated sectarian biases that moulded Ulster's political life into intractable positions. Paisley's DUP and a smaller fragment of the Unionist block, the United Kingdom Unionist Party, remained on the outside braying their warnings of treachery and betrayal.

17. *Irish Echo*, 8–14 April 1998.

18. *Irish Echo*, 16–22 September 1998.
19. However, Orange protesters continued to occupy fields near the march site, threatening 'No Surrender' until they got permission to march.

Chapter Nine

1. *The Collected Essays, Journalism and Letters of George Orwell. Volume 4: In Front of Your Nose*, edited by Sonia Orwell and Ian Angus, Penguin, London 1970.
2. *A Citizens' Inquiry: The Opsahl Report on Northern Ireland*, edited by Andy Pollak, Lilliput Press, Dublin 1993.
3. In his acceptance speech Trimble – the first Unionist and Orangeman ever awarded the Nobel Prize – seemed at times just as uncomfortable as many of his fellow Protestants with this honour, which put the spotlight of world attention on him at a time when he was mired in a stalemate with his nationalist colleagues in the assembly over the setting up of the new executive. He began by disavowing any attempt to make a 'vision' speech, which he condemned for tending to vagueness and utopianism. Instead, he invoked the scientific traditions of the Enlightenment, quoting the 18th-century Anglo-Irish political philosopher Edmund Burke's criticism of the French Revolution for unleashing dangerous tendencies towards violence and 'fascism', as Trimble termed it. This in turn he associated with Irish republicanism, using the alleged link as an excuse to attack the IRA and Sinn Fein for not disarming. In other words, the Unionist leader did not rise to the occasion, but with one eye on his constituency back home let the occasion sink to the level of local politics.

Hume in his speech could just as easily have quoted Burke about the need for magnanimity in politics and gone on to point out that the Orange Order, of which Trimble was a member, was still threatening to defy the forces of law and order in Portadown and march where their Catholic neighbours did not want them. Had local political concerns dictated his remarks, he might have been tempted to suggest that his fellow Nobel laureate address his words about the Enlightenment to his Orange brethren in Portadown. Hume's speech was about his vision of how divisions can be overcome when allegiances are in conflict. Even his supporters acknowledged it was the one he had been making without many variations for 30 years. It was just that the Nobel committee had finally caught up with him.

GLOSSARY

PARAMILITARY AND MILITARY

1. Republican

Continuity IRA: Formed in 1986 by hardline republicans who disagreed with the Provisional IRA's decision to recognize the Irish parliament. Outlawed in 1997.

Irish National Liberation Army: Formed from a split within the Official IRA mainly because of the refusal of the leadership to end its ceasefire. Outlawed in 1979. On ceasefire since 1998.

Irish People's Liberation Organization: Formed in 1986 when a faction within the INLA decided the leadership had become corrupted. Banned in 1990.

Official IRA: Formed in 1969 when the IRA split. Supported left-wing strategies of the then leadership. On ceasefire since May 1972.

Provisional IRA: Formed in 1969 by those within the IRA who wanted a more aggressive military posture and who were uneasy about the political strategies of the leadership. The biggest and most powerful of the republican organizations.

Real IRA: Formed in late 1997 by dissidents within the Provisional IRA who rejected the organization's peace strategies. Banned in 1998.

2. Loyalist

Combined Loyalist Military Command: Coordinating group for all the loyalist paramilitary organizations.

Loyalist Volunteer Force: Formed in 1996 by disaffected members of the Ulster Volunteer Force who were opposed to the peace process. Outlawed in 1997. After a brief assassination campaign, it called a ceasefire in 1998.

Red Hand Commandos: Formed in 1971. The smallest of the loyalist groups, it was involved in a brief assassination campaign before disappearing to reemerge in 1991.

Ulster Defence Association: The largest of the Protestant paramilitary groups. Formed in 1971 from bands of vigilantes in Belfast. Behind a series of assassination and bombings, it could claim twenty thousand members in 1974. It remained legal until 1992.

Ulster Freedom Fighters: Created in 1973 in order to claim responsibility for assassinations carried out by the Ulster Defence Association. Banned in 1973.

Ulster Volunteer Force: Named after the Protestant militia that at the turn of the century opposed Home Rule. It was formed in 1966 and declared illegal that same year. It became involved in widespread sectarian violence in the early 1970s.

3. Security Forces

B-Specials: A part-time paramilitary police force set up shortly after the creation of Northern Ireland to combat the IRA. It was disbanded in 1970.

MI5: Otherwise known as BOX, Britain's internal intelligence-gathering unit. Involved in Northern Ireland in mainly bugging and wiretapping operations since the 1970s working with the police and army. Took over control of all wiretapping operations in 1994.

Royal Irish Regiment: Formed in 1992 following the disbandment of the Ulster Defence Regiment as a mainly Ulster-based unit within the British Army.

Royal Ulster Constabulary: Northern Ireland's police force, created in 1922. Mainly Protestant. Reformed in 1970. Plans to introduce further reforms were part of the overall peace settlement in 1998.

Special Air Services: Crack antiterrorist undercover British army force, known also as The Troop. Introduced into Northern Ireland in 1976.

Ulster Defence Regiment: Replaced the B-Specials in 1970. Locally recruited militia under the British army. In 1992 was amalgamated with the Royal Irish Rangers to form the Royal Irish Regiment.

4. Political

Alliance Party: Formed in 1970 in an attempt to attract the support of moderates in both communities.

Democratic Left: Formed from a split within the Workers' Party in 1992. Moderate leftist. Merged with Irish Labour Party in 1999.

Democratic Unionist Party: Formed in 1971 by the Reverend Ian Paisley to promote uncompromising unionist policies.

Fianna Fail: The largest party in the Irish Republic. Founded in 1926 from republicans who left Sinn Fein.

Fine Gael: The second largest party in the Irish Republic. Founded in 1933 from various right-wing groups.

Friends of Sinn Fein: Set up in Washington, D.C., after the first IRA ceasefire in 1994 to lobby for and raise money on behalf of Sinn Fein in America.

Irish Northern Aid: Established by the Provisional IRA in New York in 1970 to raise money for republican prisoners and propagandize on behalf of republican issues in the United States.

Irish Republican Socialist Party: Formed in 1974, a left-wing republican group that split from the Official IRA and is linked to the INLA.

Nationalist Party: For many years the main political opposition to partition in Northern Ireland. Became defunct in the early 1970s.

Northern Ireland Civil Rights Association: Formed in 1967 to draw attention to discrimination against Catholics in jobs and housing.

Northern Ireland Women's Coalition: Formed in 1996 to fight women's exclusion from local politics, it campaigns for human rights and cross-community initiatives.

Orange Order: The largest Protestant organization in Northern Ireland. Formed in 1795 during a period of faction fighting between Catholics and Protestants, it now has branches worldwide. Holds marches every summer throughout Northern Ireland.

People's Democracy: Radical student's group formed in 1968 in Queen's University, Belfast.

Progressive Unionist Party: The political wing of the Ulster Volunteer Force.

Sinn Fein: The political wing of the IRA. Formed originally in 1905 to campaign for Home Rule. Has gone through many transformations. Now espouses moderate left-wing policies and a united Ireland.

Social Democratic and Labour Party: The largest nationalist party in Northern Ireland. Founded in 1970 to promote a constitutional solution to the crisis based on winning the consent of Protestants to reforming the state and building closer ties to the Irish Republic with the ultimate aim of a united Ireland.

Ulster Unionist Party: From the nineteenth century, the largest party in Ulster. After partition, its chief aim was maintaining Northern Ireland as a part of the United Kingdom.

Workers' Party: Originally Official Sinn Fein, the political wing of the Official IRA. Became the Workers' Party in 1982. Heavily influenced at one time by Soviet model of communism.

APPENDIX ONE

The IRA Family Tree

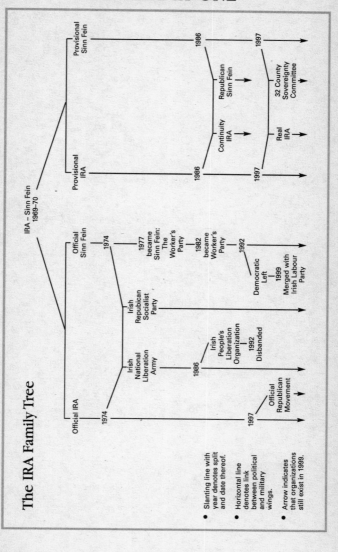

IRA – Sinn Fein 1969–70

Official IRA — 1974

Provisional IRA

Official IRA branch (1974)

Official Sinn Fein — 1974
- 1977 became Sinn Fein: The Worker's Party
- 1982 became Worker's Party
- 1992 Democratic Left
- 1999 Merged with Irish Labour Party

Irish Republican Socialist Party

Irish National Liberation Army
- 1986 Irish People's Liberation Organization — 1992 Disbanded

1997 Official Republican Movement

Provisional branch

Provisional Sinn Fein
- 1986 Republican Sinn Fein
- 1997 32 County Sovereignty Committee

Provisional IRA
- 1986 Continuity IRA
- 1997 Real IRA

Key:
- Slanting line with year denotes split and date thereof.
- Horizontal line denotes link between political and military wings.
- Arrow indicates that organizations still exist in 1999.

APPENDIX 2

A Note On Collusion

(The following statistics are derived from *Republican Roll Of Honour 1969–1994, An Index of Deaths From The Conflict in Ireland 1969–1993* by Malcolm Sutton, *Lost Lives: The Stories of the Men, Women and Children Who Died As a Result of the Northern Ireland Troubles* by David McKittrick, Seamus Kelters, Brian Feeney and Chris Thornton, and the author's own research and work including *Phoenix: Policing The Shadows. The Secret War Against Terrorism in Northern Ireland*, with Susan Phoenix.)

Accusations that the RUC and elements in the British Army have been actively colluding with the UDA and UVF in setting up members of the republican movement for murder have been made since the early 1970s. More recently, they became a controversial political matter yet again with the assassination of Rosemary Nelson, the Lurgan solicitor who defended IRA suspects and who had alleged shortly before her death that the police had threatened her, and with the publication of *The Committee*, by Sean McPhilemy. McPhilemy's book, which is based on the documentary of the same name that he produced for Channel 4 in 1991, carries the collusion allegation much further by claiming that the murder of republican 'hawks' and ordinary Catholics had been since the mid-1980s routinely organised with the assistance of leading Protestant businessmen and prominent politicians. It allegedly involved one-third of the membership of the RUC – that is some 4000 officers. McPhilemy's allegations have already been the subject of several legal actions, both by and against him. He successfully sued Times Newspapers Ltd. in 2000 and was awarded £145,000.

Such allegations are not made in a political vacuum. Six months after the murder of Nelson, the Patten independent body on policing issued its report recommending a series of reforms to the RUC including changing the force's name (See Postscript). Some nationalists, especially Sinn Fein members and fellow travellers, have used the collusion allegations to reject Patten as inadequate and advance their demand that the RUC should be disbanded completely. These arguments carry more weight in some quarters than in others. In the US they have been received almost uncritically among certain sections of Irish American opinion, especially since the publication there of *The Committee* in 1998. (It did not appear in the UK or Ireland for libel reasons.)

In the original documentary upon which the book is based, McPhilemy's source for the story, Jim Sands, (in 1991 identified only as 'A') claimed that the aim of this widespread conspiracy was to 'kill the hawks' of the republican movement. Given the alleged participation of high-ranking Special Branch officers with access to good intelligence, this would indeed be a plausible aim. One of the ways therefore of assessing the allegations would be to estimate the number of republican 'hawks' who have fallen victim to loyalists during the course of the conflict.

As far as can be estimated from the republicans' own 'roll of honour' and independent statistics, the total number of republican military activists killed between 1969 and 1994 by loyalist groups is 30. During the same period of the conflict, the same groups were responsible for approximately 1005 deaths.

What follows is a list of republican volunteers from the IRA (Official and Provisional), the INLA and the IPLO, who died at the hands of loyalists during those twenty-five years.

1969

15 August
Gerard McAuley (junior IRA), shot dead during fighting in the streets between the Shankill and the Falls roads.

1970

27 June
Henry McIlhone (Provisional IRA) fatally wounded during gun battles with loyalists around St. Matthew's Catholic Church in the Short Strand, East Belfast. He died two days later.

1972

16 December
Louis Leonard (Provisional IRA), assassinated in his butcher's shop, Derrylin, Co. Fermanagh.

1973

3 February
James Sloan (Provisional IRA) and James McCann (Provisional IRA) were both shot during a UDA drive-by attack. The two men were standing outside a pub in the Catholic New Lodge Road area of North Belfast at the time. McCann died early on 4 February.

14 April
Robert Millen (Official IRA), shot dead while on vigilante

duty by UVF gunmen in a drive-by attack on the Lower Ormeau Road, South Belfast. Millen was a Protestant.

6 July
Patrick Bracken (Official IRA), shot dead from a passing car by UVF gunmen as he left a café on the Falls Road.

1974

7 May
Frederick Leonard (Provisional IRA), shot dead in a UDA attack on a building site where he worked in a Protestant area near Newtownabbey, just north of Belfast. A Catholic workmate also died.

19 September
Patrick McGreevy (Junior Official IRA), shot dead outside a café in Clifton Street, North Belfast, by the UVF.

1975

10 January
John Green (Provisional IRA), shot dead by the UVF while on the run and hiding in a farm near Castleblaney, Co.Monaghan. He was O/C of the North Armagh Provisionals.

18 May
Francis Rice (Provisional IRA), found stabbed to death near Castlewellan, Co. Down. The UVF were responsible.

1976

13 July
Gerard Gilmour (Official IRA), shot dead by the UDA as he stood on vigilante duty outside a Catholic bar in North Belfast.

1978

8 March
Thomas Trainor (O/C INLA, North Armagh), shot dead along with a Catholic friend by the UVF after leaving a dole office. Trainor's mother and brother had been killed by loyalists in 1975 in separate attacks.

1979

25 April
Billy Carson (Provisional IRA), shot dead in the Oldpark area of North Belfast by UVF gunmen who were waiting for him in his house.

9 June
Joseph McKee (Official IRA), shot dead by the UDA in a butcher's shop near the Falls Road.

1980

15 October
Ronnie Bunting (O/C INLA Belfast) and Noel Lyttle, both Protestant republicans, shot dead in the early hours of the morning at the Bunting home near Turf Lodge in West Belfast by the UDA.

1981

23 February
James Burns (Provisional IRA Quartermaster, Northern Command), shot dead at his home in West Belfast by a UVF gunman.

1983

5 December
Joseph Craven (INLA) shot dead from a passing motor cycle by UVF as he and his two brothers (who were wounded) left a dole office in North Belfast.

1987

2 April
Laurence Marley (Third Battalion Quartermaster, Provisional IRA), shot dead by the UVF at his home in the Ardoyne, North Belfast.

1988

16 March
Caoimhin MacBradaigh (Provisional IRA) killed along with two mourners in a gun and grenade attack by a UDA man on the funeral of the three IRA members killed in Gibraltar.

25 July
Brendan Davison (Provisional IRA), shot dead at his home in the Markets area of Belfast by UVF gunmen disguised as police officers.

1989

4 April
Gerard Casey (Provisional IRA), shot dead by the UDA at his home near Rasharkin, Co. Antrim.

29 November
Liam Ryan (O/C East Tyrone Battalion, Provisional IRA),

shot dead by UVF gunmen in his pub in Ardboe, Co. Tyrone. A customer also died in the attack.

1991

3 March
John Quinn (Provisional IRA), Dwayne O'Donnell (Provisional IRA), and Malcolm Nugent (Provisional IRA) shot dead by the UVF as they arrived at a pub in Cappagh, Co. Tyrone.

16 August
Martin 'Rook' O'Prey (IPLO), shot dead by the UVF in his home near the Divis Flats, West Belfast.

1992

29 April
Conor Maguire (IPLO), shot dead by the UVF at a community centre where he worked in North Belfast.

1993

25 March
James Kelly (Provisional IRA), shot dead by UDA gunmen along with three other Catholic workmen as they arrived at a building site in Castlerock, Co. Derry.

1994

21 May
Martin Doherty (Provisional IRA), shot dead by the UVF during an attack on a Dublin pub in which a republican fundraiser was being held.

On this analysis, republican 'hawks' represent just under 3% of the total number of victims of loyalist violence. Indeed, considerably more republicans died in feuds with other republicans (47) or were 'executed' as informers (approximately 72) than died at the hands of loyalists. Even if the number of Sinn Fein members (14) and IRSP and Republican Clubs/Workers' Party activists (6) who were murdered by loyalists is added to the list, it still represents a small fraction of the total number of loyalist victims. Another important consideration that must be taken into account is that not all those republican volunteers listed above can be said to have been victims of collusion. If the circumstances of their deaths are broken down it appears that two (Gerard McAuley and Henry McIlhone) died in street battles and seven were killed as the result of random attacks directed against Catholic targets. These are James Sloan, James McCann, Robert Millen, Patrick Bracken, Frederick Leonard, Patrick McGreevy, and James Kelly. Six, Gerard Gilmore, Caoimhin MacBradaigh, Martin Doherty, John Quinn, Dwayne O'Donnell, and Malcolm Nugent were killed in attacks on places or gatherings identified by the attackers as republican.

This leaves fifteen killings in which the victims seem to have been deliberately selected because it was known that they were IRA, INLA or IPLO members. This in itself, however, would not necessarily indicate that their killers had access to intelligence since many of those who were shot were well known as republicans. But their killers possessed enough information to know where to find them. Seven, Billy Carson, Ronnie Bunting, James Burns, Larry Marley, Brendan Davison, Gerard Casey, and Martin O'Prey, were murdered at home. Three, Louis Leonard, Liam Ryan, and Conor Maguire, were murdered at their workplace. Two, Thomas Trainor and Joseph Craven, were shot leaving dole offices. Francis Rice was apparently abducted as he walked home late at night before being stabbed to death. Joseph McKee was shot in a butcher's shop near his workplace which he visited regularly.

John Green was murdered in a 'safe' house while on the run, having escaped from prison. His case, among the most controversial, would appear to be a good candidate for collusion. However, in the account of his death in *Lost Lives*, an RUC officer who had been convicted of murder and involvement with the UVF, is quoted as saying that Green was not the intended target but 'just happened to be at the house' when the UVF gunmen arrived looking for another republican.

Green is among the highest ranking republican 'hawks' to die at loyalist hands during the course of the conflict. The others are Ronnie Bunting, James Burns, Larry Marley, Liam Ryan, and Brendan Davison all of whom were at 'battalion' or 'brigade' level. What is also apparent from examining the above list is that the high-level collusion claimed by *The Committee* as having begun around 1985 (post-Anglo-Irish Agreement) seems not to have led to any significant increase in the number of republican 'hawks' killed by the UDA, UVF, RHC or other loyalist groups as compared to the previous decades. What is noticeable, however, is the post-1985 increase in the number of Sinn Fein activists killed. But that is partly explained by the fact that until 1982 Sinn Fein did not fight elections in Northern Ireland and so had no elected officials. Before that year, it had lost only three members to loyalist assassins. Between 1982 and 1993 loyalists killed twelve members including three local councillors, John Davey, Eddie Fullerton and Bernard O'Hagan.

If, as McPhilemy claims, loyalist killers had been acting on the information coming from the highest levels of the Special Branch, it seems likely that more major 'players' in the republican leadership would have fallen victim since the police had detailed information about where they lived, what cars they drove, when they visited their families, wives and girlfriends. Many were under intense surveillance, giving the alleged conspirators ample opportunities to target them. 'If there had been that kind of collusion,' a veteran Special Branch officer told the author, 'Gerry Adams, Martin McGuinness and Gerry Kelly would not be walking the streets. If the Committee existed how come they were bumping off innocent Catholics in sweet shops?' A UVF member made the same point when he told Henry McDonald, the author of *Trimble*, 'if we had half the information McPhilemy claims we were given, then there would have been hundreds more dead IRA men in graves all over the place'.

A useful comparison is to look at the operations of the SAS which had access to accurate information about republican activists from the Special Branch and army intelligence allowing it to anticipate and intercept many terrorist attacks. In the Tyrone-Armagh area between 1985 and 1992 the SAS killed 22 IRA men, several of them leading operators and practically wiped out the organisation in East Tyrone.

Simply because the case for collusion alleged in *The Committee* appears flawed is not to say that it did not exist. Clearly it did, but usually at a lower level than is claimed. The overlap between the UDR and UVF in North Armagh has been documented and information was exchanged which led to the death of IRA man John Green (though he may not have been the intended target). Something similar must have occurred elsewhere. Shortly before he was murdered, Ronnie Bunting was allegedly threatened by the RUC. As a Protestant republican, and O/C of the Belfast INLA, he had long been a target of the UDA and UVF. His killers made their way immediately to the bedroom where he was sleeping. They accessed and exited a well-patrolled republican area near Turf Lodge seemingly effortlessly. Their getaway car was never traced. It was a well-planned, well-executed operation, based on good information.

The most prominent case of alleged collusion, however,

does not relate to the murder of a prominent republican activist but of a solicitor, Patrick Finucane. The UDA shot him at his home in North Belfast in February 1989. Since the shooting, two members of the UDA linked to the incident, one of whom was Brian Nelson, have been exposed as having connections also to the security forces. Nelson was the Belfast UDA's intelligence officer while working for an army intelligence unit, the Field Research Unit. One supplied the information about Finucane and the other the guns that were used in the murder. What is interesting is that in spite of the information Nelson was allegedly receiving from FRU about republican activists, during the entire period he was active the UDA (approximately 1986–1990) succeeded in killing only one IRA volunteer, Caoimhin MacBradaigh, and he died during a wild attack on a republican funeral (see above). The most prominent paramilitary activist killed during that time was John McMichael, the overall head of the UDA's assassination gangs, blown up by an IRA booby-trap car bomb in December 1987.

In conclusion, the difficulty for those who advance the proposition that there was high-level collusion between loyalist paramilitaries and the security forces remains the fact that of all the categories of victim in the Northern conflict, it seems from the above statistics that those least likely to have died at the hands of the UDA, UVF, LVF and RHC, were its prime targets – the 'hawks' of the IRA, INLA and IPLO.

Index